FOREWORD

Who could have believed that a collection of match summaries, diaries, player and manager profiles along with hoards of statistical data – albeit painstakingly and tenderly constructed – would have come to see the light of day in such spectacular fashion? Having seen my first Brentford game back in 1970 and quickly embarking on a run of witnessing every home game bar two in a 25 year stretch, such obsessive loyalty was complemented by detailed record-keeping which included all those little snippets that can now provoke the "Oh, I remember that!" exclamation for us all. A labour of love, undoubtedly - but now through this book, providing a pathway back to some magical memories for Brentford supporters.

When, in 2010, I wondered how these treasures could be shared with other like-minded Bees fans, keen as we all are to reminisce, I approached Greville Waterman. His wonderful enthusiasm for and knowledge of all-things Brentford, provided the link to David Lane, the publisher of numerous fantastic publications including the marvellously readable *Cult Bees and Legends* series. Between the three of us, *The Big Brentford Book of the Seventies* has been brought to life, by merging the text with some wonderful pictures, personal recollections of many never-to-be-forgotten playing heroes and with an unerring desire to obtain previously untapped information. Quite how many hours Greville spent using his contacts to unearth Steve Wilkins's elusive birth date, you will never know!

The sheer pleasure in working together to produce the book has been as enjoyable as the nostalgia itself – as has witnessing first-hand the creativity that was needed to transform a life-time of record keeping into a cherished book of memories that we can all treasure.

Mark Croxford

INTRODUCTION

As the years go by your memory seems to fade – incidents merge into one another or get lost completely into the mists of time. While faces seem to blur, appointments and names are forgotten and my glasses and mobile phone remain permanently lost, but there is still one decade that remains in sharp focus to me – namely the Seventies.

Why should that be when so many other years have gone totally blank? Maybe because they were my formative years, the time of my teens, "O" and "A" levels, learning to drive, going to University (or in my case, three of them!), leaving home, my first job – even my first girlfriends. The Seventies have forged some indelible memories into my psyche that I can still remember as if they occurred only yesterday.

It was the era of Progressive Rock – all those bands with ridiculous, pretentious names like Focus, Hatfield and the North, Caravan and Gong that I am now forced, on pain of death, to listen to alone in the car with the windows wound tightly shut.

It was the time of Abba, M*A*S*H, Monty Python, Fawlty Towers, the first colour televisions, decimal currency, the Three Day Week, flared trousers, loon pants, sideburns, the baking hot Summer of 1976, the Queen's Silver Jubilee, Punk Music, The Winter of Discontent and the election of Margaret Thatcher – and you can all add your own favourites.

But bringing matters back to football, who can forget Brazil and The Beautiful Game in the 1970 World Cup?

The Gordon Banks save from Pele, mavericks such as Peter Osgood, Stan Bowles, Tony Currie, Alan Hudson and Frank Worthington, the Chelsea versus Leeds FA Cup Final replay kicking match at Old Trafford, and for me, most evocative of all, Barry Davies's iconic commentary: *"Lee... interesting... very interesting. Look at his face! Just look at his face!"* as Francis Lee's thunderous 20-yarder screamed into the roof of the Manchester City net.

As for Brentford, the Seventies saw two promotions, a relegation, and an FA Cup run to the Fifth Round – a bit tame perhaps for a normal Brentford decade given the excitement and non-stop action of subsequent years!

I can still vividly picture great talents such as Roger Cross, John O'Mara, Pat Kruse and Andy McCulloch, the brooding genius of Steve Phillips, the loyalty of characters such as Peter Gelson, Paul Bence, Alan Hawley, Gordon Phillips and Alan Nelmes along with the steely determination, skill and commitment of the man who, for me, best symbolised what being a Brentford player is all about – the immortal Jackie Graham.

[Right] Brentford fans at the Ealing Road end celebrate during the 7-2 home win over Hull City in season 1979-80

THE BIG BRENTFORD BOOK OF THE SEVENTIES

70

THE BIG BRENTFORD BOOK OF THE SEVENTIES

Legends Publishing
18 Darby Crescent
Sunbury-on-Thames
Middlesex
TW16 5LA

E-mail david@legendspublishing.net
Web www.legendspublishing.net

As for individual moments that encapsulated the decade, what better than Bobby Ross's 'coolness personified' penalty against Exeter that clinched promotion?

Any goal by John O'Mara, Roger Cross, Gordon Sweetzer, Andy McCulloch or Steve Phillips, beating Cardiff in the Ninian Park mud bath, Alex Dawson's last gasp winner against Gillingham in the FA Cup, Paul Priddy's Superman impression at Vicarage Road when he saved those two Watford penalties, poor Stan Webb attempting the impossible by replacing the legend that was John O'Mara – a real Dean Holdsworth - Murray Jones scenario.

How about Bob Booker's legendary hat-trick against Hull, Lee Holmes riding pillion on a motorbike heading to his own wedding, Bill Glazier literally throwing away the chance of an historic League Cup win at Old Trafford, the exciting, smooth-as-silk, attacking football of the Bill Dodgin promotion team and winning the first set against Crewe 6-4?

One other name to conjure with – John Bain. Bar Stan Bowles, has there been another midfielder as cultured and skilled at the club since his short stay came to such a premature end?

There was a real sense of togetherness between the players and the supporters, with many memorable trips to distant away games at far-flung and uncharted territories, such as Workington, South-port and Darlington.

Most poignantly, who can forget the packed Royal Oak, the two 18,000 plus crowds in 1971-72, a triumphant promotion season where we attracted crowds of over 10,000 to 15 League games and wonder where they have all disappeared to now?

I still bemoan the lost opportunity, maybe the last one for some considerable time, when lack of vision, ambition and investment saw the club crash straight back into the bottom division in 1973 – a calamitous fall which saw the Bees hit the bottom of the entire Football League in the very next season.

Let's not hark back on sad memories, though, instead we should concentrate on the things that gave us all so much joy.

The Big Brentford Book of the Seventies contains, in lavish and glorious detail, a cornucopia of riches and delights: match reports, pen pictures, statistics, interviews, photographs and press clip-pings covering everything that made the Seventies such an unfor-gettable decade for the club and supporters alike.

Despite my vivid recollections of the decade I have remembered so much more after leafing through these pages, with a permanent smile glued to my face and I hope that you all do too.

Greville Waterman

5

DAN TANA'S VISION

I'd been involved with football all of my life. I signed as a young player with Red Star Belgrade before I defected from Yugoslavia and, during the 1960s, I'd owned a football club in Los Angeles, the LA Toros, along with two partners, Dan Reeves and Dan Martin – the three Dans! While I was running the Toros we recruited Brentford's Ron Crisp, who was a good player and, surrounded by Brazillians, Mexicans, plus stars from a host of other nations who couldn't speak English, he was the automatic choice to become our captain.

When my daughters were eight and ten, my wife and I decided to come to England so that the girls could get a better education than they were getting in The States, and we looked at some nice schools. I also had some good friends in England that I'd made in the film industry and I have to admit that, combined with the nation's love of football, a game that has always been my first love, it meant I felt at home in this country almost straight away – despite the fact that the Seventies were tough years in England. The country was almost bankrupt and we had three days of electricity, followed by three days of blackouts, not to mention the miners' strike.

In London I became very good friends with Brian Mears, who was chairman of Chelsea, and I was invited along to a few games at Stamford Bridge, where I was also introduced to the Arsenal chairman, Denis Hill-Wood, so I visited Highbury on several occasions too. Then, because of my love for the game, and the fact that I'd been a player myself, I was also invited to join a football team called the Goal Diggers, who played to raise money for charity over at Hyde Park on Sundays. The team included the likes of Jimmy Hill, Ron Greenwood and Bobby Moore, amongst others, and we'd always follow the match with a few beers in one of the pubs along the

Fulham Road. I remember one day I was chatting to the former Chelsea player, Frank Blunstone, who I discovered was the manager at Brentford – he asked me why I'd been to Chelsea and Arsenal, but had never been down to Griffin Park. I was honest and said I didn't know where Brentford was, so when I found out how close it was, I agreed to come down and watch the Bees.

I'll be the first to admit that the match itself wasn't great – Brentford lost two or three-nil – but the combination of the red and white stripes, which were similar to the ones that I played in at Red Star, and the atmosphere generated by the fans who were singing; "We love you Brentford" and "Come on you Bees", made a real impression on me. It was love at first sight.

I was made to feel very welcome at Brentford, but it was clear that the club were in a spot of trouble, but even so, it was a bit of a surprise when, after just a handful of games, I was invited to the club AGM and asked if I wanted to join the board. I was flattered, but made it clear that I had no desire to become involved at that level and, either way, I wasn't even a shareholder, so I wouldn't be permitted to attend in any case. Somehow I was persuaded to buy five shares at 50 pence each and I went along, but at that stage, only a handful of people knew anything about me.

It soon became clear that there was a situation between the two families who were in control of the club – the Davey's and the Wheatley's – then towards the end of the meeting it was proposed that I joined the board and a seconder was called for to support the idea. But I could see there were a lot of problems that would need to be solved and I told them that I would only consider it if I was unanimously voted in among the shareholders – I didn't want to cause any further splits or make matters worse. The shareholders all backed me and, before I knew it, I was on the board! At the same time I was elected, former Supporters' Club chairman, Peter Pond-Jones joined too, which I thought was a very positive step.

At my first board meeting I realised there was another problem – an agreement between the two families to rotate the running of the club between themselves on an annual basis. One year the Davey father and son team would be chairman and vice chairman respectively, then it would be the Wheatley's turn. So I explained that, in my mind at least, there was no way we could run the club like that going forwards – but there seemed no immediate end to that situation. Then, after six months or so, in a bid to solve that continuity situation, it was proposed by the Wheatley's that I became chairman and, after some negotiating, both families agreed that I should take over the hot seat for a period of four years. I therefore became the first foreign-born chairman of an English football club – things have certainly changed in this country since then!

My demands were that the board would be run by my rules, with a meeting at least once a month, and I insisted that no meeting could ever end without everyone on the board agreeing on the outcomes. I said that we'd have to continue discussing outstanding issues until everyone was convinced about making a decision. Although not all of my ideas were well received by Denis Piggott, who was a very stubborn and military man, but he loved the club, there was no question about that. I used to attempt to replicate some of the successful ideas we'd tried in America, such as a Ladies' Day where women and children could come in for free. I visited all of the local factories in Brentford and went all around the neighbourhood with the players – we also held regular lunches with the press, which was very contrary to the archaic situation previously.

Another idea I introduced was that at least one of the directors had to have seen a potential new player before the manager bought him. We had some great scouts, but I thought it was important for the board to be fully aware of who we were buying. But the director wasn't allowed to sit in the directors' box, he had to buy a ticket and stand on the terraces with the fans and ask their views on the player – I thought the system worked very well too. I also suggested that if any our supporters, who lived all over the country and many of whom were very knowledgeable about the game, recommended a player we weren't aware of, and we subsequently signed them, the fan would be given a sum of money as a reward.

The next thing I insisted on was changing the team manager. I knew it was time to start rebuilding the club and I thought Mike Everitt was not the right person to be in charge, despite being a nice guy. So we started interviewing potential new managers and, after half a dozen or so, I'd decided that I wanted Roy Hodgson to come to Brentford and told the rest of the board. They didn't agree. I was told that the new manager should be a Brentford person, a former player, and Peter Pond-Jones nominated John Docherty, so I backed him.

John did a very good job at Brentford I thought, and brought in some very exciting players but, to this day, I have no idea what happened between him and I to make him want to walk out of the club. One day the manager came into the board meeting, which was another new development I'd insisted on, and said that he was angered at the board turning down a transfer for a new player, naming me as the person he thought had blocked the move, and he left the club over the matter. But as I say, even to this day, I really don't fully understand why Docherty resigned from Brentford.

But John's departure paved the way for Bill Dodgin to come to Brentford – Bill was a great manager for the club and we played some wonderful football with him in charge. We also introduced some new people onto the board, including the playwright Willis Hall and the rock star, Rick Wakeman, who was a big Brentford fan. It felt like it was becoming a real family club and we increased the crowd quite significantly with Bill's attractive, winning football. Great men like Eric Radley-Smith were involved too, he was so proud of having been the chairman of the club he loved.

Because of my relative inexperience of English football at that time, I always kept a close eye on the development of managers at other clubs, just in case I needed to change the manager at Brentford, and

I kept a list containing the names of two or three men. Anyway, one night I received a very late phone call at home from Glenn Frey and Don Henley, members of the band The Eagles, who were friends from Hollywood and had come to Griffin Park to watch a match as my guests while they were on their first tour of England. They'd called to invite me to a party at Elton John's house and told me that they'd been talking about me to Elton, who it emerged was about to take over at Watford, and said that I should come over and join them at the party. I told them that I'd been fast asleep and that they'd woken me up in the middle of the night, but they kept saying that Elton wanted to meet me to talk about football… "Come on Dan!" they kept urging me, so I asked my wife and she said I should get up and go.

So I was introduced to Elton and he told me all about his plans at Watford, of how he was about to appoint Bobby Moore as his new manager, and what did I think? Well, it was difficult for me, I had a great deal of respect for Bobby, he was an incredible player, but he had no experience of management, so I told Elton that if I were him, I'd be looking for somebody with a bit more experience. I then told him about the list that I kept if things didn't work out with Bill Dodgin and said that if I had to bring a new manager in straight away, the first person I'd ask would be Graham Taylor at Lincoln City. And, lo and behold, the very next day Watford had a new manager, one that took them from the Fourth Division to the First. I felt sorry for Bobby Moore, he was a friend of mine, God bless him. But the key to success, at any football club, is in having the right man in charge – a good manager is essential.

The time around Bill Dodgin's departure was very difficult, with only a handful of games to go it looked as if Brentford would get relegated and something had to be done to avoid the drop back to Division Four. The supporters had been demonstrating in the forecourt at Griffin Park prior to his departure and I'd spoken up on behalf of the

manager – telling people that he'd been good enough to get us up and I thought he was good enough to keep us up too. Bill and I spoke about the situation and, until the 6-1 defeat at Colchester, followed by the home defeat to Rotherham, he'd told me not to worry as he had every faith in being able to turn the situation around.

But after the Rotherham game Bill came over to my house and we analysed the whole situation and, on further reflection, Bill was no longer convinced that the team would escape the drop. So we came to a mutual agreement that he should step aside. I didn't sack him – Bill was a very good man. Fred Callaghan then came in and we just about escaped relegation in the final game of the season. Fred was a very good assistant manager, in fact I begged him to stay on to help Bill before he left to take over at Woking.

As well as my commitment to Brentford I'd been invited onto the FA board to replace the Arsenal chairman, Denis Hill-Wood, in representing clubs of all sizes in and around London (FA Division VII) – from the likes of Arsenal and Tottenham, to minnows like Ford United and Hendon. I spent five of the best years I've been involved in football combining the two roles before Chelsea's Ken Bates replaced me in 1983. The integrity and honesty at the FA was, and still is, second to none – but those are the two qualities which, in my opinion, meant they were always unlikely to win the World Cup bid. I had a fantastic relationship with both Ted Croker and Sir Bert Millichip, men I will always have a huge amount of respect for.

I knew that if English clubs could combine the energy and pace of the game here, with the technical skill of the continental game, the FA could oversee a situation where they possessed the strongest League in the world – which is now the case with the Premier League. Jimmy Hill and I were also the two instigators of the three points for a win system into the English game. It may have taken us

four years to get our way, but look how representation from Third Division Brentford and Second Division Fulham helped revolutionise the game.

I was also looking to import overseas talent to Brentford, so that the club could perhaps regain its place in the top flight. But I realised that the problem at Brentford was the stadium needed developing – I explained to the board that we should be a Second Division club at the very least, but beyond that, we'd need the stadium to be ready.

My vision was to improve and enlarge Griffin Park, certainly not to sell off parts of the ground and remove the ability to grow completely. So, when they came on the market, the club started buying the houses around Griffin Park to help give us scope in the future. There was also a lot of talk about relocating the club, either to the old Brentford Market site, or out towards the airport, but they were just pipe dreams without the required political will to make them happen.

Looking back to the era I was at Brentford makes me realise what good times we had and reading about the players' happy memories in the *Cult Bees & Legends* books brings it all right back. Yes, it could be frustrating at times, but overall, they were very happy days. It was great to get promoted out of Division Four and then to knock on the door of Division Two – we had some very exciting players, including Steve Phillips, Andy McCulloch, Pat Kruse, Jackie Graham and Danis Salman, who were all fantastic for Brentford.

I also have a great, great love for Brentford supporters – through all the bad times, and the few good times, it is the supporters who have stood by the football club. From grandfather, to father, to son, to grandson, and regardless of what division the club are in, the fans stay loyal to Brentford. Yes there are times when they get angry and demand that the manager, or even the chairman or board, should be replaced, but that is all part of football.

Dan Tana

1970–71

[Back Row] Brian Turner, Paul Bence, Peter Gelson, Dick Renwick
[Middle Row] Eddie Lyons, Roger Cross, Gordon Phillips, Alan Nelmes, Chic Brodie, Alan Hawley, Michael Maskell, Frank Blunstone
[Front Row] Brian Tawse, John Docherty, Gordon Neilson, Bobby Ross, Jackie Graham, Allan Mansley

Football League	Division Four
Manager	Frank Blunstone
Trainer	Eddie Lyons
Captain	Bobby Ross
Final Position	14th
FA Cup	5th Round
League Cup	1st Round
Leading Goalscorer (all competitions)	Bobby Ross – 16 goals

Frank Blunstone's first full season as manager got off to a dreadful start with six straight defeats – setting a new post war record of nine opening games without a win – twice conceding five goals in a game. Darlington were finally beaten 1-0 at Griffin Park in late September, but the victory was followed by another five defeats in the next six matches.

The loan signing of Alex Dawson from Brighton helped to turn around fortunes in emphatic fashion with a run of eight wins in nine matches, including a remarkable 6-4 home victory against York City and an equally dramatic FA Cup first round home success over Gillingham, with two late goals after 88 and 89 minutes, resulting in a 2-1 win

The remainder of the campaign was largely dominated by the Cup run and, after Division Three visitors Walsall had been dispatched in round two, the potentially lucrative third round brought about a long and unrewarding trip to Workington, where a 1-0 win set up a fourth round tie at Ninian Park against Second Division promotion-chasers Cardiff City. In atrocious conditions, on a mud-bath of a pitch, a headline-making 2-0 victory was achieved in front of more than 23,000 spectators.

The first appearance in the fifth round of the competition for 21 years drew a trip to Division Two leaders Hull City and, despite taking the lead through Bobby Ross, the home side booked a place in the quarter-finals with two late goals to the delight of the majority of the near-30,000 crowd. League results throughout the second half of the season produced sufficient points to ensure a comfortable mid-table finish.

[Previous page] John Docherty and Roger Cross during the 4-0 defeat at Colchester United

Total Home League Attendances	155,843
Average Home League Attendance	6,776
Highest Home League Attendance	10,058
Lowest Home League Attendance	4,176

		P	W	D	L	F	A	W	D	L	F	A	Pts
1	Notts County	46	19	4	0	59	12	11	5	7	30	24	**69**
2	Bournemouth	46	16	5	2	51	15	8	7	8	39	31	**60**
3	Oldham	46	14	6	3	57	29	10	5	8	31	34	**59**
4	York City	46	16	6	1	45	14	7	4	12	33	40	**56**
5	Chester	46	17	2	4	42	18	7	5	11	27	37	**55**
6	Colchester	46	14	6	3	44	19	7	6	10	26	35	**54**
7	Northampton	46	15	4	4	39	24	4	9	10	24	35	**51**
8	Southport	46	15	2	6	42	24	6	4	13	21	33	**48**
9	Exeter City	46	12	7	4	40	23	5	7	11	27	45	**48**
10	Workington	46	13	7	3	28	13	5	5	13	20	36	**48**
11	Stockport	46	12	8	3	28	17	4	6	13	21	48	**46**
12	Darlington	46	15	3	5	42	22	2	8	13	16	35	**46**
13	Aldershot	46	8	10	5	32	23	6	7	10	34	48	**45**
14	**Brentford**	**46**	**13**	**3**	**7**	**45**	**27**	**5**	**5**	**13**	**21**	**35**	**44**
15	Crewe	46	13	1	9	49	35	5	7	11	36	41	**44**
16	Peterborough	46	14	3	6	46	23	4	4	15	24	48	**43**
17	Scunthorpe	46	9	7	7	36	23	6	6	11	20	38	**43**
18	Southend	46	8	11	4	32	24	6	4	13	21	42	**43**
19	Grimsby	46	13	4	6	37	26	5	3	15	20	45	**43**
20	Cambridge	46	9	9	5	31	27	6	4	13	20	39	**43**
21	Lincoln	46	11	4	8	45	33	2	5	12	25	38	**39**
22	Newport	46	8	3	12	32	36	2	5	16	23	49	**28**
23	Hartlepool	46	6	10	7	28	27	2	2	19	6	47	**28**
24	Barrow	46	5	5	13	25	38	2	3	18	26	52	**22**

League Position throughout the Season

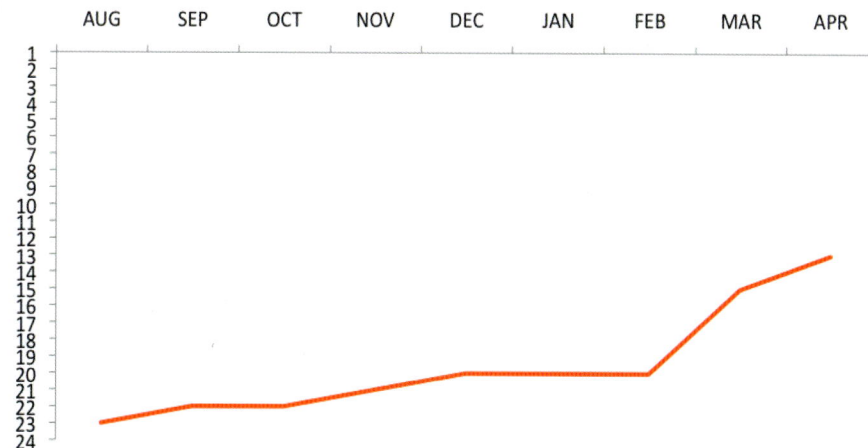

AUG	SEP	OCT	NOV	DEC	JAN	FEB	MAR	APR

15

1970-71

Sat 15th August: **Chester (H)**
Lost 1-2   **Attendance: 6,477**

On a sun-drenched afternoon the season started disappointingly when the visitors took a two-goal lead, with strikes after 37 and 42 minutes, and always looked the more likely to extend their lead throughout. With the crowd streaming towards the exits John Docherty took a 30 yard free-kick in the 85th minute and the ball sailed directly into the net as the keeper was challenged by Roger Cross.

Wed 19th August: **Aldershot (A) League Cup 1st Round**
Lost 0-1   **Attendance: 6,899**

The home side started the stronger and took the lead with the game's only goal in the 38th minute, but although the second period was more evenly contested, an equaliser rarely looked to be forthcoming and interest in the cup competition was ended at the earliest stage.

Sat 22nd August: **Lincoln City (A)**
Lost 0-2   **Attendance: 6,813**

Despite matching the hosts for long periods in open play throughout the game, goal threats were few and far between, and the home side scored twice after 10 and 81 minutes to record a comfortable victory. In the 87th minute the goalpost and crossbar collapsed onto Chic Brodie, holding the game up for 45 minutes.

Sat 29th August: **Southport (H)**
Lost 0-1   **Attendance: 5,324**

The game was played out in Bank Holiday weekend sunshine and followed a pattern similar to previous matches with two teams evenly matched, but the lack of a cutting edge in attack proved decisive as the visitors scored the winning goal after 71 minutes.

A niggling encounter saw an opposing player suffer a broken leg following a clash with Brian Turner.

Mon 31st August: **Cambridge United (A)**
Lost 0-1   **Attendance: 6,654**

The first-ever visit to the home of the Football League newcomers extended the goal-less run to 365 minutes and a solid defensive display was matched by some neat football, but it was the hosts who hit the only goal in the 10th minute to inflict a fifth successive defeat.

Sat 5th September: **Oldham Athletic (A)**
Lost 1-5   **Attendance: 4,866**

In a gale-force wind the home side started superbly, earning eight corners in the opening 20 minutes, but a goal completely against the run of play came in the 22nd minute, when Brian Tawse picked up the ball on the right flank, cut inside and hit a low 20-yard effort, which squirmed past the keeper. The hosts continued with their bombardment and, having equalised in the 44th minute, a rampant second-half display of non-stop attacking saw them hit four more goals, with a superb performance from Chic Brodie preventing an even heavier defeat.

Sat 12th September: **Peterborough United (H)**
Drew 1-1   **Attendance: 4,176**

The best performance of the season brought about the first point – but the Bees deserved both in a game which saw the visitors take a 43rd minute lead and adopt a 'what we have we hold' approach, until a 68th minute corner from Brian Tawse was headed home by Bobby Ross. The match was played in a deluge of torrential rain.

Sat 19th September: Notts County (A)
Drew 0-0   Attendance: 10,281

An enterprising first-half display deserved a share of the spoils in an entertaining draw – although the table-topping hosts dominated the second period, during which they were thwarted by an outstanding performance from Chic Brodie in goal.

Wed 23rd September: Crewe Alexandra (A)
Lost 3-5   Attendance: 1,909

A dreadful display created a new post-war record of nine games without a win at the start of a season. The home side ripped through the defence scoring three times in the opening 16 minutes and adding a fourth goal soon afterwards, following a slip from Alan Nelmes. Roger Cross headed home a cross from John Docherty in the 35th minute, and when the hosts added a fifth after 63 minutes, an avalanche looked on the cards. But a 40-yard free-kick from Dick Renwick was headed into his own net by a defender and, in the 75th minute, Brian Turner hit a 35-yard drive to reduce the arrears further. With injuries hitting hard, reserve keeper, Gordon Phillips, was named as the substitute.

Sat 26th September: Darlington (H)
Won 1-0   Attendance: 4,841

After a modest first-half, the second period produced the best all-round display of the season, and the negative visitors were overwhelmed – the one-goal margin of victory being scant reward for a fine performance. In the 67th minute a cross from Paul Bence was missed by both Roger Cross and a defender and the ball found its way to John Docherty, who ran on to fire home a cross-shot from just inside the penalty area to secure the first win.

Mon 28th September: Stockport County (A)
Lost 0-1   Attendance: 4,387

The 19 travelling supporters witnessed the debut of loanee striker Alex Dawson and, after the home side had scored a 13th minute

penalty, awarded when Dick Renwick punched a goal-bound effort over the bar, an uninspiring second-half was devoid of any entertainment or excitement.

Sat 3rd October: Northampton Town (A)
Lost 0-1   Attendance: 6,282

A resilient defensive display in the face of growing pressure from the hosts looked to have earned a point, but defeat was inflicted in the cruellest of manners when a 94th minute cross into the penalty box was diverted into his own net by the out-stretched foot of Bobby Ross. Another outstanding performance in goal from Chic Brodie was even more commendable as he chipped a bone in his arm as early as the 20th minute.

Sat 10th October: Bournemouth (H)
Lost 1-2   Attendance: 5,965

A rapturous ovation from supporters reflected a lively first-half in which the visiting league leaders were second-best and reward finally came in the 62nd minute when John Docherty's right-wing free-kick was met by a terrific 20-yard shot from Jackie Graham. But the visitors levelled just two minutes later and hit a 76th minute winner. The game lost its sparkle in the final stages.

Sat 17th October: Chester (A)
Won 2-1   Attendance: 5,834

Revenge was gained for the opening day defeat, despite the new leaders taking a 34th minute lead when Gordon Phillips fumbled a shot. But, straight after the interval, Paul Bence crossed the ball into the penalty box and the keeper spilled under pressure from John Docherty – Alex Dawson lashed home the equaliser. In the 56th minute a corner from John Docherty was scuffed into the net by Roger Cross after Alex Dawson had nodded the ball down.

Mon 19th October: **Aldershot (H)**
Lost 2-3   **Attendance: 7,648**

Following a lively opening period the visitors took the lead after 27 minutes, before Alex Dawson netted the equaliser in the 36th minute with a poacher's goal after a rasping shot from Jackie Graham was parried by the keeper. Having fallen behind again in the 62nd minute, Bobby Ross levelled for a second time with a deceptive angled lob into the goal after Peter Gelson and John Docherty had created the opening, but the visitors gained a fortuitous win in the 77th minute by virtue of long-time nemesis Jack Howarth's hat-trick of headers.

Sat 24th October: **Southend United (A)**
Lost 3-4   **Attendance: 6,052**

A cut-and-thrust, evenly-matched affair full of excitement, none-the-less brought about the 11th defeat of the season, which left Brentford in 22nd place in the table. The scoring started in the 6th minute when Jackie Graham's corner was headed back across the goalmouth by Dick Renwick for John Docherty to pivot and score from six yards. But the home side struck twice in three minutes to take the lead and added a third after 60 minutes. Alex Dawson headed home a centre from Roger Cross, but the hosts hit their fourth immediately afterwards, before Brian Turner's drive was met by a diving header from Bobby Ross in the 80th minute to set up a grandstand finale.

Sat 31st October: **Exeter City (H)**
Won 5-0   **Attendance: 5,267**

A rampant display of attacking football brought about the biggest win for more than five years. The scoring got underway after 28 minutes, when a long, diagonal ball from Alan Nelmes was headed home by the on-rushing John Docherty then, on the stroke of half-time, Alan Nelmes again set up Roger Cross to fire wide of the keeper. In the 57th minute Jackie Graham fought off a challenge and slipped between two defenders to unleash a superb long-range shot and goal number four arrived when Bobby Ross turned to lash the ball home as it dropped after he had challenged the keeper. The rout was completed in the 79th minute when Brian Turner's cross was dummied by Alex Dawson and John Docherty pounced.

Sat 7th November: **Newport County (A)**
Won 1-0   **Attendance: 2,407**

The bottom of the table and winless hosts were the better team and, in swamp-like conditions following incessant rain, a somewhat fortuitous win was achieved in the 81st minute when Jackie Graham's pass found Roger Cross – his centre was headed home by Alex Dawson.

Mon 9th November: **York City (H)**
Won 6-4   **Attendance: 5,955**

An astonishing evening produced a ten-goal thriller – after 4 minutes a fumble from Gordon Phillips gifted the opener, before Alex Dawson equalised within 90 seconds when he nodded home a lobbed cross by Brian Turner. Roger Cross' goal in the 32nd minute gave Brentford the lead, which was extended after 54 minutes, when Alan Nelmes and Brian Turner combined to set up John Docherty to score and, 9 minutes later, Roger Cross swivelled and lashed home a long-range drive after Paul Bence and John Docherty had combined well. In the 72nd minute John Docherty waltzed round the keeper to make it 5-1 and the game seemed well and truly over – but the visitors hit three goals in just two minutes, the second of which was an own goal by Alan Nelmes, before John Docherty secured the points with a strike from a Brian Turner pass, to seal his hat-trick.

Sat 14th November: **Grimsby Town (H)**
Won 2-0   **Attendance: 5,497**

Heavy rain in the preceding 24 hours had left the pitch sodden, meaning the game was played with large areas in ankle-deep mud

[Left L-R] Bobby Ross, Peter Gelson, Alan Nelmes (No.6) and Brian Turner in defensive action at Southend United

as the rain continued to teem down, but in only the 2nd minute a cross-shot from Brian Turner was fired through the legs of the keeper by Alex Dawson for the quickest goal of the campaign. The lead was doubled after 20 minutes with a penalty from Bobby Ross following a handball, but conditions deteriorated even further, making the second-half a farcical affair.

Sat 21st November: Gillingham (H) (FA Cup 1st Round)
Won 2-1   Attendance: 8,000

The visitors took a 15th minute lead and defended in numbers against a wave of attacks, but with an early cup exit looking certain, a Gordon Neilson cross was stabbed home by John Docherty at the second attempt in the 88th minute. Still-celebrating, supporters were sent into near-hysteria just a minute later, as a right-wing throw-in was assisted into the penalty box by Gordon Neilson and Jackie Graham, where Alex Dawson grabbed the winner with the follow-up after his first effort had been blocked.

Sat 28th November: Colchester United (A)
Lost 0-4   Attendance: 4,673

The five-match winning run came to a crashing end as the home side scored after 11,16, 49 and 89 minutes, recording a comprehensive victory. Highlights of the game, shown on ITV's *Big Match*, were dominated by a second-half incident in which a stray dog on the pitch clattered into Chic Brodie as he stooped to collect a back pass. The injury caused the keeper to suffer damaged knee ligaments.

Sat 5th December: Barrow (H)
Won 2-1   Attendance: 5,632

A one-sided encounter should have produced a more comprehensive victory and, in the fourth minute, Jackie Graham set up Roger Cross to fire in a 25-yard thunderbolt effort. The lead was doubled two minutes after the interval when Gordon Neilson won possession and played in Roger Cross, whose square-pass was cracked home by Bobby Ross, although Peter Gelson conceded a 76th minute penalty, which was converted to set up a nervy finale.

Sat 12th December: Walsall (H) FA Cup 2nd Round
Won 1-0   Attendance: 8,500

The Division Three visitors were dispatched from the cup with a dominating first-half display and an even better second period, in which the game's only goal arrived. In the 69th minute Brian Turner's free-kick was knocked on by Bobby Ross for Roger Cross to net from close range. With both teams changing strips to avoid a clash of colours, Frank Blunstone's team wore the away kit of yellow and black.

Sat 19th December: Lincoln City (H)
Won 2-1   Attendance: 5,966

The early honours went to the visitors but, in the 20th minute, Roger Cross burst through three challenges and his right-wing centre was met by the head of Jackie Graham darting in at speed. The visitors levelled right on half time and started the second half on top, but the game was won in the 60th minute when Alan Hawley's overlapping run ended with a cross bravely headed home through an array of boots, by a diving Paul Bence.

Sat 26th December: Scunthorpe United (A)
Drew 1-1   Attendance: 4,736

The home side took a 14th minute lead when John Docherty's intended back-pass was intercepted and Gordon Phillips fumbled the subsequent shot. A solid defensive display thereafter kept the superior hosts at bay in wet and freezing conditions and, in the 87th minute, a free-kick from Alan Hawley was chipped into the penalty box by John Docherty for Roger Cross to lift the ball over the keeper's head and into the net.

Sat 2nd January: **Workington (A) FA Cup 3rd Round**
Won 1-0   **Attendance: 5,953**

An in-depth defensive approach staved off incessant attacking from the home side and the 250 travelling fans were rewarded with a fortuitous win after a 65th minute goal. A 35-yard free-kick from Brian Turner was flicked on by Bobby Ross for John Docherty to nip in and slot past the keeper. The club's share of the £1,498.6s/11d gate receipts amounted to £400 after the deduction of expenses.

Sat 9th January: **Stockport (H)**
Won 3-0   **Attendance: 7,340**

The eighth successive home win was also the tenth win in 12 matches and the visitors were fortunate to avoid an even heavier defeat after the fourth minute opener from John Docherty who fired home following a cross from Dick Renwick. In the 20th minute a well rehearsed corner-kick routine saw Docherty play the ball to Jackie Graham 20-yards out, and his darting run and low cross was knocked in by Bobby Ross, before the win was completed after 77 minutes when Roger Cross thumped home a shot after a blocked Brian Turner effort. The achievement of 100 consecutive League games for Ross was missed by manager Frank Blunstone, who was away watching forthcoming Cup opponents, Cardiff City.

Sat 16th January: **Aldershot (A)**
Lost 0-1   **Attendance: 7,533**

A largely forgettable encounter was settled by the more impressive hosts in the 23rd minute, and despite a more evenly-matched second half, the final outcome rarely looked anything other than a home win. Brentford's six-match unbeaten run came to an end.

Sat 23rd January: **Cardiff City (A) FA Cup 4th Round**
Won 2-0   **Attendance: 23,335**

The referee deemed a shocking pitch 'playable' despite a goal-to-goal rectangle of clogging ankle-deep mud and, with teeming rain continuing to fall throughout the 90 minutes, the high-flying, Second Division hosts were undone by a superb display. A 30th minute free-kick from the centre-circle by Peter Gelson was helped on by Bobby Ross, and Jackie Graham intercepted a back-pass to slot the ball home from a narrow angle. Then, Gordon Neilson's 50th minute right-wing free-kick was headed into the net by John Docherty. The remainder of the game saw an outstanding backs-to-the-wall defensive display repel the onslaught from the home side and manager Frank Blunstone's tactical astuteness was rewarded with progression to the last 16 of the FA Cup.

Sat 6th February: **Barrow (A)**
Won 1-0   **Attendance: 2,338**

The first league double of the campaign was secured in the 62nd minute when Roger Cross picked up a blocked free-kick and played the ball out to Alan Hawley, whose right-wing cut-back was drilled home by Paul Bence. Although the lowly hosts threw everything forward in the latter stages, they failed to find a way through a resolute defence. The final whistle blew at 4.59pm meaning the players had to complete their post-match ablutions at break-neck speed before being transported to the railway station in time to catch the 5.15pm train back to London.

Sat 13th February: **Hull City (A) FA Cup 5th Round**
Lost 1-2   **Attendance: 29,709**

A thrill-a-minute Cup tie produced a tremendous performance at the home of the Division Two table-toppers, and a dream start was secured in the 11th minute when Jackie Graham's left-wing run ended with a long cross from John Docherty, for Bobby Ross to head the opener. The end-to-end encounter saw the hosts gradually take territorial control, but in the 70th minute, a crucial two-goal lead was denied when a shot from Brian Turner came back off the inside of a post. An 81st minute equaliser was conceded before Gordon Phillips dropped the ball under pressure of a dubious challenge three minutes later, which ended the dreams of 3,000 travelling fans.

| **Sat 20th February:** | **York City (A)** |
| **Drew 0-0** | **Attendance: 3,366** |

An outstanding goalkeeping performance from Chic Brodie secured a point from a match played in murky and wet conditions – the home side producing wave after wave of attacks, without achieving the breakthrough.

| **Wed 24th February:** | **Hartlepool (H)** |
| **Won 1-0** | **Attendance: 9,246** |

A game between the teams in 20th and 22nd places in the table resulted in the best attendance of the season – the crowd were treated to a pulsating affair of richly-entertaining football, with the only goal of the evening arriving in the 28th minute, when John Docherty and Roger Cross combined to set up Jackie Graham for a darting run into the penalty box, which ended with a low drive into the net.

| **Sat 27th February:** | **Exeter City (A)** |
| **Lost 0-1** | **Attendance: 3,892** |

In a disappointing performance, the home side had the better of the first-half and, despite an improved display after the break, the points were lost after an error from Peter Gelson gifted the only goal of the game, which was notable for John Docherty receiving the first booking of his 14-year career for kicking the ball away.

| **Sat 6th March:** | **Southend United (H)** |
| **Won 4-2** | **Attendance: 6,348** |

On a rock-hard pitch and, with an icy wind howling, Roger Cross opened the scoring in the 6th minute when he turned and hooked the ball into the net after Bobby Ross had flicked on a John Docherty

centre. But the lead lasted just 3 minutes as Chic Brodie fumbled a short back-pass from Alan Hawley. The advantage was restored in the 49th minute from a Bobby Ross penalty and, with 60 minutes gone, Paul Bence neatly stepped over the ball and Roger Cross fired home a first-time shot. In the 70th minute Bobby Ross scored his second spot-kick after a John Docherty effort had been handled on the line, before the visitors grabbed a last minute goal.

| **Mon 8th March:** | **Crewe Alexandra (H)** |
| **Won 3-1** | **Attendance: 7,631** |

A free-flowing game produced the first goal after 34 minutes when Bobby Ross headed on a cross from John Docherty, and Paul Bence scored. The second goal arrived in the 67th minute as Gordon Neilson converted a left-wing centre from Roger Cross. The impressive visitors halved the arrears following a mix-up between Alan Hawley and Gordon Phillips, but the points were secured when Paul Bence centred from the right bye-line, and Roger Cross headed the ball on for Bobby Ross to apply the finishing touch.

| **Sat 13th March:** | **Grimsby Town (A)** |
| **Won 5-1** | **Attendance: 3,336** |

The scoreline was fully merited following a superb performance and, in the 18th minute, Roger Cross nodded in a Jackie Graham corner that had been flicked on by both Dick Renwick and Bobby Ross. Paul Bence hit a stunning second with a shot from the edge of the penalty area, after picking up a pass from Bobby Ross. The third goal arrived when John Docherty crossed for Bobby Ross to flick a backward header into the net – it was 4-0 after just 39 minutes when Alan Hawley provided the centre for Roger Cross to add his second of the afternoon. In the 80th minute John Docherty wriggled past two defenders and set up Paul Bence, whose shot

was parried for Bobby Ross to hit a fifth before the beleaguered hosts grabbed a consolation effort two minutes later.

Mon 15th March: **Hartlepool (A)**
Drew 0-0   **Attendance: 2,936**

An uneventful encounter ended scoreless – the home side had held the upper hand in the first-half and an improved second period performance failed to separate the teams on a cold, windy evening

Sat 20th March: **Newport County (H)**
Lost 0-3   **Attendance: 8,421**

The run of 11 successive home wins came to an end at the hands of the lowly visitors, who achieved their first away win in 19 attempts and, after indecision from Chic Brodie had led to the 35th minute opener, Alan Nelmes scored a second-half own goal. A third strike soon after compounded a disappointing afternoon.

Wed 24th March: **Workington (A)**
Drew 1-1   **Attendance: 1,731**

The hosts scored first in a dour, gruelling affair played out in heavy rain – a hard-earned point was secured when a free-kick from Renwick bounced into the net off the thigh of John Docherty.

Sat 27th March: **Oldham Athletic (H)**
Drew 1-1   **Attendance: 7,207**

The visitors hit the opening goal in an uninspiring game following a 25th minute blunder from Peter Gelson and despite creating a host of chances an equaliser seemed unlikely until the 89th minute when a Brian Turner cross was miscued by Roger Cross and Dick Renwick thumped home the leveller.

Mon 29th March: **Colchester United (H)**
Won 1-0   **Attendance: 9,209**

The FA Cup giant-killers and promotion-chasing visitors were outplayed throughout in a display that showed little effects of an 11th

game in 34 days – the winner coming in the 87th minute when a long throw from Roger Cross was flicked into the net by Gordon Neilson, prompting ecstatic supporters to raise the roof in delight.

Sat 3rd April: **Southport (A)**
Lost 0-2   **Attendance: 2,026**

The Saturday evening fixture, with a 7.30pm kick-off, saw a below-par performance punished – the more resourceful home side fully deserving both points, courtesy of their two goals coming after 28 and 43 minutes.

Fri 9th April: **Northampton Town (H)**
Won 3-0   **Attendance: 10,058**

A comfortable Good Friday morning victory was achieved – Bobby Ross glanced in a 20th minute header from a Jackie Graham corner, before a Dick Renwick cross was thumped home by Brian Turner to double the lead. The third goal came in unusual circumstances when a foul on John O'Mara inside the penalty area was punished with the award of an indirect free-kick, which was lashed into the net by Bobby Ross after Brian Turner's lay-off.

Sat 10th April: **Scunthorpe United (H)**
Lost 0-1   **Attendance: 7,561**

An emphatic and dominant performance saw a host of chances wasted and numerous clear-cut goal-scoring opportunities squandered – the under-pressure visitors couldn't believe their luck when an 88th minute strike grabbed both points.

Mon 12th April: **Peterborough United (A)**
Won 2-1   **Attendance: 3,841**

Following a poor first-half, the game seemed to be drifting towards an end-of-season stalemate, but in the 72nd minute Dick Renwick was sent off for a foul and the hosts scored from the subsequent free-kick. An equaliser arrived when a Paul Bence free-kick was headed back by John O'Mara for Gordon Neilson to hit an angled shot, and another free-kick produced the winner when Bobby Ross flicked home from Brian Turner's centre.

Sat 17th April: **Bournemouth (A)**
Lost 0-1   **Attendance: 11,206**

The all-but-promoted hosts were held at bay by a sound defensive performance, which fully merited a share of the spoils – but in the 82nd minute, a dreadful error proved fatal as Alan Nelmes lost possession in attempting to let the ball run out of play and an undeserved defeat was inflicted.

Sat 24th April: **Notts County (H)**
Drew 2-2   **Attendance: 9,299**

The visit of the champions was in doubt after heavy, overnight and pre-match rain, but with proceedings being given the go-ahead, the match was evenly contested until the 27th minute, when a blunder from Gordon Phillips gifted a goal. Roger Cross hit a 20-yard left-footer to equalise in the 61st minute, before the visitors went back in front after 74 minutes. Three minutes later Peter Gelson picked out Paul Bence, and his right-wing cross was met with a spectacular diving-header from Jackie Graham to secure a draw.

Mon 26th April: **Cambridge United (H)**
Lost 1-2   **Attendance: 5,994**

A scrappy opening 45 minutes was followed by a second period in which the wastefulness in front of goal was almost embarrassing. Although the deadlock was broken in the 57th minute by John O'Mara's 12-yard header from a Brian Turner free-kick, the visitors snatched an equaliser in the 70th minute, and hit the winner immediately afterwards.

Sat 1st May: **Darlington (A)**
Lost 1-2   **Attendance: 1,629**

An improved performance nonetheless contributed to an uninspiring end-of-season encounter, highlighted in the 35th minute by a superb goal when Paul Bence hit a long free-kick from his own penalty area which was flicked on by John O'Mara on the half-way line for Roger Cross to swivel and crash home a volley from fully 35-yards. The home side equalised in the 51st minute and won the game nine minutes later.

Fri 7th May: **Workington (H)**
Won 3-0   **Attendance: 4,781**

The final game of the season proved to be anything but a Cup-Final eve epic, although the ever-mounting pressure finally paid off when a free-kick from Paul Bence was touched on by John O'Mara for Gordon Neilson to hit the opener. Early in the second half Paul Bence and Gordon Neilson combined to set up Jackie Graham for a cracking drive from the edge of the penalty area, and the curtain came down on the campaign in the 67th minute when a goal-bound shot from amateur debutant, Mickey Heath, was headed into the net by John O'Mara.

PRE-SEASON

Frank Blunstone signed three new players all on free transfers – 21-year old Paul Bence from Reading, Jackie Graham aged 24 from Guildford City and 18-year old Michael Maskell from Chelsea.

After nine months on the transfer list, Alan Hawley's name was removed at his own request and Bobby Ross was appointed as club captain.

Roy Ruffell moved to the club from Uxbridge to manage the newly-formed juniors. The junior team joined the South-East counties League with home games scheduled at Griffin Park on Saturday mornings when the first team were playing away.

AUGUST 1970

• Paul Bence missed the whole pre-season programme with a thigh strain.
• Dick Renwick was given a 28-day suspension for receiving three cautions during the 1969-70 campaign.
• Michael Maskell was sidelined by injury.

SEPTEMBER 1970

• Alan Hawley went into hospital for observation and faced a lengthy lay-off.
• Goalkeeper Gordon Phillips, the club's only other fit player, was named as substitute for the game at Crewe.
• Striker and former 'Busby Babe' Alex Dawson, aged 30, was signed on loan from Brighton.

Geoff Prevett interviews
FRANK BLUNSTONE

Q. Frank, you have come to Griffin Park after 17 years at Chelsea. What differences have you noticed?

A. In a word, money. At Chelsea money appeared to be no object. The Players would travel first class, overnight stays at hotels were common. Almost everything one desired was readily available. The staff was huge. At Brentford everyone fends for themselves and stringent economies are the order of the day. I am however extremely pleased at the help the board and Mr. Piggott have given me. We have signed several players, none of whom would have been possible without further money being made available. In addition the players dressing room has been decorated, a new bath installed and this year the lads will wear white socks, but all are extra expense.

Q. Are you settling down well at Brentford?

A. Yes, very well. At Chelsea I was Youth Team Manager and coach, and more on the coaching side. There is a difference managing a first team but I much prefer having my own ideas and putting them into practice, after my 5 year apprenticeship with the Chelsea Youth side. At the Bridge Dave Sexton looked after the first team and Ron Stuart the reserves and both of these and Tommy Docherty before them were a great help to me. Brentford have great potential and I wouldn't have left Chelsea had it not been so.

Q. Is Brentford a happy club?

A. Yes, from the Chairman to the Groundsman the Team Spirit is first class. This is essential as it enables the players to give their all. The facilities are also very good and could easily accommodate a second division team. With improvements a first division team and even now it is better than Ipswich or Blackpool.

Q. What are your views on rough play?

A. I do not like dirty play. I tell the lads to play it hard but fair. There is no need to kick their way out of the fourth division—good football will do it all the time and we have got the players who can play good football.

Q. At the end of last season the Bees were less defensive. Are we to see more attacking play this season?

A. We shall be attacking much more. Last year we were unlucky at Grimsby, Oldham and York but the new style began to pay off at Southend and Aldershot. A style cannot be changed overnight. At least we began to create chances and miss them which is better than neither creating nor missing. This year we shall score more. I am hoping, injuries permitting, for Alan Mansley, Roger Cross and John Docherty to get 20 goals apiece and with the big fellows at the back weighing in with a few each hope to see well over 70 goals scored.

[Above] Peter Gelson and Alan Nelmes in defensive action during the Cup-tie at Cardiff in January 1971

OCTOBER 1970

• Michael Maskell had his contract cancelled by mutual consent for disciplinary reasons.

• Chic Brodie played for an hour at Northampton with a chipped bone in his arm, and faced a spell on the sidelines.

• Former full-back, Ken Horne, was enlisted to assist with the coaching of the juniors.

NOVEMBER 1970

• Alex Dawson returned to Brighton at the end of his loan spell when terms could not be reached with the player after a reported £7,000 fee had been agreed between the two clubs.

• Allan Mansley was placed on the transfer-list and joined Fulham on loan.

• Brian Turner received a fine and a 14-day ban, suspended until the end of the season, for receiving three bookings.

• Peter Gelson's benefit match against West Ham raised £1,670.

• Chic Brodie suffered torn knee ligaments after colliding with a stray dog in the match at Colchester.

DECEMBER 1970

• Allan Mansley returned from his loan at Fulham and was offered a similar move to Crewe.

• Brian Tawse was placed on the transfer-list at his own request.

• A loan move for Luton striker John Collins was called off when his club suffered an injury crisis, while Frank Blunstone also expressed an interest in signing Luton striker Peter Phillips.

• At the club AGM, three new directors were appointed to the board – Colin Wheatley and Peter Davey, both sons of existing directors, and Bert Poyton.

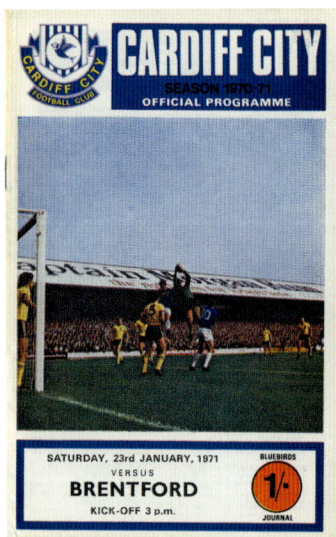

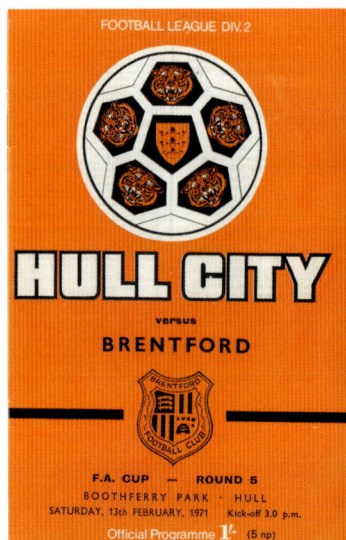

JANUARY 1971

- 3,000 supporters travelled to Ninian Park for the FA Cup match with Cardiff.
- Allan Mansley rejected the offer of a loan move to Crewe and remained transfer-listed.
- The home match with Colchester on 30th January was postponed as a result of bad weather.
- Walter Wheatley was ousted as chairman of the board of directors and replaced by Eric Radley-Smith; Wheatley became joint Club President with Frank Davis.

QUESTIONS AND ANSWERS WITH THE PLAYERS

PAUL BENCE
Q. How did you feel after scoring your first league goal ?
A. Reading v. Rotherham. I scored in the 89th minute and we won 1—0 (It was my home debut so I was over the moon).
Q. Has joining Brentford given you a better taste for scoring goals ?
A. Yes.

CHIC BRODIE
Q. What was your favourite team as a boy ?
A. Glasgow Rangers.
Q. What do you consider was your best ever save ?
A. The one I made against Leeds United in Div II taken by Bobby Collins.

ROGER CROSS
Q. Which goal gave you the greatest thrill at Brentford in front of the home fans ?
A. My first one which I scored during the Exeter City game.
Q. Where did you learn the art of a long throw and from whom ?
A. You will be interested to know that I taught myself this art.

JOHN DOCHERTY
Q. What was the spirit in the dressing room after the Cup Match against Cardiff ?
A. It was so good in the dressing room, I felt we had won the cup.
Q. What is it like to be back at Griffin Park for over a year now ?
A. As though I had never been away.

PETER GELSON
Q. Did you ever consider not becoming a professional footballer ?
A. Yes, I thought I might be a civil servant.
Q. Who was the hardest centre-forward you played against last season ?
A. Jim Fryatt of Oldham Athletic.

JACKIE GRAHAM
Q Are there any changes you would like to see in British Football ?
A. I would like to see more protection for the ball-players.
Q. Have you enjoyed your first season in the English Football League ?
A. Yes, it has been very enjoyable.

ALAN HAWLEY
Q. Which is your most memorable game ?
A. My first ever League appearance against Barrow (1962/63)
Q. Does rail-travel etc., affect your game mentally before a game.
A. Not really, but longer trips tend to be much more tiring.

GORDON NEILSON
Q. Do you come from a sporting family ?
A. Yes, members of my family both past and present.
Q. What do you consider was your best goal ?
A. The goal, which wasn't the best but, which gave me the most satisfaction was against Colchester last season

ALAN NELMES

Q. What is the most memorable game you have played for Brentford ?
A. It was against Cardiff in the F.A. Cup 4th round, 1971.
Q. How did you feel after receiving the Players 'Player of the Year' cup ?
A. The best thing to happen to me in my years at Brentford.

JOHN O'MARA

Q. How nervous were you on your home debut game for Brentford ?
A. Not very nervous, once the game had started everything was alright.
Q. What in your opinion is the most significant difference between the Southern League and the Fourth Division ?
A. The players are fitter and faster

GORDON PHILLIPS

Q. How did you come to play for Brentford ?
A. I joined the juniors and progressed through to the first team from there.
Q. What was it like to play in the 1st team after a long absence ?
A. It was really good to be back.

DICK RENWICK

Q. Do you prefer to play up front with the forwards rather than at the back ?
A. No, I much prefer playing right at the back.
Q. Which was the hardest team you played against last season ?
A. Colchester United.

BOBBY ROSS

Q. What is your greatest moment as captain of Brentford so far ?
A. While captaining the side during the great cup run last season, really tremendous.
Q. Whose was your childhood hero as a youngster ?
A. Dave Mackay.

BRIAN TAWSE

Q. What is the highlight of your career so far ?
A. It was playing for Arsenal against Spurs at Highbury in front of a capacity crowd.
Q. How did you feel after scoring your first goal for Brentford ?
A. Naturally it felt good after scoring this goal.

BRIAN TURNER

Q. What interests do you have outside football ?
A. I enjoy playing cricket and golf.
Q. Where did you learn about taking free-kicks ?
A. I learnt the technique with Chelsea.

FEBRUARY 1971

• Brian Tawse joined Folkestone on loan.
• The appearance at Hull City in the fifth round of the FA Cup was the furthest the club had reached in the competition since 1949.

MARCH 1971

• Allan Mansley was offered a free transfer and joined Notts County on loan.
• 6'3" striker John O'Mara was signed from non-league Wimbledon on transfer deadline day for a reported fee of £750, plus £250 after 20 games .
• Junior, Alan Gane, signed as an amateur.

APRIL 1971

• Local boy, Mickey Heath, signed as an amateur.
• Brian Tawse was offered an opportunity to go to the United States to play for Washington.
• Dick Renwick was sent off at Peterborough and faced a suspension at the start of the new season.

MAY 1971

• Allan Mansley signed for Notts County on a free transfer.
• The retained list was announced and free transfers were given to Chic Brodie and Brian Tawse.

1971-72

[Back Row] Paul Bence, Peter Gelson, Brian Turner, Alan Nelmes, Gordon Phillips, Mike Allen, Alan Hawley, Terry Scales
[Front Row] Gordon Neilson, John O'Mara, Bobby Ross, Jackie Graham, John Docherty, Steve Tom

Football League	Division Four
Manager	Frank Blunstone
Trainer	Eddie Lyons
Captain	Bobby Ross
Final Position	3rd
FA Cup	1st Round
League Cup	1st Round
Leading Goalscorer (all competitions)	John O'Mara – 27 goals

A season built on a philosophy of all-out attack at home, and in-depth defending on their travels, resulted in a successful campaign for Brentford, spearheaded by giant centre-forward John O'Mara. He hit 27 goals, many with his head, as numerous visiting teams were swamped at Griffin Park.

A 4-0 home win against Barrow on August Bank Holiday Monday set up a sequence of six straight victories at Griffin Park, including thumpings of Hartlepool (6-0), Peterborough (5-1) and Northampton (6-1) and, after a first round FA Cup replay against Swansea had attracted a home crowd of 15,000, a run of four consecutive victories in December culminated with 18,237 spectators flooding to the Boxing Day game against Crewe Alexandra – the biggest home attendance since 1959.

The five-week suspension of John O'Mara in January, having already amassed 22 goals, proved a difficult loss to cope with and his five-game absence resulted in three defeats and two draws – but his return to action prompted a five-game winning streak and the Good Friday fixture resulted in another massive attendance, 18,521, for the visit of Chester City.

With home crowds averaging over 11,000, promotion was secured with two games remaining following a 1-0 victory against Exeter City in the final home match – the feat was made all the more remarkable by the use of just 18 players during the entire season.

[Previous page] John Docherty, John O'Mara and Bobby Ross – who scored a total of 55 goals between them during the 1971-72 season

BRENTFORD FOOTBALL CLUB
SEASON 1971-72

Football League Division IV

BRENTFORD
versus
ALDERSHOT

GRIFFIN PARK   *Photo by courtesy of Evening Mail*

SATURDAY, 21st AUGUST, 1971
Kick-off 3.15 p.m.

Ground: Griffin Park, Braemar Road, Brentford

Official Programme Price 5p.

NEXT HOME GAMES

TUESDAY 24th AUGUST, 1971   BRENTFORD JUNIORS v. WEALDSTONE JUNIORS
F.A. Youth Challenge Cup Competition.   Kick-off 7.30 p.m.   (at Griffin Park)
1st Qualifying Round

SATURDAY, 28th AUGUST, 1971   BRENTFORD JUNIORS v. TOTTENHAM HOTSPUR
South East Counties League   Kick-off 11 a.m.   (at Ruislip Manor F.C.)   JUNIORS

MONDAY, 30th AUGUST, 1971   BRENTFORD v. BARROW
Football League Division IV   Kick-off 7.30 p.m.

Total Home League Attendances	269,985
Average Home League Attendance	11,738
Highest Home League Attendance	18,521
Lowest Home League Attendance	8,712

		P	W	D	L	F	A	W	D	L	F	A	Pts
1	Grimsby	46	18	3	2	61	26	10	4	9	27	30	63
2	Southend	46	18	2	3	56	26	6	10	7	25	29	60
3	**Brentford**	**46**	**16**	**2**	**5**	**52**	**21**	**8**	**9**	**6**	**24**	**23**	**59**
4	Scunthorpe	46	13	8	2	34	15	9	5	9	22	22	57
5	Lincoln	46	17	5	1	46	15	4	9	10	31	44	56
6	Workington	46	12	9	2	34	7	4	10	9	16	27	51
7	Southport	46	15	5	3	48	21	3	9	11	18	25	50
8	Peterborough	46	14	6	3	51	24	3	10	10	31	40	50
9	Bury	46	16	4	3	55	22	3	8	12	18	37	50
10	Cambridge	46	11	8	4	38	22	6	6	11	24	38	48
11	Colchester	46	13	6	4	38	23	6	4	13	32	46	48
12	Doncaster	46	11	8	4	35	24	5	6	12	21	39	46
13	Gillingham	46	11	5	7	33	24	5	8	10	28	43	45
14	Newport	46	13	5	5	34	20	5	3	15	26	52	44
15	Exeter City	46	11	5	7	40	30	5	6	12	21	38	43
16	Reading	46	14	3	6	37	26	3	5	15	19	50	42
17	Aldershot	46	5	13	5	27	20	4	9	10	21	34	40
18	Hartlepool	46	14	2	7	39	25	3	4	16	19	44	40
19	Darlington	46	9	9	5	37	24	5	2	16	27	58	39
20	Chester	46	10	11	2	34	16	0	7	16	13	40	38
21	Northampton	46	8	9	6	43	27	4	4	15	23	52	37
22	Barrow	46	8	8	7	23	26	5	3	15	17	45	37
23	Stockport	46	7	10	6	33	32	2	4	17	22	55	32
24	Crewe	46	9	4	10	27	25	1	5	17	16	44	29

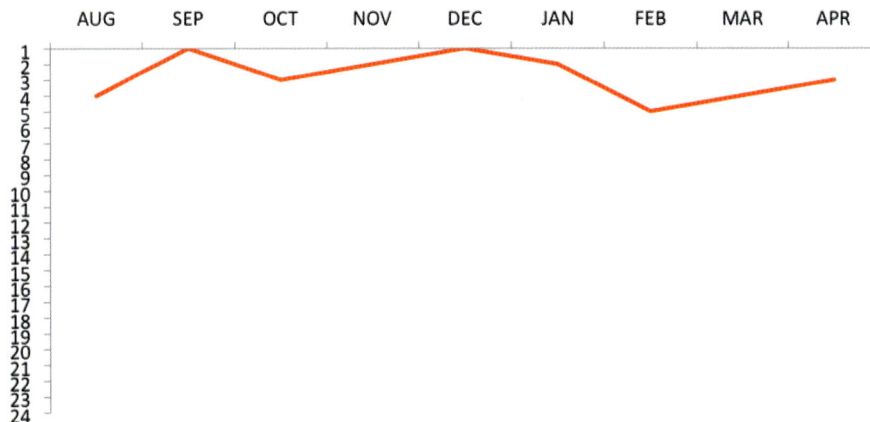

League Position throughout the Season

1971-72

Sat 14th August: **Bury (A)**
Won 2-0   **Attendance: 2,957**

An impressive display welcomed the arrival of the new season and, in the 33rd minute, a corner from Jackie Graham found its way to Peter Gelson who steadied himself, before shooting home from six yards – the points were sealed after 51 minutes when John O'Mara's cross was half-cleared for debutant Steve Tom to crack in a spectacular drive from 20 yards.

Wed 18th August: **Colchester (A) League Cup 1st Round**
Lost 1-3   **Attendance: 6,125**

Interest in the competition was extinguished with a resounding defeat that, at times, threatened to turn into a rout – goals for the hosts in the 33rd and 53rd minutes, then a twice-taken penalty conceded by Gordon Phillips, rewarded relentless pressure from the home side. In the 88th minute Roger Cross squared the ball from the right flank and Bobby Ross netted a consolation goal with a neat back-header.

Sat 21st August: **Aldershot (H)**
Drew 1-1   **Attendance: 8,920**

In front of the ITV *Big Match* cameras, a tepid first half turned into a more competitive encounter after the break and, in the 63rd minute, a deflected 15-yard shot from Brian Turner secured the lead. However, a series of squandered opportunities proved costly and the visitors equalised in the third minute of stoppage time.

Sat 28th August: **Darlington (A)**
Drew 0-0   **Attendance: 2,514**

An uninspiring game saw the points shared – the most notable moment of the goal-less encounter coming in the 55th minute when a Bobby Ross header rebounded from a post and John

O'Mara contrived to lash the ball vertically into the air from less than two yards – the effort dropping behind the goal.

Mon 30th August: **Barrow (H)**
Won 4-0   **Attendance: 8,866**

A closely-fought, enterprising first half saw the teams separated by an 18th minute goal courtesy of a back-header from John O'Mara from a left-wing Bobby Ross centre. The second half produced a display of scintillating Bees football. In the 53rd minute Roger Cross powered home a John Docherty corner and Jackie Graham then set up Brian Turner to score with a low, 20-yard drive. Bobby Ross completed the victory with a header from a Docherty centre.

Sat 4th September: **Hartlepool (H)**
Won 6-0   **Attendance: 8,712**

The biggest victory since October 1963 resulted from a one-sided encounter – the opening goal arrived in the 24th minute when Brian Turner leapt to head in a left-wing centre from Roger Cross, Brian Turner scored again after 38 minutes, with a skimming low cross-drive from the edge of the penalty area after receiving the ball from John Docherty. In the 57th minute John O'Mara converted a corner from Jackie Graham and, after 80 minutes, a pass from John Docherty found Roger Cross in space to nod home. John O'Mara completed a hat-trick with two late strikes, both set up by Brian Turner.

Sat 11th September: **Grimsby Town (A)**
Lost 1-3   **Attendance: 11,683**

The division's biggest crowd of the day saw the home side take over top spot with a deserved win despite going behind in the 4th minute when a long ball from Alan Nelmes was centred by John Docherty for John O'Mara to head home. The hosts responded with second-half strikes after 49, 55 and 84 minutes – only a superb display from Gordon Phillips kept the margin of defeat from being far greater.

Sat 18th September: **Peterborough United (H)**
Won 5-1   **Attendance: 8,770**

A display of attacking football, likely to be unsurpassed during the campaign, increased the goal tally to 15 in three home games even after the visitors had taken a 24th minute 'against the run of play' lead, which was cancelled out within four minutes when Brian Turner's powerful 30-yard run ended with his blocked shot being netted by Gordon Neilson. A dominant second half produced four further goals – firstly Paul Bence and John Docherty combining to create an opening for Jackie Graham to slide the ball beyond the keeper, before a shot from Peter Gelson was handled – John Docherty slamming home the rebound after Bobby Ross's penalty had hit a post. Docherty then flicked on a corner for John O'Mara to head the fourth and, when the keeper fumbled another corner, Bobby Ross lashed the ball into the net.

Sat 25th September: **Chester (A)**
Drew 0-0   **Attendance: 4,088**

An unyielding and unfaltering defensive display in the face of intense attacking from the dominant hosts secured a hard-earned point, backed up by another great goalkeeping performance from Gordon Phillips.

Mon 27th September: **Stockport County (H)**
Won 2-0   **Attendance: 10,445**

The bottom of the table visitors contributed fully to an evening of rich, attacking entertainment – the crucial opening goal arriving in the 60th minute thanks to a low 20-yard drive from Bobby Ross. Victory was sealed when a chipped free-kick from Brian Turner was met by a glancing back-header from Bobby Ross – the two goals brought the tally of successful strikes at the Ealing Road end of the ground to 14 out of a total of 18.

Sat 2nd October: **Northampton Town (H)**
Won 6-1   **Attendance: 11,004**

On a warm and sultry afternoon the visitors took the lead after just 38 seconds and a scrappy opening half-hour ended when the limping Peter Gelson headed home a John Docherty cross to equalise. The second period was barely underway when an exquisite through-ball from Alan Nelmes set up John Docherty to hit a low, crisp drive past the keeper then, in the 54th minute, John O'Mara headed in a Jackie Graham corner, with an identical second for O'Mara coming five minutes later. A centre from Bobby Ross was nodded down by John O'Mara for Gordon Neilson to thump home from close-range, then a 78th minute shot from Paul Bence came back off the post for John O'Mara to complete his second hat-trick of the season in another home goal-fest.

Fri 8th October: **Southport (A)**
Drew 0-0   **Attendance: 5,371**

A lively Friday evening encounter produced an exciting match in which another solid defensive performance ensured a share of the spoils – the 20 travelling supporters saw the unwanted record of never having scored a goal on a visit to Haig Avenue extended for yet another season.

Sat 16th October: **Bury (H)**
Won 2-0   **Attendance: 9,851**

Heavy pre-match rain, and persistent downpours thereafter, greeted an evenly-contested opening 45 minutes in which the visitors proved tough opposition. In the 63rd minute a corner from Brian Turner was met by the head of John O'Mara to open the scoring, then, deep into injury time, John Docherty sent in a right-wing cross and Jackie Graham's header sealed the win.

Wed 20th October: **Reading (A)**
Lost 1-2   **Attendance: 10,473**

The home side were in the ascendency throughout and goals after 51 and 57 minutes looked to be the prelude to a heavier defeat – but a late rally saw John O'Mara head home a John Docherty cross in the 81st minute and top spot was retained despite the loss.

Sat 23rd October: **Southend United (H)**
Lost 1-2   **Attendance: 14,001**

A second successive defeat, the first home loss of the season, was inflicted by visitors who took the lead on the stroke of half-time, then, just a minute into the second period, Alan Nelmes headed into his own net under no pressure to double the deficit. In the 69th minute Paul Bence set up John O'Mara to stride forward and unleash a venomous drive from the edge of the penalty area and the remaining 20 minutes produced a barrage of attacks, but all to no avail.

Sat 30th October: **Scunthorpe United (A)**
Drew 0-0   **Attendance: 6,121**

A stout rearguard action provided the basis for a fourth goal-less draw in seven away matches and early in the second half Brian Turner conceded a penalty but Gordon Phillips saved the spot-kick to leave the team sitting in third place in the league table.

Sat 6th November: **Newport County (H)**
Won 3-1   **Attendance: 10,484**

On a dark, dank, wintery afternoon John Docherty hooked the ball into the net to open the scoring after 25 minutes after Bobby Ross had headed on a long throw from Brian Turner – the lead was doubled when John Docherty was fouled and Bobby Ross converted a twice-taken spot-kick. In the 68th minute John Docherty's long left-wing cross was met by a swerving drive from Bobby Ross and, after a brief stoppage caused by a floodlight failure, the visitors netted a late consolation goal.

Sat 13th November: **Colchester United (A)**
Drew 1-1   **Attendance: 6,898**

The opening half produced the best away display of the season and, after the hosts had taken a 14th minute lead, the leveller arrived after 26 minutes when Paul Bence's cross was met by the deftest of touches from the head of John O'Mara. A 'what we have we hold' approach after the interval secured the point necessary to return to the top of the table.

Sat 20th November: **Swansea (A) FA Cup 1st Round**
Drew 1-1   **Attendance: 7,915**

Almost 2,000 travelling fans journeyed to South Wales to witness a cup-tie played in appalling weather – strong winds and a constant deluge of rain had left much of the pitch waterlogged and threatened to prevent the game running its full course. The home side took a 35th minute lead, but a 77th minute headed goal from John O'Mara, from a Brian Turner corner, earned a deserved replay.

Mon 22nd November: **Swansea (H) FA Cup 1st Round**
Lost 2-3   **Attendance: 15,000**

A superb action-packed replay provided a memorable cup-tie and the visitors took an 8th minute lead following a misjudgement from Gordon Phillips – the advantage was doubled after 24 minutes when a Steve Tom slip gifted a second goal. Bobby Ross headed home a Jackie Graham corner in the 44th minute and, backed by fervent support, the second period saw an all-out attacking display. But the visitors restored their two-goal lead when a free-kick was diverted into his own net by Brian Turner, however, a late goal from John O'Mara, flicking home a pass from Terry Scales, failed to prevent an exit from the competition.

Sat 27th November: **Gillingham (H)**
Lost 1-3   **Attendance: 10,945**

Against the run of play the visitors took a 36th minute lead with a freak goal – a 45-yard free-kick sailed straight into the net. A second goal after 43 minutes left a second-half mountain to climb. In the 51st minute a cross from John Docherty was headed on by a defender for Bobby Ross to net with a low drive, but the points were lost in the 61st minute when a poor corner from Brian Turner led to a breakaway third goal.

Sat 4th December: **Exeter City (A)**
Won 1-0   **Attendance: 3,809**

The first away success since the opening day of the season came courtesy of a 47th minute headed goal from John O'Mara following a corner from Brian Turner, after which the fog descended and the over-worked floodlights just about saw the game through to the 90th minute.

Sat 11th December: **Southport (H)**
Won 1-0   **Attendance: 9,624**

A scrappy affair promised never to linger long in the memory of football purists, and the encounter was settled in the 70th minute when Bobby Ross and Peter Gelson, making his 400th club appearance, combined to set up Jackie Graham whose left-wing cross from the by-line was diverted into his own net by a visiting defender.

Sat 18th December: **Hartlepool (A)**
Won 2-1   **Attendance: 2,199**

The top-versus-bottom clash saw the home strugglers take a 3rd minute lead, before stand-in striker, Mike Allen, hit a 39th minute equaliser with a short-range effort after Peter Gelson had nodded on a Jackie Graham corner. An identically-worked goal provided Allen with his second after 75 minutes, but not before Brian Turner had been sent off on the hour-mark having previously been booked.

Mon 27th December: **Crewe Alexandra (H)**
Won 1-0   **Attendance: 18,237**

Spring-like Boxing Day weather brought out a huge holiday crowd and, after a tepid first-half, in which the visitors offered little, the

[Right] Captain Bobby Ross, who made 167 consecutive first team starts between November 1968 and February 1972, during the home defeat to Gillingham

deadlock was broken after 63 minutes when Bobby Ross fed John Docherty who beat two defenders, before sending in a cross that John O'Mara headed home in trademark style.

Sat 1st January: **Peterborough United (A)**
Drew 2-2   **Attendance: 7,027**

The New Year fixture saw the home side ahead after 13 minutes, but a splendid display produced a magnificent fight-back, and the scores were level in the 35th minute when a long, forward ball from Terry Scales was headed home by John O'Mara. Seven minutes later a free-kick from Jackie Graham led to another headed goal from John O'Mara. In the 78th minute a home corner kick went straight through the arms of Gordon Phillips and into the net to leave the score all-square.

Sat 8th January: **Darlington (H)**
Won 6-2   **Attendance: 10,582**

On a wet and muddy pitch Bobby Ross opened the scoring after 22 minutes when he was fouled in the penalty area, then picked himself up to score from the resultant spot-kick – but the visitors equalised in the 30th minute. After an evenly-matched first-half the game burst to life with three goals in 19 minutes – firstly John O'Mara headed in Jackie Graham's corner, then a chipped free-kick from Brian Turner saw the ball prodded over the line by John Docherty after John O'Mara's effort had been blocked. In the 56th minute a wonderful move ended with Paul Bence hitting a diagonal cross to John O'Mara, who smashed the ball home from just outside the penalty area with a first-time shot. Docherty then hit a 62nd minute powerful angled shot, then two minutes later, waltzed past two defenders and netted after his first effort had hit the post The beleaguered visitors snatched an 88th minute consolation effort.

Sat 15th January: **Lincoln City (A)**
Lost 1-4   **Attendance: 7,552**

A miserable January afternoon saw a 9th minute slip from Alan Nelmes gift the hosts the opening goal and the deficit was doubled after 42 minutes, but after the interval, Brentford ran the home side ragged and, in the 74th minute, a cross from John Docherty was headed in by John O'Mara. Against the run of play the home side hit a breakaway goal to extend their lead in the 83rd minute and ended the contest with a fourth strike two minutes later. John O'Mara received his fourth booking of the campaign.

Fri 21st January: **Stockport (A)**
Won 1-0   **Attendance: 3,247**

A Friday evening performance of punch, pace and polish produced a slick exhibition of attacking football with the all-important goal finally arriving in the 78th minute – Jackie Graham seizing on a loose ball on the left flank, cut along the by-line before sending over a precision, chipped cross for Bobby Ross to head home.

Sat 29th January: **Reading (H)**
Lost 1-2   **Attendance: 12,144**

In the 10th minute Gordon Phillips fumbled a shot and Alan Nelmes' attempted clearance rebounded into the net off an opponent – the visitors then took a two-goal lead after 30 minutes, before John Docherty punished a defensive blunder by nipping between the keeper and a dithering defender to toe-poke the ball over the line. The second half produced a stuttering display and the visitors held firm as top spot in the table was conceded.

Sat 5th February: **Cambridge United (A)**
Drew 1-1   **Attendance: 6,861**

With John O'Mara starting his five-week suspension, a dour midfield battle led to a less than exciting encounter. The home side went ahead in the 51st minute before an equaliser came after 71 minutes when John Docherty crossed from the right and debutant,

[Right] John O'Mara, playing his last game before starting a five-week suspension, during the home defeat to Reading

Ken Wallace, dummied to allow Jackie Graham to lash home a 15-yard shot.

Sat 12th February: **Southend United (A)**
Lost 1-3   **Attendance: 9,841**

With the midweek home fixture against Workington having been postponed due to the threat of power cuts, the week ended with a heavy defeat – the hosts dominated proceedings throughout, scoring after 26, 35 and 65 minutes, and threatened to run riot on a rain-sodden pitch. In the 89th minute Bobby Ross converted a penalty after John Docherty had been brought down when attempting to round the keeper.

Sat 19th February: **Scunthorpe United (H)**
Lost 0-3   **Attendance: 11,912**

The visiting league leaders recorded a comprehensive victory after taking a 30th minute lead and, despite superb home support, the lack of a cutting edge up front was apparent as a misplaced pass from Ken Wallace set up the visitors for a 65th minute second – the heavy defeat was sealed after 86 minutes.

Sat 26th February: **Newport County (A)**
Drew 0-0   **Attendance: 3,271**

A grim defensive display on a quagmire of a pitch produced a stalemate in which both keepers performed well in difficult conditions – the solitary point earned saw the team slip out of the top four for the first time in the campaign.

Sat 4th March: **Colchester United (H)**
Lost 0-2   **Attendance: 9,210**

The winless run was extended to six matches as the visitors scored after 48 and 72 minutes to inflict a dismal defeat with many sup-

porters heading for the exits long before the final whistle – the only highlight of the afternoon being the splendid debut of Chelsea loanee, Stewart Houston.

Mon 13th March: **Lincoln City (H)**
Won 2-0   **Attendance: 12,065**

The postponement of the fixture at Doncaster Rovers, due to restrictions on the use of floodlights, enabled the return to action of John O'Mara and the huge crowd who turned up in expectation were rewarded with the best performance of the season. After a scintillating first-half, a 53rd minute free-kick from Brian Turner was headed home by John O'Mara to raise the roof. A magnificent display was sealed with a stunning 76th minute goal – Terry Scales hit a rocket from 25 yards after a free-kick had been cleared.

Sat 18th March: **Aldershot (A)**
Won 2-1   **Attendance: 6,989**

After 8 minutes a cross from Terry Scales, after a corner had been cleared to him, was nodded past the keeper by John O'Mara. The home side then took control and equalised on the stroke of half-time. The winner arrived in the 55th minute when Jackie Graham's corner was headed on by both Mike Allen and Stewart Houston for Bobby Ross to flick home and a firm defensive display kept the home side at bay until the end.

Tue 21st March: **Doncaster Rovers (A)**
Won 3-0   **Attendance: 5,256**

The best away performance for many seasons produced an outstanding display of non-stop action and thrills. Brian Turner's foraging run and cross enabled Jackie Graham to open the scoring from close range after just 2 minutes, before Stewart Houston's cross saw Bobby Ross turn the ball into the net for a second goal with just seven minutes on the clock. A memorable win was secured in the 85th minute when Jackie Graham drove home a cross-shot following a long free-kick from Brian Turner.

Sat 25th March: **Grimsby Town (H)**
Won 2-0   **Attendance: 14,635**

The main event of the ITV *Big Match* programme provided a great spectacle with a thrilling first half, in which the visiting keeper ensured that the scores were level at the interval. The deadlock was broken in the 63rd minute when Jackie Graham emerged from a mass of players in the penalty area to set up John Docherty for a low shot into the net. The rapturous applause had barely died down when John Docherty's dashing run and square pass was swept home by John O'Mara less than sixty seconds after the first goal.

Mon 27th March: **Workington (H)**
Won 2-0   **Attendance: 13,972**

Gordon Phillips was the busier of the two keepers in a first-half dominated by a gale-force wind – John Docherty hit a 53rd minute half-volley following a flowing move involving Stewart Houston, Jackie Graham and John O'Mara. After the heavens had opened, accompanied by a violent thunderstorm, Stewart Houston clinched the win in the 80th minute with a crashing angled shot having been played in by John Docherty.

Fri 31st March: **Chester (H)**
Drew 1-1   **Attendance: 18,521**

The biggest home attendance since 1959 witnessed the Good Friday encounter. Captain-for-the-day, John Docherty, nodded in a 22nd minute corner from Brian Turner, which had been flicked on by Stewart Houston, before the visitors levelled with their first attack 8 minutes later – thereafter the game turned into a ragged affair which drifted towards an inevitable conclusion.

Sat 1st April: Crewe Alexandra (A)
Lost 1-2 Attendance: 2,072

The visit to the Football League's bottom club produced the worst performance of the season and, with the pitch ankle-deep in mud, Alex took a two-goal lead after strikes in the 11th and 35th minutes. With speculation rife surrounding the circumstances of the half-time substitution of John O'Mara, a slightly improved second half display saw John Docherty curl in a 72nd minute shot from the tightest of angles – but a damaging defeat had been inflicted.

Mon 3rd April: Northampton Town (A)
Drew 0-0 Attendance: 5,314

The Easter programme ended with an entertaining draw in which a host of squandered first-half opportunities proved costly – the second period was more evenly-contested as both defences dominated.

Sat 8th April: Cambridge United (H)
Won 2-1 Attendance: 9,061

The visitors were aided by a strong wind in the opening period and took the lead in first-half injury-time against the run of play. But the scores were levelled in the 52nd minute when John Docherty out-witted two defenders on the right touch-line and fired in a 25-yard swerving effort, which beat the keeper. The winner arrived in the 74th minute as a corner was only half-cleared – Stewart Houston laid the ball off to Jackie Graham, who slammed it into the net.

Sat 15th April: Gillingham (A)
Won 1-0 Attendance: 5,819

Two precious points were gained with the seventh away win of the season – the all-important goal came after 29 minutes when Steve Tom headed the ball out of the centre circle to Bobby Ross and his flick found John Docherty, who burst forward and steadied himself, before firing home from 20 yards. The hard-fought victory was secured in the face of incessant home pressure and with an outstanding goalkeeping display from Gordon Phillips.

[Right] Bees players celebrating in the bath, following the 1-0 promotion clincher at home to Exeter City

Mon 17th April: Doncaster Rovers (H)
Won 2-1 Attendance: 13,484

With the prize of promotion tantalisingly close, a tension-filled evening was on the cards. But after a good opening spell the scoring got underway in the 23rd minute when Stewart Houston played in John O'Mara, who let the ball run past him before turning and firing home a low drive. In the 40th minute an up-and-under from Peter Gelson dropped just beyond the half-way line for John O'Mara to race forward and elude the keeper's dive to score. The nervousness of the second period was not aided by a delay when one of the floodlights failed and, after a misplaced back-pass from Peter Gelson gifted the visitors an 81st minute goal, the remaining time produced an agonising and suspense-ridden finale – immense relief greeted the final whistle.

Sat 22nd April: Exeter City (H)
Won 1-0 Attendance: 14,540

A perfect start saw a penalty awarded in the 14th minute after John O'Mara was pushed in the back – Bobby Ross converted the spot-kick with a low drive, but a string of good moves failed to produce further rewards. After the interval, anxiety crept in with passes going astray and the tension from the terraces transmitted itself to the pitch – the visitors took advantage, turning erstwhile breakaways into sustained attacks. However, the minutes ticked by slowly until the final whistle, then the dream of promotion became reality and supporters spilled onto the pitch in celebration.

Mon 24th April: Barrow (A)
Won 3-0 Attendance: 2,646

On a bone-hard and bumpy pitch Stewart Houston nodded in a right-wing cross from John O'Mara in the 32nd minute and a well-marshalled defensive display kept the advantage until the

[Left] Bobby Ross in aerial action as The Bees attack the Ealing Road end during the home defeat by Gillingham

73rd minute when Mike Allen hit a 20-yard shot following a cross from John Docherty. The win was sealed after 80 minutes as John Docherty crossed for Jackie Graham to fire home and consign the hosts to the end of their time as a Football League club.

Sat 29th April: **Workington (A)**
Lost 0-3   **Attendance: 1,751**

The season ended on a wind-swept afternoon and the rampant home side opened the scoring after 26 minutes – a two-goal half-time advantage was extended to three goals with 50 minutes gone and a potential rout looked on the cards. But the game ended with the disappointment of defeat heavily over-shadowed by the overall success of the campaign, and the train travellers amongst the 200 travelling supporters celebrated with the players on the return journey back to London.

PRE-SEASON

Dick Renwick received an eight-week suspension as a result of his disciplinary record during the previous season but requested a free transfer which was granted and he left the club.

Alan Hawley was placed back on the transfer list at his own request, and Eddie Lyons, who had been assisting on a part-time basis since November 1969, was appointed as full-time trainer.

Frank Blunstone signed 19-year old left-back Terry Scales from West Ham United and 20-year old midfielder Steve Tom from Queens Park Rangers, both on free transfers. A one-month trial was offered to former amateur Nigel Saywood. Junior team matches were to be played at Ruislip Manor in the new season instead of at Griffin Park.

Five amateur players were available for selection: Dave Collyer would act as understudy to Gordon Phillips and would also play for Woking, Paul Priddy (Hayes), Mickey Heath (Walton & Hersham), Alan Gane and Paul Devis.

Director Ted Rogers was awarded an MBE in the Honour's List.

AUGUST 1971

- The final pre-season friendly, scheduled to be played at Walton, was postponed as a result of an injury crisis.
- Nigel Saywood left the club on the completion of his trial.

LETTER FROM THE CHAIRMAN

Dear Supporters,

I would like to keep you in the picture about the present position of the Club in relation to the transfer of Cross.

When our last Team Manager left us in the Autumn of 1969, we were in the top four of the Fourth Division. From a very large field of applicants, Mr. Frank Blunstone was chosen unanimously by the Board and he has continued to have our support ever since. He kept us in the top four during the Winter of 1969/70, but early in the New Year advised us—which was obvious to everyone—that our chances of promotion would be enhanced if we could get a further striker. His choice was Roger Cross of West Ham and the fee was in the region of £12,000. The Board agreed with his advice that if a good young player was bought, not only would it increase the chance of our promotion but, in the longer term, would not be a bad transaction as with further experience of playing League football and with the benefit of Frank's coaching, his value must increase. The sum was, for us, a large one and all that money was not available at the moment. So much did the Board support Frank's opinion that three Directors personally made available £6,000 to make the purchase possible and those three Directors are still on the Board.

Unfortunately, through no fault of Frank's, we slipped from the top four in the last crucial week and the Cross purchase had failed in one of its immediate objects, but I still feel we were right to have bought him.

It is not easy to persuade players to move from the First Division to the Fourth and Cross was promised that if a Club from a superior Division made a reasonable offer in the future, Brentford would not stand in his way.

A number of Clubs have enquired for Cross. Before the Barrow match on Bank Holiday evening, the Manager of a Northern First Division club informed Mr. Blunstone that he was coming to watch Cross and wanted the Board to decide the figure they would require. After full discussion, the figure of £30,000 which Frank had recommended was agreed by the board. Whether that Manager ever came to see the match is unknown, but certainly he did not approach Frank to hear what the figure was.

On Tuesday, 7th September, Fulham offered £25,000 and that was the first concrete offer ever received.

We did our best to get even more, but finally accepted £30,000. During the lengthy discussions, Frank naturally had to tell us that he did not want Cross to go, and indeed we all shared his view, but he also reminded us of our promise not to stand in Cross' way if a reasonable offer came from a Club in a higher Division.

The first instalment of £15,000 has been received and is to be used for the purchase of players. Frank advises us that his immediate requirements are two players, one of whom is clearly a replacement for Cross. When a good player leaves us, naturally we are all sad, but we have to look at the broader picture. By this transaction, more money is available to Frank for the purchase of players than he had when he bought Cross and I sincerely believe that when he has got these new players, the team will be even better.

Intense activity has been taking place to get a new player. Already, a player with a Second Division club has been selected, but the deal has not yet been completed. Another player for temporary loan has been approached. However, Frank insists, quite rightly, that he wishes to choose carefully and spend wisely, even if this means not having the player for this Saturday.

Protests and criticism are inevitable when a good player leaves us and we fully understand and share the disappointment which must be felt. However, some letters received show that there are those amongst our supporters who appreciate the reasons for our decision to let Cross go. The object was certainly not to pay off the overdraft as one National Daily has suggested, but to provide money for the two players needed and to honour our promise to Cross.

SEPTEMBER 1971

- Roger Cross was sold to Fulham for a club record fee of £30,000.
- A writ was issued against *The Sun* newspaper and journalist Frank Nicklin, following an article about the transfer of Cross and the suggestion that the money received would be used to pay off club debts.
- Alan Hawley joined Fulham on loan.
- 25-year old midfielder Trevor Dawkins was signed on loan from Crystal Palace.
- A trial was given to Brian Carnaby who had returned from playing in South Africa.

OCTOBER 1971

- An £8,000 fee was paid to Middlesbrough for 22-year old midfielder Mike Allen.
- Alan Hawley returned from his loan at Fulham.
- Trevor Dawkins returned to Crystal Palace at the end of his loan spell.
- Gordon Neilson was transfer-listed at his own request.
- Paul Priddy suffered a broken ankle in the London Challenge Cup defeat at Millwall.

NOVEMBER 1971

- On 16 November, the final repayment (£19,600) of the loan of £104,000, which kept the club alive in February 1967, was presented to Walter Wheatley.

DECEMBER 1971

- Brian Turner was sent off in the match at Hartlepool.
- A one-month trial was given to former Chelsea striker, Joe Fascione, who had been playing for Durban City (South Africa).
- The crowd of 18,237 for the home game with Crewe was the biggest League attendance at Griffin Park since September 1959.

JANUARY 1972

- John O'Mara, with 22 goals to that point, received a five week ban, taking in five matches, as a result of his poor disciplinary record. The punishment included a suspended sentence imposed the previous season while he was at Wimbledon.
- Joe Fascione's trial was terminated when his South African club indicated that they would require a transfer fee.
- A trial was given to 18-year old Bob Spink, who had paid his own air fare from Australia for the opportunity.
- Eric Radley-Smith was replaced as chairman by Les Davey and Walter Wheatley, who would share the responsibilities.

FEBRUARY 1972

- 19-year old striker, Ken Wallace, was signed from West Ham United on loan with a view to a permanent transfer.
- Bobby Ross was dropped for the game against Scunthorpe after 167 consecutive starts, a run stretching back to November 1968.

COMEBACK GOAL ENDS BEES SLIDE

KING JOHN has returned — and so has that promotion look at Griffin Park. John O'Mara, out of soccer because of a harsh five-week suspension, came back against Lincoln last night and promptly headed home Brentford's first goal as if he hadn't been out of the game.

Now for the championship!

Brentford keep up winning run

MARCH 1972

• Ken Wallace returned to West Ham United at the end of his loan period.

• Highly-rated 22-year old Stewart Houston was signed on loan from Chelsea, initially for one month, but then extended until the end of the season.

• A transfer deadline-day bid of £10,000 for Luton striker Robin Wainwright, was rejected.

• Brian Turner was fined £20 and suspended for one week by the FA as a result of his disciplinary record, but he did not miss any matches.

• Former Windsor and Eton centre-half, Phil Jarrett, was appointed as the new junior team manager – Roy Ruffell took charge of scouting in the south of England but retained overall responsibility for junior football at the club.

[Above] The three non-playing members of the squad – Steve Tom, Paul Bence and Brian Turner – celebrate with Eddie Lyons and Frank Blunstone after the Exeter game

APRIL 1972

• Promotion to Division Three was clinched after the home win over Exeter.

MAY 1972

• Free transfers were given to Brian Turner, Gordon Neilson and Steve Tom.
• The squad was rewarded with an end-of-season break in Guernsey, where two games were played.

BRENTFORD'S BUSIEST BEE...

BRENTFORD have bounced back to football fame on a shoe-string, 25 years after losing their First Division status.

They won promotion to the Third Division by finishing in third place. And, they are out of the "red" for the first time for many years, having paid off an outstanding loan of £104,000.

Who has put the buzz back into the Bees? Most of the credit goes to Frank Blunstone who has only spent just over two years as team boss of Brentford. He could still have been in charge of Chelsea's successful Youth section, but decided the time had come to have a shot at running his own show as a League club manager.

It has been a hard slog for Blunstone at Brentford. He works on average 70 hours a week, training his team, planning their tactics and seeking out new talent.

"SHOE STRING" SQUAD

Five days before the start of last season five of Brentford's "shoe string" squad of only 14 professionals were being treated for injuries, and that began an ever recurring nightmare for Blunstone of possibly not having enough fit men on his books to make up a team each week.

Then the club decided to sell their top marksman Roger Cross to Fulham for £30,000. Blunstone went shopping and bought midfield man Mike Allen from Middlesbrough for around £10,000.

Meanwhile, however, he had to give the chief goal-scoring role to his "bargain buy" from non-League Wimbledon. The 6ft. 3½ ins. striker John O'Mara did not let him down.

O'Mara — rated by Blunstone as his most exciting capture for Brentford — has been a big success. He cost Brentford £750 down and another £250 after 20 games. In those first 20 games for Brentford O'Mara scored 15 goals and the club were only too

Manager Frank Blunstone

happy to pay Wimbledon the extra cash.

Blunstone now thinks it was worthwhile getting up early one morning in March of last year to meet engineer O'Mara outside the gates of the factory where he was working an early day shift. He clinched the deal with O'Mara before the factory whistle went for the start of another day's work on the early shift.

O'Mara has become such a key man in the team that before the home game with promotion rivals Southport in December, Blunstone drove him to Brentford hospital one hour before the match to have a painkilling injection so that he could play with bruised ribs.

FRANK'S STRATEGY

What was the secret behind Brentford's promotion last season? Frank explains: "We attack at home and counter-attack away. We go all out for goals at home, but playing away from home we try to score by breaking out of defensive positions whenever the chance arises. In season 1970-71 we went looking for goals away but paid for it by being caught out at the back too many times. 'Win at home, draw away' is the recipe for promotion."

How have Brentford managed to do so well with so few reserves to call upon?

Says Frank: "We know we cannot afford injuries with such a small staff so we go all out to avoid them. By that I don't mean we shy away from tackles. We train very hard and put our players under a lot of physical stress to lessen the danger of pulled or strained muscles in matches."

Gates at Griffin Park last season averaged a healthy 10,000, and remember, Brentford have to compete for fans in an area of London housing such clubs as Chelsea, Fulham and Queen's Park Rangers, all of whom are in higher Divisions.

"We have a good hard-core of supporters and a crowd at Griffin Park who are very fair," says Manager Blunstone. "They have given the boys great encouragement — just what we needed when we were struggling. We wanted to go up as much for them as for ourselves.

"We're looking forward to pleasing our fans even more with Third Division football next season!"

Brentford's leading goal-scorer last term . . . big John O'Mara. He was bought for a mere £750.

BRENTFORD'S POST-WAR UPS AND DOWNS:

1946-47 Relegation from the First Division.
1953-54 Relegation to the Third Division (South).
1957-58 Runners-up and entry to the newly-formed Third Division instead of the Fourth.
1961-62 Relegation to the Fourth Division.
1962-63 Fourth Division Champions, gaining promotion to the Third.
1965-66 Relegation to the Fourth Division.
1967-68 The club faces extinction but resists Q.P.R. take-over.
December 1971 the club announces that an outstanding loan of £104,000 has been paid off. Brentford hold leadership of the Fourth Division.
1971-72 Promotion to the Third Division!

1972-73

[Back Row] Alan Hawley, Alan Nelmes, Paul Bence, Paul Priddy, Gordon Phillips, Terry Scales, Mike Allen, David Court, Peter Gelson **[Front Row]** John Docherty, David Jenkins, Stewart Houston, Bobby Ross, Jackie Graham, Alan Murray, John O'Mara

Football League	Division Three
Manager	Frank Blunstone
Trainer	Eddie Lyons
Captain	Bobby Ross / Alan Hawley
Final Position	22nd
FA Cup	1st Round
League Cup	2nd Round
Leading Goalscorer	John Docherty
(all competitions)	& Alan Murray – 7 goals

The summer signings of David Jenkins (Tottenham Hotspur), David Court (Luton Town) and Alan Murray (Middlesbrough) failed to provide the necessary quality needed to compete in the higher division and, despite a promising opening month, including home wins against Blackburn Rovers (4-0) and Bolton Wanderers (2-1), the early season departures of John O'Mara, sold to Blackburn Rovers for £50,000, and Bobby Ross proved to be a fatal blow as their replacement, Stan Webb, made little impact.

Defeat at Rotherham in the League Cup in early September triggered an unbelievable run of 17 successive defeats on the road, which included hammerings at Southend United (4-0), Grimsby Town (4-0) and Tranmere Rovers (6-2) – the dire sequence finally ended in March with consecutive victories at Rochdale and York.

Home form kept the threat of relegation at bay for much of the campaign with a seven-match winning sequence between September and December and a notable 5-0 victory over Port Vale in February, in which 19-year old Andy Woon hit a hat-trick on his first start.

The signings of Roger Cross (returning from Fulham) and Barry Salvage from Queens Park Rangers, for a total outlay of £25,000, proved too little too late – seven defeats and three draws from the final 12 games confirmed relegation back to Division Four after just one season. The 4-1 defeat at Wrexham in the penultimate game proving to be the final nail in the coffin.

A season of ultimate failure led to manager Frank Blunstone quitting in the summer, citing a lack of ambition by the board for the immediate return to the bottom tier.

[Previous page] Strike partners, Stewart Houston (left) and John O'Mara, during the pre-season friendly against Portsmouth

SEASON 1972-73

BRENTFORD F.C.
FOUNDED 1888

Football League
Division III

© Brentford Football and Sports Club Limited, 1972

BRENTFORD

versus

HALIFAX TOWN

SATURDAY, 12th AUGUST, 1972
Kick-off 3.15 p.m.

Ground: Griffin Park, Braemar Road, Brentford

NEXT HOME GAMES

WEDNESDAY, 16th AUGUST, 1972
Football League Cup - First Round

BRENTFORD v. CAMBRIDGE UNITED
Kick-off 7.30 p.m.

SATURDAY, 19th AUGUST, 1972
*South East Counties League,
Division 1*

BRENTFORD JNRS v. IPSWICH TOWN
JNRS
*Kick-off 11.00 a.m.
(at Ruislip Manor)*

SATURDAY, 26th AUGUST, 1972
Football League Division III

BRENTFORD v. BLACKBURN ROVERS
Kick-off 3.15 p.m.

Official Programme Price 5p

Total Home League Attendances	201,064
Average Home League Attendance	8,742
Highest Home League Attendance	11,803
Lowest Home League Attendance	6,067

		P	W	D	L	F	A	W	D	L	F	A	Pts
1	Bolton	46	18	4	1	44	9	7	7	9	29	30	**61**
2	Notts County	46	17	4	2	40	12	6	7	10	27	35	**57**
3	Blackburn	46	12	8	3	34	16	8	7	8	23	31	**55**
4	Oldham	46	12	7	4	40	18	7	9	7	32	36	**54**
5	Bristol Rov	46	17	4	2	55	20	3	9	11	22	36	**53**
6	Port Vale	46	15	6	2	41	21	6	5	12	15	48	**53**
7	Bournemouth	46	14	6	3	44	16	3	10	10	22	28	**50**
8	Plymouth	46	14	3	6	43	26	6	7	10	31	40	**50**
9	Grimsby	46	16	2	5	45	18	4	6	13	22	43	**48**
10	Tranmere	46	12	8	3	38	17	3	8	12	18	35	**46**
11	Charlton	46	12	7	4	46	24	5	4	14	23	43	**45**
12	Wrexham	46	11	9	3	39	23	3	8	12	16	31	**45**
13	Rochdale	46	8	8	7	22	26	6	9	8	26	28	**45**
14	Southend	46	13	6	4	40	14	4	4	15	21	40	**44**
15	Shrewsbury	46	10	10	3	31	21	5	4	14	15	33	**44**
16	Chesterfield	46	13	4	6	37	22	4	5	14	20	39	**43**
17	Walsall	46	14	3	6	37	26	4	4	15	19	40	**43**
18	York City	46	8	10	5	24	14	5	5	13	18	32	**41**
19	Watford	46	11	8	4	32	23	1	9	13	11	25	**41**
20	Halifax	46	9	8	6	29	23	4	7	12	14	30	**41**
21	Rotherham	46	12	4	7	34	27	5	3	15	17	38	**41**
22	**Brentford**	**46**	**12**	**5**	**6**	**33**	**18**	**3**	**2**	**18**	**18**	**51**	**37**
23	Swansea	46	11	5	7	37	29	3	4	16	14	44	**37**
24	Scunthorpe	46	8	7	8	18	25	2	3	18	15	47	**30**

League Position throughout the Season

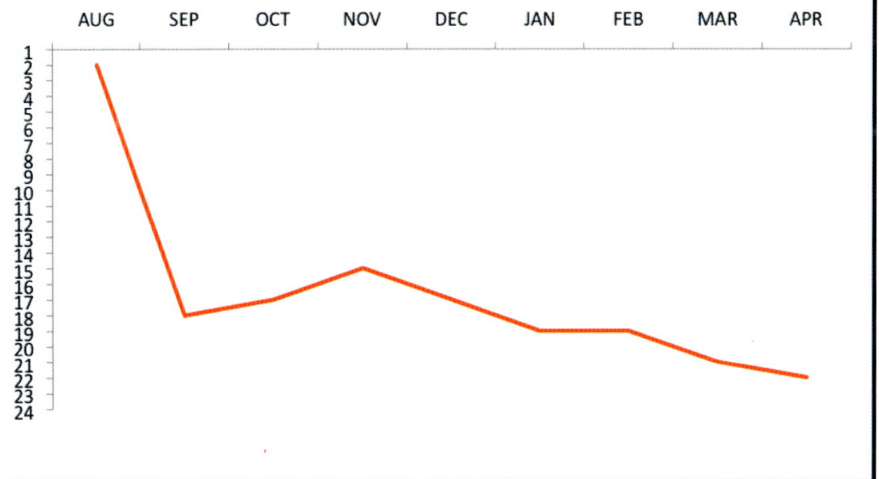

AUG	SEP	OCT	NOV	DEC	JAN	FEB	MAR	APR

57

1972-73

[Right] Stewart Houston puts in a cross during the opening day defeat to Halifax Town as team-mate Terry Scales looks on

Sat 12th August: **Halifax Town (H)**
Lost 0-1 **Attendance: 10,164**

The new campaign started in disappointing fashion when the defensive-minded visitors snatched an 85th minute winner after an error by the debutant, amateur keeper Paul Priddy, who palmed a cross straight to the feet of a lurking striker.

Wed 16th August: **Cambridge Utd (H) League Cup 1st Round**
Won 1-0 **Attendance: 7,750**

John Docherty's 31st minute flick, after an Alan Murray free-kick had deflected off the defensive wall, was enough to secure a passage through to the second round of the competition for the first time in four seasons – a win achieved despite Bobby Ross missing an early penalty, which was saved by the keeper after John Docherty had been fouled in the penalty area.

Sat 19th August: **Oldham Athletic (A)**
Drew 1-1 **Attendance: 6,106**

The first point of the season was gained courtesy of a goal scored after just 69 seconds – Stewart Houston headed home John Docherty's cross after good work from Bobby Ross. The host's equaliser came just a minute later, when an air-kick by Alan Hawley presented his opponent with an open goal.

Sat 26th August: **Blackburn Rovers (H)**
Won 4-0 **Attendance: 9,427**

A scintillating performance got underway when the visitor's Ben Arentoft, under pressure from David Jenkins, lofted a 25-yard backpass over the head of his keeper into his own net and, after Stewart Houston thumped a header against the cross bar, he nodded in a David Jenkins cross to double the lead in the 42nd minute. Eight minutes after the break John O'Mara headed in Alan Murray's

centre – the rout was completed on 80 minutes when Mike Allen's free-kick was knocked on by Alan Murray for Jackie Graham to fire the fourth goal of the game.

Mon 28th August: **Bolton Wanderers (H)**
Won 2-1 **Attendance: 11,803**

An outstanding game of football saw the visitors take the lead in the 19th minute, but they only held the advantage for five minutes before Mike Allen rose to meet a cross from Jackie Graham and netted a backward header. The winner arrived in the 42nd minute when Alan Murray fired home after receiving the ball from David Jenkins.

Sat 2nd September: **Plymouth Argyle (A)**
Won 1-0 **Attendance: 7,833**

The match was settled in highly controversial circumstances in the 73rd minute when Alan Murray received a long pass from Stewart Houston and fired a shot goalwards. The ball appeared to go through the back of the net and ended up behind the goal but protests from the home players prompted the referee to inspect the netting – it was found that the net lifted easily from the ground and the general consensus was that the ball had entered the net via the side-netting. The 'goal that never was' was allowed to stand and it proved to be the winner.

Tue 5th September: **Rotherham (A) League Cup 2nd Round**
Lost 0-2 **Attendance: 4,996**

A goal in each half settled the cup tie in favour of the home side – the opening strike in the 32nd minute being followed by the deciding goal scored after 69 minutes – the Yorkshiremen progressed to round three.

Sat 9th September: **Swansea City (H)**
Lost 0-2   **Attendance: 9,986**

The visitors took the lead in the 9th minute when Alan Nelmes mis-cued a header to the feet of an opposing striker, who fired the ball into the net. The second goal, in the 75th minute, was clouded in controversy when a long-range shot hit the underside of the crossbar and appeared to bounce back into play, but the lines-man signalled a goal. The decision stood after consultation with the referee.

Sat 16th September: **Port Vale (A)**
Lost 0-1   **Attendance: 4,663**

A good display failed to reap its deserved rewards when Vale snatched a last-gasp winner – a corner was flicked on and the ball found its way past Paul Priddy and into the net.

Wed 20th September: **Chesterfield (A)**
Lost 0-3   **Attendance: 6,507**

A comprehensive defeat was on the cards from as early as the 6th minute when the hosts took the lead, which was doubled in the 51st minute when Peter Gelson appeared to be fouled as he tried to play a back-pass to his keeper, but the referee played on and the home side went 2-0 up. Gelson was also involved in the third goal when his attempted clearance rebounded back off an opposing striker and ricocheted into the net from the edge of the penalty area.

Sat 23rd September: **Bournemouth (H)**
Drew 1-1   **Attendance: 11,100**

A first-minute corner brought the opening goal when Mike Allen's kick was missed by the keeper and John Docherty poked the ball home from virtually on the goal-line. The visitors equalised on 11 minutes when ace marksman, Ted MacDougall, headed against the top of the post and pounced to net the rebound.

Mon 25th September: **Bristol Rovers (H)**
Won 2-1   **Attendance: 9,720**

After an evenly start, a freak own-goal opened the scoring in the 41st minute – Paul Bence's free-kick into a crowded penalty box was punched into the net by the visiting goalkeeper. David Jenkins added the second with his first goal for the club on 65 minutes, moving onto John Docherty's through ball and slotting it past the keeper, but the advantage was halved with 17 minutes remaining.

Sat 30th September: **Notts County (A)**
Lost 0-1   **Attendance: 8,152**

A dominant performance by the home side brought them only one goal, scored in the 8th minute, but the result was rarely in doubt. The only surprise was the lack of further goals.

Sat 7th October: **Scunthorpe United (A)**
Lost 0-1   **Attendance: 3,378**

After an impressive first-half display that failed to bring a goal, despite several attempts by John Docherty and Stewart Houston, the decisive strike came in the 49th minute when the hosts grabbed the lead and held on to take the points.

Mon 9th October: **Tranmere Rovers (H)**
Won 2-0   **Attendance: 8,154**

John Docherty scored the opener in the 10th minute when Stewart Houston headed on Peter Gelson's long-range free-kick for the little winger to net a downward header. Three minutes after the half-time break a move involving Paul Bence and Jackie Graham resulted in a visiting defender prodding the ball past his own keeper to seal the victory.

Sat 14th October: **Walsall (H)**
Won 2-0   **Attendance: 9,493**

A victory more comprehensive than the scoreline suggests com-prised of Stewart Houston's 44th minute header, which powered into the net from the underside of the bar after a cross from Mike Allen, then, in the 89th minute, a clearance from defence was helped on by David Jenkins to John Docherty who slotted home a simple second goal.

Sat 21st October: Southend United (A)
Lost 0-4 Attendance: 7,205

The dismal away run continued with a sixth successive defeat, without a single goal being scored – the thrashing saw the home side two goals in front at the break, the second courtesy of a headed own goal by Peter Gelson on 39 minutes, adding to the opener after 18 minutes. Further second half strikes, in the 56th and 72nd minutes, compounded a miserable afternoon.

Sat 28th October: Rochdale (H)
Won 1-0 Attendance: 9,201

An early goal from John Docherty on five minutes proved to be the match-winner although it was not without controversy as the winger received the ball in a clearly offside position but the officials deemed that there had been a deflection via an opposing defender and allowed the goal to stand. The other noteworthy incident of the match saw new signing Stan Webb being stretchered off on his debut, the striker having been the victim of a crunching tackle from Ex-Bee Dick Renwick who was roundly booed by fans for the remainder of the game.

Sat 4th November: Bristol Rovers (A)
Lost 1-3 Attendance: 7,916

An early 4th minute goal set the scene for another away defeat and although Stewart Houston's equaliser on the hour ended a drought of 614 minutes without a goal on the road, two late errors proved costly. On 84 minutes Gordon Phillips allowed a cross to slip past him into the net and in the final minute Peter Gelson's poor headed clearance set up a third goal for the hosts.

Sat 11th November: Chesterfield (H)
Won 3-1 Attendance: 8,078

Chesterfield took a 16th minute lead in a dismal half, when Gordon Phillips could only parry a shot into the air, the ball dropping over the line behind him. The second period saw a big improvement and, on 56 minutes, a penalty was awarded after Mike Allen was fouled – Alan Murray converted the spot-kick, followed soon after, by Stan Webb lashing home a cross from Stewart Houston for his first goal in club colours. With 10 minutes remaining a Mike Allen cross was thumped high into the net by Stewart Houston to seal the victory.

Sat 18th November: Yeovil Town (A) FA Cup 1st Round
Lost 1-2 Attendance: 9,447

A poor, dispirited display, in front of 1,500 travelling supporters, resulted in an ignominious cup exit to Southern League opposition – despite taking a 50th minute lead when a John Docherty cross spun into the net off the knee of Mike Allen. Two goals in three minutes (70th and 73rd) gave the minnows a richly-deserved victory and all the headlines.

Sat 25th November: York City (H)
Won 2-0 Attendance: 7,111

An entertaining encounter was settled by two 'out of the ordinary' goals – the first on 28 minutes, when the visitor's goalkeeper pushed the ball onto his own bar and as it dropped Stan Webb used his hip to nudge it over the line, the second in the 61st minute was scored directly from a corner by Jackie Graham.

Tue 28th November: Charlton Athletic (A)
Lost 1-2 Attendance: 6,192

The first visit to The Valley for 26 years extended the run of consecutive away defeats to nine, although a bright start saw John Docherty take advantage of a terrible back-pass and crack home an angled drive via the underside of the crossbar in the 43rd minute. Charlton equalised in the 58th minute and, with a draw looking the likely outcome, an innocuous shot from the host's substitute was dropped over the line by Paul Priddy – the howler coming in the 86th minute and proving to be the costliest of errors.

Sat 2nd December: **Shrewsbury Town (A)**
Lost 0-2   **Attendance: 2,079**

Two early goals for the home side, in the 11th and 14th minutes, set up another predictable away day defeat and created a new post-war club record of ten successive away games without a win.

Sat 16th December: **Grimsby Town (A)**
Lost 0-4   **Attendance: 9,110**

A first-half horror show saw the hosts hit four goals in an 18-minute spell, the second of which was credited as an own goal by Peter Gelson – his attempted clearance only helped the ball into his own net. With the game lost before the break, the second half became a damage-limitation exercise – no further punishment was inflicted.

Sat 23rd December: **Wrexham (H)**
Won 1-0   **Attendance: 6,067**

The season's smallest crowd witnessed a pre-Christmas spectacle that was settled by a John Docherty goal on 37 minutes – he received a pass from Alan Murray, then rounded the keeper with ease. In a game that saw the visitors reduced to ten men as a result of a sending-off just before the interval, the delight at winning was marred by the broken collar-bone injury to Terry Scales.

Tue 26th December: **Bournemouth (A)**
Lost 2-3   **Attendance: 14,372**

An impressive first-half performance by the home side brought just one goal, scored in the 34th minute, and their failure to capitalise on their dominance was punished when Stewart Houston headed an equaliser from a corner on the stroke of half-time. Two quick goals early in the second period, in the 50th and 57th minutes, looked to have put the result beyond doubt, but a late strike by Jackie Graham gave the score-

line a closer look. The final goal was a successful execution of a well-rehearsed and often-tried free-kick, in which two players feigned annoyance with each other over an apparent misunderstanding, in the midst of which, the ball was tapped to another player, in this case Jackie Graham, to shoot past the bemused opposing defence and goalkeeper.

Sat 30th December: **Oldham Athletic (H)**
Drew 1-1   **Attendance: 7,719**

A run of seven consecutive home victories came to an end when the visitors grabbed an 86th minute equaliser. The opening goal had arrived only 12 minutes before, when Alan Hawley exchanged passes and his goal-bound shot deflected off a defender into the path of Stan Webb, who scored from close range.

Sat 6th January: **Blackburn Rovers (A)**
Lost 1-2   **Attendance: 6,534**

A good performance failed to bring about a change in fortune away from home and, after taking a 7th minute lead, when Stewart Houston headed David Court's cross into the path of Jackie Graham to slot the ball home, the home side's pressure finally told with a 67th minute equaliser and a late winner eight minutes from time.

Sat 13th January: **Rotherham United (H)**
Drew 1-1   **Attendance: 7,446**

Although another home point was dropped, the disappointment was tempered by the goal-scoring second 'debut' of Roger Cross, re-signed after his spell with Fulham – his 81st minute strike, after a John Docherty corner had not been cleared, looked to have won both points, but the visitors equalised just three minutes later.

Sat 20th January: **Plymouth Argyle (H)**
Lost 0-2   **Attendance: 7,075**

A calamitous goalkeeping error by Gordon Phillips after just four minutes, when his attempt to push a long-range effort over the bar resulted in him fisting the ball into his own net, seemed to drain the confidence from his colleagues. A dire performance resulted in the visitors scoring the second and decisive goal on the hour mark. The performance was greeted with jeers and slow handclapping – a match deemed to be one of the poorest for a long time.

Fri 26th January: **Swansea City (A)**
Lost 1-2   **Attendance: 2,119**

In a game played in torrential South Wales rain, the home side took the lead on 5 minutes – a cross from the left squirmed out of Gordon Phillips' hands on the sodden pitch, leaving the scorer with a simple tap-in. A second goal followed soon after the interval when Roger Cross was deemed to have raised his foot too high on the edge of his own penalty box and the resultant free-kick ended up in the back of the net. A 70th minute consolation arrived courtesy of Alan Murray, who fired home after the keeper could only parry Terry Scales' centre into his path.

Fri 2nd February: **Tranmere Rovers (A)**
Lost 2-6   **Attendance: 6,650**

With the game under threat from thickening fog, Tranmere struck twice, in the 4th and 7th minutes, and had extended their lead to three inside 23 minutes. David Court hit back with a thunderous 25-yard volley in the 33rd minute, but as the fog lifted for the second half, the fight-back was over within five minutes – Alan Murray's short back-pass was intercepted to make the score 4-1 – and a fifth goal followed nine minutes later. Murray atoned, slightly, for his error when he beat the keeper from 18-yards to reduce the deficit, but when Stewart Houston's deflected own-goal gave the hosts a sixth with twenty minutes to go, the club record of never having conceded more than seven goals in a game looked under threat.

[Right] Alan Hawley, Paul Bence and Peter Gelson look on as loanee goalie, Kieron Baker, gathers the ball during the home win against Scunthorpe United

Sat 10th February: **Port Vale (H)**
Won 5-0   **Attendance: 6,694**

A change of formation and personnel in an attempt to reverse the win-less trend reaped almost instant dividends when Andy Woon, making his full debut, headed in a Roger Cross centre after just 71 seconds and, in the 23rd minute, Jackie Graham scored directly from a corner. The second half saw Barry Salvage, another debutant, score when he raced onto a Roger Cross pass and rifled home a superb left-foot shot from the edge of the box. Andy Woon completed an incredible hat-trick in the 89th and 90th minutes when he netted from a cross by Barry Salvage, then thumped home a fierce left-footed drive after being set up by John Docherty.

Sat 24th February: **Grimsby Town (H)**
Lost 0-1   **Attendance: 9,302**

The game followed a familiar pattern, with a host of missed chances, which had become all the more important after the visitors scored an early goal when the ball was chipped over the head of the advancing Gordon Phillips, dropping neatly into the back of the net. The strike proved to be the decisive moment of the game.

Mon 26th February: **Charlton Athletic (H)**
Won 1-0   **Attendance: 9,929**

With new loanee goalkeeper Kieron Baker making his debut, the action at the other end of the pitch was immediate – Roger Cross thumped a long-range effort against the crossbar and the ball rebounded to Barry Salvage who scored. The goal was officially timed at 24 seconds after kick-off, making it one of the fastest goals in the club's history.

Sat 3rd March: **Scunthorpe United (H)**
Won 1-0   **Attendance: 7,896**

A tepid affair, against opponents embroiled in the relegation battle, was settled in the 63rd minute when Alan Murray headed home from Jackie Graham's corner to secure another vital home victory.

Tue 6th March: **Rotherham United (A)**
Lost 1-2   **Attendance: 3,758**

After a run of four successive home games, the first away trip for over a month failed to bring about a change in fortune and the club's 2,000th League fixture since joining the Football League in August 1920, ended in the 16th consecutive loss, Brentford's worst ever run. Stan Webb's equaliser had levelled the scores by half-time but an own goal from Stewart Houston settled the encounter.

Sat 10th March: **Walsall (A)**
Lost 0-3   **Attendance: 4,192**

Another defensive blunder set the tone for the afternoon – Alan Nelmes handled a corner in the 13th minute, and the resultant penalty gave Walsall the lead. The hosts added further goals just after half-time and again six minutes from the end, which reflected their dominance.

Sat 17th March: **Southend United (H)**
Lost 1-2   **Attendance: 8,051**

Despite taking an 11th minute lead – Roger Cross heading home a Barry Salvage's corner, the visitors gradually took over and, having equalised on 42 minutes, grabbed the winner on 70 minutes.

Mon 19th March: **Watford (H)**
Drew 1-1   **Attendance: 8,232**

The pantomime free-kick routine, which had proved successful earlier in the season at Dean Court on Boxing Day, worked a treat again just two minutes before half-time – Roger Cross rifled the ball home from outside the box but the visiting neighbours scored an equaliser three minutes after the break to leave the prospect of relegation looking ever more likely.

Sat 24th March: **Rochdale (A)**
Won 1-0   **Attendance: 1,747**

The abysmal run of 17 consecutive away defeats finally ended at Spotland when, in the 65th minute, a counter-attack was instigated after the home side's corner, and the ball was cleared via Barry Salvage and Roger Cross to Mike Allen. He cut in from the right and sent a long-range effort into the back of the net via the foot of a post.

Sat 31st March: **York City (A)**
Won 1-0   **Attendance: 2,307**

After achieving a first away win in almost seven months in the previous game, the feat was repeated by the same scoreline, and with the same goal scorer. Mike Allen's 54th minute headed goal coming after a Roger Cross effort was deflected out via the goalkeeper's legs.

Wed 4th April: **Halifax Town (A)**
Lost 2-3   **Attendance: 970**

A pitiful attendance, which included around 40 Bees fans, witnessed a first-half display of clinical finishing by the home side who clocked up a 3-0 lead with goals in the 6th, 17th and 28th minutes. Stan Webb provided a glimmer of hope in the 74th minute, when he headed a ball from Roger Cross into the net, then Mike Allen scored a bizarre second when his low 40-yard free-kick from the touchline passed through a crowded penalty box and continued into the back of the net. But an equaliser was not forthcoming.

Sat 7th April: **Shrewsbury Town (H)**
Lost 1-2   **Attendance: 6,758**

A splendid first half display was rewarded when Barry Salvage fired a left-foot shot high into the net from just outside the penalty box after 22 minutes, following a fine move involving Roger Cross, Mike Allen and John Docherty. The visitors equalised in the 63rd minute then struck a devastating blow after 82 minutes, when hesitation by Gordon Phillips allowed the ball to be chipped beyond him for the winner.

Sat 14th April: **Watford (A)**
Drew 2-2   **Attendance: 7,813**

In a game crucial to hopes of avoiding relegation, the worst possible start saw a short back-pass from Alan Nelmes intercepted to give the hosts a 3rd minute lead. Roger Cross equalised five minutes later, though, converting a centre from Barry Salvage. On the half-hour mark Stan Webb's flicked header set up Alan Murray to race away and unleash a low drive, which entered the net via the foot of a post. By the time the scores had been levelled in the 75th minute, the game had been overshadowed by the loss of John Docherty with a broken ankle.

Fri 20th April: **Notts County (H)**
Drew 1-1   **Attendance: 11,658**

The final home game, against opponents almost certain to be promoted, required nothing less than a win to stave off impending relegation, but two goals in two first-half minutes meant that the shares were spoiled. Jackie Graham equalised 60 seconds after the visitor's opener on 20 minutes, firing home Alan Murray's cross from 12 yards.

Mon 23rd April: **Wrexham (A)**
Lost 1-4   **Attendance: 2,611**

Any slim, lingering hopes of avoiding the drop back to Division Four were extinguished within two minutes – the home side took a lead that they doubled ten minutes after the break. Almost immediately Stan Webb nodded home a centre from Roger Cross, but in the 70th minute, the hosts increased their lead again and the fourth goal simply hammered the final nail in the relegation coffin.

Sat 28th April: **Bolton Wanderers (A)**
Lost 0-2   **Attendance: 21,917**

With relegation already confirmed, and Bolton having claimed the Division Three championship trophy, the game was little more than an exhibition for both sides – goals in the 52nd and 62nd minutes sealed a predictable outcome to the last match of the season.

PRE-SEASON

Manager Frank Blunstone rejected the offer of a coaching position with First Division Everton, while Stewart Houston was signed on a permanent basis from Chelsea for a reported £15,000 fee, following his loan spell.

22-year old midfielder Alan Murray (Middlesbrough) and striker David Jenkins, aged 25 (Tottenham Hotspur) were both signed on free transfers.

25-year old Peter Chadwick, previously assistant manager at Southall, took over as junior team manager and two of the juniors, Kevin Harding and Richard Poole, were signed as apprentice professionals. Paul Priddy would continue to play as an amateur, whilst assisting Southall.

Director Ted Rogers, who suffered a stroke during the promotion-clinching game with Exeter, died at the age of 78. The libel action taken against 'The Sun' newspaper following the transfer of Roger Cross was settled out of court, with the newspaper paying costs and damages.

AUGUST 1972

• Experienced, former Arsenal midfielder, David Court, aged 28, was signed on a free transfer from Luton Town.
• John O'Mara was sent off in a friendly at Hillingdon and received a three match suspension.
• Alan Hawley was taken off the transfer list at his own request.
• Gordon Phillips suffered an injury on the eve of the season and amateur Paul Priddy was called up to the first-team.

SEPTEMBER 1972

• John O'Mara was transferred to Blackburn Rovers for a reported club record sale of around £50,000.
• A bid to sign 23-year-old striker Ron Wigg failed to progress after Watford asked for a £25,000 trasnfer fee.
• John Docherty entered hospital to have his tonsils removed and also underwent a minor leg operation.
• Both Stewart Houston and Jackie Graham suffered injuries sidelining them for several weeks.

OCTOBER 1972

• Captain Bobby Ross had his contract cancelled by mutual consent and signed for Cambridge United.
• Frank Blunstone's long-time transfer target, Stan Webb, was signed from Carlisle United for a reported fee of £10,000.

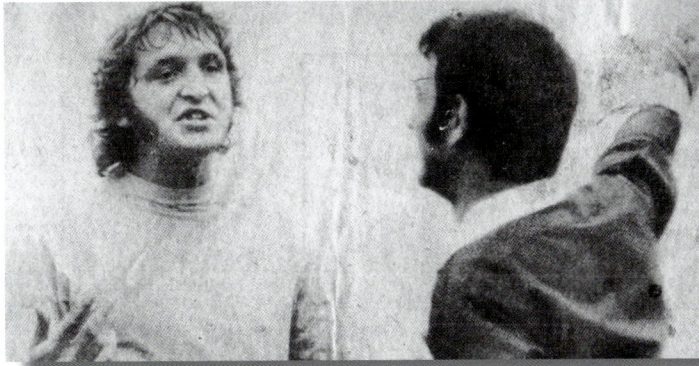

Priddy turns pro

By NICHOLAS CLARKE

AMATEUR goalkeeper Paul Priddy, who has been keeping Gordon Phillips out of Brentford's Division 3 side this season, today signed professional forms for the club.

Plastic . . . not me, says John

HE MUST BE the most different footballer ever. He's a man who's got something to say and is not afraid to say it. He's a man who fought his way into the limelight from a colliery coal face . . . and almost decided he wanted to go back down the mines.

He's John O'Mara, the rangy Brentford centre forward whose goals rocketed the North London club into the Third Division last season. But football is not everything to O'Mara . . . he's a deep thinker and an articulate talker on everything from politics to the star treatment lavished on top footballers nowadays.

O'Mara was voted Fourth Division Player of the Season in an exclusive poll conducted among Football League managers for The Football League Year Book 1972-73. An outstanding player—and not just because of his 6ft 3 inches—in an outstanding side, John O'Mara is featured in an engrossing article in the book.

Among some of the system shattering things he has to say is: "I treat newspaper stories about myself like gossip. It's not the papers fault, they're writing for a fickle public. I'm a realist who accepts that however much you disagree with the 'system' there's not a great deal you can do to change it.

"Football is not the be all and end all for me. It's a job for which I'm paid. I don't want to be a 'plastic' player who always does, says and reacts the way people want him to."

- Andy Woon, a 20-year old amateur with Bognor Regis, was signed as a professional.
- Paul Priddy, who had retained his place as first-team goalkeeper, signed professional terms.
- Alan Hawley was appointed as club captain in succession to Bobby Ross.
- Four new associated schoolboys were signed: Mickey Tripp, Billy Stagg, Peter Cobb and Mark Farrer.

NOVEMBER 1972

- Jackie Graham made a successful return from injury.
- Paul Priddy dislocated his shoulder and faced a month out of action.

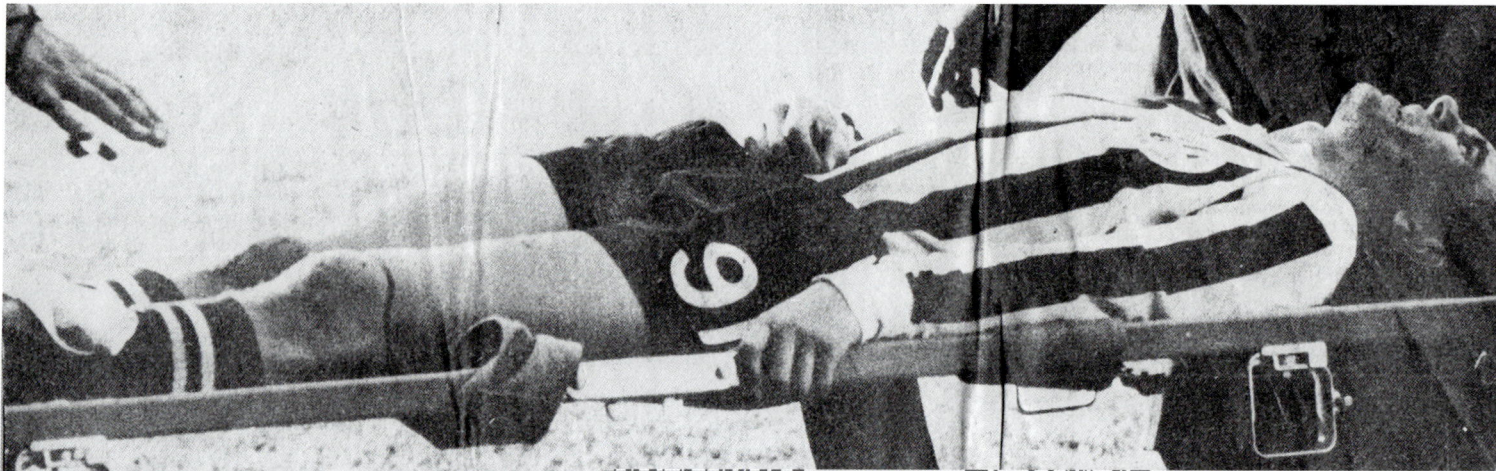

BRENTFORD'S new striker, Stan Webb, is carried off in his debut match on Saturday following a tackle by former Bees full back Dick Renwick.

• Mike Allen faced a lengthy absence after an operation to remove his tonsils.

• Joint-chairman, Walter Wheatley, announced that the club had no plans to relocate to a new site, unless a better location than Griffin Park became available.

DECEMBER 1972

• Alan Hawley received a two-match suspension following an accumulation of bookings.

• Mike Allen continued to struggle to regain fitness.

• Terry Scales suffered a broken collarbone in the game against Wrexham.

• Both David Jenkins and David Court were made available for loan or transfer.

Blunstone chases former striker

Bees bid for Cross return

By Nicholas Clarke

BRENTFORD have agreed terms with Fulham to buy back their former striker Roger Cross. And manager Frank Blunstone was today waiting for Cross to contact him and try and come to terms.

BEES CRASH TO DEFEAT No. 17

No excuses Bees, you were well beaten!

Yeovil 2, Brentford 1

JANUARY 1973

• Striker Roger Cross [pictured left] was re-signed from Fulham for a £16,000 fee, 16 months after his record transfer sale.
• The 13th successive away defeat at Blackburn Rovers equalled the worst ever run in the club's history, set in 1925.
• Bob Higgins was appointed as schoolboy scout.

FEBRUARY 1973

• Winger Barry Salvage was signed from Queens Park Rangers, the 26-year old costing a reported £9,000 fee.
• Paul Priddy was likely to be out of action for another month with a pulled muscle.
• After unsuccessful attempts to sign goalkeepers Jim Eadie (Cardiff) and Bob Tooze (Shrewsbury) on loan, Kieron Baker was signed on loan from Bournemouth until the end of the season.
• The away trip to Halifax was postponed as a result of bad weather.
• Andy Woon scored a hat-trick on his full debut against Port Vale.
• Barry Salvage's goal against Charlton was scored 24 seconds after kick-off.
• Mike Allen's battle to regain fitness was further hampered when he suffered an ankle injury.
• Peter Gelson, who had indicated that he intended to retire from professional football, announced that he had changed his mind.
• Alan Nelmes's absence from the team against Port Vale ended a run of 145 consecutive games.
• Tom Whiteside was signed on schoolboy terms.

MARCH 1973

• David Jenkins joined Hereford United on loan, initially for a month and then extended until the end of the season.
• Kieron Baker was recalled from his loan by Bournemouth.
• Paul Bence received a two-match suspension following a number of bookings.
• The away match at Rotherham was the club's 2,000th League game since joining the Football League in August 1920.

APRIL 1973

• John Docherty suffered a broken ankle in the game at Watford [pictured right].
• The defeat at Wrexham confirmed immediate relegation back to the Fourth Division.

MAY 1973

• Free transfers were given to Alan Murray, Gordon Phillips and David Court.

[Right] Stewart Houston in the final home game of the season against Notts County as the campaign ended in relegation

BRENTFORD GO DOWN FIGHTING!

Blunstone quits Brentford –'I have no alternative'

1973-74

[Back Row] Paul Bence, Alan Nelmes, Stan Webb, Paul Priddy, Garry Towse, Roger Cross, Stewart Houston, Terry Scales
[Middle Row] Andy Woon, John Docherty, Peter Gelson, Alan Hawley, Jackie Graham, Barry Salvage, Mike Allen
[Front Row] Kevin Harding, Neil Oliver, Richard Poole

Football League	Division Four
Manager	Mike Everitt
Trainer	Jess Willard
Captain	Alan Hawley / Gordon Riddick
Final Position	19th
FA Cup	1st Round
League Cup	1st Round
Leading Goalscorer (all competitions)	Roger Cross – 17 goals

Little-known new boss Mike Everitt's arrival from non-league Wimbledon, just days before the start of the new campaign, after Frank Blunstone's resignation, left pre-season plans in tatters. The first week of the season produced two league defeats without a goal being scored and elimination from the League Cup in the first round.

Despite the signings of experienced players, Dave Metchick and Gordon Riddick, the manager failed to endear himself to both players and supporters. The team continued to struggle and a 4-1 defeat at Scunthorpe in October saw the club slip to 92nd place in the Football League for the first time in its history. Disharmony and in-fighting in the boardroom failed to help the situation.

December saw Stewart Houston sold to Manchester United for £50,000, after requesting a transfer, then stalwarts Paul Bence, Alan Nelmes and Jackie Graham joined Barry Salvage and Paul Priddy in requesting moves elsewhere.

A 2-1 FA Cup first round exit at Plymouth Argyle started a run of just one win in 14 games and cemented a place in the bottom four of the division – before the arrival of experienced Scottish international, Jimmy Gabriel from Bournemouth, and his involvement on the coaching side along with John Docherty, produced an unexpected and welcome revival.

The final 15 matches resulted in just two defeats being incurred and the embarrassing ignominy of a re-election application was avoided by two points – the season ended with further off-field antics in the boardroom making more of the headlines.

[Previous page] Roger Cross, Andy Woon and Stan Webb during the 2-1 home defeat to Bury

Total Home League Attendances	116,454
Average Home League Attendance	5,063
Highest Home League Attendance	8,717
Lowest Home League Attendance	3,166

		P	W	D	L	F	A	W	D	L	F	A	Pts
1	Peterborough	46	19	4	0	49	10	8	7	8	26	28	**65**
2	Gillingham	46	16	5	2	51	10	9	7	7	39	33	**62**
3	Colchester	46	16	5	2	46	14	8	7	8	27	22	**60**
4	Bury	46	18	3	2	51	14	6	8	9	30	35	**59**
5	Northampton	46	14	7	2	39	14	6	6	11	24	34	**53**
6	Reading	46	11	9	3	37	13	5	10	8	21	24	**51**
7	Chester	46	13	6	4	31	19	4	9	10	23	36	**49**
8	Bradford	46	14	7	2	45	20	3	7	13	13	32	**48**
9	Newport **	46	13	6	4	39	23	3	8	12	17	42	**45**
10	Exeter *	45	12	5	6	37	20	6	3	13	21	35	**44**
11	Hartlepool	46	11	4	8	29	16	5	8	10	19	31	**44**
12	Lincoln	46	10	8	5	40	30	6	4	13	23	37	**44**
13	Barnsley	46	15	5	3	42	16	2	5	16	16	48	**44**
14	Swansea	46	11	6	6	28	15	5	5	13	17	31	**43**
15	Rotherham	46	10	9	4	33	22	5	4	14	23	36	**43**
16	Torquay	46	11	7	5	37	23	2	10	11	15	34	**43**
17	Mansfield	46	13	8	2	47	24	0	9	14	15	45	**43**
18	Scunthorpe *	45	12	7	3	33	17	2	5	16	14	47	**42**
19	**Brentford**	46	9	7	7	31	20	3	9	11	17	30	**40**
20	Darlington	46	9	8	6	29	24	4	5	14	11	38	**39**
21	Crewe	46	11	5	7	28	30	3	5	15	15	41	**38**
22	Doncaster	46	10	7	6	32	22	2	4	17	15	58	**35**
23	Workington	46	10	8	5	33	26	1	5	17	10	48	**35**
24	Stockport	46	4	12	7	22	25	3	8	12	22	44	**34**

** Newport had one point deducted for fielding an illegible player /* Exeter and Scunthorpe did not complete
their fixtures, the points were awarded to Scunthorpe

League Position throughout the Season

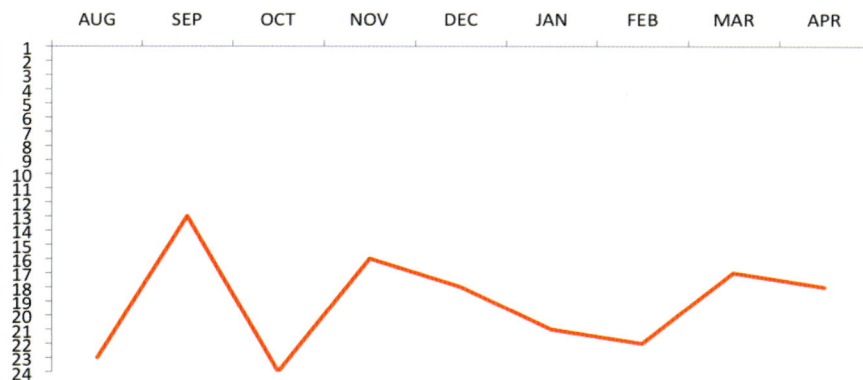

79

1973-74

Sat 25th August: **Hartlepool (A)**
Lost 0-1   **Attendance: 3,447**

The new season started in familiar fashion with a goal-less away defeat, albeit under new manager Mike Everitt, but with no new faces in the playing line-up. The only goal of the game came in the 79th minute – enough to ensure a long, fruitless journey home.

Tue 28th August: **Orient (H) League Cup 1st Round**
Lost 1-2   **Attendance: 6,620**

The Division Two visitors went ahead after 22 minutes when Stewart Houston's attempted back-pass evaded Paul Priddy and an opposing striker nipped in to prod the ball over the line to avoid the embarrassment of an own goal. The deficit was doubled in the 33rd minute and, although Stan Webb pulled a goal back in the 49th minute, when he scored from Mike Allen's headed flick-on, it wasn't enough to avoid a first round cup exit.

Sat 1st September: **Exeter City (H)**
Lost 0-1   **Attendance: 4,814**

A 43rd minute header for the visiting team proved to be the only goal of a dismal match in which the performance reached rock-bottom in terms of quality – the frustrations of the fans were heard long and loud during the latter stages and at the final whistle.

Sat 8th September: **Darlington (A)**
Won 2-1   **Attendance: 2,287**

The first goals and points of the season arrived in a match played in sweltering heat and, despite the hosts taking advantage of some poor defending to grab a 38th minute lead, the equaliser arrived three minutes into the second half when, from a Barry Salvage corner, Roger Cross flicked the ball to Andy Woon, who netted from close range. The winner came in the final minute when John Docherty's pass found Andy Woon – he returned the favour of the first goal by flicking on to Roger Cross to fire home the decider.

Mon 10th September: **Torquay United (H)**
Drew 0-0   **Attendance: 5,581**

A one-sided encounter, in which the visitors failed to remotely test debutant goalkeeper Garry Towse, ended in the first goal-less draw for 60 games, although a host of chances created throughout should have brought a better reward.

Sat 15th September: **Doncaster Rovers (H)**
Won 2-0   **Attendance: 4,957**

A comfortable win was achieved courtesy of two goals by Roger Cross, the first of which arrived in the 35th minute and was a trademark 25-yard left-foot screamer, having been cleverly set up by John Docherty. Barry Salvage created the second goal on 75 minutes with a low centre that Cross finished with a neat backwards flick.

Mon 17th September: **Reading (H)**
Lost 0-1   **Attendance: 8,717**

The biggest crowd of the season witnessed a match dominated by the visitors, although the solitary goal did not arrive until the 64th minute when a misunderstanding between Alan Nelmes and Garry Towse resulted in a corner, which was headed home to secure the win. The evening was also notable for an astonishing miss when a long punt forward was completely missed by keeper Towse, the ball bouncing over his head and the on-rushing Reading striker ran on and contrived to head the ball over the bar of the gaping, empty goal.

Sat 22nd September: **Bury (A)**
Lost 0-3   **Attendance: 4,329**

The comprehensive defeat was based on the award of two penalties, the first of which arrived in the 29th minute when Stewart Houston was adjudged to have pushed his opponent, and the second, converted after 54 minutes, having been awarded for another foul by Houston. Two minutes later a third goal put the result beyond any doubt.

Sat 29th September: **Barnsley (H)**
Won 5-1   **Attendance: 5,010**

The game was decided by three goals in the first 12 minutes, and two more in the final four, to give an overall flattering look to the scoreline. Terry Scales's darting run into the penalty area in the 3rd minute resulted in his close-range shot being helped over the line by an opposing defender, before John Docherty provided the 10th minute cross for Andy Woon to head in the second. Two minutes later, Docherty himself was on the end of a Roger Cross pass to nod home. The visitors pulled a goal back on 57 minutes, but the 86th minute brought a debut goal for Dave Metchick with a powerful 20-yard blast beyond the keeper – Andy Woon provided the icing on the cake 60 seconds later with a header from a John Docherty cross.

Wed 3rd October: **Reading (A)**
Lost 0-1   **Attendance: 11,267**

Although suffering an early season double defeat to Berkshire-based rivals, a spirited performance deserved better than the single goal loss, which was inflicted with an 80th minute close range tap-in for the home side.

Sat 6th October: **Lincoln City (A)**
Lost 2-3   **Attendance: 4,056**

Andy Woon's 7th minute opener, having been set up by a through ball from Dave Metchick, provided the foundations for a splendid first half display, which was further enhanced on the half-hour mark when a free-kick five yards outside the penalty box was touched by Dave Metchick to Roger Cross, who fired home powerfully into the roof of the net. However, the second half saw the rampant home side lay siege, and goals in the 53rd, 75th and 83rd minutes completed a devastating comeback to seal the win for City.

Sat 13th October: **Peterborough United (H)**
Lost 0-1   **Attendance: 6,141**

A lacklustre game of few chances was settled in the 49th minute when a long-range shot was parried by Paul Priddy, but he was unable to prevent the ball from rolling into the net to give the visitors a lead – one that they were determined to hold onto without looking to add further to their tally.

Sat 20th October: **Rotherham United (H)**
Drew 1-1   **Attendance: 4,419**

The dismal Autumn weather was replicated on the pitch and, after a scoreless first half, the lead was secured when Barry Salvage's 40-yard run ended with a low cross that the visiting keeper fumbled to enable Stan Webb to poke the ball home. With time almost up at the end of the 90 minutes, Salvage turned villain as his attempted dribble on the edge of his own penalty box saw him lose possession and enabled Rotherham to snatch a last-gasp equaliser.

Wed 24th October: **Torquay United (A)**
Lost 0-3   **Attendance: 4,445**

A spectacular long-range strike in the 30th minute gave the hosts the lead – the quality of the goal was bettered in first-half injury-time when another powerful, swerving rocket from close to the touchline flew ferociously into the net. If the first two goals had been worthy winners, the third, in the 75th minute, was a comedy of errors – Jackie Graham slipped over in possession of the ball in his own penalty area, providing a gift goal to his opponent.

Sat 27th October: **Scunthorpe United (A)**
Lost 1-4   **Attendance: 2,523**

With manager Mike Everitt away on a scouting mission, a catastrophic start to the game saw United sweep into a four-goal lead inside the opening 17 minutes. A strike from a free-kick started the debacle in the second minute and, just two minutes later, a defensive mix-up between Garry Towse and Peter Gelson presented the hosts with a gift. Further goals in the 12th and 17th minutes put the game beyond reach and presented a real possibility of a cricket-score being chalked up. A 40th minute consolation from Roger Cross, tapping home from an Alan Hawley centre, was the only other notable action. The result saw the club propping up the entire Football League in 92nd place for the first time in its history.

Sat 3rd November: **Mansfield Town (H)**
Won 4-1   **Attendance: 4,331**

A 37th minute goal for the visitors looked to spell further gloom, but the game turned around in the second half, which was only two minutes old when Alan Hawley's free-kick was headed home by Stewart Houston. Six minutes later Roger Cross lobbed the ball over the keeper's head and into the net. The game appeared to be won in the 71st minute when Andy Woon's snap-shot in a goalmouth melee rebounded to Roger Cross, who rattled in his second goal. A 77th minute penalty, awarded when a Dave Metchick shot was handled, gave Cross the opportunity to complete his hat-trick.

Sat 10th November: **Workington (A)**
Won 2-0   **Attendance: 970**

A game played in a virtually empty stadium, which had once held over 21,000 spectators, was devoid of any atmosphere and two second half goals ended the home side's proud record of 27 league games unbeaten on their own pitch. The first goal came in the 55th minute when Roger Cross beat the offside trap and raced through to take the ball wide of the keeper, before squaring it to give Andy

Woon a simple tap-in. Terry Scales's 70th minute free-kick saw Woon set up Gordon Riddick to fire home and seal victory.

Mon 12th November: **Stockport County (A)**
Drew 1-1   **Attendance: 1,948**

A heavy rain-soaked pitch and a strong wind did not prevent one of the best displays of the season being seen at Edgley Park, although the 29th minute goal came about largely as a result of the conditions. Gordon Riddick, on receiving the ball back from his throw-in, attempted a centre which curled in the wind and sailed high into the net over the keeper's head. The 51st minute equaliser for the home side could also be attributed to the conditions – Paul Priddy failed to hold a low shot, which slipped from his grasp to the feet of an opposing forward.

Sat 17th November: **Chester City (H)**
Won 3-0   **Attendance: 5,166**

Roger Cross became the proud owner of a club record – two hat-tricks in successive home games – as the fine run of results and goal-scoring continued. The match kicked off at 2.15pm, a result of the energy crisis sweeping the country. Cross's first goal came in the 10th minute when he back-flicked Gordon Riddick's header into the net following a Barry Salvage corner then, on 41 minutes, he diverted Dave Metchick's shot in from the edge of the penalty box – the treble was completed in the 58th minute when he slammed the ball into the net after another mazy Barry Salvage run had paved the way.

Sat 24th November: **Plymouth Argyle (A) FA Cup 1st Round**
Lost 1-2   **Attendance: 11,050**

Around 1,000 Bees fans travelled to South Devon and witnessed a splendid cup-tie, which saw end-to-end excitement. The home side took the lead in the 51st minute, before Dave Metchick was sent off on 70 minutes for violent retaliation to a challenge on him. Nine minutes later the ten-men equalised when Gordon Riddick's

defence-splitting pass found Mike Allen in the clear and he slotted the ball past the keeper. With a replay looking all but certain, tragedy struck in the 87th minute. Stewart Houston's attempted back-pass from outside his penalty box sailed over the head of Paul Priddy and dropped into the net, sending the Third Division side through to the next round.

Sat 1st December: **Gillingham (H)**
Lost 0-3   **Attendance: 5,748**

A hard frost-covered pitch made for difficult conditions, but nonetheless, a host of chances were created and missed before the visitors took the lead in the 38th minute. Although somewhat fortunate to be in front at the interval, they took full advantage in the second half with two goals arriving on 55 and 61 minutes.

Sat 8th December: **Bradford City (A)**
Drew 1-1   **Attendance: 3,243**

In the 9th minute a John Docherty corner was misjudged by the keeper and Stan Webb took advantage to head the ball into the net – but the lead was short-lived. On the half-hour mark a goalmouth skirmish saw the ball poked towards goal and Mike Allen, on the line, appeared to clear comfortably. But the linesman signalled a goal, which was awarded despite long and vociferous protests.

Sat 15th December: **Darlington (H)**
Drew 0-0   **Attendance: 3,166**

A combination of the now-accustomed early kick-off, in order to avoid adding to the energy crisis by use of the floodlights, and the alternative option of Christmas shopping, contributed to the crowd being the lowest home attendance since 1963 – they witnessed a frustrating game in which the visitors set their stall out for a point and achieved it with relative ease.

Sat 22nd December: **Barnsley (A)**
Lost 1-2   **Attendance: 2,458**

Two goals midway through the first half failed to separate the teams – the home side's 29th minute opener being equalised just three minutes later when Roger Cross produced another of his left-foot specials – a low, powerful 20-yard effort that beat the keeper. The winner arrived in the 54th minute and was a disaster for Peter Gelson, whose back-pass from 12 yards lacked any strength. The ball travelled no more than half its intended distance, before being intercepted and prodded into the net, leaving the centre-back with his head in his hands.

Wed 26th December: **Newport County (H)**
Drew 1-1   **Attendance: 5,445**

An entertaining holiday encounter, in which both sides attacked throughout, resulted in a fair sharing of the points. Barry Salvage set up Jackie Graham to fire into the top right-hand corner of the net from 25 yards after half an hour, but the visitors drew level five minutes before the break. The game, the last for Stewart Houston before his transfer to Manchester United, also marked the 1,000th consecutive Brentford match covered by the Middlesex Chronicle's legendary sports editor, George Sands (pictured).

Tue 1st January: **Exeter City (A)**
Lost 1-2   **Attendance: 5,754**

Just three minutes into the New Year's Day action, Roger Cross played in Barry Salvage, who ran on and shot low into the net from the left corner of the penalty box. The early lead was held until the 56th minute, when Jackie Graham's handball in the area was punished with a penalty-kick. The home side snatched the points at the death with a 90th minute winner. An unusual incident meant the game almost started with no Brentford substitute as Dave Metchick overslept and missed the coach, leaving just 11 players to set off – Metchick had to drive himself to Devon, arriving with seconds to spare before the team sheets were handed in.

Sat 5th January: **Swansea City (H)**
Lost 0-2   **Attendance: 3,501**

Despite a flurry of attacking play, the visitor's solid defence held firm, and once they had taken a 14th minute lead, the task to break them down became even tougher. With an all-out attacking policy as the game approached the closing stages, a break-away sealed the win for the Welshmen in the 84th minute – both Paul Priddy and Peter Gelson slipped in the muddy conditions attempting to clear the ball and left a gaping goal behind them.

Sat 12th January: **Doncaster Rovers (A)**
Won 2-1   **Attendance: 3,009**

With the fuel crisis biting even harder, and rail travel extremely unpredictable, the game was almost a non-event when the team coach failed to arrive at Griffin Park and the players had to travel north in a fleet of cars – and find room for the kit basket. However, the trauma only had a positive effect, despite the home side taking a 19th minute lead. Andy Woon equalised two minutes later when, from Mike Allen's cross, he headed against the post and thumping home the rebound then, ten minutes before the break, from another Mike Allen cross, Woon seized on a misdirected punch from the keeper to slot the ball home.

Sat 19th January: **Hartlepool (H)**
Lost 1-2   **Attendance: 4,646**

From their first corner the visitors took an unexpected lead in the 15th minute, when Alan Nelmes headed into his own goal – although another corner levelled the scores on the stroke of half time when Barry Salvage's cross was flicked on by Andy Woon, for Mike Allen to nod into the net. A disappointing second-half display was compounded when, in the 72nd minute, Peter Gelson's poor headed clearance fell straight into the path of an opposing striker, who gratefully accepted the gift to win the game.

Sat 26th January: **Crewe Alexandra (A)**
Drew 0-0   **Attendance: 1,380**

A second successive non-appearance of the team coach resulted in another hurried journey north in a convoy of cars and, despite a mud-bath of a pitch, and torrential rain, an entertaining goal-less draw was played out. The point gained being in no small way attributable to an outstanding goalkeeping display from Paul Priddy.

Sat 2nd February: **Northampton (A)**
Drew 0-0   **Attendance: 4,130**

Another scoreless draw lacked the thrills of the previous week and a dour game was played out with goal scoring chances few and far between – some of the spells of inactivity being more suited to the adjoining cricket pitch.

Sat 9th February: **Bury (H)**
Lost 1-2   **Attendance: 4,015**

Heavy rain prompted a pitch inspection to see if the game could go ahead and, with both teams trying to adapt to the boggy conditions, it took until the 43rd minute for the first goal to arrive – Dave Metchick's right-wing centre was slammed home by Roger Cross after Andy Woon's initial effort had been blocked. Just a minute later another Metchick free-kick was fired in by Andy Woon but,

having given the goal, the referee was informed by his linesman that the ball was moving when the kick was taken and the goal was ruled out. It proved costly when the visitors equalised in the 49th minute and then grabbed a late winner.

Sat 16th February: **Peterborough United (A)**
Lost 0-1   **Attendance: 7,645**

The visit to the home of the champions-elect proved to be a tough challenge and incessant attacking from the hosts meant that the match was almost a rearguard action for the entire 90 minutes. The single goal came in the 43rd minute, when Paul Bence inadvertently deflected a low cross into his own net.

Sat 23rd February: **Lincoln City (H)**
Won 2-1   **Attendance: 4,171**

A run of six consecutive home games without a win ended despite the visitors taking a 4th minute lead – Paul Priddy failed to hold a long range shot. The equaliser came in the 17th minute when Dave Metchick sent Barry Salvage away to fire home from the edge of the penalty box – the tally was doubled just before the hour mark when Andy Woon found Roger Cross, who slotted the ball into the net from eight yards out. Barry Salvage missed an opportunity to cement the win when his penalty was saved by the keeper, but it ultimately didn't change the outcome of the match.

Sat 2nd March: **Newport County (A)**
Drew 1-1   **Attendance: 2,167**

In possibly the best away performance of the season, it took just 15 minutes for the first goal to arrive – Barry Salvage collected the ball on the left touchline, waltzed past two opponents in a run towards the corner of the penalty box, then hit a fierce low drive into the net. The remainder of the game produced a performance that would have delighted manager Mike Everitt, who was absent on a scouting mission, but with just over a minute remaining, a richly deserved win was denied by a headed equaliser.

Sat 9th March: **Scunthorpe United (H)**
Won 2-1   **Attendance: 4,053**

Having been set up by a move involving Dave Metchick and Gordon Riddick, Barry Salvage claimed his third goal in consecutive games – speeding down the left flank and leaving two defenders in his wake, before planting a low cross-drive beyond the keeper and into the net. The goal came after ten minutes and, just eight minutes later, Mike Allen doubled the lead when he took advantage of a frantic scramble in the penalty box to prod the ball home. The visitors scored almost immediately at the start of the second half when Steve Sherwood failed to hold a long range shot and led to a nervous finale.

Sat 16th March: **Rotherham United (A)**
Drew 1-1   **Attendance: 2,536**

In blazing sunshine, and with two debutants in Jimmy Gabriel and Dave Simmons, a defeat looked likely when the hosts took the lead in the 68th minute. But, with nine minutes remaining, a well-rehearsed free-kick move saw the ball played from the edge of the area to Dave Metchick on the left, who took the ball almost to the bye-line before firing in from the acutest of angles.

Mon 18th March: **Northampton Town (H)**
Won 3-1   **Attendance: 3,686**

An attendance of over 3,500 could be considered extremely good bearing in mind the kick-off time of 5.15pm would have seen many supporters just leaving work, but their presence was rewarded after 34 minutes of intense pressure when Dave Metchick's low centre was converted by Roger Cross. Four minutes later, Dave Simmons' headed goal came from a Barry Salvage cross. Northampton's threat increased after pulling a second-half goal back, but Barry Salvage continued his rich vein of scoring and hit a typical low drive after a strong run to seal the victory in the 77th minute.

Sat 23rd March: **Workington (H)**
Drew 1-1   **Attendance: 5,008**

Paul Bence was the architect of the 16th minute goal that opened the scoring – his right-wing cross was headed on by Dave Simmons for Roger Cross to nod the ball home. The equalising goal for the visitors came on the hour mark – another goal to fall into the 'gift' category. A lofted ball into the penalty box caught Steve Sherwood napping, leaving an easy header for the on-running striker.

Tue 26th March: **Swansea City (A)**
Drew 0-0   **Attendance: 2,220**

A splendid away performance produced some excellent football, which was largely orchestrated by Jimmy Gabriel in the midfield – showing the qualities that had seen him playing at the highest level for many years. Despite a game full of incident and thrills, the scoreline remained goal-less at the final whistle.

Sat 30th March: **Mansfield Town (A)**
Drew 1-1   **Attendance: 1,909**

The home side's superiority in the first half reflected an excellent home record throughout the season, so it was little surprise when they took the lead after 26 minutes. The second half was a different story and a vastly improved performance was rewarded in the 68th minute when Jimmy Gabriel's left-wing centre was back-headed into the net by Jackie Graham.

Mon 1st April: **Crewe Alexandra (H)**
Won 3-0   **Attendance: 5,552**

A return to floodlit football extended the unbeaten run to nine games, and it took only 12 minutes before a ball from Jimmy Gabriel was headed on by Dave Simmons for Roger Cross to score a rare right-footed goal. Midway through the second half, with the visitors threatening a revival, a Barry Salvage corner was cleared only as far as Dave Metchick, who crashed a 25-yard thunderbolt into the roof of the net – Dave Simmons' late header, from a perfect cross-field pass by Metchick, provided the cap on a fine display.

Sat 6th April: **Stockport County (H)**
Drew 0-0   **Attendance: 5,625**

With an unchanged line-up for a seventh successive game, the undefeated run continued, although the game was a tepid affair with both sides struggling to make any impact. The final whistle proved to be a blessing for the majority of those at Griffin Park.

Fri 12th April: **Colchester United (A)**
Lost 1-2   **Attendance: 8,155**

In a game that virtually assured the hosts of promotion, they took the lead in the 15th minute – Steve Sherwood mishandled a corner and dropped the ball, presenting an easy scoring opportunity. Brentford levelled against the run of play early in the second-half – Dave Metchick's cross was headed home by Dave Simmons against his old team. But an inevitable winner for the home side arrived soon after.

Sat 13th April: **Chester City (A)**
Drew 0-0   **Attendance: 2,775**

Despite only travelling north on the morning of the game, and having played another away fixture just 24 hours earlier, a strong and committed display resulted in the seventh 0-0 draw of the season, as the rival defences dominated throughout this Easter weekend clash.

Tue 16th April: **Colchester United (H)**
Drew 0-0   **Attendance: 7,478**

A return fixture, just four days after the first meeting, was somewhat unusual and the encounter brought together two teams at opposite ends of the table. While the visitors were already assured of promotion, points were still needed by The Bees to stave off the increasingly unlikely prospect of a re-election application. A somewhat experimental line-up more than matched the high-flyers and an entertaining, yet scoreless draw resulted.

Sat 20th April: **Bradford City (H)**
Won 2-0   **Attendance: 5,224**

After a slow start, the proceedings were livened up 16 minutes into the second half when a half-hit shot from Bees striker Dave Simmons was inexplicably dropped behind the goal-line by the visiting keeper. Then, when Barry Salvage and Gordon Riddick paved the way for 16-year-old Richard Poole to run on and thump the ball past

the keeper from the edge of the penalty box for a second goal in the 81st minute, any lingering re-election fears were extinguished.

Sat 27th April: **Gillingham (A)**
Lost 0-1   **Attendance: 9,319**

With the hosts already assured of promotion there was little but pride riding on the outcome and the 69-hour long season had just three minutes remaining when the home side grabbed the winning goal in chilly and windswept conditions.

Blunstone in hospital after M-way smash

PRE-SEASON

One week before the start of pre-season training Frank Blunstone, who was not under contract, resigned as manager to join Manchester United as youth team manager. On the same day he was involved in a serious car accident and suffered multiple injuries. Trainer Eddie Lyons also resigned. Alan Hawley and other senior professionals supervised the pre-season work whilst the manager's post was advertised.

21-year old goalkeeper Garry Towse was signed from Crystal Palace on a free transfer. David Jenkins signed permanently for Hereford United on a free transfer following his loan spell. Goalkeeper Neil Oliver was signed as an apprentice professional. Both Gordon Phillips and Alan Hawley were awarded testimonial matches.

Bill Berry was appointed as promotions manager, having previously held a similar position with Doncaster Rovers. The board issued a statement announcing that an enquiry had been made to the council regarding the possible re-development of the old Brentford Market site as a new ground.

FOOTBALL LEAGUE, Div. I.

(Each club plays 42 fixtures).

Pos.		P.	W.	L.	D.	For	Agt.	P.
1*	Brentford	29	14	8	7	48	36	35
2	ARSENAL	28	14	8	6	53	32	34
3	Wolverh'pton	26	14	6	6	46	32	34
4	Leeds United	28	11	6	11	46	40	33
5*	Preston N. E.	28	10	7	11	45	33	31
6	Charlton Ath.	25	10	5	10	38	29	30
7	Bolton Wan.	28	10	8	10	46	41	30
8*	Sunderland	28	10	8	10	38	40	30
9	Middlesbrough	27	12	10	5	46	44	29
10	Derby County	28	10	8	10	46	58	28
11	Stoke City	27	10	10	7	42	32	27
12	Chelsea	27	10	10	7	49	49	27
13*	Huddersfield T.	28	11	13	4	36	44	26
14*	Manchester C.	26	10	11	5	50	45	25
15	Everton	28	11	15	2	48	50	24
16	W. Bromwich	26	9	11	6	42	48	24
17	Liverpool	27	8	11	8	39	47	24
18	Grimsby Town	28	6	10	12	32	43	24
19	Leicester City	28	9	13	6	36	48	24
20	Birmingham	27	5	9	13	32	37	23
21	Portsmouth	28	6	13	9	38	53	21
22	Blackpool	29	7	15	7	33	48	21

* = In 6th Round of Cup Competition.

TOP TO BOTTOM IN 35 YEARS !

BRENTFORD, top of the First Division? It seems hard to believe, as they are now bottom of Division Four, but it did happen — in 1938.

Alas, their success was short-lived. They took only 10 points from their last 13 games and finished sixth.

Brentford were in the First Division from 1935 until 1947. Their highest end of season placing was fifth, in 1935-36.

This league table is taken from an old Arsenal programme in a colleague's collection. Starring at Finsbury Park Empire that week were Carrol Levis and his Radio Discoveries and Jack Payne with his band, and admission to the first team games was 1s. (5p)!

Phillips made his farewell in style

THE BRENTFORD public shunned the testimonial game for former keeper Gordon Phillips at Griffin Park on Monday. Only 1,461 turned up to pay tribute to a player who appeared in 227 games for the club, and receipts were a mere £595.

However, with the addition of programme sales, donations, etc., Gordon will collect over £700.

The match itself, between Brentford and a team comprising former Brentford players, resulted in a win for the ex-Bees by four goals to three, although it must be stated, due to injuries over the weekend, there were three absentees in the ex-Bees' side, and Brentford came to their rescue with Stan Webb and 16-years-old apprentice professionals Kevin Harding and Richard Poole.

The eyes of those supporters who did attend were firmly fixed on big John O'Mara who hit 27 goals in their promotion year, and he did not disappoint his former fans on this occasion when he hit two fine goals in his old style.

Brentford drew first blood with a goal in the eighth minute created by Barry

GORDON PHILLIPS

Salvage and converted by Andy Woon.

After a shot by Dave Metchick had hit a post, Phillips showed his old agility with a super catch from a Paul Bence drive. After 19 minutes O'Mara flashed into the picture when racing on to a Poole through-ball to thump the ball well wide of the advancing Paul Priddy.

On the half-hour mark the fourth division side went ahead again, Salvage bending the ball past Phillips from a Bence cross, but the equaliser came inside a minute with a typical O'Mara header from a Dave Jenkins' corner. Three minutes later the ex-Bees edged ahead when Steve Tom headed splendidly home from Webb's centre.

Mike Allen limped off to be replaced by Roger Cross, who was quickly in action with a powerful shot which Gordon Phillips saved in fine style. He also did well with a great overhead save from Alan Hawley.

The ex-Bees went further ahead with their fourth goal after 70 minutes when Cliff Myers' 25-yard effort turned in off a post. The final goal went to the home side, Metchick heading home from Bence five minutes from the end, but Brentford's problems increased in the dying stages when Jackie Graham went off with a twisted ankle.

The players lined up to cheer off Gordon Phillips who, despite the poor attendance, had a memorable game for his last appearance at Brentford.

Brentford: Priddy, Hawley, Scales, Bence, Gelson, Nelmes, Graham, Allen, Woon, Metchick, Salvage, Sub: Cross.

Ex-Bees: Phillips, Harding, Renwick, Higginson, Tom, Richardson, Webb, Poole, O'Mara, Myers, Jenkins.

AUGUST 1973

- From a shortlist of 36, non-League Wimbledon's 32-year old manager, Mike Everitt, was appointed as player-manager, but indicated that he would only play in the event of an injury crisis. The former Arsenal, Northampton, Plymouth and Brighton midfielder would not be able to take up his new post until 16th August.
- 49-year old Cecil 'Jess' Willard ended a 20-year long association with Crystal Palace to become the new trainer and chief scout.
- A 29-day trial period was offered to amateur Alan Gane, who had been playing for Wycombe Wanderers.
- Jackie Graham faced a lengthy spell out of action with a leg injury.
- Garry Towse suffered a fractured finger in training.
- Alan Hawley missed the opening match as he completed the suspension imposed at the end of the previous season.

SEPTEMBER 1973

- Former Fulham midfielder, Dave Metchick, aged 30, signed for a 28-day trial, having returned from playing for Atlanta Apollo in the USA.
- 22-year old centre-back Mick Brown was signed on loan from Brighton.
- Having agreed a fee with Northampton Town, the transfer of Gordon Riddick was called off when the player failed to agree personal terms.

- Alan Gane rejected the offer of another 28-day trial period and signed for Hereford United.
- John Docherty suffered a broken rib in training and faced several weeks out of action.
- Peter Gelson and Paul Priddy were both injured in the match at Darlington.
- Roy Ruffell left the club to join Crystal Palace as a scout.

OCTOBER 1973

- Gordon Riddick finally signed from Northampton Town, the 29-year old midfielder costing a reported £4,000 fee.
- Dave Metchick signed a contract until the end of the season following his trial period.
- Mick Brown was recalled by Brighton after his loan spell.
- 23-year old winger Hugh Reed was signed on a one-month loan from Plymouth Argyle.
- Paul Bence and Alan Nelmes were both transfer-listed at their own request.
- Defeat at Scunthorpe left the team in 92nd place in the League.

[Above] A Brentford team face Ex-Bees in a testimonial game played for Gordon Phillips

NOVEMBER 1973

- Hugh Reed returned to Plymouth Argyle at the end of his loan spell.
- Stan Webb was made available for loan or transfer.
- Dave Metchick was sent off at Plymouth and given a three-match ban.
- John Docherty recovered from his broken rib but Barry Salvage fractured his wrist in a training accident.
- Gordon Riddick was appointed as the new club captain in place of Alan Hawley.
- The board disharmony was emphasised when joint chairman, Walter Wheatley, issued a statement regarding the club's position near the foot of the table, following which Eric Radley-Smith refuted the statement, criticising the views expressed and indicating that they did not reflect the views of the whole board.

DECEMBER 1973

- Stewart Houston was sold to Manchester United for a reported record-equalling £50,000 fee, after requesting a transfer.
- Paul Bence joined Hillingdon Borough on a one-month loan.
- Junior centre-back, Gary Smith, signed professional terms.
- The board announced that a reserve team would be re-introduced for 1974/75 and would play in the Midweek Football League – although there would no longer be a competitive junior team.

BRENTFORD manager Mike Everitt did not mince his words after see ing his team crash to defeat after holding a 2-0 interval lead at Lincoln on Saturday, writes Nicholas Clarke.

"I am sick, the directors are sick and the players are sick" he said.

"The team collectively played badly with only Peter Gelson doing well. This performance was thoroughly unprofessional.

"Two goals up at the break, we should never have lost this match and only started playing in the second half when we went 3-2 down. We had three men in mid-field compared with Lincoln's two and yet we never looked like doing anything there.

"We had 11 men in our penalty area for the free kick that resulted in Lincoln's winning goal yet they still managed to score."

Everitt's verbal lashing was perfectly justified for Brentford folded completely in the second half to literally present Lincoln with the points.

The mid-field trio might just as well not have been playing for all the effect they had on the game. Every time the Defence pumped the ball clear it came straight back.

JANUARY 1974

- 20-year old goalkeeper, Steve Sherwood, was signed on loan from Chelsea for the rest of the season.
- Garry Towse was released from his contract and left the club.
- Paul Bence returned following his loan at Hillingdon Borough.
- Barry Salvage requested a transfer claiming that the club lacked ambition.
- A fee was agreed with Blackburn Rovers for the return transfer of John O'Mara, but the player was unable to agree terms.
- Walter Wheatley became sole chairman of the club with Eric Radley-Smith assuming the role of vice-chairman.

FEBRUARY 1974

- Cambridge United rejected a bid for their striker Dave Simmons.
- A loan deal, with a view to a permanent move, was agreed with Peterborough for striker Peter Price, but the player rejected the deal.
- Alan Hawley was loaned to Hillingdon for the rest of the season but returned after a few days in order to join Aldershot on a one-month loan deal.
- Jackie Graham and Paul Priddy were both placed on the transfer list at their own request.
- Alan Nelmes asked to come off the transfer list.
- Richard Poole became the first of the apprentices to break through into the first team.
- John Docherty, who had been instrumental in the development of the junior set-up and had been coaching the schoolboys, assisted Mike Everitt with the first-team coaching for the remainder of the season.

MARCH 1974

• Following an improved offer, 25-year old Dave Simmons signed from Cambridge United on transfer deadline day for a £12,000 fee.

• Former Scottish international, and Everton and Southampton midfielder, Jimmy Gabriel, signed from Bournemouth until the end of the season.

• Alan Hawley returned from his loan spell at Aldershot.

• Three of the directors (Les Davey, Peter Davey and Bert Poyton) called an extraordinary board meeting to call for the removal of Walter Wheatley, Frank Davis and Eric Radley-Smith as directors, and the appointment of Ron Blindell. Colin Wheatley announced that he would resign if the motion was carried. At the meeting, the proposals were passed but Les Davey and Peter Davey were also voted off the board and, with only three directors remaining, the board was left unable to conduct any business.

APRIL 1974

• Paul Bence was taken off the transfer list at his own request.

• Steve Johnson and Billy Stagg were signed as apprentice professionals.

• One of the three remaining directors, Bert Poyton, announced that he would resign when a new board was constituted.

MAY 1974

• Free transfers were given to John Docherty, Stan Webb and Alan Hawley.

Bees watch Simmonds

CAMBRIDGE United striker Dave Simmonds is one of the players that Brentford manager Mike Everitt has watched in a bid to strengthen his team.

But Cambridge manager Bill Leivers was angry today that news had been leaked of a deal between the two clubs for the player.

"There is no deal in the offing," said Leivers and Brentford also claim that Simmonds is just one of many players they have been watching.

Former skipper Alan Hawley is joining Hillingdon Borough on loan and hopes to make his debut for the Southern League club against Chelmsford at the Leas Stadium on Saturday.

"I hope to play on Saturday. At least this move will give me a chance of playing instead of sitting around doing nothing," said Hawley.

"I fixed the move up myself with Jim Langley and am on a 24-hour recall with Brentford."

Jimmy Gabriel: command of a leader

MOVEMENT IN SPORT

Gabriel's mission

There comes a time when great footballers must decide, either to retire at the top as Greaves and the Charltons did, or to take the Fourth Division route towards obscurity. Jimmy Gabriel, who with Everton won every honour in the game, was tracked down yesterday in the League basement at Brentford. ROB HUGHES found him full of hope and looking up.

"THE BRAIN speeds up, but the legs slow down slightly." That's Jimmy Gabriel, with succinct turn of phrase, a whitened head and a weathered look about his play, describing life in Division IV. Yesterday's goalless draw against Stockport, which with even competent finishing might have finished 6-1 in Brentford's favour was Gabriel's seventh game for the club, the seventh without defeat in a run which has hauled Brentford away from the traumatic prospect of applying for re-election to the Football League.

What then is Gabriel, a great warhorse in his time, doing in the League's £40 a week basement? The move from Bournemouth rated only four lines in the London evening papers last month, after a career which started in Dundee almost 20 years ago as a Scottish international schoolboy, progressed to full international at 20, and then a championship and an FA Cup winner's medal before the age of 25 with Everton. All told with Everton, Southampton and Bournemouth, over 600 League games.

"Great?" echoes Jimmy. "I've seen great players and I've played with great players. I don't include myself as one of them. I wouldn't delude myself."

Oh, but you were, Jim, you were. Not a mercurial artiste, but a great fighting leader. My memory of Jimmy Gabriel is a fiery, blond right half at Wembley who never shirked a tackle, who sprayed zest and enthusiasm around and had the legs and heart to demand a frenzied, unremitting team effort. It would be wrong, as well as cruel, to say that you have altogether gone to seed. But what I saw yesterday wasn't the same man I saw in his prime. Gabriel Division IV-style is no less of a man, but there are adjustments to be made: like asking a grand pianist to revert to honkytonk.

He agrees, almost. "I have seen the players with nothing left to give being by-passed by time, killing memories by playing on. But if I can't give the urgency or the fire I can still tackle, still lay off good paced balls and still help a team that needed my experience."

Gabriel appreciates he's lost a fraction of pace, no more, but enough. If he had not he'd expect at 33 to be at the top still. He looks at Derek Dougan, a year his senior and still in Division I, and says: "The Doog still has this enthusiasm for actually playing. My own enthusiasm is as fresh as the day my father first coached me, but it's being overtaken by a fanaticism for coaching or managing."

The job at Brentford is virtually coaching on the field, guiding players with encouraging words, picking up loose balls where once they were won with swashbuckling tackles. Doing everything nice, safe and sensible, and keeping the team's morale on the level.

"I'm finding the game mentally exhilarating as well as sometimes frustrating. I enjoy the intimacy and the repartee with smaller crowds and without the pressures of television cameras and all the rest."

Candidly he explains that money enticed him out of the First Division to Bournemouth who were paying him "the best money outside Division I."

And it is his driving ambition to become a manager which has led Gabriel to accept the fall down soccer's ladder. "If I stayed in Division I all my life I would have learnt only about life at the top. I'm finding out quite a few little things in the lower divisions which would even be useful put into practice at the very top."

Weather: Sunny. **Ground:** Firm. **Brentford** (4-3-3): Sherwood; Bence, Neimes, Gelson, Allen, Graham; Gabriel, Metchick, Simmons, Cross, Salvage. **Stockport Co** (4-4-2): Ogley; Charter, Trevis; Ableson, Ormrod, Fogarty; Collier, Young, Kirk, Hollis, Lawther. **Referee:** R. Tinkler (Boston).

1974-75

[Back Row] Mike Everitt, Dave Simmons, Gordon Riddick, Andy Woon, Roger Cross, Paul Priddy, Keith Lawrence, Alan Nelmes, Gary Smith, Jess Willard **[Middle Row]** Paul Bence, Terry Scales, Dave Metchick, Barry Salvage, Jackie Graham, Mike Allen, Peter Gelson **[Front Row]** Mickey Tripp, Billy Stagg, Richard Poole, Steve Johnson, Kevin Harding

Football League	Division Four
Manager	Mike Everitt / John Docherty
Trainer	Jess Willard / Eddie Lyons
Captain	Gordon Riddick
Final Position	8th
FA Cup	2nd Round
League Cup	2nd Round
Leading Goalscorer (all competitions)	Dave Simmons – 13 goals

Despite the only signing summer being 20-year novice centre-half Keith Lawrence on a free transfer from Chelsea, the campaign got off to a decent start with three wins in the opening four matches and a first round League Cup victory over Aldershot was rewarded with a second round trip to Anfield to face Liverpool where a promising display nonetheless produced inevitable elimination (1-2).

Results began to decline thereafter and just two wins in fourteen games preceded a trip to Slough Town (4-1) in the first round of the FA Cup whilst a notable departure was Peter Gelson who was released at his own request after 516 club appearances.

The arrivals of new signings Terry Johnson (£15,000) from Southend United and striker Willie Brown (£4,000) from Newport County sparked a mini-revival of five wins in seven games but after the New Year got underway without a victory in three games, newly appointed chairman Dan Tana acted quickly to replace manager Mike Everitt with former playing favourite John Docherty.

Results steadily improved with the remaining 19 matches producing nine wins, six draws and just four defeats as the move towards mid-table security gave the new manager the opportunity to give teenagers Mickey French and Nigel Smith, who both followed the new boss from Queens Park Rangers, their first-team debuts.

[Previous page] An angled finish from Dave Simmons with Terry Johnson (No.7) in amongst the Exeter City defenders

BRENTFORD

NORTHAMPTON TOWN SATURDAY 17 AUGUST 1974 KO 3 PM
OFFICIAL MATCHDAY MAGAZINE & LEAGUE REVIEW — 10p

		P	W	D	L	F	A	W	D	L	F	A	Pts
1	Mansfield	46	17	6	0	55	15	11	6	6	35	25	68
2	Shrewsbury	46	16	3	4	46	18	10	7	6	34	25	62
3	Rotherham	46	13	7	3	40	19	9	8	6	31	22	59
4	Chester	46	17	5	1	48	9	6	6	11	16	29	57
5	Lincoln	46	14	8	1	47	14	7	7	9	32	34	57
6	Cambridge	46	15	5	3	43	16	5	9	9	19	28	54
7	Reading	46	13	6	4	38	20	8	4	11	25	27	52
8	**Brentford**	**46**	**15**	**6**	**2**	**38**	**14**	**3**	**7**	**13**	**15**	**31**	**49**
9	Exeter	46	14	3	6	33	24	5	8	10	27	39	49
10	Bradford	46	10	5	8	32	21	7	8	8	24	30	47
11	Southport	46	13	7	3	36	19	2	10	11	20	37	47
12	Newport	46	13	5	5	43	30	6	4	13	25	45	47
13	Hartlepool	46	13	6	4	40	24	3	5	15	12	38	43
14	Torquay	46	10	7	6	30	25	4	7	12	16	36	42
15	Barnsley	46	10	7	6	34	24	5	4	14	28	41	41
16	Northampton	46	12	6	5	43	22	3	5	15	24	51	41
17	Doncaster	46	10	9	4	41	29	4	3	16	24	50	40
18	Crewe	46	9	9	5	22	16	2	9	12	12	31	40
19	Rochdale	46	9	9	5	35	22	4	4	15	24	53	39
20	Stockport	46	10	8	5	26	27	2	6	15	17	43	38
21	Darlington	46	11	4	8	38	27	2	6	15	16	40	36
22	Swansea	46	9	4	10	25	31	6	2	15	21	42	36
23	Workington	46	7	5	11	23	29	3	6	14	13	37	31
24	Scunthorpe	46	7	8	8	27	29	0	7	16	14	49	29

Total Home League Attendances — 118,946
Average Home League Attendance — 5,172
Highest Home League Attendance — 6,485
Lowest Home League Attendance — 3,983

League Position throughout the Season

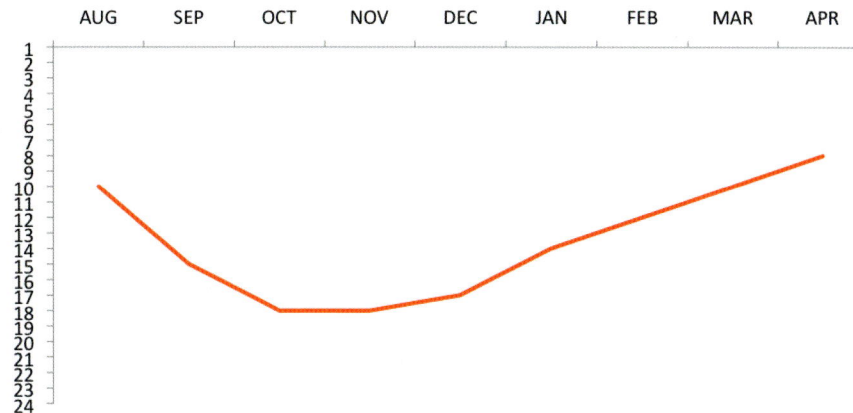

AUG SEP OCT NOV DEC JAN FEB MAR APR

1974-75

[Right] (L-R) Peter Gelson, Keith Lawrence, Mike Allen and Steve Sherwood fail to prevent Liverpool's Phil Boersma scoring in the Anfield cup-tie

Sat 17th August: **Northampton Town (H)**
Won 1-0 **Attendance: 5,147**

After an evenly-matched first half, a 62nd minute goal from Andy Woon sealed the points when he pounced on a save by the keeper – although his initial effort hit the crossbar, the stabbed rebound found the net. The crowd was the largest Fourth Division attendance of the day.

Wed 21st August: **Aldershot (H) League Cup 1st Round**
Won 3-0 **Attendance: 5,702**

Roger Cross opened the scoring with a penalty, awarded for handball in the 27th minute, and eight minutes later, Terry Scales cracked home a half-volley from ten yards – Andy Woon sealed the win with a late third goal, when he raced onto a Keith Lawrence through-ball to beat the keeper.

Sat 24th August: **Southport (A)**
Lost 0-3 **Attendance: 1,285**

A goalkeeping error by Steve Sherwood gave the hosts their first goal on 12 minutes, and the home side doubled their lead two minutes after half-time. Jackie Graham was sent-off in the 65th minute for retaliation to a challenge inside his own penalty box – the success of the subsequent spot-kick signalled a poor 3-0 defeat.

Sat 31st August: **Swansea City (H)**
Won 1-0 **Attendance: 4,908**

In a far from impressive performance the only goal arrived after just four minutes – a low left-wing cross from Barry Salvage was flicked goalwards by Roger Cross and the keeper allowed the ball to slip under his body and trickle into the net.

Sat 7th September: **Chester City (A)**
Lost 0-2 **Attendance: 2,625**

A gale force wind, which at times resembled a hurricane, dominated proceedings and the home side took the lead in the 49th minute when a scramble in the penalty box resulted in Keith Lawrence's clearance rebounding off a home player and into the net. An 87th minute second goal confirmed another away-day defeat.

Tue 10th September: **Liverpool (A) League Cup 2nd Round**
Lost 1-2 **Attendance: 21,413**

At the home of the Merseyside giants, a shock lead was provided for the 500 travelling fans when Roger Cross took a through ball from Terry Scales and fired home from just inside the penalty box after ten minutes. Goals before the break from Ray Kennedy and Phil Boersma saw the First Division leaders through to the next round, although not with the ease that might have been expected.

Sat 14th September: **Cambridge United (H)**
Won 1-0 **Attendance: 5,313**

A modest, at best, performance followed the midweek cup excitement – the only goal of the game arrived in the 83rd minute when Dave Metchick fed Mike Allen, overlapping down the left-wing, and his long, far-post cross was headed home across the goal by Dave Simmons.

Mon 16th September: **Rotherham United (H)**
Lost 3-4 **Attendance: 5,979**

An early two-goal lead was secured when Dave Simmons headed in a Gordon Riddick cross in the fourth minute, then Dave Metchick fired home from 30-yards after 22 minutes – but the dogged opponents hit back with two goals in three minutes just prior to the

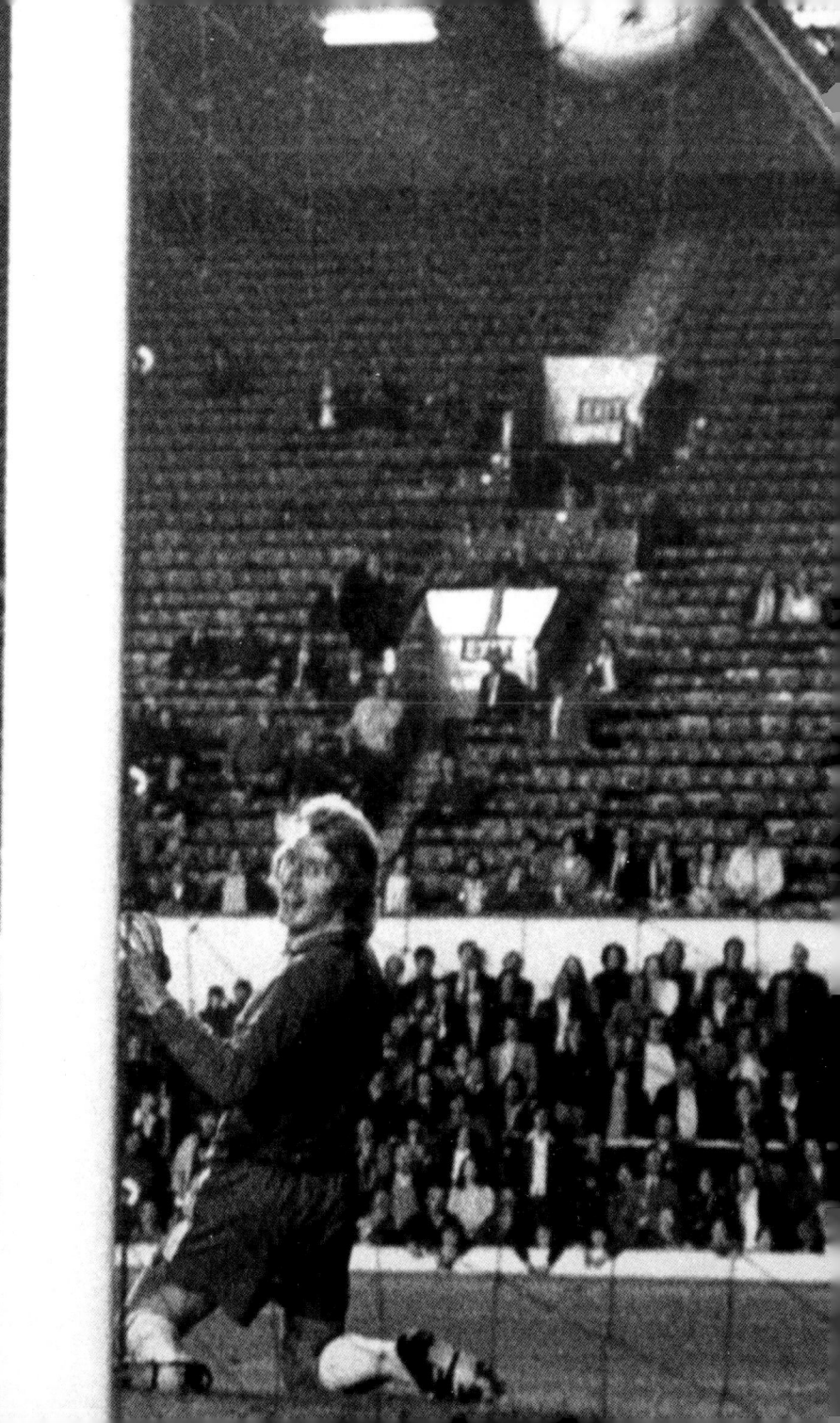

half-time break and then went 3-2 up in the 49th minute. Another 30-yard screamer, this time from Paul Bence, levelled the scores – but the visitors sealed the points with a late winner. The thrilling game proved to be Peter Gelson's last-ever appearance in a Brentford shirt.

Sat 21st September: **Newport County (A)**
Lost 0-1   **Attendance: 3,022**

An 80th minute County goal inflicted a defeat in a game which saw Paul Bence sent off for retaliation in the final few minutes – the away goal drought continued and the hosts deserved their win on the balance of play and chances created.

Mon 23rd September: **Rochdale (A)**
Drew 0-0   **Attendance: 1,587**

An entertaining and exciting draw was kept score-less by two superb goal-keeping performances. The game was also notable because of 16-year old apprentice Billy Stagg's debut and the drama of the broken jaw sustained by Mike Allen.

Sat 28th September: **Crewe Alexandra (H)**
Won 1-0   **Attendance: 5,442**

The game's only goal arrived in the 53rd minute when Dave Metchick found Barry Salvage on the left wing and his low cross was stubbed in by Dave Simmons via the foot of a post and the leg of defender Snookes – this after the table-topping visitors had controlled proceedings in the first half.

Mon 30th September: **Stockport County (A)**
Drew 1-1   **Attendance: 1,982**

Andy Woon scored the first away goal of the season to reward a good first-half performance with the lead in the 16th minute – he followed up Dave Simmons's long-range effort, which was spilled by the keeper before the home side equalised in the 49th minute.

Sat 5th October: **Doncaster Rovers (A)**
Lost 1-2   **Attendance: 1,692**

Despite going behind to a goal inside the first two minutes, Dave Simmons equalised midway through the first half when his glancing header, from a left-wing free-kick by Dave Metchick, crept into the net via a defender. The winning goal for the home side arrived in the 69th minute – but the scoreline failed to reflect their superiority.

Sat 12th October: **Lincoln City (H)**
Drew 1-1   **Attendance: 4,973**

Keith Lawrence scored his first ever League goal when a 29th minute corner from Barry Salvage was headed back across goal by Gordon Riddick for the young centre-back to nod home. But the visitor's equaliser came in the 88th minute after Barry Salvage had unwittingly contributed to a second goal by squandering possession trying the keep the ball in play near the corner flag.

Sat 19th October: **Shrewsbury Town (A)**
Lost 0-1   **Attendance: 4,099**

A 24th minute penalty, conceded by Kevin Harding, proved to be the only goal of a game – a spirited and determined performance was not matched by the quality of the finishing and the poor sequence of away results continued.

Wed 23rd October: **Bradford City (A)**
Lost 0-1   **Attendance: 2,932**

Another single goal away defeat was settled in the 34th minute – the home side scored the winning goal with a headed effort from a free-kick in a classic game of two halves. But again, a lack of fire power proved fatal.

Sat 26th October: **Torquay United (H)**
Won 3-1   **Attendance: 4,496**

Dave Simmons opened the scoring in the 15th minute when he ran onto a pass from Andy Woon, hooking the ball over the head of the on-coming goalkeeper – Simmons doubled the lead 10 minutes later, capitalising on a goalkeeping error, with a short-range tap-in. The points were sealed in the 62nd minute when a low left-wing cross from Dave Simmons was converted by Jackie Graham but the two-goal hero missed a late penalty before the visitor's 88th minute consolation goal.

Sat 2nd November: **Barnsley (A)**
Drew 1-1 **Attendance: 4,158**

Mike Everitt, on a scouting mission elsewhere, missed seeing Dave Simmons 74th minute goal when he headed in Andy Woon's flick from a Keith Lawrence free-kick, but the home side's agonising equaliser came from a last-gasp free-kick.

Mon 4th November: **Bradford City (H)**
Drew 0-0 **Attendance: 5,131**

A superb goalkeeping display by Steve Sherwood ensured a clean-sheet was kept in an otherwise poor goal-less draw, which lacked quality despite offering more 'near-misses' than might have been anticipated – the seventh blank attacking foray of the season.

Sat 9th November: **Mansfield Town (H)**
Lost 2-3 **Attendance: 5,553**

The league leaders scored the only goal of the first half in the 28th minute – the equaliser coming in the 55th minute after an away defender put through his own goal trying to clear a Dave Simmons' cross – Simmons then headed home a Roger Cross centre for a second goal in the 74th minute. The visitors pulled it back to 2-2 after 80 minutes, then grabbed the winner four minutes later.

Sat 16th November: **Hartlepool United (A)**
Lost 2-3 **Attendance: 2,864**

Despite falling behind to a 12th minute goal from the home side, Dave Simmons equalised five minute afterwards when he headed in Barry Salvage's corner. The hosts took the lead again in the 53rd

minute with a free-kick deflected in off Keith Lawrence – then sealed the points with a third goal shortly after – a late Terry Johnson debut goal proved to be no more than a consolation.

Sat 23rd November: **Slough (A) FA Cup 1st Round**
Won 4-1 **Attendance: 3,394**

In a game played in sodden conditions at Walton's ground, an early lead against the Isthmian Leaguers was secured with Jackie Graham's 12th minute 20-yard thunderbolt – this was quickly followed by Paul Bence's right-wing cross being converted by the head of Dave Simmons. The non-League outfit pulled a goal back midway through the half, but two goals from Andy Woon – a left-footed lob from the edge of the box and a diving header – ended the game's scoring after just 37 minutes.

Sat 30th November: **Workington (A)**
Won 1-0 **Attendance: 1,325**

A 50th minute headed goal by Willie Brown, from Paul Bence's right-wing centre, secured the first away win in ten months, ending a run of 20 successive league games without success at the home of the perennial strugglers, found propping up the Football League.

Sat 7th December: **Darlington (H)**
Won 3-0 **Attendance: 4,925**

Two home debutants marked their first appearances with goals – Terry Johnson's 18th minute opener, scored from an acute angle, was doubled on the half-hour mark when Paul Bence set up Willie Brown to fire home from 12 yards. A last minute, low shot from Willie Brown, after being set-up by Barry Salvage, added some-what of a gloss to the scoreline.

Sat 14th December: **Brighton (A) FA Cup 2nd Round**
Lost 0-1 **Attendance: 13,287**

Pre-match preparation for the squad at a health-spa failed to provide a victory spur and an 11th minute goal enabled the higher Division hosts to proceed into the third round of the FA Cup, although their passage was anything but comfortable having been forced to play second fiddle for the vast majority of an entertaining encounter. A combination of splendid goalkeeping and the woodwork denied a deserved equalising goal.

Sat 21st December: **Scunthorpe United (H)**
Won 2-0 **Attendance: 4,364**

Willie Brown opened the scoring with an astute lob over the keeper in the 37th minute and there were no further goals, until the 76th minute, when Brown added his second to seal the win against opposition whose performance belied their lowly league position.

Thu 26th December: **Cambridge United (A)**
Lost 0-2 **Attendance: 3,959**

Goals in the 53rd and 55th minutes gave the hosts a comfortable Boxing Day win – they dominated the match and deserved more than a two-goal victory as their reward from a one-sided encounter.

Sat 28th December: **Exeter City (H)**
Won 2-0 **Attendance: 5,608**

A re-shuffled line-up, after the debacle 48 hours earlier, saw Dave Simmons open the scoring after just 92 seconds – he ran onto Terry Johnson's through-ball and beat the keeper from a tight angle. The second and decisive goal arrived in the 74th minute, when Terry Johnson ended a 30-yard run by firing low into the net.

Sat 4th January: **Northampton Town (A)**
Drew 0-0 **Attendance: 4,735**

A goal-less draw was the outcome from a game in which the Bees were the better team in the first-half and, although Northampton dominated the second period, a sound defensive display ensured that a point was retained.

Sat 11th January: **Darlington (A)**
Lost 1-2 **Attendance: 2,095**

[Right] Andy Woon in aerial action against Reading in John Docherty's first game as Bees manager

Terry Johnson opened the scoring in the 7th minute when he ran onto a long goal-kick from Steve Sherwood, taking advantage of a misjudgement by a home defender to fire home a low cross-shot into the net. An equaliser arrived in the 17th minute from Ex-Bee Stan Webb – the hosts then snatched the points with a last-minute winner as the match proved to be the end of the road for manager Mike Everitt, who was sacked days later.

Sat 18th January: **Workington (H)**
Drew 2-2 **Attendance: 3,983**

In a game where trainer Jess Willard selected the team, the pitch was only deemed playable 90 minutes before kick-off. A 7th minute header from Willie Brown, direct from Barry Salvage's corner, opened the scoring before the visitors equalised three minutes from the break. After 55 minutes Dave Simmons restored the lead with a stooping header from Paul Bence's free-kick, but the struggling opposition equalised for a second-time in the 87th minute.

Sat 25th January: **Reading (H)**
Won 1-0 **Attendance: 6,485**

The highest league crowd of the season greeted the start of John Docherty's reign as manager and a memorable win was sealed by a 50th minute goal from Willie Brown, who followed up when the keeper was unable to hold a long-range shot from Mike Allen.

Sat 1st February: **Mansfield Town (A)**
Drew 1-1 **Attendance: 11,362**

A performance as good as any away from Griffin Park for some time saw an early setback – although the runaway league leaders went ahead in the 12th minute, the scores were brought level again in the 45th minute when Barry Salvage's header rebounded from the keeper and the ball was nodded home by Jackie Graham.

Tue 4th February: **Rotherham United (A)**
Lost 0-3   **Attendance: 4,541**

Goals in the 6th and 51st minutes all but sealed the points for the home side, then a catastrophic third goal came in the late stages when Steve Sherwood was lobbed with ease after a weak clearance went straight to a Rotherham striker to complete a poor evening for the on-loan goalkeeper.

Sat 8th February: **Barnsley (H)**
Won 3-0   **Attendance: 5,080**

Dave Simmons scored a 30th minute goal with a header from a Paul Bence free-kick before substitute debutant Mickey French's spectacular overhead kick in the 79th minute secured the win. An 87th minute goal by Willie Brown, converting French's cross, was the icing on the cake.

Sat 15th February: **Reading (A)**
Lost 0-1   **Attendance: 6,013**

The game was settled by a 12th minute goal – Paul Bence's attempted back-pass stuck in the mud on a rain-soaked pitch and a home striker nipped in to put the ball into the net for the game's only goal and secure a most fortuitous win.

Sat 22nd February: **Hartlepool (H)**
Won 1-0   **Attendance: 5,516**

The goal that decided a match, where the result was more pleasurable than the performance, came in the 71st minute when Terry Johnson latched onto a parry from the goalkeeper from Barry Salvage's shot and fired home through a crowd of players.

Fri 28th February: **Swansea City (A)**
Won 1-0   **Attendance: 1,706**

A performance that fully merited a reward was settled by a 30th minute goal from Willie Brown –heading in Mickey French's flick-on from a Terry Johnson centre to secure a 1-0 win thereby achieving the second away success and the first double of the season.

Sat 8th March: **Rochdale (H)**
Won 3-0   **Attendance: 4,460**

A convincing, third straight win was started by Terry Johnson in the 9th minute – he volleyed home from 12 yards after being set up by Paul Bence and Roger Cross. The second goal came three minutes before half-time – Jackie Graham smashing the ball into the net following a save by the keeper from Mickey French. The rout was competed after 55 minutes when Roger Cross ran half the length of the field to score with ease.

Sat 15th March: **Crewe Alexandra (A)**
Drew 1-1   **Attendance: 2,356**

After falling behind, to a goal deflected off the head of Gordon Riddick in the 67th minute, a defeat looked to be looming until nine minutes from time – Dave Simmons won the ball in the centre circle and raced towards goal, only to see his effort come back off the bar to be converted by the incoming Terry Johnson.

Sat 22nd March: **Chester City (H)**
Drew 1-1   **Attendance: 5,827**

Having taken a 12th minute lead, the promotion-chasing visitors were content to sit back on their advantage until the 62nd minute, when Dave Simmons headed a Paul Bence free-kick onto Roger Cross, who finished things off with a neat nod into the net to earn a deserved share of the spoils.

Mon 31st March
Lost 0-1

Exeter City (A)
Attendance: 3,301

Following the postponement of the Easter Saturday clash at Scunthorpe, the holiday programme finally got under way with a trip to South Devon and a goal-less draw seemed the likely outcome until in the 85th minute, when Steve Sherwood spilled a low shot and the ensuing scramble saw the ball end up in the back of his net – the host's winner just about being deserved.

Tue 1st April
Drew 0-0

Newport County (H)
Attendance: 5,569

The second game of the four-day Easter programme ended score-less – a dismal affair produced jeers and slow-hand-clapping from disgruntled supporters in a match poor on quality and bereft of scoring action or entertainment.

Sat 5th April
Lost 2-3

Torquay United (A)
Attendance: 2,555

In a game played in unseasonal snowy conditions, the home side took the lead on six minutes but, seven minutes later, Roger Cross headed home Mike Allen's left-wing cross to equalise. The home side scored again midway through the first half, after a poor back-pass from Gordon Riddick, and another defensive blunder after 63 minutes further extended their lead. The scoring ended in the 81st minute when Terry Scales fired home from distance after a surging run from Alan Nelmes.

Mon 7th April
Won 3-0

Stockport County (H)
Attendance: 4,434

Another freezing, wintry night saw Gordon Riddick open the scoring in the 31st minute, shooting high into the net from 15-yards after a goalmouth melee. The encounter was all but settled thanks to two Mickey French goals in four minutes during the second half, the first of which came when he ran onto a Dave Metchick pass to fire under the keeper from 20 yards, then headed a second with a deft flick from another Metchick free-kick.

[Left top] Steve Sherwood leans on Keith Lawrence for support during the FA Cup defeat at Brighton

[Left bottom] Jackie Graham crosses the ball in the mud against Workington

Sat 12th April: **Doncaster Rovers (H)**
Drew 1-1   **Attendance: 5,147**

A match devoid of entertainment saw the visitors take the lead in the 40th minute, although Mickey French equalised two minutes after the break – thumping the ball home from eight yards following a cleared corner-kick. A headline that arose from the game was that both teams lined up to mark the retirement of top referee Gordon Hill before he officiated in his final Football League match.

Tue 15th April: **Scunthorpe United (A)**
Won 2-1   **Attendance: 1,556**

The re-arranged Easter Saturday match was played before a pitifully low crowd, which included just over twenty Bees fans. A Roger Cross goal on 12 minutes opened the scoring, heading home following a cross from Mike Allen. A bizarre goal settled the game on 60 minutes, though, Terry Johnson running onto a clearance from Steve Sherwood, then almost nodding the ball out of the on-rushing keeper's hands and into an empty net. The home side's consolation goal came in the 82nd minute.

Sat 19th April: **Lincoln City (A)**
Drew 1-1   **Attendance: 6,956**

A draw at the home of the division's high-flyers was achieved in the final away game of the season, despite going behind after 22 minutes. And although Roger Cross grabbed a 55th minute equaliser, after being set up by Terry Johnson's mazy run, the result failed to do justice to the hosts who did the lion's share of the attacking throughout.

Mon 21st April: **Southport (H)**
Won 1-0   **Attendance: 4,796**

An end of season affair saw 17-year old 'A' level student Nigel Smith make his debut – the game was settled by a 73rd minute free-kick when Roger Cross claimed the fierce strike, which had deflected into the net off the chest of colleague Mickey French.

Sat 26th April: **Shrewsbury Town (H)**
Won 2-1   **Attendance: 5,810**

Although the already-promoted visitors went ahead in the 24th minute, Jackie Graham scored an equaliser within three minutes – slotting home from inside the box having received a pass from Roger Cross. With 20 minutes remaining, Cross grabbed the second goal, latching onto a long kick from Steve Sherwood, to bring the league season to an end in impressive style.

PRE-SEASON

20-year old centre-back Keith Lawrence was signed on a free transfer from Chelsea. An unsuccessful bid was made to sign goalkeeper Roy Brown from Notts County, Mickey Tripp was awarded an apprenticeship but Roy Cotton was not offered terms.

Deposed director Les Davey made a bid to return to the board with his son Peter, whilst also proposing the election of Dan Tana and Peter Pond-Jones. Colin Wheatley indicated that he would not work with Les Davey, who accordingly withdrew his application, although the three other nominees were elected. A further late development saw Davey offered a place as a director by the new board, and he was subsequently elected as chairman.

Former player and Hillingdon Borough striker Joe Gadston, working as a physical education teacher, was to coach the schoolboys, assisted by Alan Humphries who would also act as chief scout.

AUGUST 1974

• Steve Sherwood was re-signed on loan from Chelsea, for the whole season.
• Graham Smith was signed on a 28-day trial period, the 23-year old midfielder having been released by Wimbledon.
• Jackie Graham was sent off at Southport and received a three match ban and would miss the League Cup trip to Anfield.
• Kevin Harding fractured a toe in the friendly game at Stevenage.
• Alan Nelmes, suffering from an achilles injury since March, failed to respond to a period of rest and required an operation that would sideline him for a number of months.

F.A. CUP WINNERS   1973-74   1964-65

FOOTBALL LEAGUE CUP—2nd Round
LIVERPOOL
VERSUS
BRENTFORD
TUESDAY, SEPTEMBER 10, 1974
Kick-off 7.30 p.m.

THE ANFIELD REVIEW
Price 7p

(Two reviews for the price of one)

U.E.F.A. CUP WINNERS 1973
LEAGUE CHAMPIONS: 1973, 1966, 1964, 1947, 1923, 1922, 1906, 1901

BRENTFORD SO NEAR TO GLORY

By CHRIS JAMES

Liverpool . . . 2
Brentford . . . 1

LIVERPOOL, unbeaten First Division leaders, squeezed through to the next round of the League Cup, but brave little Brentford gave them such a fright.

The battling Bees had stunned Liverpool in the ninth minute by taking the lead.

Terry Scales sent Roger Cross sprinting through a square defence to hold off Phil Thompson's challenge and calmly slide the ball past Ray Clemence.

It could have been two five minutes later as Dave Simmons found Barry Salvage unmarked. But instead of chipping the ball over Clemence, Salvage tried to take the ball round him.

Liverpool finally levelled when Ray Kennedy maintained his record of scoring in every match he's played.

Phil Boersma put Liverpool ahead with the last kick o fthe first half, but Brentford fought on and only a headed clearance off the line by Emlyn Hughes late on stopped Gordon Riddick snatching a replay.

SEPTEMBER 1974

- 19-year old midfielder, Ian Filby, was signed on one-month's loan from Orient.
- Graham Smith had his trial period extended.
- Paul Bence was sent off in the defeat at Newport.
- Mike Allen suffered a serious long-term facial injury at Rochdale.
- Former chairman, Walter Wheatley, issued a threat to sue the club for non payment of the outstanding interest on his loan, amounting to £4,600. The board offered to pay £2,500 immediately, with the balance to be paid as soon as possible.

OCTOBER 1974

- After 15 years, two testimonials and 516 games – the second highest in the club's history – 33-year old Peter Gelson asked to be released from his contract and was given a free transfer.
- Paul Priddy had his contract cancelled by mutual consent.
- Ian Filby returned to Orient on completion of his loan period.
- Mike Everitt agreed a £10,000 fee with Aldershot for the transfer of striker Terry Bell, but the player failed his medical and the deal was cancelled.
- A deal to sign goalkeeper John Dunn from Charlton was also unsuccessful.
- 26-year old goalkeeper, Barry Gordine, was signed – having previously played for Oldham Athletic.

NOVEMBER 1974

- 25-year old winger Terry Johnson was signed from Southend United for a reported £15,000 fee.
- Willie Brown joined on loan from Newport County, the 24-year old striker signing with a view to a permanent move.
- Graham Smith signed a contract until the end of the season.
- Graham Springett signed schoolboy forms.
- The FA Cup match at Slough Town was switched to Walton & Hersham's ground.
- Les Davey resigned as chairman and was replaced by Dan Tana, with Peter Pond-Jones being appointed as vice chairman.
- The new chairman declared that the club was entering a new era and gave a public vote of confidence to manager Mike Everitt.

Brentford sack Mike Everitt

by GEORGE SANDS, Sports Editor

AFTER 17 months as team-manager of Brentford involving 72 league matches and six cup-ties, Mike Everitt was given notice to quit on Wednesday.

The club are now seeking their 12th post-war manager, following in the wake of Harry Curtis, Jackie Gibbons, Jimmy Bain, Tommy Lawton, Bill Dodgin (senior), Malcolm McDonald, Tommy Cavanagh, Billy Gray, Jimmy Sirrell, Frank Blunstone and Mike Everitt.

I have attended every Brentford first-team match, and travelled more than 6,000 miles in Mike's company.

I was present at the question panel meeting at Griffin Park on Tuesday evening and everything went through smoothly, with nothing in the air to suggest that there were any managerial problems.

Mike, in fact, was frequently applauded for his answers to questions from supporters concerning the playing staff; and his wife, Janet, conducted the draw for the raffle.

After the interval, however, a supporter asked if there was any foundation for the paragraph in a Sunday paper to the effect that the manager was willing for two of his players to go to other clubs on loan, with a view to final transfer. Mike agreed that it was so, and club chairman, Dan Tana, immediately declared that neither he nor the board had been informed of such a proposal. But obviously the manager's dismissal must have been in the pipe-line before that.

In a statement on Wednesday Mike Everitt told me: "I am extremely disappointed with the decision, as I went to Brentford in August, 1973, to rebuild a side that had been relegated at the end of the previous season and was lacking in confidence. Until November last year there was disharmony in the boardroom, which, as we all know, creates problems throughout the club. On December 20, at the club's annual meeting, Dan Tana, the new Brentford chairman, stated that I had his 110 per cent support and confidence and that he realised it took two or three years to rebuild and strengthen a football side. Now, less than four weeks have passed and I am sacked as team-manager. Why make such a statement in the first place, if he did not intend to honour it?"

Dan Tana, who accompanied Brentford Reserves to the away match with Orient that evening, made the following response:

"True, I said that Mike had 110 per cent support from the board only a month ago and I have continued to give him that support. But recent events have caused me to change my mind and I would say that it was the unanimous decision of the board that he should be sacked."

Everitt began his professional career as a wing-half with Arsenal, and went on to Northampton, where he played as Foley's partner at full-back in the club's sensational climb from the Fourth Division to the First in the 60's. Subsequently he had spells with Brighton, Plymouth Argyle and Plymouth City before going to Wimbledon, of the Southern League, as player-manager. He took charge at Brentford in August 1973.

DECEMBER 1974

• Willie Brown signed permanently on completion of his loan period for a reported £4,000 transfer fee.
• At the club's AGM Dan Tana announced that the manager had 110% support from the board.

JANUARY 1975

• Following the defeat at Darlington, Mike Everitt was sacked as team manager.
• Dan Tana announced that recent events had caused him to retract the views that he had recently expressed.

• Jess Willard selected the team for the match against Workington.
• Former player, 34-year old John Docherty, was appointed as the new manager, commencing his fourth spell at the club, having been coaching at Queens Park Rangers.
• Eddie Lyons re-joined the club as trainer and Jess Willard had his contract terminated.

FEBRUARY 1975

• 19-year old striker Mickey French was signed on one month's loan from QPR.
• Former Chelsea youngster, Tony Potrac, was offered a trial, having returned from a spell in South Africa.

- Andy Woon was given a free transfer and left the club.
- Graham Smith was loaned back to former club Wimbledon.
- Barry Salvage came off the transfer list at his own request.
- Bob Pearson was appointed as chief scout on a part-time basis.

MARCH 1975

- Following his loan spell Mickey French signed a permanent contract in a £2,000 transfer from Queens Park Rangers.
- Willie Brown was sold to Torquay United for a reported £5,000 fee.
- Kevin Harding was not offered a professional contract on completion of his apprenticeship.
- Tony Potrac was released at the end of his trial period.
- Peter Davey resigned from the board of directors.

APRIL 1975

- Gary Smith joined Wimbledon on loan for the rest of the season and then had his contract cancelled by mutual consent.
- 17-year old defender Nigel Smith followed John Docherty from Queens Park Rangers and was signed as a professional as soon as he left school.

MAY 1975

- Free transfers were given to Dave Metchick, Graham Smith and Barry Gordine.
- Steve Sherwood returned to Chelsea at the end of his season-long loan.

IDENTITY CARD NOT ON, SAYS DENIS PIGGOT

by George Sands

THE suggestion that football fans should be issued with identity cards would not work, would be too expensive and would increase not decrease the risk of violence, Brentford FC general manager Mr. Denis Piggott, said this week.

Mr. Piggott, one of soccer's senior administrators, who celebrated 28 years at Griffin Park on Wednesday, said the Brentford board had not discussed the identity card suggestion, made by Mr. Denis Howell, Minister of Sport, but Mr. Piggott said that he, personally, felt the idea impracticable.

Explained Mr. Piggott: "The main problem is that it would turn gatemen, who are difficult enough to recruit anyway, into security officers, and that in itself would create violence if there was a dispute over the admission of an individual to the ground.

"It would obviously very much slow down the speed at which the public could go through the turnstiles. I think we should have to have police stationed outside every turnstile to prevent possible violence, and the expense would be enormous. Even then, without a photograph, the system could be abused, as if a card was withdrawn, doubtlessly the individual could make a fresh application in another name, or get someone else to apply on his behalf.

"Also, if Cup Final tickets can be forged, how much easier it would be to forge identity cards? Then there is the problem of the casual visitor. What if we drew at Liverpool and they came back to us for a replay? Many youngsters who have never been to Griffin Park might want to see the game, and we could even get overseas visitors who would also wish to bring their children to see a professional game—and then not getting admission."

Asked what he thought could be a solution to the violence problem, Mr. Piggott said: "Undoubtedly tougher penalties. I think this must involve prison sentences or Borstal, or whatever form of detention is applicable according to age. Football is being used as an excuse for violence, not the cause of it, and I don't think that the Press and media have helped, as the fans of certain teams have built up an image for trouble and now seem to have to live up to it."

1975-76

[Back Row] John Docherty, Eddie Lyons, Alan Nelmes, Richard Poole, Graham Cox, Bill Glazier, Keith Lawrence, Mike Allen, Gordon Riddick, Peter Pond-Jones **[Front Row]** Dave Simmons, Nigel Smith, Mickey French, Terry Johnson, Paul Bence, Mickey Tripp, Jackie Graham, Terry Scales

Football League	Division Four
Manager	John Docherty
Trainer	Eddie Lyons
Captain	Paul Bence
Final Position	18th
FA Cup	3rd Round
League Cup	2nd Round
Leading Goalscorer (all competitions)	Roger Cross – 16 goals

An impressive nine-game unbeaten start to the campaign included the notable scalp of Third Division Brighton and Hove Albion in a two-legged League Cup tie – the winning opening was punctuated only by a defeat to Manchester United (2-1) in a glamorous cup-tie at Old Trafford in the second round of the competition

A dramatic change in fortunes saw six defeats in seven games – the sudden and unexpected retirement of experienced, new goalkeeper Bill Glazier after just 12 appearances majorly upsetting John Docherty's plans.

Despite nine goals at home in three days (5-2 against Scunthorpe and 4-0 against Workington) and the emergence of teenage striker Gordon Sweetzer contributing towards a sequence of seven victories in nine matches, results began to decline steadily after the New Year with just three wins in 23 games – although Second Division Bolton Wanderers were taken to a replay in the third round of the FA Cup.

As the season faded into lower mid-table obscurity, hopes for the future were re-ignited by the arrival of record transfer signing Andy McCulloch from Oxford United for £25,000. The 5-1 home thrashing of Exeter City on Easter Saturday was the highlight of a run of three wins and four draws in eight matches and a disappointing campaign ended with the team finishing just three points outside of the re-election zone.

[Previous page] Gordon Sweetzer in typical attacking mode, challenges the Tranmere Rovers goalkeeper

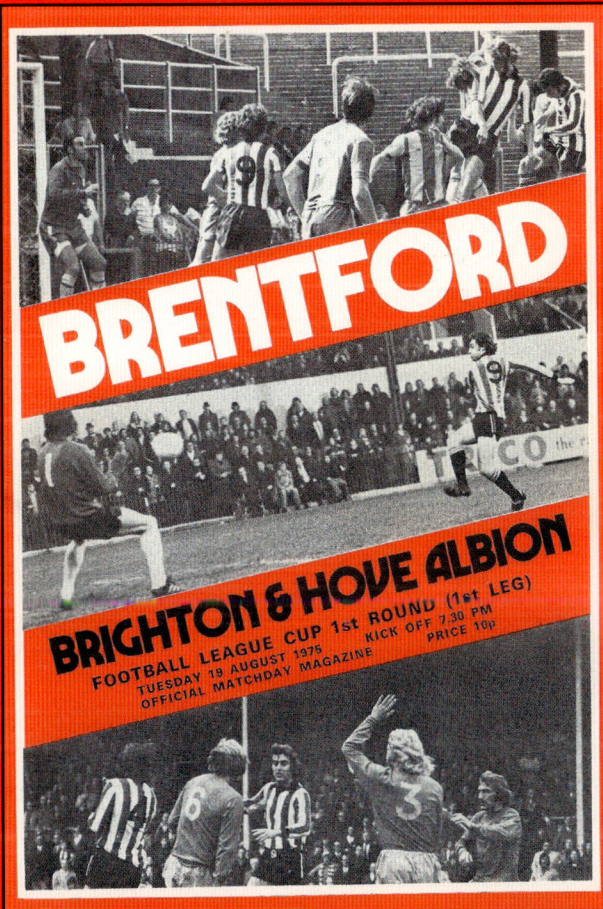

BRENTFORD

BRIGHTON & HOVE ALBION

FOOTBALL LEAGUE CUP 1st ROUND (1st LEG)
TUESDAY 19 AUGUST 1975   KICK OFF 7.30 PM
OFFICIAL MATCHDAY MAGAZINE   PRICE 10p

		P	W	D	L	F	A	W	D	L	F	A	Pts
1	Lincoln City	46	21	2	0	71	15	11	8	4	40	24	**74**
2	Northampton	46	18	5	0	62	20	11	5	7	25	20	**68**
3	Reading	46	19	3	1	42	9	5	9	9	28	42	**60**
4	Tranmere	46	18	3	2	61	16	6	7	10	28	39	**58**
5	Huddersfield	46	11	6	6	28	17	10	8	5	28	24	**56**
6	Bournemouth	46	15	5	3	39	16	5	7	11	18	32	**52**
7	Exeter City	46	13	7	3	37	17	5	5	11	19	30	**50**
8	Watford	46	16	4	3	38	18	6	2	15	24	44	**50**
9	Torquay	46	12	6	5	31	24	6	8	9	24	39	**50**
10	Doncaster	46	10	6	7	42	31	9	5	9	33	38	**49**
11	Swansea	46	14	8	1	51	21	2	7	14	15	36	**47**
12	Barnsley	46	12	8	3	34	16	2	8	13	18	32	**44**
13	Cambridge	46	7	10	6	36	28	7	5	11	22	34	**43**
14	Hartlepool	46	10	6	7	37	29	6	4	13	25	49	**42**
15	Rochdale	46	7	11	5	27	23	5	7	11	13	31	**42**
16	Crewe	46	10	7	6	36	21	3	8	12	22	36	**41**
17	Bradford	46	9	7	7	35	26	3	10	10	28	39	**41**
18	**Brentford**	**46**	**12**	**7**	**4**	**37**	**18**	**2**	**6**	**15**	**19**	**42**	**41**
19	Scunthorpe	46	11	3	9	31	24	3	7	13	19	35	**38**
20	Darlington	46	11	7	5	30	14	3	3	17	18	43	**38**
21	Stockport	46	8	7	8	23	23	5	5	13	20	53	**38**
22	Newport	46	8	7	8	35	33	5	2	16	22	57	**35**
23	Southport	46	6	6	11	27	31	2	4	17	14	46	**26**
24	Workington	46	5	4	14	19	43	2	3	18	11	44	**21**

Total Home League Attendances	**117,218**
Average Home League Attendance	**5,096**
Highest Home League Attendance	**10,612**
Lowest Home League Attendance	**3,453**

League Position throughout the Season

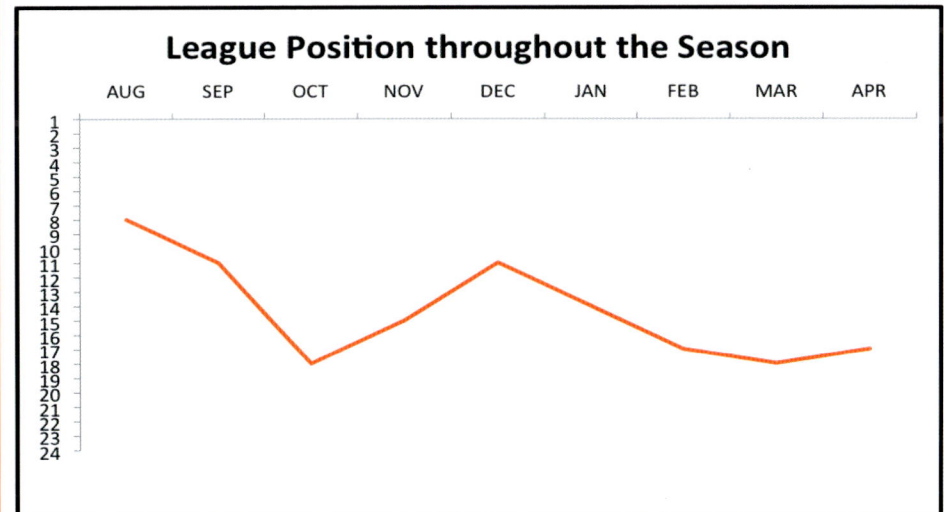

1975-76

[Right] Brentford midfielder Terry Scales in action during the 3-1 defeat by Newport County

Sat 16th August: **Bradford City (A)**
Drew 1-1 **Attendance: 2,385**

The opening game of the new campaign saw the home side take the lead on 39 minutes, before Terry Johnson equalised three minute later with a cross-shot after running onto a through-ball from Paul Bence.

Tue 19th August: **Brighton (H) League Cup 1st Round**
Won 2-1 **Attendance: 5,360**

A bizarre goal gifted the visiting side the lead on the stroke of half-time – Bill Glazier inadvertently palming an indirect free-kick into his own net after it had struck the bar without touching anyone else. Terry Johnson scored the equaliser from the penalty spot seven minutes into the second half, after Dave Simmons had been fouled. The winner came in the dying seconds when a Paul Bence corner was slammed home by substitute Roger Cross.

Sat 23rd August: **Hartlepool (H)**
Drew 1-1 **Attendance: 4,948**

Roger Cross scored when he smashed the ball home from Jackie Graham's corner in the 11th minute but, as further chances were frittered away, the visitors struck back with ten minutes to go.

Wed 27th August: **Brighton (A) League Cup 1st Round**
Drew 1-1 **Attendance: 11,016**

An early penalty was conceded when Alan Nelmes and Keith Lawrence combined to foul a home striker, but Roger Cross scored the equaliser, which ensured progress to the next round when he converted a right-wing cross from Paul Bence from 15 yards.

Sat 30th August: **Torquay United (A)**
Won 3-2 **Attendance: 3,179**

Although the hosts from Devon took the lead in the 37th minute, Roger Cross equalised just before the break, netting the rebound after Terry Johnson's shot came back off the post. In the final 10 minutes of the second half Mike Allen scored a freak goal, his free-kick sailing over the keeper's head and into the net – a third goal came when a well-rehearsed move saw Paul Bence's free-kick left by Dave Simmons and Jackie Graham slotted home. The home side's last minute goal was no more than a consolation.

Sat 6th September: **Barnsley (H)**
Won 1-0 **Attendance: 5,605**

A stunning display by the visiting goalkeeper kept the game goalless until the 87th minute, when an Alan Nelmes free-kick from the corner of the penalty box was headed on by Mike Allen for Roger Cross to nod the ball into the net and secure the win.

Wed 10th September: **Man United (A) League Cup 2nd Round**
Lost 1-2 **Attendance: 25,286**

After a first half without goals, Paul Bence's free-kick from just out-side the penalty box was headed into the net by Keith Lawrence to grab a shock lead, which lasted just 4 minutes. Bill Glazier then fumbled Lou Macari's free-kick and dropped the ball over the goal-line. Sammy McIlroy scored the second, and ultimately winning goal, for the Old Trafford giants, but Dave Simmons conspired to somehow miss an open goal in the dying seconds – blazing the ball over an empty net from six yards to the dismay of almost 1,000 travelling Bees supporters.

Mon 15th September: **Doncaster Rovers (A)**
Drew 1-1   **Attendance: 6,353**

An entertaining game, which was highlighted by a superb goal-keeping display from Bill Glazier, saw Terry Johnson score the opener on the hour mark – Mickey French's well-rehearsed free-kick was dummied by Dave Simmons's step-over. The equalising goal arrived with ten minutes remaining.

Sat 20th September: **Stockport County (H)**
Won 2-1   **Attendance: 6,282**

An opening strike from Dave Simmons came courtesy of an intercepted back-pass in the 15th minute – an equaliser arrived ten minutes later. After surviving a second-half of intense pressure from the visitors, an 86th minute corner from Paul Bence was twice hammered against the bar by Dave Simmons and Mickey French, before Gordon Riddick dived full-length to head the winning goal.

Wed 24th September: **Bournemouth (A)**
Lost 0-3   **Attendance: 4,113**

The first league loss in 12 games was all but settled after the opening 20 minutes – the home side went two goals up, and the third, in the 70th minute, simply sealed a convincing defeat.

Sat 27th September: **Huddersfield Town (A)**
Lost 1-2   **Attendance: 4,160**

Following a scoreless first half on a heavy and slippery pitch, the home side took the lead in the 56th minute, a lead that was doubled soon afterwards. In the 84th minute, a cross from Paul Bence was headed home by substitute debutant Gordon Sweetzer to halve the arrears, but without affecting the final outcome.

Sat 4th October: **Newport County (H)**
Lost 1-3   **Attendance: 5,678**

Two goals in three minutes (12 and 14 minutes) put the visitors in control, but although Jackie Graham converted a pass from Roger Cross in the 28th minute to reduce the arrears, a third goal, conceded after 65 minutes, sent the points back to Wales.

Sat 11th October: **Lincoln City (A)**
Lost 1-3   **Attendance: 6,312**

Three goals in quick succession settled issues for the home side. Two first half goals, arriving just minutes apart before the interval, with a third after six minutes of the second half. Jackie Graham's 76th minute 25-yard pile driver was little more than a consolation.

Sat 18th October: **Southport (H)**
Won 1-0   **Attendance: 4,515**

A dismal display was brightened slightly by a 27th minute goal from Terry Johnson – side-footing home from six yards after a free-kick by Gordon Riddick, but the match lacked any real quality.

Tue 21st October: **Northampton Town (A)**
Lost 1-3   **Attendance: 6,225**

Town took the lead in the 17th minute and, just three minutes later, capitalised on a defensive error by Gordon Riddick to double their advantage. In the 48th minute, Mike Allen's foraging run down the left flank saw him square the ball to Terry Scales, who fired into the back of the net from just inside the penalty box. But almost immediately, the home side scrambled a third goal and sealed the win.

Sat 25th October: **Cambridge United (A)**
Lost 1-2   **Attendance: 2,596**

United took the lead after just 59 seconds and, although Mickey French equalised, driving home a weak clearance from a free-kick in the 26th minute, the host's winner arrived midway through the second period to spoil an otherwise encouraging performance.

Sat 1st November: **Scunthorpe United (H)**
Won 5-2   **Attendance: 4,227**

Mickey French opened the scoring in the 25th minute when he

headed in a cross from Mike Allen and, five minutes later, following a corner-kick, Terry Johnson swivelled just inside the penalty box to hit home a powerful left-footer. Although the visitors pulled a goal back in the 56th minute, three minutes later, Roger Cross converted another Mike Allen cross and Jackie Graham quickly made it 4-1. Another defensive lapse was quickly followed by a crisp strike from Roger Cross after a Jackie Graham pass to make it five.

Mon 3rd November: **Workington (H)**
Won 4-0   **Attendance: 5,379**

A one-sided encounter produced the opening goal in the 15th minute – a fine move ended with Mickey French curling a left-footed effort under the bar after good work from Roger Cross and Terry Johnson. A second goal, from Gordon Sweetzer, arrived before the interval and the same player was instrumental in the third, after 60 minutes, when he was pulled down in the box by the keeper – Terry Johnson converted the penalty. A scorching left-footer from outside the penalty area from Roger Cross completed the rout.

Fri 7th November: **Tranmere Rovers (A)**
Lost 1-5   **Attendance: 4,326**

First-half goals by Rovers in the 24th and 30th minutes were off-set when Terry Johnson headed on Jackie Graham's corner for Roger Cross to crack home a fine goal. But another three second half goals from the hosts sealed a convincing win in a game that saw debutant loanee goalkeeper, Graham Horn, taken to hospital to have stitches to repair a partially severed ear – Keith Lawrence was also detained in hospital with serious concussion.

Sat 15th November: **Watford (H)**
Won 1-0   **Attendance: 6,934**

The only goal of the game arrived in the 70th minute – Paul Bence's through ball found Terry Scales who slammed a cross shot into the net. The match, which saw 15-year old schoolboy Danis Salman become the club's youngest ever League player, was also notable for an off the field incident when chairman, Dan Tana, moved into the crowd to make a citizen's arrest for abusive language.

Sat 22nd November: **Northampton Town (H) FA Cup 1st Round**
Won 2-0   **Attendance: 6,645**

Progress in the FA Cup came courtesy of two goals from Gordon Sweetzer, the first of which came in the 59th minute when he received a pass from Paul Bence and brushed off the challenge of three defenders, before firing home from the edge of the penalty area. Three minutes later he notched his second – nodding home Mike Allen's centre from inside a packed penalty box.

Sat 29th November: **Crewe Alexandra (A)**
Lost 0-1   **Attendance: 2,248**

A 7th successive away defeat was sealed as early as the 11th minute when keeper, Graham Horn, fumbled a shot on the muddy pitch and the loose ball was then prodded past him.

Sat 6th December: **Rochdale (H)**
Won 3-0   **Attendance: 4,853**

A quiet first half in which an early penalty, given after a foul on Gordon Riddick, had been converted by Terry Johnson, was followed by an eventful second period. In the 61st minute Roger Cross doubled the lead from a corner, before Gordon Sweetzer was sent off for a second booking – then a goalmouth clash saw both Terry Johnson and the Rochdale keeper red carded. In the final minute, Gordon Riddick's back-header, from Paul Bence's cross, made it three.

Sat 13th December: **Wimbledon (A) FA Cup 2nd Round**
Won 2-0   **Attendance: 8,375**

The Southern League outfit were dispatched with two first half goals. In the 26th minute, Terry Johnson finished a neat move involving Mike Allen and Roger Cross by hooking the ball into the net after a smart turn then, seven minutes later, Johnson got his second goal from the penalty spot following a foul on Gordon Sweetzer.

Sat 20th December: **Darlington (H)**
Won 3-0   **Attendance: 4,193**

In a comprehensive victory, Gordon Sweetzer opened the scoring in the 15th minute with a bullet header from a Paul Bence free-kick. Sweetzer followed it up after 65 minutes when he sent a cross-shot into the net after a long throw from Roger Cross had resulted in a goalmouth scramble. The win was sealed in the 78th minute when Roger Cross turned and struck the ball home firmly as supporters were treated to an impressive refereeing display from Jack Taylor who, 18 months earlier, had officiated during the World Cup Final.

Fri 26th December: **Exeter City (A)**
Drew 0-0   **Attendance: 4,912**

An 8.00am Boxing Day coach departure produced no ill-effects for the players and brought about the first away point since September – the two teams fought out an entertaining festive goal-less draw.

Sat 27th December: **Reading (H)**
Drew 2-2   **Attendance: 10,612**

In front of the highest crowd of the season, Terry Johnson slammed home an 9th minute cross from Paul Bence, and when Terry Scales hit a right-footed screamer from outside the penalty box on the hour mark, the game seemed to be settled. However, a 74th minute Reading goal preceded the sending-off of Roger Cross for retaliation and, with almost the last kick of the game, the visitors equalised direct from a corner.

Sat 3rd January: **Bolton Wanderers (H) FA Cup 3rd Round**
Drew 0-0   **Attendance: 12,452**

The largest home crowd since March '72 witnessed an entertaining Cup-tie against Second Division opposition – the clash produced plenty of thrills, numerous chances but, ultimately, no goals.

Tue 6th January: **Bolton Wanderers (A) 3rd Round Replay**
Lost 0-2   **Attendance: 18,538**

Following on from the goal-less draw in the first tie, it took until the 66th minute for the deadlock to be broken in the replay – but the opening goal for the hosts was added to by a second ten minutes later to settle the lively encounter played in murky conditions.

Sat 10th January: **Torquay United (H)**
Drew 1-1   **Attendance: 5,687**

A 21st minute penalty, awarded for handball against Keith Lawrence, gave the visitors the lead, but Terry Johnson's equaliser, nine minutes later, came after Paul Bence and Alan Nelmes exchanged passes – the latter set up the scoring chance just inside the penalty box. Despite intense second half pressure, a winner never arrived.

Fri 16th January: **Stockport County (A)**
Lost 0-2   **Attendance: 2,267**

After falling a goal behind to a 9th minute free-kick, the game became an uphill struggle – the hosts scored their second in the 58th minute and effectively sealed the Friday night win.

Sat 24th January: **Doncaster Rovers (H)**
Lost 0-1   **Attendance: 4,885**

The second home defeat of the season arrived courtesy of a 19th minute Rovers goal, which proved to be the winning strike in a game played in freezing conditions – the falling snow adding to the gloomy atmosphere.

Sat 31st January: **Northampton Town (H)**
Won 2-1   **Attendance: 4,114**

A penalty, awarded for handball, was successfully converted by Terry Johnson in the 22nd minute, then Gordon Sweetzer's right-wing cross enabled Roger Cross to head a second goal midway through the second half. High-flying Northampton reduced the arrears in the 78th minute to set up a nervy finale.

[Left] Roger Cross and Terry Johnson, during the 0-0 draw at home to Cambridge United

Sat 7th February: **Workington (A)**
Drew 1-1   **Attendance: 1,231**

Mickey French opened the scoring in the 31st minute when he neatly side-stepped the keeper and hooked the ball into the net after being set-up by Gordon Sweetzer. The home side levelled things up four minutes into the second half with a penalty-kick, awarded for a Nigel Smith foul.

Sat 14th February: **Tranmere Rovers (H)**
Lost 0-1   **Attendance: 4,725**

After taking a 44th minute lead, with a scrambled goal following a free-kick, the visitors adopted a defensive strategy throughout the second period and successfully held onto both points as the game petered out into mediocrity.

Sat 21st February: **Watford (A)**
Lost 2-3   **Attendance: 6,223**

A bizarre own goal in the 10th minute, when Gordon Riddick's long up-field punt was headed backwards over his own keeper by a home defender, was equalised by the hosts in the 25th minute. But, just a minute later, Jackie Graham seized on a poor clearance from a corner and crossed for Gordon Sweetzer to touch the ball home from almost under the bar. The hosts dominated the second half and, after levelling things up again in the 52nd minute, Watford grabbed a winner, and twice hit the woodwork.

Mon 23rd February: **Bournemouth (H)**
Lost 1-2   **Attendance: 4,585**

Jackie Graham's fifth goal of the season came in the 14th minute after Mickey French sent a right-wing cross into the penalty box that enabled the midfielder to head firmly into the net. The Bees dominated much of the remainder of the match, until the visitors unexpectedly equalised against-the-run-of-play in the 85th minute – Mickey French inadvertently played a long back-pass straight to an opposing striker. Two minutes later worse was to follow – the south-coast side grabbed an even more unlikely winner.

Sat 28th February: **Cambridge United (H)**
Drew 0-0   **Attendance: 4,095**

A dismal performance was described by manager John Docherty as the worst he had seen his team play – the visitors held the upper hand throughout the 90-minute but could not score – and the home side left the pitch to a chorus of boos and jeers.

Sat 6th March: **Scunthorpe United (A)**
Lost 1-2   **Attendance: 3,377**

In icy cold conditions, Scunthorpe took the lead in the 39th minute, and their second goal in the 84th minute, appeared to settle things in their favour. But just 60 seconds later, substitute Tom Sharp netted a neat downward header from a Terry Johnson cross to set up an anxious ending – but an equaliser could not be found.

Mon 8th March: **Newport County (A)**
Lost 0-1   **Attendance: 1,150**

An uneventful match, played out under woefully inadequate flood-lights, was settled by a 36th minute strike from County – the most notable event being the debut of new, record fee signing Andy McCulloch, which had been delayed from the previous Saturday following a training ground mishap.

Sat 13th March: **Lincoln City (H)**
Won 1-0   **Attendance: 5,386**

The champions-elect were beaten courtesy of a 32nd minute goal created when Andy McCulloch set up Paul Bence to cross from the right flank, Terry Johnson flicked the ball on to Roger Cross, who nodded into the net for the winner.

Tue 16th March: **Southport (A)**
Lost 0-2   **Attendance: 1,506**

A 52nd minute goal from the bottom of the table strugglers was followed by a second soon afterwards. Only some solid defending kept the scoreline down to two from there on in. Haig Avenue remained a ground that Brentford had never scored at.

Sat 20th March: **Crewe Alexandra (H)**
Drew 0-0   **Attendance: 3,851**

A stereotypical end of season affair, almost totally devoid of incident and entertainment, did nothing to quell the frustrations of supporters – many of whom had left long before the final whistle after witnessing another poor, goal-less draw.

Sat 27th March: **Rochdale (A)**
Won 2-1   **Attendance: 894**

The first away win for seven months, and the first double of the season, was prompted by Andy McCulloch's first goal for the club – heading home a Paul Bence corner in the 15th minute. It was 2-0 after 67 minutes, Mickey French running onto a through-ball from Mike Allen to slot past the keeper. The hosts grabbed a late consolation in the 84th minute.

Mon 29th March: **Darlington (A)**
Lost 0-2   **Attendance: 1,758**

The long away trip resulted in another loss, which started when Keith Lawrence diverted a long-range shot into his own net after 28 minutes and a classic headed goal from the hosts midway through the second half ensured that the points stayed up north.

Sat 3rd April: **Bradford City (H)**
Drew 2-2   **Attendance: 3,453**

The smallest home crowd of the season witnessed the visitors race into a two-goal lead with strikes in the 23rd and 25th minutes – but, on the stroke of half-time, Terry Scales crossed for Andy McCul-

[Right] Keith Lawrence watches No.4, Terry Johnson, surrounded by Crewe Alexandra defenders

loch to halve the deficit. After the Bantams lost their goalkeeper through injury, Roger Cross salvaged a point in the 85th minute when he cracked home a sizzling left-foot drive.

Mon 5th April: **Huddersfield Town (H)**
Drew 0-0   **Attendance: 4,413**

A catalogue of missed chances, some of which fell into the 'sitter' category, resulted in another scoreless encounter – but the visiting promotion contenders travelled back north grateful for a point.

Sat 10th April: **Barnsley (A)**
Drew 1-1   **Attendance: 3,877**

Mike Allen conceded a penalty in the 5th minute to give the hosts a lead that they held until the 68th minute, when Roger Cross collected a through-ball from Paul Bence and hit a swerving left-footed shot, which struck the crossbar and dropped into the net.

Fri 16th April: **Swansea City (H)**
Won 1-0   **Attendance: 4,623**

The Good Friday encounter proved to be an exciting affair and was settled with just five minutes remaining – Alan Nelmes sent a searching pass forward to Andy McCulloch, who in turn found Terry Johnson to fire a low 20-yarder beyond the keeper.

Sat 17th April: **Exeter City (H)**
Won 5-1   **Attendance: 4,175**

After Paul Bence had opened his account for the season with a 30-yard effort that the keeper fumbled into the net in the 15th minute, the visitors were reduced to ten men and, on the stroke of half-time, Mickey French added a second with a low drive. Although Exeter pulled a goal back in the 54th minute, Mickey French scored again from a Mike Allen cross, and another centre from Allen enabled

[Left] Paul Bence in a race with a Rochdale defender during the 3-0 home win

Andy McCulloch to head home the fourth. An 89th minute tap-in by Roger Cross gave the scoreline a very flattering look.

Mon 19th April: **Reading (A)**
Lost 0-1   **Attendance: 12,972**
Promotion chasing Reading dominated much of the 'derby' match proceedings and scored the only goal of the game on the hour-mark when prolific striker, Robin Friday, powered through the defence to set up the winner.

Sat 24th April: **Hartlepool United (A)**
Lost 0-1   **Attendance: 1,276**
An uneventful encounter, played in the Spring sunshine, was settled in the 25th minute – after which the hosts took control of the game and retained the points with comparative ease, but Hartlepool could not add to their tally.

Mon 26th April: **Swansea City (A)**
Drew 2-2   **Attendance: 1,480**
Entertainment was at a premium in the final match of the campaign, fought out by two teams with little to play for. Against the run of play Mickey French scored from a Roger Cross pass in the 27th minute to give The Bees the lead at half-time then, two minutes after the re-start, a Paul Bence corner was dropped by the keeper at the feet of Terry Johnson who made no mistake. Swansea got back into the game when Terry Johnson's handball conceded a penalty in the 57th minute and City's equaliser arrived with just five minutes to go.

Last-minute miss upsets Bees after great display

JOHN DOCHERTY stood outside the dressing rooms at Old Trafford last night a mixture of frustration, bewilderment and downright anger.

He had just seen his Brentford team—which has lived in the backwaters of London Soccer for more years than they care to remember—come agonisingly close to knocking Manchester United out of the League Cup.

WELCOME TO OLD TRAFFORD
UNITED REVIEW
The official programme of Manchester United Football Club Ltd

FOOTBALL LEAGUE CUP COMPETITION
ROUND 2 No. 5

UNITED
v
BRENTFORD

10th SEPTEMBER 1975
Kick-off 7.30 p.m.

10p

PRE-SEASON

Former England international goalkeeper 31-year old Bill Glazier signed from Coventry City for a fee of £4,000.

Ken Foggo arrived on a one-month trial, having been released by Portsmouth. Barry Salvage had his contract cancelled, at his own request and left the club.

18-year old striker Richard Poole was offered a professional contract on the expiry of his apprenticeship.

Paul Bence was appointed as the new club captain, taking over from Gordon Riddick. Graham Cox was awarded an apprenticeship, but both Billy Stagg and Steve Johnson left the club.

Bill Berry resigned as promotions manager to join Fulham.

AUGUST 1975

- Ken Foggo was released at the end of his trial period.
- Gordon Sweetzer, an 18-year old Canadian striker, was offered a two-month trial following his release by Queens Park Rangers.
- Two new schoolboys were signed – Danis Salman and Paul Walker.

SEPTEMBER 1975

- Gordon Sweetzer was offered a full professional contract.
- Paul Priddy, released eleven months earlier, was re-signed as goalkeeping cover for Bill Glazier.
- Former Portsmouth apprentice Gordon Bartlett was given a trial.
- George Thomas became the new promotions manager.

OCTOBER 1975

- Bill Glazier [pictured above with John Docherty] announced his retirement from football in order to concentrate on his business interests and his contract was cancelled by mutual consent – although his registration was retained.
- Gordon Bartlett left following his trial and signed for Slough Town.
- Nigel Smith was called up for training with the England under-18 squad.

GLAZIER – Why I quit Brentford!

By NICHOLAS CLARKE

BILL GLAZIER, the goalkeeper who has just quit Brentford after playing only 12 games, spoke from his Brighton hotel today of having let the club down.

The 32-year-old former Crystal Palace and Coventry man talked of the difficulty he faced running his newly-acquired hotel while at the same time being with a London club.

"I have taken over a hotel in Brighton and found it harder to run it when I was not there. I feel I have let Brentford down a bit, especially John Docherty who is a fine manager," Glazier said.

"But I had to think of the family. I felt I could not give John 100 per cent and unless I could give Brentford and myself 100 per cent I didn't want to carry on.

"I had hoped to combine running the hotel and playing soccer, but it just didn't work.

"I also had niggling little injuries which meant that I was going home and resting while my wife was doing all the work.

"But if I had done the work instead of resting my injury, it would have been unfair on the club. I felt it was wrong to take the money if I was not fulfilling my job properly.

"I'm packing up football completely — I have always said that when I give up I'll give up completely.

"I am disappointed from Brentford's point of view, but you've got to make decisions and I made mine very much from the family's point of view.

"On the travelling side, though this was not so important, I was used to living next to the training ground at Coventry. I didn't mind the travelling at first at Brentford, but it got harder. I was doing 200 miles a day when I was living at Leamington and about 120 after I had moved to Brighton.

"But then I'm no different from a lot of other players — for instance Paul Bence lives down in Sussex and a couple of Brentford players live elsewhere away from Brentford.

"I've enjoyed my stay at Brentford, they are a great bunch of lads."

NOVEMBER 1975

- Dave Simmons was transferred back to his previous club, Cambridge United, for a nominal fee.
- Luton Town's 21-year old goalkeeper, Graham Horn, was signed on a month's loan from Luton Town.
- Schoolboy, Danis Salman, made his debut as substitute against Watford and became the club's youngest ever player at 15 years, 8 months and 3 days old, beating the previous record set by Alan Hawley in 1962.
- Bob Pearson became the club's first full-time chief scout for 25 years.
- Chairman Dan Tana went into the crowd during the match against Watford and made a citizen's arrest after a supporter shouted obscenities at the director's box.

DECEMBER 1975

- Graham Horn returned to Luton at the end of his loan spell.
- Three players were sent-off in the game against Rochdale, including Terry Johnson and Gordon Sweetzer, but as the dismissals were for persistent misconduct, no suspensions were imposed.
- Roger Cross was sent off against Reading.

JANUARY 1976

- QPR rejected a record £25,000 bid for midfielder Martyn Busby.
- Tom Sharp, an 18-year old Scottish defender, was signed on loan from Everton.
- A one month trial was offered to Scotland under-18 captain, David Oxley.
- The home cup tie with Bolton Wanderers produced record gate receipts of £8,032.
- Dan Tana was re-appointed as chairman. The board dispensed with the role of vice-chairman, instead giving each director specific responsibility for one area of work. Ron Blindell assumed responsibility for scouting, Colin Wheatley for the stadium, Bert Poyton for finance and Peter Pond-Jones for advertising and public relations.

THE BIG BRENTFORD BOOK OF THE SEVENTIES

Brentford's gamble doesn't worry striker

'TWO DIVISIONS DROP PLAYS ON MY MIND'

McCulloch aims to score enough to bound back

Andy McCulloch at home with his mother, Margaret, and father Adam.

ANDY McCULLOCH has become Fourth Division Brentford's biggest-ever soccer investment. £25,000 for his ability to score goals.

This is the equivalent of a £300,000 transfer fee for the likes of Manchester United and Derby County. Which also makes it a colossal gamble.

McCulloch was previously Oxford United's record buy at £75,000 — from Cardiff City—and that move never really came off. How does he feel about being put in a similar position again?

Needed cash

"The responsibility of being Brentford's costliest-ever buy doesn't worry me in the slightest," says McCulloch. "I have come to Brentford to score goals. That's all I'm thinking about.

"I didn't ask Oxford for a transfer. I gather they needed the money."

Over the last decade

Brentford have become experts at managing their financial affairs.

They wiped out an over-draft of more than £100,000 by careful "housekeeping." Chopped the reserve side for several years. Operated on a bare staff of 14 professionals.

Signed only free transfer men or amateurs. Sold the occasional home - produced player—like striker John O'Mara to Blackburn for £25,000 — to balance the books.

But the arrival last season of Dan Tana as chairman at Griffin Park marked a new

phase. A more ambitious out-look coupled with the arrival of John Docherty as man-ager.

A fee of £10,000 brought goalkeeper Bill Glazier from Coventry — a deal which backfired when Glazier decided to give up the game.

A League Cup-tie at Man-chester United, and two FA Cup third round games with high-flying Bolton Wanderers earned Brentford around £20,000.

Now they have used the cash to sign the striker they feel could turn them into a Third Division side.

"I'm sure I can score goals for Brentford. I want to get my stay at Oxford out of my system," McCulloch goes on.

"A string of injuries (knee ligaments, cartilage operation and Achilles tendon) prevented me from playing very many games. Nothing against Oxford as a club, but I lost all my confidence there.

"I feel I did quite well at Cardiff (in 58 games he scored 24 goals). I have faith in my scoring ability. I can't wait to get amongst the goals again.

"It does play on my mind, of course, that I've dropped down two divisions. But I hope to score enough goals to get me back there eventually. No matter where you are, if you keep scoring you get noticed."

THE MAJOR'S LOG

ANDY McCULLOCH made a quiet debut for Brentford in this defeat at Newport last night, but did sufficient for manager John Docherty to believe that the club's record £25,000 splash-out was worth it.

FEBRUARY 1976

- 17-year old David Oxley was offered a contract until the end of the season.
- Tom Sharp had his loan extended for a second month.
- Terry Johnson was transfer-listed at his own request.
- Groundsman, John Stepney, died after a short illness.

MARCH 1976

- Andy McCulloch was signed from Oxford United, with a new club record fee of £25,000 being paid for the 26-year old former Queens Park Rangers striker.
- Tom Sharp was signed on a permanent con-tract following his loan spell.
- Paul Walker was named as captain of the Eng-land schoolboy team.

APRIL 1976

- Jackie Graham suffered a shoulder injury and was ruled out for the remainder of the season.

MAY 1976

- Free transfers were given to Alan Nelmes, Keith Lawrence and Richard Poole whilst David Oxley also left the club.

Griffin Park admission prices going up

ADMISSION prices at Griffin Park will go up next season to a minimum of 65p as decided by the Football League at their recent meeting. Brentford general manager Denis Piggott says: "It was, of course, inevitable that prices would increase in view of the current inflation and if we had been free agents it is quite likely that we would have not gone to as high as 60p but we have no choice."

He and indeed the Brentford Board are aware of the escalating costs of soccer not only in admission prices but in travelling expenses to the ground and they have therefore made one or two new approaches to the problems of season tickets.

Quite clearly these have not been related to the admission prices in the past and in fact the club are aware that several people bought a season ticket for Block E last season and stood in the Braemar Road enclosure as it was cheaper to come into the games via a season than to pay for admission at each match.

While recognising the value of the season ticket holders in providing money when the club most need it in the close season and a revenue which applies whether or not they attend all matches they have been compelled to increase season ticket prices from £15 to £24 for the most expensive seats and £12 to £22 for the less expensive.

However, these are still excellent value and have been calculated on the basis of giving supporters three free entries. For example it will next season cost £1.20 to attend a game and have a seat in Stand C whereas a season ticket for 23 home Fourth Division games will only cost £24 thus saving the supporter who attends every match £3.60.

In addition a season ticket guarantees the holder his own seat for an FA Cup Tie and for the first two rounds of the Football League Cup he has only to pay admission for the enclosure and he gets his actual seat free.

Other advantages of season tickets are that the participant is automatically included in the draw for FA Cup Final and England v Scotland tickets and would not suffer any increase in price if due to inflation a further increase took place during the season as happened last year.

But for a super buy the club are making a special ticket available at £18 which guarantees a seat in Stand B although not necessarily the same seat for each game. In addition old age pensioners can still get a seat in Stand G for as little as 30p per match in addition to the fact that the Supporters Club have an allocation for tickets for pensioners in Stand X free of charge.

There was much discussion at the League Meeting as to whether juniors should be aged 12, 14 or 16 and Brentford have opted for junior admission price of 30p under 16 so the club, while facing the harsh facts of inflation are doing the best they can to see that the loyal supporter gets a square deal.

Brentford swoop for more youngsters

BRENTFORD manager John Docherty, who has already brought several highly promising youngsters to Griffin Park, has swooped to bring two more teenagers to the club.

For Docherty has returned to his native Scotland to persuade mid-field player David Oxley to come south for trials with the club, and has also signed Everton reserve centre-half Tom Sharp on a month's loan.

– but the future still looks bright

THE season of disappointment in the Fourth Division could be pointing Brentford in the right direction for the future.

Mike Everitt was sacked for achieving a better position in the League than John Docherty, but a manager's achievements should never be measured on one complete season.

This was supposed to be the promotion season. Docherty said so, and so did chairman Dan Tana . . . but they were inevitable words from men of ambition.

What else could they say?

To predict a modest season of team building would only discourage supporters from watching the team.

The club depends on the turnstiles clicking and the supporters want success, so managers have to do a selling job.

In the eyes of the fans Docherty has failed to deliver the goods. Brentford are still anchored in the Fourth Division.

☐

But there is more to the grey picture than low position in Division 4. There is a bit of youthful colour, too.

Docherty, with a limited budget, has built a promising foundation for the future with his obvious eye for young talent.

Five players under 20 have appeared in the first team this season, and with the others still maturing in the reserves are the

COMMENT — BY RICK JAMIESON

key to Brentford's future.

Nigel Smith at 19 is already wanted by many higher status clubs after impressive displays at centre-back.

Fifteen-year-old Danny Salman was 'blooded' in the Football League against Bournemouth in February, and new signing Tom Sharp, Gordon Sweetzer, Richard Poole and goalkeeper Paul Priddy are all 20 or under.

The majority of Division I clubs would have been delighted to win the signature of dynamic schoolboy midfield player Paul Walker.

But the England schoolboy international from Slough signed associated schoolboy forms for Brentford and will figure prominently in Docherty's long term plans.

These are players who have come to Brentford without a transfer fee and at a time of soaring prices it is important that clubs build in this way.

When Docherty took over from Everitt, he could not have a mass clear-out and completely rebuild because that would cost money — money which is just not available in such quantity.

So he has started building slowly and cheaply, the youngsters can provide a tremendous launching pad for future success.

1976-77

[Back Row] Jackie Graham, Danis Salman, Steve Russell, John Fraser, Steve Aylott, Terry Scales **[Middle Row]** John Docherty, Nigel Smith, Tom Sharp, Paul Priddy, Bobby Goldthorpe, Gordon Riddick, Graham Cox, Keith Pritchett, Mike Allen, Eddie Lyons **[Front Row]** Gordon Sweetzer, Mickey French, Terry Johnson, Paul Bence, Roger Cross, Andy McCulloch, Gary Rolph

Football League	Division Four
Manager	John Docherty / Bill Dodgin
Trainer	Eddie Lyons
Captain	Paul Bence / Jackie Graham
Final Position	15th
FA Cup	2nd Round
League Cup	1st Round
Leading Goalscorer (all competitions)	Gordon Sweetzer – 23 goals

John Docherty's summer re-jigging of the squad saw the arrival of four free transfers, but was undone by an horrendous injury crisis as the new season kicked-off. And, after a 1-1 draw at Watford in the two-legged first round of the League Cup, the depleted team suffered four straight defeats.

The failure to register a win in the opening six matches saw John Docherty leave the club in early September, to be replaced as manager by the experienced Bill Dodgin, who immediately embarked on a complete overhaul of the playing squad. Despite winning his first match, 3-0 against Southport, the dire run of results continued and only two more League wins had been achieved by the end of December – home victories over Workington (5-0) and Bournemouth (3-2).

With Brentford's lowest-ever League attendance being recorded (3,158) and wholesale changes to the team continuing, a re-election application looked certain – the turn of the year produced a woeful sequence of 12 defeats in 14 matches, including a 4-1 home loss to Colchester and a 5-0 thrashing at Doncaster Rovers.

February saw the signings of Steve Phillips, Paul Shrubb and John Bain shortly afterwards, Pat Kruse completed Bill Dodgin's new-look jigsaw and fortunes changed dramatically – the team hit sparkling form to produce 14 victories in the remaining 18 games with just two defeats being suffered during that sequence.

With Gordon Sweetzer contributing a staggering 22 goals in 23 matches, the run produced some scintillating displays of attacking football, and included comprehensive victories over high-flying opponents Bradford City (4-0), Swansea City (4-0) and Watford (3-0) which saw The Bees end the season in a comfortable mid-table position and pave the way for the following season's promotion push.

[Previous page] Roger Cross in opening day action during the home clash with Barnsley

BRENTFORD

OFFICIAL CLUB MATCHDAY MAGAZINE Price 12p

TUESDAY
17 AUGUST 1976
KICK OFF 7.30 PM

FOOTBALL LEAGUE CUP
1st ROUND 2nd LEG

WATFORD

		P	W	D	L	F	A	W	D	L	F	A	Pts
1	Cambridge	46	16	5	2	57	18	10	8	5	30	22	**65**
2	Exeter	46	17	5	1	40	13	8	7	8	30	33	**62**
3	Colchester	46	19	2	2	51	14	6	7	10	26	29	**59**
4	Bradford	46	16	7	0	51	18	7	6	10	27	33	**59**
5	Swansea	46	18	3	2	60	30	7	5	11	32	38	**58**
6	Barnsley	46	16	5	2	45	18	7	4	12	17	21	**55**
7	Watford	46	15	7	1	46	13	3	8	12	21	37	**51**
8	Doncaster	46	16	2	5	47	25	5	7	11	24	40	**51**
9	Huddersfield	46	15	5	3	36	15	4	7	12	24	34	**50**
10	Southend	46	11	9	3	35	19	4	10	9	17	26	**49**
11	Darlington	46	13	5	5	37	25	5	8	10	22	39	**49**
12	Crewe	46	16	6	1	36	15	3	5	15	11	45	**49**
13	Bournemouth	46	13	8	2	39	13	2	10	11	15	31	**48**
14	Stockport	46	10	10	3	29	19	3	9	11	24	38	**45**
15	**Brentford**	**46**	**14**	**3**	**6**	**48**	**27**	**4**	**4**	**15**	**29**	**49**	**43**
16	Torquay	46	12	5	6	33	22	5	4	14	26	45	**43**
17	Aldershot	46	10	8	5	29	19	6	3	14	20	40	**43**
18	Rochdale	46	8	7	8	32	25	5	5	13	18	34	**38**
19	Newport	46	11	6	6	33	21	3	4	16	9	37	**38**
20	Scunthorpe	46	11	6	6	32	24	2	5	16	17	49	**37**
21	Halifax	46	11	6	6	36	18	0	8	15	11	40	**36**
22	Hartlepool	46	8	9	6	30	20	2	3	18	17	53	**32**
23	Southport	46	3	12	8	17	28	0	7	16	16	49	**25**
24	Workington	46	3	7	13	23	42	1	4	18	18	60	**19**

Total Home League Attendances	117,777
Average Home League Attendance	5,121
Highest Home League Attendance	8,951
Lowest Home League Attendance	3,158

League Position throughout the Season

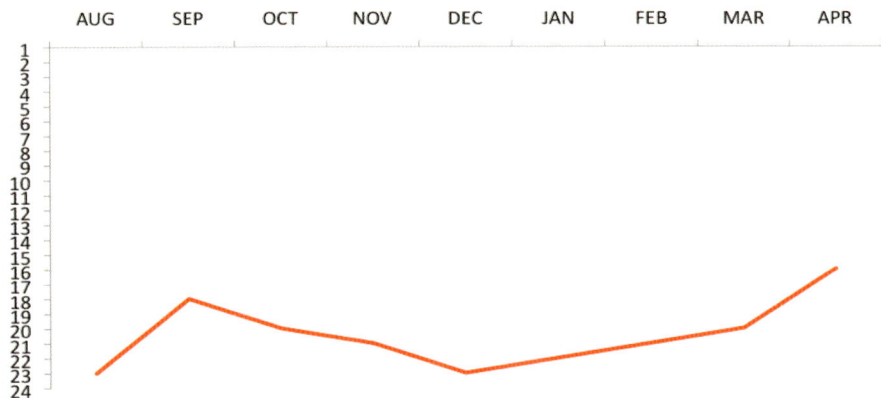

AUG SEP OCT NOV DEC JAN FEB MAR APR

135

1976-77

Sat 14th August: **Watford (A) League Cup 1st Round**
Drew 1-1   **Attendance: 4,827**

An injury-hit start to the new season saw 15-year-old schoolboy Paul Walker make history as the youngest ever first team player, and he took the corner that led to the opening goal in the 32nd minute – Bobby Goldthorpe flicked the ball on for Roger Cross to score. Watford equalised in the 80th minute when Paul Priddy was caught off his line and the ball was lobbed over his head.

Tue 17th August: **Watford (H) League Cup 1st Round**
Lost 0-2   **Attendance: 5,542**

A dismal game produced a laborious performance in which Paul Priddy was the busier keeper – the match looked to be heading for extra-time before the visitors dominance was rewarded with two late goals to send them through to the next round.

Sat 21st August: **Barnsley (H)**
Lost 0-1   **Attendance: 3,903**

In front of the lowest opening day attendance since the club joined the Football League in 1920, another punch-less display up front saw the visitors grab the only goal in the 38th minute, when a swift counter-attack saw Nigel Smith out-paced for the winner.

Mon 23rd August: **Stockport County (A)**
Lost 0-2   **Attendance: 3,191**

The dominance of the home side resulted in almost non-stop pressure and, in a one-sided encounter, only some splendid goalkeeping from Paul Priddy, and some desperate defending, kept the scoreline down to two goals, which were scored in the 23rd and 80th minutes.

Sat 28th August: **Huddersfield Town (A)**
Lost 0-1   **Attendance: 4,559**

A much improved performance failed to bring the first League goal or point of the new season as a hatful of chances were spurned – the hosts scored on the stroke of half-time to seal the win.

Sat 4th September: **Doncaster Rovers (H)**
Drew 2-2   **Attendance: 3,804**

Despite an early goal after just six minutes, when Steve Aylott's lob was headed on by Mickey French for Terry Johnson to drive the ball into the net, the visitors controlled the game and, although French scored a second against the run of play early in the second half, converting a Roger Cross centre – the lead was squandered. Two late goals were conceded, the second of which arrived with just 90 seconds left on the clock. The match proved to be the last for manager John Docherty, who left the club three days later.

Fri 10th September: **Aldershot (A)**
Drew 1-1   **Attendance: 5,129**

Trainer, Eddie Lyons, selected the team and watched on as Mickey French hit a 30-yard cross-cum-centre that deceived the keeper and dipped into the net. The home side equalised with a scrambled effort on 53 minutes, as already mounting injury woes worsened with trialist Harry Redknapp's debut lasting just 38 minutes.

Sat 18th September: **Southport (H)**
Won 3-0   **Attendance: 4,185**

New manager, Bill Dodgin, got off to a winning start, but a sterile performance against a poor side was not reflected by the score-line. A cross by Terry Johnson enabled Jackie Graham to net with a downward header that bounced high into the net for the first-half opener, and Johnson settled the game after 71 minutes when he pounced to score after the keeper spilled a shot from Terry Scales. Roger Cross hit the late third from a Terry Johnson centre.

Sat 25th September: **Torquay United (A)**
Drew 1-1   **Attendance: 2,456**

A superb 33rd minute opener from Roger Cross saw him lash home from 30 yards, but a promising overall performance was spoiled 12 minutes from time when a horrendous error from Paul Priddy gave Torquay their equaliser – he fumbled the ball when trying to prevent a corner, presenting an easy chance for a waiting striker.

Sat 2nd October: **Bradford City (A)**
Lost 2-3   **Attendance: 4,809**

Terry Scales set up the opening goal in the 7th minute – his pass enabled Roger Cross to score and, despite an equaliser eight minutes later, Cross scored again, from a Keith Pritchett centre, to take a 2-1 lead into half-time. The home side responded in the second period and goals in the 58th and 80th minutes gave them the win.

Sat 9th October: **Newport County (H)**
Drew 1-1   **Attendance: 5,894**

A 26th minute goal for the visitors was the signal for them to shut up shop and a negative performance looked set to bring them reward – until the 60th minute when a Keith Pritchett lob into the box was headed on by Roger Cross, and although the keeper saved his effort, Bobby Goldthorpe hit home the rebound.

Fri 15th October: **Swansea City (A)**
Lost 3-5   **Attendance: 3,656**

A goal feast started in the 8th minute when Mike Allen sped down the left flank and hit a powerful 20-yard, low drive into the net, but straight from the kick-off, Allen turned a cross into his own net for the equaliser. The Swans took the lead on 35 minutes, before Keith Pritchett volleyed home from a Terry Johnson centre five minutes later. In the 55th minute, Bobby Goldthorpe rose to head home a Danis Salman free-kick but the home side took over and scored further goals after 64, 66, then a fifth with three minutes to go, which sealed a flattering victory.

Sat 23rd October: **Darlington (H)**
Lost 0-3   **Attendance: 4,303**

The ineptness of the performance led to jeers and cries of "what a load of rubbish" at the half-time interval, even although the score-line was goal-less. Strikes from the visitors in the 50th, 63rd and 65th minutes fueled further protests from frustrated supporters.

Mon 25th October: **Workington (H)**
Won 5-0   **Attendance: 3,158**

Following the debacle just 48 hours earlier, the lowest ever League crowd at Griffin Park witnessed a complete turn-around. After just three minutes Gordon Riddick's centre was headed against the post by Bobby Goldthorpe and Roger Cross hit home the rebound. It was two after 25 minutes – Jackie Graham found Gordon Sweetzer wide on the right, who smashed a 20-yard shot into the net. The best goal arrived five minutes before half-time – Allan Glover accelerated past four defenders and sent over a cross that was flicked on by Roger Cross for Andy McCulloch to score – a goal that was almost bettered when John Fraser powered home a long range effort after the break. The fifth goal came when McCulloch rose unmarked to head in Jackie Graham's free-kick.

Sat 30th October: **Colchester United (A)**
Lost 1-2   **Attendance: 3,607**

Despite an 18th minute opener from Colchester, Roger Cross equalised just a minute later – heading in from a cross by Andy McCulloch. A furious goalmouth scramble in the 24th minute saw the hosts take the lead again, which proved to be the end of the scoring with McCulloch forced into a makeshift centre-back role.

Wed 3rd November: **Exeter City (A)**
Lost 2-3   **Attendance: 2,779**

A goalkeeping error from Paul Priddy presented the hosts with their opening goal in the 20th minute, but the levelling strike came on 53 minutes when Andy McCulloch headed home from an Allan Glover

[Left] A goal in the 5-0 win against Workington, celebrated by Roger Cross, Bobby Goldthorpe (No.5) and Gordon Sweetzer

corner. The reprieve was short-lived, though, the home side scored twice more before Jackie Graham showed exquisite skills before firing home from 20 yards – the best goal of the match.

Sat 6th November: **Bournemouth (H)**
Won 3-2   **Attendance: 4,254**

In the absence of manager Bill Dodgin, who was elsewhere seeking new recruits, a vastly improved display saw Roger Cross snatch the lead in the 15th minute – John Fraser's cross was flicked on by McCulloch. But a penalty conceded for handball by Gordon Riddick five minutes later brought the visiting equaliser, which was followed on 50 minutes by a second for the south-coast team. A stunning goal levelled the scores on 70 minutes, when Mickey French lashed home a volley after Andy McCulloch had headed into his path and, with the game in its final minute, McCulloch nodded home a precision cross from Jackie Graham to seal the win.

Sat 13th November: **Hartlepool (A)**
Lost 0-2   **Attendance: 1,888**

A disappointing display produced little in the way of attacking threat and the home side took the lead on 20 minutes, when Gordon Riddick conceded a penalty. The points were sealed midway through the second half when Paul Priddy failed to hold a header and, in the resulting confusion, the ball found its way into the net.

Sat 20th November: **Chesham (H) FA Cup 1st Round**
Won 2-0   **Attendance: 5,633**

The Isthmian leaguers made life difficult with a gritty display and held out until early in the second half, when Dave Carlton flicked the ball into the penalty box and Mickey French prodded the ball into the net. The decider arrived in the 75th minute when French was the provider for Roger Cross to score.

Sat 27th November: **Cambridge United (H)**
Lost 0-2   **Attendance: 5,040**

Cambridge produced a well-organised and hard-working performance and won the game without too much difficulty – scoring their first in the 40th minute and wrapping up the points with an embarrassingly easy goal in the 78th minute.

Sat 11th December: **Colchester United (A) FA Cup 2nd Round**
Match Abandoned 0-0

A farcical match, played in frozen and icy conditions on a skating-rink of a pitch, was halted by the referee after 65 minutes, but not before Terry Johnson had fallen and broken his arm on the rock-hard surface.

Mon 20th December: **Colchester United (A) FA Cup 2nd Round**
Lost 2-3   **Attendance: 4,730**

A disastrous opening period saw the hosts score twice, after 6 and 7 minutes, before Brentford's 'goal-of-the-season' arrived in the 43rd minute – a fine move between Mickey French and Roger Cross enabled young debutant, Gary Rolph, to draw the keeper before firing home. In the 85th minute Rolph crossed for Roger Cross to shoot and, when his effort was cleared off the line, John Fraser fired the equaliser. But disaster struck two minutes later when Bobby Goldthorpe's first touch as a late substitute was a mistimed tackle to concede a penalty and end any hopes of a cup run for another season.

Mon 27th December: **Southend United (A)**
Lost 1-2   **Attendance: 9,239**

After 10 minutes young loanee debutant Steve Scrivens sprinted past the home defenders and, as he rounded the keeper, was brought crashing down – Roger Cross scored from the resultant penalty. The hosts grabbed an equaliser in the 22nd minute and won the match with their second goal on 80 minutes.

Sat 1st January: **Bournemouth (A)**
Lost 1-3   **Attendance: 4,268**

The scoring was started by Roger Cross in the 15th minute, when he curled a centre into the penalty box and saw the ball sail over everyone and into the roof of the net. The hosts equalised from the penalty spot after 31 minutes, when 17-year old debutant goal-keeper, Graham Cox, misjudged a low cross and hauled down one of his opponents trying to redeem his error. A second penalty was awarded just before half-time for a trip by Nigel Smith and the third and final goal, late in the second half, sealed the points.

Mon 3rd January: **Colchester United (H)**
Lost 1-4   **Attendance: 4,629**

A first half lead, courtesy of a 26th minute goal when a Steve Scrivens corner was nodded on by Gordon Riddick for Andy McCulloch to score, promised a turnaround in fortunes, but the second half was a different story. The visitors equalised when Graham Cox failed to hold a shot – a second goal all but sealed the win. Two more late goals (82 and 87 minutes) sealed the rout.

Sat 8th January: **Crewe Alexandra (A)**
Lost 2-3   **Attendance: 2,198**

Despite another game in which the lead was taken – Andy McCul-loch scoring from a Steve Scrivens cross in the 15th minute, an equaliser came prior to the interval, by which time, injuries to Gordon Riddick and Andy McCulloch had reduced the team to ten men. Although substitute Gordon Sweetzer scored seven minutes after the break, when he sprinted away to flick the ball past the keeper, the Railwaymen scored two goals to wrap up the points before the 65th minute, inflicting a sixth consecutive defeat.

Sat 15th January: **Stockport County (H)**
Won 4-0   **Attendance: 3,981**

A fine win was set up after just 3 minutes when John Fraser hit home a Jackie Graham cross after the keeper had failed to hold

the ball – Gordon Sweetzer added a second in the 31st minute, running onto a Fraser pass to score with a neat flick. It was three after 47 minutes when, from a Gordon Riddick free-kick, Roger Cross set up Sweetzer for his second – the young striker com-pleted his hat-trick in spectacular fashion in the 70th minute with a diving header from a left-wing centre by Roger Cross. The game was notable for a comical touch-line incident when the reluctance of two different players to be substituted led to trainer, Eddie Lyons, throwing the number cards to the ground in frustration.

Sat 22nd January: **Barnsley (A)**
Lost 0-2   **Attendance: 4,095**

A goal-less, evenly-matched first-half gave little hint of Barnsley's dominance after the break – their total control of the proceedings was rewarded with goals in the 51st and 69th minutes.

Tue 25th January: **Scunthorpe United (A)**
Lost 1-2   **Attendance: 2,867**

A goal, after just 45 seconds, from the head of Gordon Sweetzer, served purely to inspire United to take control and a one-sided first-half ended level. The second period saw more intense pressure from the hosts, but the winner didn't arrive until the 90th minute.

Sat 29th January: **Halifax Town (H)**
Won 2-1   **Attendance: 4,517**

Against fellow re-election-strugglers, Gordon Sweetzer scored the opening goal when he ran on to a Mickey French header to beat the keeper with a deft flick – although the visitors levelled things up on the stroke of half-time, Sweetzer headed on a Neil Smillie centre on for Mickey French to net the winner on the hour mark.

Sat 5th February: **Huddersfield Town (H)**
Lost 1-3   **Attendance: 4,833**

Despite an 11th minute first-career goal for Danis Salman, when he sprinted into the box before firing home, a poor overall display saw the visitors score twice, after 23 and 26 minutes, and a potential lifeline was thrown away in the 38th minute when a twice-taken penalty was twice missed – Steve Aylott hit the first effort over the bar and, from the re-take, Gordon Riddick hit the post. A second half own goal by Nigel Smith gave the score a more realistic look.

Sat 12th February: **Doncaster Rovers (A)**
Lost 0-5   **Attendance: 4,095**

Outplayed throughout, the opening goal after 13 minutes marked the start of a long and difficult afternoon – the second goal arrived just four minutes later. Second-half strikes in the 57th and 60th minutes were followed by another own goal from Nigel Smith to complete a miserable drubbing.

Sat 19th February: **Aldershot (H)**
Lost 0-1   **Attendance: 4,542**

With Bill Dodgin's new-look team starting to take shape, a much improved performance against resolute opposition proved fruitless as a second-half goal was the cue for the visitors to shut up shop.

Tue 22nd February: **Rochdale (H)**
Won 3-2   **Attendance: 3,307**

Rochdale scored after 30 minutes to secure a half-time lead, but the second period was a different story – five minutes after the break Terry Johnson capitalised on a defensive mix-up to equalise. Johnson was the creator for the second goal, when his left-wing centre was headed on by Gordon Sweetzer for Steve Phillips to score and, in the 80th minute, the win was secured when John Fraser's right-wing cross was headed home by Sweetzer. The visitor's injury-time second was no more than a late consolation.

Sat 5th March: **Torquay United (H)**
Won 3-2   **Attendance: 4,172**

Two defensive blunders by the visitors presented Gordon Sweetzer with goals in the 35th minute, when he gained possession,

before running on to score the opener, then on the stroke of half-time, he picked up a misplaced back-pass to fire powerfully home. Sweetzer completed his second hat-trick of the season after 60 minutes when he converted a penalty after Mike Allen's centre had been handled. Two goals for the visitors, after 65 and 89 minutes, ensured that the scoreline was a more realistic reflection of the game and opposition centre-half Pat Kruse did enough to convince Bill Dodgin to sign him just days later.

Tue 8th March: **Southport (A)**
Won 2-1   **Attendance: 969**

The first away win of the season was finally achieved and Terry Johnson laid the foundation with a penalty early in the second half, after he was brought down by the keeper following a mazy run into the box. Although the home side equalised, the winner arrived 15 minutes from the end when a free-kick was flicked across the goalmouth by John Bain – Steve Phillips headed the ball on and Gordon Sweetzer added the final touch, the first goals ever scored by Brentford at Southport.

Sat 12th March: **Bradford City (H)**
Won 4-0   **Attendance: 5,742**

A comprehensive win was on the cards from as early as the 5th minute when Paul Shrubb, making his full debut, played a one-two with Gordon Sweetzer and fired home from just inside the penalty box. Terry Johnson added a second on the hour mark, when he headed in a cross from Jackie Graham, and when Mike Allen's centre resulted in a scramble in the six-yard box, John Bain flicked home his first goal. Then, in injury time, Steve Phillips outpaced his marker and calmly flicked the ball into the net.

Fri 18th March: **Newport County (A)**
Lost 1-3   **Attendance: 1,747**

Despite taking a 9th minute lead, courtesy of a Gordon Sweetzer header, the hosts drew level just 60 seconds later and took the lead after 15 minutes. A penalty was awarded for a handball by John Fraser after 56 minutes and it was converted to seal the win for the home side.

Wed 23rd March: **Watford (H)**
Won 3-0   **Attendance: 7,602**

A blistering start saw all three goals arrive inside the opening fifteen minutes against the promotion-chasing Hornets – Gordon Sweetzer raced onto a Terry Johnson pass after four minutes, shrugged off his marker then slotted the ball past the keeper. Just two minutes later, he repeated the feat – chasing a long ball from Mike Allen and drilling home a low shot. Jackie Graham thundered the ball into the roof of the net after receiving a pass from Terry Johnson in the 15th minute and the remainder of the game saw a man-of-the-match display from Paul Priddy to keep the scoreline intact.

Sat 26th March: **Swansea City (H)**
Won 4-0   **Attendance: 6,201**

Another goal-feast got underway with a 34th minute penalty from Terry Johnson, after Jackie Graham's run into the box had been halted by a foul. The second goal arrived on 55 minutes when Dave Carlton's thunderbolt was palmed upwards by the keeper and Gordon Sweetzer continued his rich scoring vein by flicking home with his head. Steve Phillips converted a Dave Carlton cross, before Johnson smashed in a free-kick from outside the area after 75 minutes to complete another impressive display.

Sat 2nd April: **Darlington (A)**
Drew 2-2   **Attendance: 1,681**

A match played in gale-force winds saw the hosts take a two-goal first-half lead, before a spectacular 60th minute goal reduced the arrears – Terry Johnson, with his back to goal, managed to launch himself from the ground to score from an ingenious overhead kick. Gordon Sweetzer hit the equaliser in the 86th minute when his miss-hit shot went through the keeper's legs and into the net.

[Right] Gordon Sweetzer awaits the outcome of John Bain's one-on-one with the Swansea goalkeeper

Fri 8th April: **Southend United (H)**
Won 1-0   **Attendance: 8,951**

A scrappy Good Friday game was settled after 73 minutes when John Bain lofted a 25-yard free-kick into the goalmouth and Steve Phillips nipped in between a mass of defenders to slip the ball into the net to secure a sixth successive home win.

Sat 9th April: **Watford (A)**
Won 1-0   **Attendance: 9,382**

A tense, local derby produced just the one goal, which arrived in the 20th minute – John Fraser's centre was powerfully headed home by Andy McCulloch, making his return from a three-month injury lay-off. The match was most notable for two separate penalty saves by Paul Priddy – the first, after 21 minutes, from Dennis Bond following John Fraser's handball, and the second, in the dying minutes from Alan Mayes after a handball offence by Pat Kruse.

Tue 12th April: **Exeter City (H)**
Won 1-0   **Attendance: 7,641**

The outstanding run of results was enhanced by a superb display of attacking football, and a hugely entertaining match was settled by an 80th minute goal that was a culmination of everything good about the performance. John Fraser won the ball with a crunching tackle and sent Terry Johnson bursting away down the right flank, and when he pulled the back with a deep infield cross, Gordon Sweetzer rose majestically to head the winner.

Sat 16th April: **Workington (A)**
Won 3-1   **Attendance: 1,032**

The breakthrough against the division's bottom side came as early as the 9th minute – Gordon Sweetzer side-footed home from a

John Fraser cross, although the home side equalised just five minutes later. The lead was regained after 54 minutes with a goal of real quality – John Bain's deep centre was hit low across the box by Phillips for McCulloch to fire home powerfully. An individual effort from Steve Phillips sealed the victory with 18 minutes remaining when he cheekily chipped the ball over the keeper.

Tue 19th April: **Halifax Town (A)**
Drew 0-0   **Attendance: 1,464**

A strong rearguard action ensured a share of the spoils in a hard-fought and sometimes dour encounter, in which Pat Kruse stole the headlines by producing an outstanding display at centre-back.

Sat 23rd April: **Hartlepool (H)**
Won 3-1   **Attendance: 5,978**

A 15th minute corner from Jackie Graham was met by a diving header from Pat Kruse to open the scoring, but just a minute later, a howler by Paul Priddy saw him fumble a harmless-looking header over the line to gift the visitors with an equaliser. The lead was restored after 20 minutes when another Jackie Graham corner was headed home by the on-rushing McCulloch and the third and final goal arrived in the 70th minute, when Gordon Sweetzer was fouled in the penalty area and converted the spot-kick himself.

Sat 30th April: **Cambridge United (A)**
Lost 2-3   **Attendance: 5,617**

The visit to the champions-elect was a sterile encounter between two teams with differing styles – the game was all but sealed by a 16-minute second half hat-trick from United striker Tom Finney. Two late goals from Gordon Sweetzer and Jackie Graham were not enough to steal a point.

Mon 2nd May: **Crewe Alexandra (H)**
Drew 0-0   **Attendance: 5,842**

A tedious affair, played between two teams with little to play for, produced very few chances, despite both sides looking to play a passing game.

Sat 7th May: **Scunthorpe United (H)**
Won 4-2   **Attendance: 5,298**

The home campaign finished on a high-note, and although the visitors took a 5th minute lead, an equalizer arrived after 26 minutes when Jackie Graham's corner was headed home at full-stretch by Pat Kruse. Five minutes later Gordon Sweetzer scored to make it 2-1, then grabbed his second after 40 minutes flicking home a tight by-line centre from Steve Phillips – the strike was Sweetzer's 23rd goal in just 24 matches. The Iron pulled another goal back in the 61st minute but Andy McCulloch headed down John Bain's centre for Steve Phillips to net an 88th minute fourth goal.

Sat 14th May: **Rochdale (A)**
Won 3-2   **Attendance: 977**

One goal behind at the interval, after a 30th minute strike from Dale, the game turned with two goals in three minutes right at the start of the second period. The first came when Paul Shrubb slotted home after collecting a poor attempted clearance and then Dave Carlton fired home a left-footed volley from distance. The home side drew level again after an hour, but the 70th minute winner had more than a hint of good fortune about it as Danis Salman's speculative shot was deflected into the path of Steve Phillips, who stroked the ball into the net.

MANCINI TO JOIN BEES THIS WEEK

By STEVE JAMES

ARSENAL centre-half, Terry Mancini is certain to be a Brentford player by the end of the week.

The former Eire international was at Griffin Park for Saturday's game with Barnsley and the Brentford board agreed to accept his terms.

Although he was given a free transfer by Arsenal at the end of the season, he will cost the Division 4 club quite a sum, but they are not revealing just how much.

Chairman, Dan Tana explained: "Manager John Docherty and I met with Terry on Saturday and told him that although we couldn't meet offers from Division 1 and 2 sides, we could still make him a good offer.

"He said that he would like to play for Brentford more than any other club, and asked for certain terms.

"At a meeting after the game, the board agreed all his terms, and told him so. He has agreed to sign for us on Wednesday, as he wants to play in a reserve game against Spurs on Tuesday,". said Tana.

"As far as I am concerned, Mancini is a Brentford player."

● **TERRY MANCINI** casts an eye over Brentford during Saturday's game against Barnsley. Brentford director Peter Pond-Jones is on his right

Brentford give up all-green strip

GEORGE SANDS COLUMN

BRENTFORD have decided to dispense with the all-green livery they wore in many away games last season and are reverting to their former blue outfit when a clash of colours makes a change necessary.

Probably most of their supporters, who watch them only at Griffin Park or in very near "derbies" have never seen them in green, and although the rig-out looked quite attractive, it did not bring a lot of success.

Taking part in the most important match of his life, goalkeeper Paul Priddy gets married this Saturday. Living at Isleworth, he attended Syon School and first played for the Bees as a junior. Two other Brentford players of last season, Keith Lawrence and Richard Poole, are also coming off the single list this summer.

FORMER West Ham winger Harry Redknapp is expected to sign for Brentford on a two-month trial and play in this evening's (Tuesday) Mid-week League reserve game at home to Southend, kick-off 6 p.m.

Winger Redknapp, pictured at the Brentford-Doncaster match at Griffin Park on Saturday, has been freed by Bournemouth and is keen to try out his luck at Brentford, despite the offer of a coaching job in the United States.

PRE-SEASON

John Docherty made four new signings, all on free transfers – John Fraser, a 23-year old defender signed from Fulham, 24-year old midfielder Steve Aylott arrived from Oxford United, 22-year old full-back Keith Pritchett signed from Queens Park Rangers and Bobby Goldthorpe, a 25-year old centre-back who had previously been a junior back in 1967, joined from Charlton Athletic.

Director and team boss quit

By Leon Stork

AN emergency meeting of the Brentford directors on Tuesday evening to discuss the problems confronting the club erupted in angry words, resulted in the immediate resignation of manager John Docherty and led to the subsequent resignation of the youngest director Ron Blindell.

Assistant manager Eddie Lyons takes charge immediately while the club advertise for a replacement.

When I spoke to Docherty on Wednesday he expressed his regret at having left Brentford, but he was adamant that "there was no way he could have stayed on" and Brentford chairman Dan Tana echoed these sentiments with "we might have been able to patch it up at the meeting last night, but after he resigned John said some unforgivable things, and that was that. We are now looking for a new manager."

The meeting was called for on Saturday

after Brentford's drawn game against Doncaster. Dan Tana explains:

"At the previous home game this season when Brentford lost to Barnsley, Docherty called an emergency meeting after the game to discuss our team problems. He did the same on Saturday, but as it isn't always convenient to have a meeting after a game, I called it for Tuesday instead."

Neither John Docherty nor Dan Tana was prepared to divulge what was said at the board meeting, which lasted approximately 20 minutes before Docherty went in. Dan Tana was, however, prepared to admit that a motion proposed by the youngest director, Ron Blindell, had been defeated. He refused to say what the motion had been.

Mr. Blindell was more forthcoming when I spoke to him.

"I was amazed when after the game on Saturday Dan Tana came up to me and said that he didn't want John to stay on as manager. He asked me to tell him," he claims. "I found this a strange request and disagreed with it, but I told John, who was very upset, and insisted on an emergency meeting being called."

Ron Blindell said that until then no one, to his knowledge, had ever expressed doubts about retaining Docherty as manager.

In fact, when I interviewed John

Docherty the previous week I got the impression that all was well at the Griffin Park ground and that there was complete harmony among members of the board. It now emerges, however, that a clash of personalities had been simmering underneath the calm waiting to erupt.

The board meeting took an unexpected turn when Ron Blindell proposed a motion of no confidence in the chairman Dan Tana and asked for his resignation if the club were to keep John Docherty as manager.

The motion was not seconded and subsequently thrown out.

UNTENABLE

Docherty then joined the meeting saying that he believed Dan Tana had expressed a desire for his resignation.

He told me he then asked the board to either confirm or deny this, and when it refused to do either he felt his "position had become untenable" and he resigned.

When I asked Ron Blindell why he wanted his chairman to go, he said:

"I think Dan Tana has done very little for the club. I wanted Docherty to stay on. He's good for the game and good for Brentford."

Strangely, Dan Tana said that he wanted Docherty to stay.

"It's all lies," he said. "I never said I wanted him to leave. I would have wanted him to stay on at least until his injured players were back in action to prove themselves. John is a hard worker, and the "game needs men like him. Now, unfortunately, the situation is impossible. Harsh words were spoken."

And on Wednesday Brentford received its second bombshell of the week when Ron Blindell resigned as a director. He explained why:

"It wasn't so much because Docherty had left, but because I felt I was misled by certain members of the board who had promised over the weekend to support my motion asking for the chairman's resignation. But when the crunch came on Tuesday evening none was willing to stand up to be counted. As a result I find myself unable to continue as a director."

Earlier in the week, Brentford received their first shock when centre-back Gordon Riddick announced his retirement from the game. An ankle injury had kept him out since August 7, and on the advice of his doctor he decided to call it a day.

Riddick joined Brentford from Northampton in 1973 after previous experience with Luton, Gillingham, Charlton and Orient. He had over 400 league and cup games to his credit, and he scored five times for the Bees in 97 appearances.

Danis Salman and Gary Rolph, both 16-years old, were signed as apprentice professionals. Mickey Tripp was not offered a full contract on completion of his apprenticeship. Steve Russell, released by Luton, was signed on a one-month trial.

Terry Johnson came off the transfer list at his own request, while stalwart, Alan Nelmes, was awarded a testimonial match.

Eric Radley-Smith, voted off the board in March 1974, was invited to become a director again.

AUGUST 1976

• Terry Mancini, Arsenal's 34-year old former Eire international centre-back, agreed terms to join the club, but John Docherty withdrew from the deal at the last minute declaring that he was unaware of the player's age.
• Steve Russell was released at the end of his trial period.
• With a number of early season injuries, 15-year-old Paul Walker made his debut at Watford.

SEPTEMBER 1976

• John Docherty resigned as team manager three days after the draw with Doncaster, after failing to get a satisfactory denial from the chairman that he no longer wanted him to continue as manager.
• Director, Ron Blindell, who had informed Docherty of the chairman's comments regarding his position, proposed a motion of no confidence in the chairman, but when it was not backed, Blindell resigned from the board himself.
• Eddie Lyons was appointed as caretaker manager for the games against Aldershot and Luton.
• Bill Dodgin was appointed as the new manager in readiness for the game against Southport – the 44-year old former Fulham manager having left Northampton Town in the summer after guiding them to promotion.
• Chief Scout, Bob Pearson, left the club but Eddie Lyons kept his role as physiotherapist.
• John Docherty's last signing was 29-year old former West Ham United winger Harry Redknapp on a trial basis, but the lengthening injury list saw Harry Redknapp, Andy McCulloch, Gordon Sweetzer,

DEATH OF GEORGE SANDS

WE were all grieved to hear of the death of former Chronicle Sports Editor George Sands (story, page 1).

His favourite reply to anyone who wanted to know how he managed to sustain his amazing sequence of 1,126 Brentford matches without a miss was that he had "an arrangement" to be ill only during the summer.

It was a typically humorous assessment of a serious problem, and to those who approached me for an answer to his durability, I always mentioned his great sense of humour.

I had the privilege of being his colleague for the last seven years of his working life and I shall remember "that when one is dealing almost exclusively with the ego's of people, it paid to see the funny side of the most serious situation."

I remember his words well. George Sands was a unique person, a man married to his job, and serving his community in a rather special way. His feat of covering Brentford for such a long period is entered in the Guinness Book of Records and will never be equalled or bettered. George belonged to a rare breed—regrettably a dying breed.

**LEON STORK
SPORTS EDITOR**

Steve Aylott and Mike Allen all facing several weeks out of action.
• Gordon Riddick announced his retirement following a troublesome ankle injury. His contract was cancelled by mutual consent.

OCTOBER 1976

• 23-year old midfielder, Dave Carlton, followed the new manager from Northampton Town, signing for a reported fee of £3,000.
• Allan Glover, a 25-year old midfielder, arrived on a month's loan from West Bromwich Albion.
• Harry Redknapp was released and left the club at the end of his trial.
• A bid from Torquay United for Roger Cross, was rejected.
• Paul Bence was dropped for the game at Swansea – following 99 consecutive appearances.
• Jackie Graham was named as the new club captain, replacing Paul Bence.
• Gordon Riddick made a comeback from retirement on a non-contract basis.
• The crowd against Workington (3,158) was the lowest ever league attendance at Griffin Park.

• 44-year old Gordon Quinn, a former Plymouth and Queens Park Rangers player, was appointed as the new Chief Scout.
• Playwright and author, Willis Hall, was appointed to the board of directors.

NOVEMBER 1976

• Keith Pritchett was sold to Watford for a reported £4,000 transfer fee.
• Paul Bence joined Torquay United on loan with a view to a permanent transfer.
• Bill Dodgin was unable to negotiate a deal with West Bromwich Albion for the transfer of Allan Glover and the player returned on completion of his loan.
• The manager indicated that he believed that Paul Priddy was a year off being ready for the first team, and he was searching for a new keeper.

DECEMBER 1976

• Bad weather caused the postponement of the games against Scunthorpe (away), Rochdale (home) and Watford (home).
• The cup-tie at Colchester was abandoned due to icy conditions and after Terry Johnson fell and broke his arm.
• 19-year old winger, Steve Scrivens, signed from Fulham on one month's loan.
• Paul Bence's loan at Torquay was extended by a second month.
• Middlesex Chronicle sports editor, George Sands, died after a long illness at the age of 75. He missed only two games in 40 years and saw 1,126 consecutive matches until the end of the 1975-76 season.

Dodgin has angered the supporters

"BILL DODGIN is not the man I thought he was, the sooner he goes back to Northampton the better!" They are the words of a Brentford supporter who has followed the club for nearly 21 years.

Stan Willis is a great favourite with his fellow supporters at Griffin Park and goes everywhere with Brentford but at the moment he is very discontent with the Bees.

The two most important things in Stan's football life were watching Brentford win and also watching Roger Cross play.

Cross, transferred to Millwall last week, was a favourite with the fans and his departure has caused a lot of upset.

Just before the supporters embarked on their long trip to Scunthorpe, Chronicle Sport asked them for their views.

Stan Willis, of 3 Garrick Road, Richmond, said:

"I think the selling of Roger Cross is the daftest thing since QPR tried to buy us out. Bill Dodgin is not the man I thought he was, the sooner he goes back to Northampton the better. No manager in the Fourth Division should sell his leading scorer."

Charles Kamp, of 235 Ealing Road, Brentford, is 88 years old and still follows Brentford away, he said: "I don't think much of the selling of Cross at all. I don't believe in signing goalkeepers when we want people up front. This is one of the worst sides I have ever seen."

Ron Jacobs of 132 The Drive, Hounslow, has followed Brentford for 22 years and he said: "As a Brentford supporter for many years, I was shocked but not surprised that Brentford sold Roger Cross.

"He was the leading scorer and the best player and Brentford always have let the top players go. That is why we are a POOR FOURTH DIVISION side. Let's now hear the excuses from our wonderful Board of Directors and manager!"

Brian Jennings, of Doghurst Avenue, Harlington, is also a true supporter and has followed the Bees for 20 years and said: "With the present position of the team, the selling of Cross was a retrograde step. For to get out of the re-election zone you must keep your best players, especially the leading scorer. Bill Dodgin might have given the season up as lost but to the paying customers who travel away we expect to get something for our money."

THE Chronicle agrees that everyone has their view but it should be remembered that Bill Dodgin is a newcomer and may still prove himself.

- Steve Scrivens was re-called by Fulham at the end of his loan.
- Neil Smillie, an 18-year old winger was signed on one month's loan from Crystal Palace.
- Experienced 32-year old goalkeeper, Tony Burns, also arrived on loan from Crystal Palace.
- After rejecting a bid from Peterborough United for Roger Cross, the striker was sold to Millwall for a reported fee of £9,500.
- Paul Bence returned from his loan at Torquay and the club announced that he would be given a free transfer at the end of the season, along with Terry Scales and Bobby Goldthorpe.
- Andy McCulloch entered hospital for a cartilage operation and would be out of action for several months.

FEBRUARY 1977

- The game at Southport was postponed as a result of a waterlogged pitch.
- A reported fee of £4,000 was paid to Northampton Town for 22-year old midfielder, Steve Phillips.
- 21-year old former Fulham midfielder, Paul Shrubb, joined the club from Hellenic FC in South Africa.

Division 2 in three years—Tana

BRENTFORD chairman Dan Tana chats to new manager Bill Dodgin ... the man he believes can still bring Second Division football to Griffin Park by 1979.

I WAS A REBEL— PHILLIPS

STEVE PHILLIPS . . . "I was out nearly every night. I followed the wrong people. It nearly finished me."

STEVE STAMMERS reporting

BRENTFORD'S new boy Steve Phillips, signed from Northampton last week, is rebuilding the football career which he nearly ruined through a love of the good life.

Four years ago Tottenham-born Phillips scored England's winner in the little World Cup Final against East Germany in Italy.

Phillips was then playing for Birmingham and his future looked bright.

But he confesses: "I ignored good advice and followed the example of the wrong people. It nearly finished me in football."

TEMPTATIONS

Phillips, now 22, went to Birmingham at 16 straight from school and struggled to cope with the newly-found freedom and the temptations that it offered.

"I was out nearly every night of the week, living it up most of the time," he says.

"When all the people that mattered were trying to put me right, I just ignored them and did the opposite to what I was told.

"Things went wrong after I had a few games in the first team and I was seriously thinking about packing up the game when I met my wife Kay."

The new responsibilities reformed Phillips who began to take his football seriously again.

DETERMINED

Birmingham eventually sold him to Northampton, then in the Fourth Division and managed by Bill Dodgin, his new boss at Griffin Park.

"Now I am back on an even keel. I'm even dreaming of getting back into the First Division again.

"My wife and my daughter Kelly have helped to bring a new sense of drive and determination into my life."

Phillips was reluctant to leave St Andrew's and only did so because Dodgin impressed him so much.

"He is dead straight, and the players at Northampton still think the world of him," he says.

"He has some great ideas about the game and he makes you want to play for him."

CLASSY

Phillips has already responded for Brentford, scoring in their 3-2 win over Rochdale on Tuesday night in only his second game for the club.

He showed enough classy touches to prove that he will be a valuable asset and a bargain buy from Northampton at £5,000.

Phillips adds: "We are determined to fight our way out of trouble. Bill Dodgin will get it right. He knows how to get the best out of people.

"Brentford won't be in this position this time next year. That's a promise."

- An unsuccessful bid was made to sign Reading captain, Gordon Cumming.
- Neil Smillie and Tony Burns both returned to Crystal Palace after their loan spells ended.
- 19-year old midfielder, John Bain, was signed on loan for the rest of the season from Bristol City.
- Mickey French was sold to Swindon for a reported £7,000 transfer fee.

- Gordon Riddick had his non-contract registration cancelled and left the club.
- Paul Walker was informed he would be offered an apprenticeship at the end of the season, after he had left school.
- Former Fulham player and Enfield manager, Fred Callaghan, was brought in to assist with the coaching.
- After the game against Rochdale, Bill Dodgin declared that he now had the basis of a successful team.

MARCH 1977

- A club record fee for a defender, £20,000, was paid to Torquay United for 23-year old centre-half Pat Kruse (pictured above).
- Paul Bence and Terry Scales had their contracts cancelled by mutual consent and both left the club.

I give Mum £5 a week— it's all I can manage

...he just can't afford to score with the girls

Another great EXCLUSIVE

WHO has scored most goals in the Football League this year?

Forget your super-stars. It's a 20-year-old called Gordon Sweetzer. Sweetzer has 22 goals for Brentford in 25 games since the start of January.

And who's the lowest-paid player in the League? The same Gordon Sweetzer must be running close for that also.

"After paying tax and insurance I take home £30 a week," he told me. Out of that £30 he pays his mother £5; "I should give her more but can't afford it."

He pays an average £12 a week on petrol to get from home in Bracknell to Brentford in the car he shares with his father.

"I often have to buy meals at lunchtime and buy my own clothes. The rest I spend on my one night out — Saturday night after the match," he says.

Young Sweetzer hasn't a steady girl-friend: "I can't afford one." He never gambles and won't be going on holiday this summer because he can't afford that, either.

Callaghan rejoins former boss Dodgin

FRED CALLAGHAN, who steered Enfield to the Isthmian League championship last season, has teamed up again with Brentford manager Bill Dodgin.

Callaghan played for Dodgin when the Brentford boss was manager at Fulham and is now helping him as a coach at Griffin Park.

The popular former Fulham defender, who quit as manager of Enfield earlier this season, started assisting Dodgin's team building plans this week.

"He has brought a bit more life to the place and I need someone to help me because I can't look after the team and be looking at players at the same time," said Dodgin.

Callaghan is pleased to be back in football so quickly after his unhappy Enfield episode, particularly in the Football League.

He spent more than 10 years at Fulham and says: "I left Enfield after a difference of opinion — they didn't think only four defeats in 35 games was good enough.

"Bill is looking for new players and he can't be in two places at once so he asked me if I would like to help him until the end of the season.

"I hope I can help him build a good future for Brentford. I'm sure he is on the right lines and he knows what he wants.

"While he is looking for new players I can look after the coaching for him," added Callaghan.

And Dodgin is still out looking for players to strengthen his squad, hoping to beat the transfer deadline a week tomorrow.

One player who has left Griffin Park is Neil Smillie the Crystal Palace striker who has completed a month's loan.

APRIL 1977

• Gordon Sweetzer's goal against Hartlepool was his 20th in 21 games.
• Paul Priddy saved two penalties in the win at Watford.
• Maximum points were obtained over the Easter weekend for the first time since 1965.
• Andy McCulloch made a successful comeback from his knee operation.

MAY 1977

• Free transfers were given to Paul Priddy, Bobby Goldthorpe and Tom Sharp.
• Paul Walker was signed as an apprentice professional.

The real supporter

TRAVELLING from one side of England to the other to see a football match is, in some people's minds, a very strange occupation. If the match is between Manchester United and Liverpool then it becomes a little more understandable but when it is Hartlepool and Brentford, thoughts of straight jackets and white coats come to mind.

At 9 am on Saturday morning, approximately 30 Brentford supporters gathered at King's Cross Station to prepare for a trip north to see their side.

King's Cross is an ugly station with grimy architecture and impersonal staff. On a Satur-day morning it is even worse, and with a four-hour train journey in front of you, it takes on the character of a mortuary.

Once the train had started its long journey, they settled back in their seats and enjoyed conversations concerning players, memories, or how much British Rail food prices had gone up.

As the journey progressed, they gathered momentum knowing that Hartlepool was only another two hours away.

There was little foul language for other travellers to complain about, and absolutely no vandalism. The Brentford players were also on the train, but in another carriage.

One or two supporters visited them and sent their best wishes for the game, but most were content to stay in their seats and talk about football and anything else to do with Brentford.

Once in Hartlepool, after changing at Dar-lington, the followers dispersed and found pubs or restaurants.

Then they made their way to the ground. Once inside, the real excitement began. Brentford came out on to the field and were met by the customary boos from the home crowd, which effectively cut out any noise from the away support.

Hartlepool took the lead and Brentford tried to come back, but a second goal from the home side meant defeat for Brentford.

Straight after the match it was time to get back to the station and catch the train to Darlington and change, and then wait for the London connection.

"You can have a good laugh on these trips, and they are a great crowd," said one as he sipped his umpteenth beer.

"One day we'll really start getting success," said another as he looked at his sausage roll, obviously questioning its origin.

Then, the highspot of the day. A handful of Brentford players came to the bar as well and mixed freely with their admirers.

After a few drinks, player and supporter alike were singing tributes to Brentford, and the memories of a defeat were being forgotten.

When the train eventually arrived back, the supporters started to go their own separate ways, but before they did there was still one ritual to perform.

The talk of the next away game — which happens to be at Scunthorpe. The enthusiasm for the future was beyond an ordinary person's grasp. "See you at Scunthorpe," said one chirpy supporter. Only death would stop these hard-core followers from seeing their team and, let's face it, if it wasn't for them Brentford Football Club might not exist, and British Rail would be the first to notice that!

1977-78

[Back Row] Tommy Baldwin, Andy McCulloch, Alan Easterbrook, Steve Aylott, John Fraser [Middle Row] Denis Piggott, Bill Dodgin, Barry Lloyd, Pat Kruse, Len Bond, Dave Carlton, Danis Salman, Graham Cox, Gary Rolph, Mike Allen, Eddie Lyons, Gordon Quinn [Front Row] Paul Walker, Paul Shrubb, Steve Phillips, Dan Tana, Jackie Graham, Willie Graham, Nigel Smith, Doug Allder

Football League	Division Four
Manager	Bill Dodgin
Trainer	Eddie Lyons
Captain	Jackie Graham
Final Position	4th
FA Cup	2nd Round
League Cup	1st Round
Leading Goalscorer	Steve Phillips – 36 goals
(all competitions)	

Bill Dodgin's pre-season promise of an exciting campaign became a reality – fluent, attacking football, with goals galore, was the order of the day throughout and, despite a few blips, a top four finish, and promotion, was rarely in doubt.

After a first round League Cup exit to Crystal Palace, 6-3 on aggregate, the opening two home games produced victories by 3-0 (Northampton) and 4-1 (Wimbledon) and the goal glut was reinforced two matches later with an astonishing ten goal thriller – a 6-4 win at Crewe Alexandra.

The top of the table home clash with Watford in October attracted a crowd of 14,500, but a 3-0 defeat prompted a mini-slump of four games without a win and, despite the goal-scoring exploits of strikers Steve Phillips, Andy McCulloch and Gordon Sweetzer, the mid-season dip produced just one win, 5-1 at home to Crewe Alexandra, in the ten games between December and February.

The shock sale of Gordon Sweetzer, with 14 goals in 20 games, to Cambridge United in March for £30,000, failed to have any negative impact – the team embarked on a winning streak of ten victories and four draws in the remaining 17 matches, including some crucial wins against promotion rivals Aldershot (2-0), Barnsley (2-0) and away at Huddersfield (3-1), before a 2-0 home win against Darlington sealed promotion with two games to spare.

With Doug Allder's wing play providing much of the ammunition, the strike partnership of Steve Phillips and Andy McCulloch produced an impressive 58-goal haul – with the diminutive Phillips leading the national scoring charts with 36 goals.

[Previous page] Andy McCulloch, during the League Cup tie against Crystal Palace at Griffin Park

BRENTFORD

BRENTFORD FOOTBALL & SPORTS CLUB LTD.
Griffin Park, Braemar Road,
Brentford, Middlesex TW8 0NT.
Telephone: 01-560 2021
President: F A DAVIS
Directors: D TANA Chairman L F DAVEY W HALL
P H POND-JONES B J POYTON Hon. Treasurer
C W WHEATLEY
E J RADLEY-SMITH MS, FRCS, LRCP
Hon. Con. Surgeon
Chief Administrator/Secretary/Registrar
D R PIGGOTT
Manager BILL DODGIN
Physiotherapist EDDIE LYONS
Promotions Manager G W THOMAS
Club Medical Officer Dr. D D KINN
Life Vice-President F E EDWARDS
Annual Vice-Presidents C BEVAN W J OLD
RICK WAKEMAN

CRYSTAL PALACE

SATURDAY
13 AUGUST 1977
KICK OFF 3.00 PM

FOOTBALL LEAGUE
CUP 1st ROUND 1st LEG

OFFICIAL MATCHDAY MAGAZINE 15p

		P	W	D	L	F	A	W	D	L	F	A	Pts
1	Watford	46	18	4	1	44	14	12	7	4	41	24	71
2	Southend	46	15	5	3	46	18	10	5	8	20	21	60
3	Swansea	46	16	5	2	54	17	7	5	11	33	30	56
4	**Brentford**	**46**	**15**	**6**	**2**	**50**	**17**	**6**	**8**	**9**	**36**	**37**	**56**
5	Aldershot	46	15	8	0	45	16	4	8	11	22	31	54
6	Grimsby	46	14	6	3	30	15	7	5	11	27	36	53
7	Barnsley	46	15	4	4	44	20	3	10	10	17	29	50
8	Reading	46	12	7	4	33	23	6	7	10	22	29	50
9	Torquay	46	12	6	5	43	25	4	9	10	14	31	47
10	Northampton	46	9	8	6	32	30	8	5	10	31	38	47
11	Huddersfield	46	13	5	5	41	21	2	10	11	22	34	45
12	Doncaster	46	11	8	4	37	26	3	9	11	15	39	45
13	Wimbledon	46	8	11	4	39	26	6	5	12	27	41	44
14	Scunthorpe	46	12	6	5	31	14	2	10	11	19	41	44
15	Crewe	46	11	8	4	34	25	4	6	13	16	44	44
16	Newport	46	14	6	3	43	22	2	5	16	22	51	43
17	Bournemouth	46	12	6	5	28	20	2	9	12	13	31	43
18	Stockport	46	14	4	5	41	19	2	6	15	15	37	42
19	Darlington	46	10	8	5	31	22	4	5	14	21	37	41
20	Halifax Town	46	7	10	6	28	23	3	11	9	24	39	41
21	Hartlepool	46	12	4	7	34	29	3	3	17	17	55	37
22	York City	46	8	7	8	27	31	4	5	14	23	38	36
23	Southport	46	5	13	5	30	32	1	6	16	22	44	31
24	Rochdale	46	8	6	9	29	28	0	2	21	14	57	24

Total Home League Attendances   197,302
Average Home League Attendance   8,578
Highest Home League Attendance   14,496
Lowest Home League Attendance   5,492

League Position throughout the Season

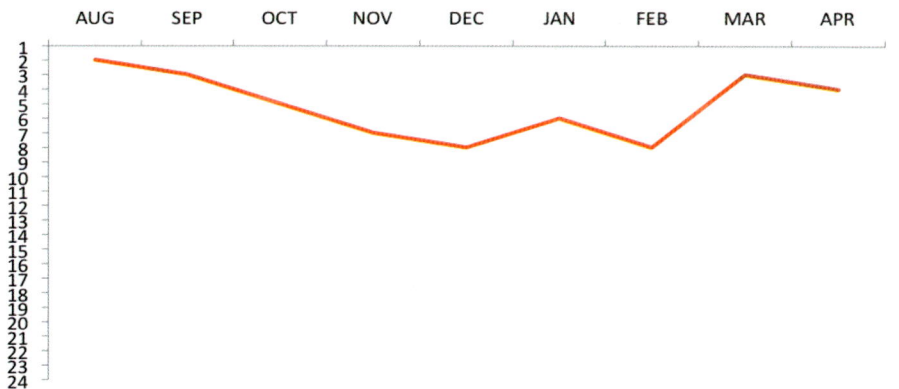

157

1977-78

Sat 13th August: **Crystal Palace (H) League Cup 1st Round**
Won 2-1   **Attendance: 8,929**

A match marred by fighting and disturbances on the terraces saw the higher-division visitors take a 32nd minute lead, although Gordon Sweetzer equalised 12 minutes into the second half – volleying in a bye-line centre from Steve Phillips. Sweetzer grabbed his second and the winner, in the 89th minute, when his diving header rocketed into the net from Paul Shrubb's curling cross.

Tue 16th August: **Crystal Palace (A) League Cup 1st Round**
Lost 1-5   **Attendance: 11,586**

A soft 5th minute goal gave the hosts the early impetus – the lead was doubled five minutes into the second half, before Andy McCulloch set up Steve Phillips to fire home on 66 minutes to level the aggregate scores. But the tie was settled with three goals in 11 minutes for the Second Division team. John Fraser deflected the ball into his own net in the 74th minute, then goals in the 83rd and 85th minutes gave the final scoreline a rather one-sided look.

Sat 20th August: **Northampton Town (H)**
Won 3-0   **Attendance: 5,492**

Despite a jittery first-half performance, Barry Lloyd hit a superb 34th minute goal – firing home from the edge of the box after exchanging passes with Jackie Graham – then Andy McCulloch dived low to net from Barry Lloyd's centre five minutes before the break. The second half was one-way traffic and, in the 50th minute, Andy McCulloch chipped the ball to Steve Phillips, who lobbed the keeper from fully 25 yards to seal an opening day league victory. The fixture was originally deemed an away game, but switched due to cricketing commitments at the County Ground.

Mon 22nd August: **Wimbledon (H)**
Won 4-1   **Attendance: 11,001**

The Football League newcomers were overwhelmed in a spectacular display of fluent, attacking football – Andy McCulloch headed home a curling right-wing centre from Steve Phillips after just five minute. Despite scoring an equaliser, the visitors went behind again in the 31st minute, when Jackie Graham's centre was headed down by Andy McCulloch for Steve Phillips to smash the ball into the net. The third goal arrived in the 54th minute, Sweetzer tapping in from three yards after Jackie Graham's shot had been parried by the keeper – the rout was completed on 78 minutes when McCulloch's header was fired home by the on-rushing Barry Lloyd.

Sat 27th August: **Reading (H)**
Drew 1-1   **Attendance: 8,176**

A game lacking in excitement saw both teams cancel each other out and the match seemed destined for a scoreless draw until a 35-yard 'out of the blue' thunderbolt gave the visitors the lead with just four minutes remaining. But, straight from the re-start, a Steve Phillips centre was handled and Gordon Sweetzer's penalty salvaged a point to the relief of the home fans.

Sat 3rd September: **Crewe Alexandra (A)**
Won 6-4   **Attendance: 1,837**

A crazy game was scoreless for 24 minutes, before the two teams embarked on a ten-goal scoring spree. A Nigel Smith error presented the hosts with the lead, but four minutes later, an Andy McCulloch centre saw a headed own-goal level the scores. Dave Carlton headed home a right-wing cross from Steve Phillips, only to see an almost immediate equaliser, then Gordon Sweetzer's 37th minute header was cancelled out once again by a 44th minute equaliser. The home side took a 4-3 lead in the 70th minute, only to be pegged back themselves within 60 seconds – Dave Carlton fired home from a Steve Phillips cross, before another Phillips centre, after 75 minutes, saw Gordon Sweetzer glance a header into the net. The sixth goal, with just two minutes remaining, completed a hat-trick for Sweetzer as he ran onto McCulloch's through-ball to slot low into the goal.

Sat 10th September: **Bournemouth (H)**
Drew 1-1   **Attendance: 7,702**

In a game of few chances, and little notable incident, a dull display produced a dreadful first half for the fans. That was until Steve Phillips, having been set up by Jackie Graham and Barry Lloyd, opened the scoring in the 52nd minute – his soft shot trickled past the keeper and into the net. But the visitors equalised after 70 minutes, when they beat the off-side trap to create their opening.

Tue 13th September: **Rochdale (A)**
Won 2-1   **Attendance: 1,164**

The scoreline failed to reflect a dominant performance, which oozed class – a display of controlled, attacking football. Andy McCulloch opened the scoring in the 31st minute, when his back-header was fumbled into the net by the keeper after Pat Kruse had flicked on a corner and, although the hosts equalised after 51 minutes, it took just nine more to restore the lead – Steve Phillips' cross following a corner was headed firmly home by Pat Kruse.

Sat 17th September: **Doncaster Rovers (A)**
Lost 1-3   **Attendance: 3,044**

The unbeaten start to the league season came to an end in controversial circumstances and, after the home side had taken a 10th minute lead, the game came to life in the second half when the deficit became 0-2 after 48 minutes. Just moments later the referee missed a blatant punch off of the goal-line by a home defender, following an Andy McCulloch header, and in the ensuing protest Gordon Sweetzer was shown a red card. Steve Phillips pulled a goal back in the 70th minute, when he ran half the length of the pitch to slot past the keeper, but the hosts sealed the game three minutes later.

Sat 24th September: **Scunthorpe United (H)**
Won 2-0   **Attendance: 6,115**

Despite dominating the opening half, a toothless display in front of goal kept the scoreline goal-less until the 62nd minute when Andy McCulloch netted with a half-volley from 20 yards. Sweeping rain made conditions difficult after the opener, but the game was settled late on when Barry Lloyd's accurate through-ball was nudged on by Jackie Graham for Steve Phillips to beat the advancing keeper.

Mon 26th September: **Stockport County (A)**
Drew 1-1   **Attendance: 4,121**

The opening goal arrived mid-way through the first-half, Gordon Sweetzer beating the keeper to a seemingly well-judged back pass, then netting from an acute angle. However, seven minutes later, Sweetzer was felled by the keeper while attempting to round him for a second time but the same player saw his spot-kick saved. County equalised in the 75th minute, then applied extreme pressure for the remainder of the game but failed to snatch a winner.

Sat 1st October: **Halifax Town (H)**
Won 4-1   **Attendance: 6,239**

Despite the comprehensive scoreline it was a laboured performance against opposition who packed their defence. Halifax held out until the 38th minute, when Steve Phillips netted from 15 yards after Andy McCulloch's header had come back off the foot of the post, but the lead was doubled after 49 minutes, when Steve Phillips scored a penalty, awarded for a push on McCulloch and, although the visitors pulled a goal back three minutes later, the win was sealed in the 80th minute when Jackie Graham fired home from a direct free-kick on the edge of the box. Barry Lloyd put the icing on the cake in the 87th minute, scoring from close range after McCulloch's diving header had been parried.

Mon 3rd October: **Watford (H)**
Lost 0-3   **Attendance: 14,496**

A first home defeat since February came courtesy of a comprehensive beating by the local visitors, who scored in the 19th and 22nd minutes, then went on to control the remainder of the game – adding a third in the 80th minute to clinch the top-of-the-table clash played in front of a bumper crowd.

Sat 8th October: **Torquay United (A)**
Lost 1-2   **Attendance: 2,538**

A game of two-halves saw Brentford control proceedings in the opening period – and the display was rewarded in the 31st minute when John Fraser's right-wing run ended with a pass to Gordon Sweetzer whose shot was parried, leaving Andy McCulloch with a simple tap-in. The second period was a different affair and a transformed home side scored after 61 and 79 minutes, as they threatened to run riot – Torquay deservedly took the points.

Sat 15th October: **Southport (H)**
Drew 0-0   **Attendance: 6,141**

In a game bereft of excitement or much entertainment, the lowly visitors were seen to pack eight or nine players behind the ball, and the inability to break them down resulted in bouts of slow hand-clapping from frustrated Bees supporters who'd witnessed the woodwork being struck three times, but little else of note.

Sat 22nd October: **Hartlepool United (A)**
Lost 1-3   **Attendance: 2,470**

A third defeat in four matches came courtesy of tremendous 30-yard free-kick in the 42nd minute – then a decisive second headed goal just minutes after the interval. Steve Phillips pulled a goal back midway through the second period, but the hosts sealed the points with another headed effort.

[Right] Pat Kruse, Steve Phillips and Andy McCulloch compete in the FA Cup match against non-League Folkestone

Sat 29th October: **Southend United (H)**
Won 1-0   **Attendance: 7,435**

A dull first-half was more than compensated for by a tense, exciting second period from the two promotion rivals. The all-important goal arrived in the 70th minute, when Steve Phillips crossed the ball from the right flank and Jackie Graham sent a powerful shot goalwards – the keeper could only parry the ball and, as it trickled along the goal-line, Andy McCulloch dived in to prod home.

Sat 5th November: **York City (H)**
Won 1-0   **Attendance: 5,985**

After taking a 9th minute lead, when Steve Phillips calmly chested the ball down and drove home after Paul Shrubb's 25-yard effort had cannoned off the underside of the crossbar, a solid display was almost undone when the visitors pressed forward in the final stages and almost grabbed an equalising goal.

Sat 12th November: **Barnsley (A)**
Drew 0-0   **Attendance: 4,209**

Continuous rain, then a violent hailstorm and swirling winds, made playing conditions almost impossible – but an impressive and determined all-round team performance was enough to earn a deserved and vital point in another top of the table clash.

Sat 19th November: **Swansea City (H)**
Lost 0-2   **Attendance: 6,337**

A dogged performance from the Welsh visitors proved effective as their tough-arm tactics earned the points – despite being reduced to 10-men for the last half hour. The opening goal came in the 11th minute, when a poor decision by Pat Kruse, and a weak challenge from John Fraser, enabled an opening to be created, then three

minutes later, it was 2-0, when Pat Kruse was again beaten to the ball. There was no way back after that.

Sat 26th November: **Folkestone (H) FA Cup 1st Round**
Won 2-0   **Attendance: 5,981**

The non-League part-timers made life difficult throughout a tricky Cup-tie and, after the opening goal arrived in the 32nd minute, when a clearance from Doug Allder was fired against the shins of Steve Phillips and rebounded into the net, a host of further chances were squandered. The tie was settled in the 71st minute, when a long-range, swerving drive from Doug Allder came back off the chest of the keeper and Steve Phillips netted with ease.

Fri 2nd December: **Darlington (A)**
Won 3-1   **Attendance: 2,058**

An early, 4th minute goal for Darlington, following a misjudgement from Len Bond, got the game off to a poor start, but a magnificent second-half performance fully merited both points. In the 54th minute the equaliser arrived when Andy McCulloch fired home, after blocked efforts from Jackie Graham and Dave Carlton, then in the 70th minute, Gary Rolph came on as substitute and, with almost his first touch, he crossed from the right for Steve Phillips to net after the keeper had parried the centre. A third goal came in the dying seconds – Andy McCulloch chasing a back-pass and the ball ricochetted off the keeper to Gary Rolph, who calmly slotted the ball into an empty net.

Sat 10th December: **Grimsby Town (H)**
Won 3-1   **Attendance: 5,762**

Another impressive display saw The Bees score after only 6 minutes – Barry Lloyd found Andy McCulloch on the edge of the penalty box and he fired the ball firmly into the net. The visitors grabbed an equaliser four minutes into the second half, before Steve Phillips scored on the hour with a superb lob over a crowded penalty area and into the net, after McCulloch's shot had been blocked.

The clinching goal arrived in the 81st minute, when a Willie Graham corner was headed down by Steve Phillips, and Andy McCulloch forced the ball over the line.

Sat 17th December: **Swindon Town (A) FA Cup 2nd Round**
Lost 1-2   **Attendance: 8,447**

Despite facing opposition from a higher division, a wonderful display of attacking football, matched with skill and determination, produced a performance to be proud of for the 1,000 travelling fans. A 60th minute penalty from Steve Phillips, after Willie Graham had been tripped, was the very least the display deserved. The hosts equalised after 77 minutes, then cruelly snatched an undeserved victory with just three minutes remaining.

Mon 26th December: **Aldershot (A)**
Lost 0-1   **Attendance: 8,175**

A soft, first-half goal was conceded when Len Bond mis-punched a cross onto the head of a home striker, and the promotion clash was all but settled when Andy McCulloch was sent-off in the 57th minute for an alleged head-butt, following an ugly clash with opponent Joe Joplin, who escaped punishment.

Tue 27th December: **Newport County (H)**
Drew 3-3   **Attendance: 8,972**

The Bees played some delightful football and a two-goal lead was established early on – the first after 18 minutes when Barry Lloyd's through-ball released Gordon Sweetzer, who was then hauled down in the area – Steve Phillips converted the penalty. A second goal came ten minutes later, when Lloyd again set up Doug Allder, who clipped the ball over the head of the stranded keeper. But the visitors roared back to level with two goals before half-time, then took the lead in the 75th minute. Brentford levelled, though, when Tommy Baldwin coolly lobbed home from outside the penalty box to earn a point with seven minutes to go.

Sat 31st December: York City (A)
Lost 2-3 Attendance: 2,329

An early York goal was equalised 15 minutes later when, from Gordon Sweetzer's cross, Andy McCulloch held off several challenges to score. Three minutes after the break, the hosts missed a penalty, awarded for handball by Pat Kruse, and they were punished for the miss when Gordon Sweetzer's header was knocked off the goal-line for Steve Phillips to score the rebound from a corner. The lead lasted only four minutes and the home side then secured the win with their third goal in the 75th minute.

Mon 2nd January: Huddersfield Town (H)
Drew 1-1 Attendance: 9,475

Huddersfield's visit to Griffin Park lacked the excitement of the previous few matches, and after falling behind to a tremendous 40-yard strike, an equaliser arrived in the 37th minute, when Andy McCulloch knocked the ball back to Paul Shrubb, who powerfully shot home from 12 yards.

Sat 7th January: Wimbledon (A)
Drew 1-1 Attendance: 5,411

Despite dominating much of the opening 45 minutes against lowly-placed opposition, and taking a 29th minute lead when Doug Allder's low, hard cross was nudged on by Steve Phillips for Gordon Sweetzer to prod the ball into the net from six yards, the home side pressed throughout and capitalised during a more even second half with a 70th minute equaliser to take a share of the spoils.

Sat 14th January: Northampton Town (A)
Drew 2-2 Attendance: 4,050

A disastrous opening 20 minutes saw Northampton race into a two-goal lead, but the turning point came when the hosts missed a penalty. This proved to be the catalyst for a determined fight back, started in the 56th minute, when a goalmouth scramble, in which Steve Phillips had three efforts blocked, ended when Andy McCul-

loch headed into the net. A further spell of intense pressure was rewarded 19 minutes later when another McCulloch goal, courtesy of a rasping header from a Doug Allder cross, levelled the scores.

Sat 28th January: Crewe Alexandra (H)
Won 5-1 Attendance: 6,871

A 5th minute opener from Alex, and a poor opening 20 minutes, gave little indication of what was to follow – despite a 22nd minute equaliser, when a Nigel Smith free-kick was rocketed into the net from the head of Andy McCulloch. The second half deluge of goals started in the 47th minute, when Steve Phillips neatly headed Doug Allder's centre beyond the keeper and he grabbed his second eight minutes later, converting a penalty awarded for handball. The fourth goal came in the 73rd minute from a superb diving header by Willie Graham, then two minutes later, the rout was completed with a Gordon Sweetzer header.

Sat 4th February: Bournemouth (A)
Lost 2-3 Attendance: 3,417

Atrocious weather conditions contributed to an error-ridden game, and the home side's 41st minute goal was a farcical affair – Doug Allder and Len Bond collided in the muddy penalty-area, presenting an open goal for a lead which was doubled soon afterwards. Pat Kruse's own goal presented the hosts with their third on the hour mark, but a late fight-back was sparked by Andy McCulloch's 72nd minute scrambled effort, following a Mike Allen cross into the penalty box. With ten minutes remaining Danis Salman's right-wing centre was headed home by Gordon Sweetzer, but a deserved equaliser failed to materialise before the final whistle.

Sat 25th February: Halifax Town (A)
Drew 1-1 Attendance: 1,764

A fortuitous goal in the first minute was credited to Dave Carlton – Doug Allder's cross smacked into his face from an attempted clearance and the ball rebounded into the net. The home side equalised

163

in the 15th minute when a double-blunder by Len Bond gifted the hosts a goal, but Bond made amends after 52 minutes when he superbly saved a penalty to ensure a valuable away point.

Sat 4th March: **Torquay United (H)**
Won 3-0   **Attendance: 6,551**

A poor opposition was outclassed throughout and fast attractive football brought two first-half goals, the first of which saw neat midfield play set up Andy McCulloch to round two defenders and cross for Gordon Sweetzer to convert from six yards whilst the second goal was courtesy of an opposing defender who deflected Doug Allder's low cross past his own goalkeeper. The solitary second-half strike came from the penalty spot after McCulloch was fouled by the keeper and Sweetzer netted his second.

Mon 6th March: **Rochdale (H)**
Won 4-0   **Attendance: 7,215**

The crowd left Griffin Park buzzing after a scintillating display had overwhelmed the visitors. Dale fell behind after 15 minutes, when Willie Graham and Gordon Sweetzer combined brilliantly, before Danis Salman crossed from the touchline and Andy McCulloch headed home powerfully. Steve Phillips missed a penalty before striking the second, directly from a 25-yard, curling, free-kick. A wave of attacks preceded the third goal in the 58th minute – Doug Allder's cross was headed home by Gordon Sweezter and a late fourth came when Barry Lloyd latched on to a McCulloch chest-down and rocketed the ball high into the net.

Sat 11th March: **Southport (A)**
Won 3-1   **Attendance: 1,691**

An evenly-matched first-half came to a close when Phillips opened the scoring after a neat exchange of passes with McCulloch. The hosts grabbed a deserved equaliser after 70 minutes, but just six minutes later, Phillips netted a goal almost identical to his first and returned the compliment to his strike partner in the 86th minute, crossing low for McCulloch to seal the win.

Tue 14th March: **Scunthorpe United (A)**
Drew 1-1   **Attendance: 3,053**

Two differing styles of play made for a poor spectacle – one that the hosts seemed set to win after taking a first-half lead. But a determined and dogged performance brought its reward in the 86th minute – Dave Carlton's cross was headed home by substitute John Murray, via a fumble from the goalkeeper.

Sat 18th March: **Hartlepool United (H)**
Won 2-0   **Attendance: 7,499**

Brentford made hard work of beating a poor opposition and were far from convincing – although the first-half was lit up by a superb diving header from McCulloch to open the scoring. Steve Phillips sealed the crucial victory with a 25-yard free-kick mid-way through the second period.

Fri 24th March: **Southend United (A)**
Lost 1-2   **Attendance: 11,810**

The Good Friday promotion clash ended in defeat, despite Steve Phillips opening the scoring in the 24th minute, netting from a superb Doug Allder cross. But after dominating proceedings, a miscue from Jackie Graham on the stroke of half-time, enabled Southend to go in level at the break. Just 58 seconds into the second period Barry Tucker headed a harmless-looking centre past Len Bond and into his own net, to gift the game to the hosts.

Sat 25th March: **Newport County (A)**
Won 2-1   **Attendance: 4,953**

An outstanding performance saw County suffer their first defeat on their own ground for 11 months, despite taking a 67th minute lead. Substitute Jackie Graham struck a glorious 20-yard equaliser and,

after Len Bond had produced a string of magnificent saves, Andy McCulloch calmly controlled a cross from Doug Allder and shot past the goalkeeper to win the game in the 86th minute.

Mon 27th March: **Aldershot (H)**
Won 2-0   **Attendance: 12,579**

A brilliant through-ball from Mike Allen enabled Steve Phillips to lob over the keeper in the 32nd minute and give the home side an advantage, which was doubled in the second-half when a penalty was awarded for handball – Phillips netted his 26th goal of the season to see off another promotion rival.

Sat 1st April: **Huddersfield Town (A)**
Won 3-1   **Attendance: 6,345**

The home side led 1-0 at half-time, courtesy of a 36th minute goal and the game could have been out of sight but for a string of fine saves from Len Bond. Steve Phillips equalised after 48 minutes and scored again seven minutes later, when he converted a bye-line centre from Andy McCulloch. This prompted intense pressure from the hosts, but a late move involving Jackie Graham and Doug Allder ended with Phillips prodding the ball home, to notch a hat-trick and seal a fortunate, yet critical, win.

Mon 3rd April: **Stockport County (H)**
Won 4-0   **Attendance: 11,674**

Thrills, spills and action throughout produced a superb evening's entertainment – the scoring commenced after just three minutes when a Barry Tucker through-ball was flicked on by Andy McCulloch for Steve Phillips to hammer home. Phillips snatched his second in first-half stoppage time when he tapped in from a left-wing centre by McCulloch. A Steve Phillips header rebounded off of the keeper's legs for McCulloch to score mid-way through the second-half and the pair combined again in the 70th minute, when Pat Kruse and Phillips set-up McCulloch for his second strike.

Sat 8th April: **Barnsley (H)**
Won 2-0   **Attendance: 12,139**

Another promotion rival was beaten – Doug Allder opened the scoring after 15 minutes, when he latched onto a through-ball from Andy McCulloch, shrugged off two challenges and fired the ball left-footed past the keeper. The second, and decisive, goal came in the 45th minute, after Steve Phillips was somewhat harshly adjudged to have been fouled in the penalty-box – he stepped up to thump home his 32nd goal of the season.

Wed 12th April: **Reading (A)**
Drew 0-0   **Attendance: 7,384**

A hard-fought game saw both sides share control of one half each – but goal-scoring chances were few and far between. There was certainly more action on the terraces than on the pitch, with scuffles breaking out throughout the course of the 90 minutes.

Sat 15th April: **Swansea City (A)**
Lost 1-2   **Attendance: 16,152**

Another top of the table clash got off to a calamitous start – Pat Kruse misjudged a long ball allowing the home side to go in front in the 17th minute, a lead that was doubled on 34 minutes thanks to a tremendous strike. Willie Graham scored in the 83rd minute when he flicked home a Steve Phillips pass, but it proved no more than a consolation, on a day when results elsewhere limited any serious damage to promotion prospects.

Tue 18th April: **Doncaster Rovers (H)**
Drew 2-2   **Attendance: 11,512**

A tense night saw Rovers take a first-half lead, but a dramatic turn-around at the break produced the equalizer after 53 minutes, when a

BOURNEMOUTH BASHING
GRIMSBY GRINDING
SWANSEA SLAYING
BARNSLEY BEATING
TORQUAY TAKING
READING RUNNING
HUDDERSFIELD HOUNDING
SOUTHEND SLAUGHTERING
ALDERSHOT ANNIHILATING
WATFORD WALLOPING

'IT 'EM ON THE 'EAD!!!'

PROMOTION WINNING
BRENTFORD

dashing run by Doug Allder took him to the bye-line and his cross was met by Steve Phillips, who swivelled and rifled in a shot off the post. Just three minutes later it was 2-1 – Phillips scored again, this time glancing home a centre from Willie Graham. The points looked to have been won, but the visitors grabbed a 92nd minute spoiler to dash the premature promotion celebrations.

Sat 22nd April: **Darlington (H)**
Won 2-0   **Attendance: 11,934**

A diving header by Andy McCulloch, following great work by Willie Graham, on 16 minutes settled the nerves, and when Steve Phillips converted a 39th minute penalty, after a foul on Doug Allder, the points were sealed. The second-half was played out without further incident, until the referee's final whistle signalled that promotion had been achieved and the celebrations commenced.

Tue 25th April: **Watford (A)**
Drew 1-1   **Attendance: 16,544**

More than 5,000 Brentford supporters continued the promotion party at the home of the champions, who took a 42nd minute lead when Willie Graham mis-controlled a centre to gift an easy opener – but Andy McCulloch ensured that the celebrations continued when he side-footed home a Willie Graham corner in the 84th minute.

Sat 29th April: **Grimsby Town (A)**
Lost 1-2   **Attendance: 4,712**

A triumphant season ended in anti-climax – a uninspiring game saw the home side take a 4th minute lead, before Steve Phillips scored his 36th goal of the campaign after half an hour. The hosts won the game in the 85th minute, but it mattered little as a The Bees waved farewell to Division Four.

DODGIN NETS HIS KEEPER

PRE-SEASON

Fred Callaghan left the club to seek a full-time management post.

Former Fulham captain, Barry Lloyd, aged 28, was signed from Hereford United on a free transfer.

18-year old striker Terry Glynn, released by Orient, was offered a one-month trial.

Danis Salman signed full professional terms as a 17-year old.

Terry Johnson had his contract cancelled by mutual consent to enable him to return to the north-east.

Bill Dodgin made several unsuccessful bids to bring in a new goalkeeper and attempts to sign Torquay's Terry Lee, Aldershot's Glen Johnson and former Swindon keeper Jim Barron, were all fruitless.

AUGUST 1977

• Goalkeeper Len Bond was signed from Bristol City, the 23-year old costing a reported £8,000 transfer fee.
• 18-year old midfielder, Willie Graham, signed on a free transfer from Northampton Town following a trial period.
• Johnny Ayris, a 24-year old winger freed by West Ham United, was signed on one month's trial.
• The home match with Wimbledon produced record gate receipts of £8,451.
• Crowd disturbances marred the home League Cup tie with Crystal Palace.
• The Kuwait national team visited Griffin Park for a friendly match as part of their World Cup preparation.

SEPTEMBER 1977

• Both Terry Glynn and Johnny Ayris left the club at the end of their trial periods.

Brentford to resist bids for stars

By Nicholas Clarke

BRENTFORD manager Bill Dodgin will resist offers for his star players.

"No one will leave this club unless I want them to go" Dodgin told the annual meeting at Brentford Supporter's Association at Griffin Park last night.

"The directors will not force me to sell any players as has happened at other clubs.

"But I could not stop players like Gordon Sweetzer and Pat Kruse going to really big clubs if they really wanted to, and if the right offers came.

"If I had stopped Neal going to Liverpool when I was at Northampton I would have had it on my conscience all my life."

On the question of hooliganism, director Colin Wheatley said he felt, that "it is not a question of if fences are put up — it's when."

He added: "We will do what is necessary to keep the friendly informality at Griffin Park as long as possible.

"We are buiding up a body of stewards to help with crowd control."

Presenting the association chairman's report David Nott said he was fearful for the coming season.

"I think we will have a good season and feel it in my boots that we will win promotion," he said.

"And with the success will come bigger crowds and a bigger hooliganism element.

"We must set an example, weed out transgressors and not be afraid to name names.

"We have had trouble on away trips. It is difficult to pinpoint the people responsible once they have left the train or coach.

"We don't want hooligans as members and intend to have more stewards on trains."

On a financial note, Nott commented on the £7,808 profit with £5,100 being given to the football club.

He warned: "In these inflationary times we cannot afford to be complacent — it took a lot of hard work to reach last season's figure and to improve on it will be very difficult."

● Dodgin told the association that he was not appointing a successor to coach Fred Callaghan.

"I have enough senior players to help me in this field," he said.

● Gordon Sweetzer was sent off in the defeat at Doncaster and received a one match suspension.

OCTOBER 1977

● Former Millwall winger, 25-year old Doug Allder, was signed on a one-month trial following a similar period at Watford.
● Unsuccessful bids were made to sign Dave Moreline from Reading (£15,000) and Les Barrett from Fulham (£10,000).
● Tommy Baldwin was signed on non-contract terms; the 32-year old former Chelsea striker had been playing for the reserves.
● A 28-day trial was offered to Robbie Anderson who had been released by Tottenham Hotspur.
● Gordon Sweetzer required an operation to remove a cyst from a knee cartilage and would be absent for several weeks.
● Record gate receipts were again taken from the clash with Watford (£11,160).

NOVEMBER 1977

● Doug Allder signed a full contract following his successful trial.
● Robbie Anderson was not offered a contract and left the club.
● Trials were offered to Derek Williams, a winger from Epsom, and striker, Alan Easterbrook, from St Albans.

DECEMBER 1977

● Andy McCulloch was sent off in the Boxing Day defeat at Aldershot.
● Gordon Sweetzer returned after his knee operation but John Fraser, Dave Carlton and Jackie Graham all suffered long-term injury problems.
● At the club's AGM, Peter Pond-Jones stood down as a director and was replaced by Ron Blindell, who had previously resigned from the board in September 1976.

Why I sold Sweetzer — Bees boss

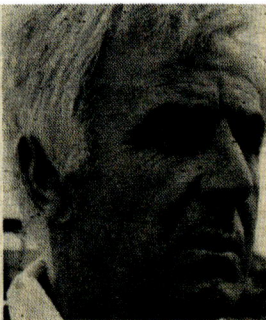

● Bill Dodgin

BRENTFORD boss Bill Dodgin this week revealed why he sold striker Gordon Sweetzer to third division Cambridge for £30,000.

Sweetzer had hit 44 goals in 74 appearances for the Bees and was a great favourite with the Griffin Park crowd.

But Dodgin decided to let him go when former Brentford boss John Docherty, the man who took Sweetzer to Griffin Park made a forth bid of £30,000 before last week's transfer deadline.

WANTED

Dodgin said: "I am sure I did the right thing.

"Some people wanted me to keep him just because he scored goals. But often he did little else.

"And he tended to go in the same positions as Andy McCulloch up front.

"Unitl I came I think he'd got seven goals in 29 games. And I'm sure it was only the players that I got around him that made the difference and helped him get more goals.

"Besides he only played in about half the games because of injury."

"We had a tentative offer from America but Cambridge were the only side to come in with firm bids.

"And I thought their last offer was good enough, especially with freedom of contract coming up, when we probably wouldn't have got so much for him.

"The player wanted away and the fee was right for us."

And the Bees didn't seem to miss Sweetzer on Saturday with replacement Steve Phillips hitting two goals in a 3-1 win at Southport — their first away victory in three months.

Dodgin joked: "Stevie didn't do bad as a replacement did he — scroing two and making the other for Andy McCulloch.

"I feel he is better playing further forward — he's scored 22 goals already this season — and John Murray came on as substitute and looked lively up front."

Phillips played as striker on Saturday after a spell in midfield with Jackie Graham returning after a five-week lay-off. Murray was signed

from Reading for only £3,000 last month and gives the Bees cover up front.

And, barring injury at Scunthorpe on Tuesday night, the Bees are likely to be unchanged for Saturday's home match with struggling Hartlepool.

Victory at Southport on Saturday kept up their promotion hopes by taking them into fourth place. And a win against Hartlepool would be a big boost before a tough spell of matches.

SILLY

Dodgin said: "We played well on Saturday. They had four at the back plus a sweeper but we might have had more goals.

"Len Bond made a couple of good saves and we have stopped throwing away silly goals away from home.

"There's more common sense now with Shrubbie and Barry Tucker at the back. And it's rubbing off on people like Len Bond and Pat Kruse."

JANUARY 1978

• The fixture at Reading was postponed as a result of bad weather.
• Paul Walker signed as a professional on completion of his apprenticeship at the age of 18.
• Alan Easterbrook and Derek Williams were not offered contracts, but were given the opportunity to remain with the club on a non-contract basis.
• Two former players, Bobby Childs and Dave Metchick, were playing for the reserves on a non-contract basis to help the youngsters.
• Club President and former chairman, Frank Davis, who first joined the board in 1928, died aged 86.

FEBRUARY 1978

• The severe winter weather caused the postponement of the games with Doncaster (home) and Scunthorpe (away).
• 25-year old Welsh full-back, Barry Tucker, signed from Northampton Town for a reported £10,000 transfer fee.
• A nominal fee was paid to Reading for 29-year old striker John Murray.
• A £30,000 bid for Andy McCulloch from Mansfield Town was rejected.
• Queens Park Rangers made an enquiry about the availability of Danis Salman.
• Dave Silman was signed on a trial basis, having been released by Wolverhampton Wanderers – Malcolm Folley joined the club from Guildford City for a trial, on the recommendation of Paul Shrubb.

Rock toast to a hat-trick

CHEERS, Stevie! Rock superstar and Brentford vice-president Rick Wakeman hands over one of 12 bottles of scotch to the Bees' scoring sensation Steve Phillips before Saturday's promotion clash with Barnsley at Griffin Park.

While Rick is a smash hit with the country's music fans Steve is making his own headlines on the goal trail this season and he is currently leading marksman in the Football League.

He received this latest award after scoring a hat-trick in the 3-1 win at Huddersfield earlier this month. Another goal — his 32nd of the season — came in Brentford's 2-0 win on Saturday.

Report and pictures — page 46.

● A new sports complex costing £1 million is being planned by Brentford Football Club.

The club says it wants to develop its ground at Griffin Park to provide 25,000 seats and room for 15,000 standing.

Brentford, who are all set to reach the third division this year, also want to provide facilities for squash, badminton and tennis.

Chairman Dan Tana said: "It is at a very early stage and we have to draw up detailed plans and then get planning permission. But I foresee the possibility of a new sporting complex embracing all other sports."

Dodgin denies £100,000 Spurs bid

BRENTFORD boss Bill Dodgin has denied reports of a £100,000 bid from Tottenham for leading scored Steve Phillips.

Phillips, 23, has finished up as the leading scorer in the country with 36 goals this season. And several leading clubs including Spurs and West Ham have watched him this season.

But Dodgin said yesterday: "We haven't heard a thing from Tottenham. I know Bill Nicholson was here the other week but nothing came out of it."

And only last week Phillips told Gazette Sport: "Frankly I wouldn't want to go anywhere else apart from Brentford. I'm happy here and that means a lot to me."

Ironically Phillips was born just down the road from Tottenham — in Edmonton — and he supported Spurs as a kid.

But clearly at the moment he is happy to stay at Brentford and they want to keep him.

Phillips and manager Dodgin have a great mutual respect for one another — Phillips played under him before at Northampton — and that could be the key factor in keeping him at Griffin Park.

Dodgin also names his retained list this week. Defender Steve Aylott will probably be freed and Mike Allen and Nigel Smith may also be released — but they are the only likely changes.

The Bees ended off their season with a disappointing 2-1 defeat at Grimsby on Saturday.

They fell a goal behind after only five minutes. And although Phillips grabbed an equaliser just before the break a defensive mix-up cost them a point five minutes from time.

And — more important — it also meant the Bees finish in fourth promotion spot and not third after Swansea won at home to Halifax.

BAD

Dodgin said afterwards: "It wasn't a bad display and I thought we deserved a point, But then we gave the goal away right near the end.

"They had looked quite impressive early on but we got more into it as the game wore on. And I thought we'd got a point until that defensive mix-up."

Phillips lone goal took him to 36 — so he finishes one short of the Bees record for goals in a season held jointly by Jack Holliday and Jim Towers.

The Bees had testimonials scheduled at Staines on Tuesday and then Folkestone last night (Wednesday). And they also had a team in the Hendon Five-A-Sides at Wembley last night.

Then next Tuesday they have the Alan Nelmes testimonial match before a well-earned break in Guernsey.

However one player who won't be going to Guernsey is double-winning Player of the Year Andy McCulloch.

Andy, who hit 22 goals this season, flew off to America yesterday (Wednesday) to play for Oaklands in the States.

Before flying out Andy said: "It'll be a great experience going to the States and playing out there.

"I don't think Oaklands are that good a side so they probably won't reach the play-off stage. And that means I'll be back for the start of next season at Brentford."

The only sour note

CHELSEA'S notorious hooligan element threatened the friendly atmosphere of Griffin Park on Tuesday.

During a thoroughly sporting and entertaining evening about 400 Chelsea fans invaded the Royal Oak end of the ground forcing Brentford fans to run to safety.

Fighting seemed to have been their only objective and there was surely no more damming evidence that these louts have absolutely no interest in football.

A chilling note was added to the happy atmosphere early on when the public address system called out:

"We welcome the players, officials and supporters of Chelsea Football Club — the true supporters that is, not the mindless idiots behind the goalposts spoiling for trouble. If Brentford supporters want to watch the game in peace then they should move away from behind the goal."

One true Chelsea fan, a regular at home and away matches said afterwards:

"They are not true Chelsea fans. I doubt if many of them even go to the home games. They are youngsters trying to act big. What was the point of starting trouble at Brentford? Lots of Chelsea fans come to Griffin Park when Chelsea aren't playing. We like the Club."

It is a sad commentary on the times we live in that an ambitious club like Brentford should perhaps already dread the day when they will be playing in the top two divisions.

Long and short of it

■ Diminutive Bees striker Steve Phillips dwarfed by Chelsea's Mickey Droy.

Brentford lose a loyal friend

MR. FRANK DAVIS, one of Brentford's and football's great men, died in West Middlesex Hospital on Tuesday evening last week at the age of 86.

Frank was a loyal, dedicated servant to Brentford and the game as a whole and his death brings to the end an era at Griffin Park.

His love for the club was amply demonstrated in 1967 when he stood firm against the QPR take-over bid.

His relationship with the club began in 1902 — before Brentford even played at Griffin Park. He was then a programme seller but "rose through the ranks" to become a director in 1929. In 1935 he became vice-chairman and with his brother Harry was the major force behind the club's rise to the First Division.

He remained on the board until 1974, an incredible 45 years, before moving to president. Outside Griffin Park he became an FA councillor and was honoured for his service to the game by being made an FA life member.

Even at his advanced age Frank watched Bees play at every opportunity. His last away game was at Swindon in September. He seldom captured the headlines but will always be remembered as a man who brought dignity to the game he loved.

MARCH 1978

- Gordon Sweetzer, with 14 goals in 20 games, was sold to Cambridge United for a reported £30,000 transfer fee.
- 18-year old Gary Rolph was offered full professional terms at the end of his apprenticeship.
- Dave Silman had his trial period extended for another month but Malcolm Folley was released.

- Record receipts were received from the Aldershot clash (£11,430).
- Bill Dodgin was named as Bell's Manager of the Month for the Fourth Division.

APRIL 1978

- Promotion was secured in the home win against Darlington and Bill Dodgin declared it to be his most satisfying moment in football.
- 28-year old defender Dave Silman signed a one year contract following his extended trial period.

MAY 1978

- Barry Lloyd and Steve Aylott were given free transfers.
- Alan Nelmes's testimonial match, during which he scored a trademark own goal, netted him receipts of £6,800.

The Jackie Graham column

THAT magic moment when the Aldershot result was announced on Saturday moved me very close to tears.

All our hard work throughout the season was rewarded in that one minute and the way everyone's faces sparkled and lit up was tremendous.

It is the younger players I really feel for. When we won promotion in 1971/72 I was one of the less experienced and it was rather surprising to see the older lads so emotional and excited.

This time I was like that whereas I don't think it will really hit the younger ones like Willie Graham and Danis Salman until they read about it in the papers.

Tommy Baldwin has been a fantastic help and influence during the season. He was particularly helpful in getting players to relax.

And others like John Fraser and Mickey Allen have also played important roles. Even though both were forced out of the side by injuries they continued to play an important part.

When we went up last time we had not been preparing for the higher division. He only had a squad of 15 players and when we sold John O'Mara he wasn't replaced.

This time is a completely different story. Bill knows what has to be done and he isn't afraid to do it. This is why I'm confident we won't finish next season lower than midway up the table.

THREE cheers for Bees!

A special salute to promotion '78

Now watch us go says Bill

PROMOTION to Division Three is just the start of great things to come — that's the message from Bees boss Bill Dodgin.

Dodgin promised promotion by the end of the 1977-78 season when he took over at Griffin Park in September 1976. He's over that first step with flying colours and reckons the club are on their way to emulate those First Division glory days of the 1930s.

Dodgin said: "I've known what this club could achieve ever since my dad was manager here.

"Now I know we can go all the way to the top.

"Funnily enough I was at QPR at the time of the take-over talks with Brentford back in 1967 and I couldn't wait to get down here."

"I knew what the club was like and was so excited at the prospect."

But Brentford withstood the take-over bid and Dodgin had to wait another nine years before he moved into Griffin Park.

Now he's making up for lost time and can't wait to see the Bees overtaking Rangers.

He said: "When I started off at QPR it was almost the same situation as when I took over here two years ago. Yet Rangers only had a hard core of 4,000 support-

ers while we had a basic support of about 6,000 when I took over at Brentford.

"The catchment area here is tremendous and we can top Rangers as a football club.

"Brentford will always be one of the big clubs in London."

And Dodgin reckons the Bees only need two or three more players to shine in the Third Division next season — then it's up to him to help them up again.

He said: "Look at that game near the end of the season. I know we were going for promotion but we had almost 12,000 against Stockport County.

"That many to see Stockport — it's marvellous.

"And the reception the lads got throughout the game and at the end was tremendous.

"Once you start getting numbers like that in you've got no excuses.

"It's going to be my job to buy and sell players I think I want or can let go.

"There's naturally been talk about letting Steve Phillips go after all the goals he's got but I wouldn't sell him unless he wanted to go.

"I couldn't afford to let him go either."

Dodgin could find clubs coming in for other players like England youth interna-

tional defender Danny Salman and outstanding centreback Pat Kruse. But he hopes to keep them happy by playing in a successful side — and by giving the players a wage rise.

He said: "We've got to offer them what I think we can reasonably afford.

"The gates we have got justify paying them more and that's something that will be sorted out during the close season."

And as far as playing goes, Dodgin reckons he can keep the Bees on the success trail next season.

He said: "I think we probably need two or three more players to strengthen the squad. But basically it's down to telling the players they can play in a higher division and getting them in a confident mood from the start of the season.

"You probably find clubs have a couple of better players in the third but that's all."

And looking back on the present season Dodgin points to the signing of full-back Barry Tucker for £10,000 from former club Northampton as his trump card in the promotion push.

Tucker has added steel, aggression and most of all confidence to the Bees' defence since his transfer in February — and it's rubbed off on the rest of the side.

"Some of our passing and football has also been a joy to watch this season — that's something that's been especially pleasing.

"I put a lot of our good passing down to our training ground at the London Transport Ground in Osterley. It really encourages people to play better training on a surface like that."

Dodgin's biggest confrontation with the fans came when he sold striker Gordon Sweetzer to Cambridge for £30,000 on the eve of the transfer deadline.

But he's been proved right with the new twin strike force of Steve Phillips and Andy McCulloch looking more effective and hitting more than 50 goals between them.

Dodgin said: "I took a calculated risk selling Sweetzer. I knew I was right but knew some of the fans wouldn't agree."

So he's won one battle with the fans and hopes to give them more success in the third next season.

He quit Northampton after taking them up from the fourth two seasons ago because he wanted to return to London.

Now he has the chance to show his worth in the third with Brentford — a club he reckons can make it back to the top.

1978-79

[Back Row] Paul Walker, Nigel Smith, Gary Rolph, John Fraser, Paul Shrubb **[Middle Row]** Danis Salman, Doug Allder, Graham Cox, Dave Silman, Len Bond, Pat Kruse, Mike Allen **[Front Row]** Eddie Lyons, Dave Carlton, John Murray, Barry Tucker, Bill Dodgin, Jackie Graham, Steve Phillips, Willie Graham, Tommy Baldwin

Football League	Division Three
Manager	Bill Dodgin
Coach	Tommy Baldwin
Physio	Eddie Lyons
Captain	Jackie Graham
Final Position	10th
FA Cup	1st Round
League Cup	1st Round
Leading Goalscorer	Steve Phillips
(all competitions)	& Andy McCulloch – 14 goals

Without any notable summer additions to the playing squad, plus the absence of goalkeeper Len Bond due to injury, the campaign started badly. A heavy (7-1) aggregate League Cup first round exit, at the hands of Watford, combined with a poor start to the League campaign, produced just three victories in the opening 13 matches and fears were raised of a struggle to come to terms with the higher level of football.

The Autumn double-signings of Jim McNichol, for a record £33,000 from Luton Town, and Dean Smith, £25,000 from Leicester City, prompted a 2-0 home win against Tranmere Rovers and helped to start a gradual improvement in results – although victories were sparse, as only three more wins were recorded before the end of January – against Oxford United (3-0), Walsall (1-0) and Plymouth Argyle (2-1) – while interest in the FA Cup ended at the first round stage as The Bees went down 1-0 at Exeter City.

The poor mid-winter weather saw a number of matches postponed but on the resumption of the league programme and spurred on by a 6-0 home win against Chester a run of five wins in six matches late in the season finally banished lingering fears of being dragged into a relegation battle.

The season ended with a 2-1 home defeat against Swindon Town, which attracted a crowd of 13,320 and, with boss Bill Dodgin rejecting the offer of the assistant manager's job at Chelsea, growing optimism of a promotion challenge the following year seemed justified.

[Previous page] A cross from Chelsea loanee, Lee Frost, during the home win against Tranmere Rovers

BRENTFORD

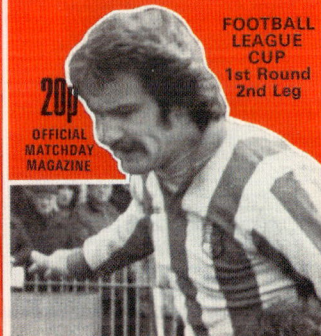

WATFORD

TUESDAY 15th AUGUST 1978
KICK-OFF 7.30 PM

FOOTBALL
LEAGUE
CUP
1st Round
2nd Leg

20p

OFFICIAL
MATCHDAY
MAGAZINE

		P	W	D	L	F	A	W	D	L	F	A	Pts
1	Shrewsbury	46	14	9	0	36	11	7	10	6	25	30	61
2	Watford	46	15	5	3	47	22	9	7	7	36	30	60
3	Swansea	46	16	6	1	57	32	8	6	9	26	29	60
4	Gillingham	46	15	7	1	39	15	6	10	7	26	27	59
5	Swindon	46	17	2	4	44	14	8	5	10	30	38	57
6	Carlisle	46	11	10	2	31	13	4	12	7	22	29	52
7	Colchester	46	13	9	1	35	19	4	8	11	25	36	51
8	Hull	46	12	9	2	36	14	7	2	14	30	47	49
9	Exeter	46	14	6	3	38	18	3	9	11	23	38	49
10	**Brentford**	**46**	**14**	**4**	**5**	**35**	**19**	**5**	**5**	**13**	**18**	**30**	**47**
11	Oxford	46	10	8	5	27	20	4	10	9	17	30	46
12	Blackpool	46	12	5	6	38	19	6	4	13	23	40	45
13	Southend	46	11	6	6	30	17	4	9	10	21	32	45
14	Sheff Wed	46	9	8	6	30	22	4	11	8	23	31	45
15	Plymouth	46	11	9	3	40	27	4	5	14	27	41	44
16	Chester	46	11	9	3	42	21	3	7	13	15	40	44
17	Rotherham	46	13	3	7	30	23	4	7	12	19	32	44
18	Mansfield	46	7	11	5	30	24	5	8	10	21	28	43
19	Bury	46	6	11	6	35	32	5	9	9	24	33	42
20	Chesterfield	46	10	5	8	35	34	3	9	11	16	31	40
21	Peterborough	46	8	7	8	26	24	3	7	13	18	39	36
22	Walsall	46	7	6	10	34	32	3	6	14	22	39	32
23	Tranmere	46	4	12	7	26	31	2	4	17	19	47	28
24	Lincoln City	46	5	7	11	26	38	2	4	17	15	50	25

Total Home League Attendances   **171,458**
Average Home League Attendance   **7,455**
Highest Home League Attendance   **13,873**
Lowest Home League Attendance   **5,140**

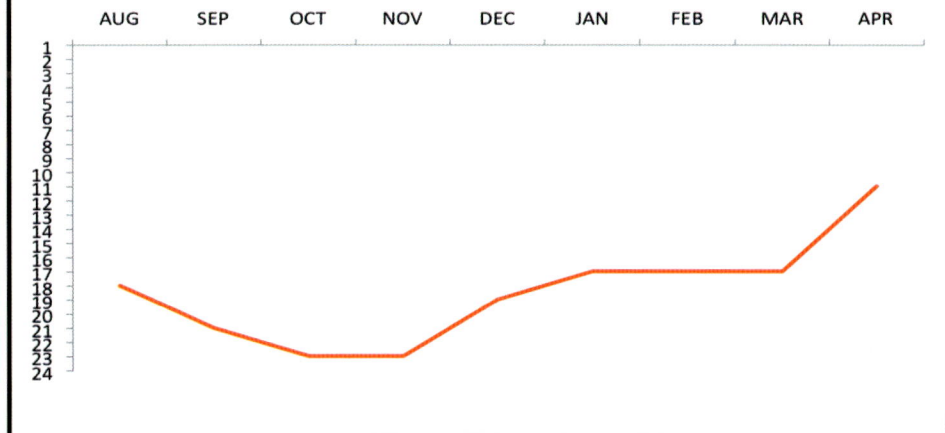

League Position throughout the Season

1978-79

Sat 12th August: **Watford (A) League Cup 1st Round**
Lost 0-4   **Attendance: 9,292**

A poor Pat Kruse back-pass after just two minutes led to Watford's opening goal, despite goal-line clearances from Trevor Porter and Barry Tucker and set the tone for a dismal afternoon. It took until the 67th minute for the Hornets to get their second goal and a third arrived eight minutes later – a blistering long-range effort completed the rout after 77 minutes.

Tue 15th August: **Watford (H) League Cup 1st Round**
Lost 1-3   **Attendance: 7,414**

A near-impossible task was made even worse after 13 minutes when the visitors scored to make it 5-0 on aggregate – their lead on the night was doubled in the 48th minute. Steve Phillips compounded a miserable evening by missing a 57th minute penalty, and although Gary Rolph did score after 76 minutes when he got his studs to a low Phillips cross to divert the ball into the net, a slip by Paul Shrubb three minutes later gave the visitors a seventh goal of the two-legged tie.

Sat 19th August: **Shrewsbury Town (A)**
Lost 0-1   **Attendance: 2,346**

Despite some highly creative, positive football, a 29th minute penalty conceded by John Fraser proved to be the match-winning strike as the Third Division campaign got off to a losing start.

Mon 21st August: **Colchester United (H)**
Won 1-0   **Attendance: 6,802**

A dominant display saw Pat Kruse score the game's only goal in the 14th minute when, from Willie Graham's corner, the keeper missed the ball under pressure from Andy McCulloch, which enabled the centre-back to score with a thunderous header. An eventful

evening also saw manager Bill Dodgin ordered from the touchline and keeper Trevor Porter stretchered off in the 88th minute – to be replaced in goal by Paul Shrubb.

Sat 26th August: **Chesterfield (H)**
Lost 0-3   **Attendance: 6,162**

An exceptionally poor display was underlined in the 25th minute when Steve Phillips made a 30-yard back-pass straight to an opposing forward, who gladly accepted the gift – the deficit was doubled seven minutes later. The performance deteriorated further in the second half and the visitors added a third when Paul Shrubb's soft header towards his keeper, presented another goal to the opposition.

Sat 2nd September: **Exeter City (A)**
Drew 2-2   **Attendance: 3,645**

The opening goal came after 12 minutes when Dave Carlton and Willie Graham combined well to enable Barry Tucker to cross low and hard for Andy McCulloch to blast the ball home – although the lead lasted just nine minutes. Brentford's advantage was regained less than 30 seconds later – McCulloch netted again, following an overhead kick from Steve Phillips, but the hosts secured a point with an equaliser in the 74th minute.

Sat 9th September: **Hull City (H)**
Won 1-0   **Attendance: 6,528**

An entertaining match was settled in the 36th minute when Willie Graham sent over a corner – Pat Kruse headed goalwards and Steve Phillips turned sharply to knock the ball into the net from four yards out to record his first goal of the season.

Tue 12th September: **Swindon Town (A)**
Lost 0-2   **Attendance: 6,902**

After a scoreless first half-hour, the odds seemed to tilt against Swindon, who were reduced to ten men after 36 minutes but they scored a decisive goal from a free-kick in the 61st minute and added a second four minutes from the end.

Sat 16th September: **Peterborough United (A)**
Lost 1-3   **Attendance: 5,884**

The home side scored a text-book opener after eight minutes and added a second 20 minutes later. A 43rd minute corner from Willie Graham was met by the head of Pat Kruse to reduce the arrears, but a third Posh goal, on 66 minutes, settled the encounter.

Sat 23rd September: **Gillingham (H)**
Lost 0-2   **Attendance: 6,977**

In the absence of manager Bill Dodgin, away scouting for new players, a costly error from John Fraser saw him mis-control the ball and present Gillingham with the opening goal in the 57th minute – the game was over six minutes later when the deficit was doubled.

Mon 25th September: **Lincoln City (H)**
Won 2-1   **Attendance: 6,107**

Jackie Graham blasted the ball into the net from inside the penalty area after neatly controlling a through ball after just three minutes – the dream start was extended 60 seconds later when trialist, Billy Eames, marked a superb debut by hitting home a blistering 10-yard drive after Andy McCulloch had headed the ball on to him. The visitors pulled a goal back in the 41st minute, but the points were retained despite a nail-biting finale.

Sat 30th September: **Swansea City (A)**
Lost 1-2   **Attendance: 11,370**

The Swans took the lead in the 16th minute but an equaliser wasn't far behind – Paul Walker swung in a corner which brushed against the underside of the crossbar and dropped perfectly for Andy McCulloch to volley home five minutes later. The game appeared to be heading for a draw until a stunning 80th minute strike gave the hosts both points.

Sat 7th October: **Bury (H)**
Lost 0-1   **Attendance: 5,855**

After a dull first half, the visitors snatched the game's only goal in the 70th minute against the run of play – capitalising on a defensive mix-up to steal the points with their first win in 19 attempts.

Sat 14th October: **Watford (A)**
Lost 0-2   **Attendance: 15,180**

A lifeless performance saw the game still scoreless at half-time as a result of a string of fine saves from Len Bond – but Watford took the lead two minutes after the break and, following a melee on the pitch and fighting on the terraces, the game was settled when the hosts scored a second with ease in the 77th minute.

Tue 17th October: **Rotherham United (A)**
Lost 0-1   **Attendance: 3,881**

A much-improved display saw Rotherham out-played for much of the game – but it was United who scored the all-important goal in the second half and held on grimly to take both points.

Sat 21st October: **Tranmere Rovers (H)**
Won 2-0   **Attendance: 5,883**

The 32nd minute opening goal was created by Lee Frost, whose looping cross to the far post was headed home powerfully by Andy McCulloch – the striker grabbed his second after 56 minutes, coolly slotting the ball into the net after being set up by debutant Dean Smith and Steve Phillips. Eleven minutes later a penalty was awarded when Lee Frost was fouled – McCulloch spurning the chance of a hat-trick when his effort was saved.

Sat 28th October: **Chester City (A)**
Lost 1-3   **Attendance: 4,495**

A strong first-half performance was rewarded with Andy McCulloch's 23rd minute goal – not Dean Smith, as reported by the

national press and football authorities. The home side hit-back with a blistering eighteen minute hat-trick from Welsh international striker, Ian Edwards, who netted after 52, 56 and 70 minutes.

Sat 4th November: **Oxford United (H)**
Won 3-0   **Attendance: 6,863**
The visitors were run ragged throughout – Andy McCulloch broke the deadlock after 16 minutes, when he met a pin-point cross from Dean Smith, to head home. Nine minutes later a carbon copy saw Steve Phillips provide the centre for Dean Smith to nod an immaculate second, and the striker doubled his personal tally immediately after half-time when reacting quickest to net from a Paul Shrubb shot that came back off the post. Len Bond saved an 89th minute penalty, awarded against Danis Salman, to preserve a clean sheet.

Sat 11th November: **Exeter City (H)**
Drew 0-0   **Attendance: 6,387**
Scoring chances for both teams were few and far between in a match that never reached the heights of the previous weekend – the visitors made clear their intentions to settle for their point early on in the proceedings.

Sat 18th November: **Chesterfield (A)**
Drew 0-0   **Attendance: 4,584**
A workmanlike performance in the wind and rain ended a run of six straight away defeats – this was a match between two teams with very differing styles, which cancelled one another out.

Sat 25th November: **Exeter City (A) FA Cup 1st Round**
Lost 0-1   **Attendance: 3,810**
Despite dominating the game the goal drought was extended to 307 minutes – even a deserved replay was denied when Barry

Tucker mis-cued a clearance in the 84th minute, creating a goal for the home side's university student midfielder, Dick Forbes.

Sat 2nd December: **Walsall (H)**
Won 1-0   **Attendance: 5,140**
A 'huff-and-puff' performance, which often saw the visitors in the ascendency, ended up with a fortunate win courtesy of a 33rd minute gifted goal – the visiting keeper dropped Paul Shrubb's corner at the feet of Andy McCulloch, who gratefully tapped the ball into the net.

Sat 9th December: **Mansfield Town (A)**
Lost 1-2   **Attendance: 4,003**
Mansfield were in front after just five minutes – Len Bond prevented a certain goal by conceding a penalty kick, which was converted, and the lead was doubled in the 41st minute. A much more disciplined and determined second-half performance brought the reward of a 78th minute header by Andy McCulloch from Jim McNichol's cross.

Sat 23rd December: **Southend United (A)**
Drew 1-1   **Attendance: 13,703**
A tremendous 64th minute strike from Steve Phillips, having been set-up by Andy McCulloch, rewarded a display in which Southend were outplayed throughout – the match ended in controversy, though, as Paul Shrubb was adjudged to have conceded a penalty, despite the foul taking place a clear yard outside the box. The equaliser proved to be a double punishment, as Shrubb was dismissed for his protestations.

Tue 26th December: **Plymouth Argyle (H)**
Won 2-1   **Attendance: 7,367**
A thrilling Boxing Day encounter produced three goals in a pulse-tingling 20 minute second-half spell – the first arrived after 55 minutes, when Barry Tucker's short back-pass was intercepted

to present the visitors with the opener before Dean Smith scored twice in quick succession. His first in the 71st minute was a header from a Doug Allder cross and, having received a pass from Jackie Graham three minutes later, he fired home again from five yards to seal the victory.

Sat 30th December: **Carlisle United (H)**
Drew 0-0   **Attendance: 6,477**

The year ended with a goal-less draw played out in freezing conditions – both teams endeavouring to produce entertaining football and the visiting goalkeeper having by far the busier workload of the two number ones.

Sat 20th January: **Peterborough United (H)**
Drew 0-0   **Attendance: 5,760**

The unbeaten run was extended to four games, but another off-day by the strikers, who failed to capitalise on a dominant midfield display, proved frustrating for supporters who punctuated an undistinguished game with cries of "rubbish" during the second half.

Sat 27th January: **Gillingham (A)**
Drew 0-0   **Attendance: 6,899**

On a weekend where few matches survived the arctic conditions, the game went ahead after two pitch inspections and an entertaining encounter took place with a hard-working display producing one of the best performances of the season against promotion contenders.

Sat 10th February: **Swansea City (H)**
Won 1-0   **Attendance: 7,264**

A performance ranking as one of the best of the manager's reign saw the high-flying visitors over-whelmed – even the likes of Tommy Smith, Ian Callaghan and John Toshack were unable to prevent the 60th minute winner from Dave Carlton, forcing home a cross from Steve Phillips after the Swans keeper made a rare mistake.

Sat 24th February: **Watford (H)**
Drew 3-3   **Attendance: 13,873**

The ITV *Big Match* cameras were present to witness a thrilling derby encounter. The table-topping visitors took a 13th minute lead from the penalty spot after Jim McNichol had handled, before Dean Smith hooked in a Jackie Graham pass over the keeper to equalise five minutes later. Another seven minutes passed before Dave Carlton's free-kick was headed on by Pat Kruse for Steve Phillips to snatch the lead, but Watford drew level in controversial circumstances in the 35th minute – Len Bond failed to hold the ball from a corner and his defenders appeared distracted by a whistle blown from the crowd. Five minutes into the second half the Hornets were back in front, before the final goal came courtesy of a hotly-disputed penalty – converted by Steve Phillips.

Sat 3rd March: **Tranmere Rovers (A)**
Won 1-0   **Attendance: 1,882**

A depressing spectacle, in which neither side showed much in the way of initiative, was settled by a 73rd minute goal when Dave Carlton's free-kick was parried by the keeper and Allan Glover squared the ball back for Steve Phillips to score from close range. After Len Bond was stretchered off, following a clash of heads in the 27th minute, centre-back Jim McNichol took over in goal and kept a clean sheet during his hour between the sticks.

Tue 6th March: **Hull City (A)**
Lost 0-1   **Attendance: 3,418**

The 72nd minute winner, which ended an eight-match unbeaten run, came at a time when the hosts were second best, but the scrappy strike saw the ball rebound from Jim McNichol following a corner to present a gift goal and settle the encounter.

185

Sat 10th March: **Chester City (H)**
Won 6-0   **Attendance: 6,421**

A fine team performance was encapsulated by a 14-minute four-goal purple patch in the second half, although the rout had started as early as the 9th minute when Steve Phillips flicked home a right-wing cross from Dean Smith. The scoring spree began with a vengeance after an hour as a brilliant through-ball from Paul Shrubb was hammered into the net by Allan Glover and, less than 60 seconds later, Dean Smith released McCulloch down the left and the big striker fired home through the keeper's legs. Glover scored again in the 73rd minute when he controlled a Steve Phillips square-ball, before netting with precision. Almost from the re-start Doug Allder sent over a perfect centre for Phillips to nod home. The thrashing was complete in the dying seconds when Glover's right-wing cross was met by the head of Steve Phillips for his hat-trick.

Tue 13th March: **Sheffield Wednesday (A)**
Lost 0-1   **Attendance: 10,383**

A battling display on a treacherous pitch went unrewarded as the match was settled by a 14th minute goal for The Owls which was enough to earn both points. Heavy rain turned to snow as the match progressed.

Wed 21st March: **Lincoln City (A)**
Lost 0-1   **Attendance: 2,060**

The division's bottom team secured a rare win with a 40th minute strike after having the better of much of the first half – City absorbed considerable pressure in the second period until Andy McCulloch was sent off following a clash with home striker Mick Harford with ten minutes remaining.

Sat 24th March: **Colchester United (A)**
Drew 1-1   **Attendance: 3,528**

An evenly matched first half was played in a swirling wind on a rain-soaked pitch – Danis Salman crossed from the right in the

66th minute for Steve Phillips to chest the ball into the path of Paul Shrubb, who lashed the ball home. The hosts equalised eight minutes later when Salman conceded a penalty. In the absence of manager Bill Dodgin, away on a scouting mission, the team were forced to borrow QPR's second strip.

Mon 26th March: **Shrewsbury Town (H)**
Lost 2-3   **Attendance: 7,756**

A deserved lead came after 17 minutes when Andy McCulloch forced the ball over the line from close range following a Jackie Graham corner, before Len Bond saved a penalty conceded by Jim McNichol in the 24th minute. But the visitors grabbed an equaliser just two minutes later, then took the lead in the 40th minute. A corner in the 51st minute produced an identical goal to the opener – Dean Smith forcing home Dave Carlton's centre, but the game was finally lost to a 68th minute goal.

Sat 31st March: **Blackpool (H)**
Won 3-2   **Attendance: 6,364**

A dramatic afternoon got off to the worst possible start when the visitors took a 10th minute lead, then doubled it on the half hour. But a storming Bees second half secured the points. Three minutes after the re-start Jim McNichol stabbed the ball into the net after a Paul Shrubb shot had been blocked, and four minutes later, McNichol headed home his second after the keeper had mis-punched a corner. The winner came in the 60th minute – Steve Phillips side-footing the ball into the net from McNichol's free-kick.

Wed 4th April: **Oxford United (A)**
Won 1-0   **Attendance: 5,242**

The winning goal came in the 72nd minute – Steve Phillips was fouled inside the penalty area but the referee awarded an indirect

free-kick in the box, from which Dave Carlton tapped the ball to Paul Shrubb who hammered a rising drive into the roof of the net.

Sat 7th April: **Walsall (A)**
Won 3-2 **Attendance: 3,840**

An early goal from Pat Kruse, who lashed in a shot after Danis Salman's cross from a corner, set the tone for a one-sided game – Steve Phillips doubled the lead after 25 minutes when he scored from a rebound after Jim McNichol's free-kick. The game was all but over 14 minutes later when Phillips lobbed into the net. Two late Walsall goals, after 83 and 89 minutes, the second an own goal from Pat Kruse, gave the score a flattering look for the hosts.

Fri 13th April: **Southend United (H)**
Won 3-0 **Attendance: 11,509**

An emphatic victory, and a fourth successive win, was set up by a goal on the stroke of half-time – Andy McCulloch headed in a free-kick from Barry Tucker, and a 74th minute second goal from Pat Kruse, heading home Doug Allder's corner, sealed the points. A third strike followed four minutes later when McCulloch crossed low for Danis Salman to score with a left-foot shot.

Sat 14th April: **Plymouth Argyle (A)**
Lost 1-2 **Attendance: 6,344**

The home side dominated proceedings early on and made the breakthrough in the 38th minute – a penalty awarded after Jim McNichol had committed the foul. The lead was doubled 16 minutes into the second half. A tremendous fight-back almost brought its rewards, but Dave Carlton's angled drive after 84 minutes proved to be no more than a consolation.

Tue 17th April: **Sheffield Wednesday (H)**
Won 2-1 **Attendance: 9,050**

Third Division status was all but assured when Jim McNichol scored twice inside two minutes in the first half – the first of which arrived in the 32nd minute, when he smashed home a cracking low shot from 30 yards direct from a free-kick and, a minute later, he was on hand to head home a corner kick from Doug Allder. The visitors pulled a goal back against the run of play in the 86th minute.

Sat 21st April: **Carlisle United (A)**
Lost 0-1 **Attendance: 3,967**

Despite dominating much of a tedious match, a whole host of chances were squandered and the home side eventually sealed a somewhat fortuitous victory with the only goal of the game in the 70th minute.

Mon 23rd April: **Rotherham United (H)**
Won 1-0 **Attendance: 6,758**

After outplaying the visitors for much of the match, with a display of fast, adventurous football, the encounter was settled courtesy of a 38th minute goal. Andy McCulloch controlled Jim McNichol's free-kick and played the ball to Dave Carlton who set up Barry Tucker for a fine run and low cross from the left which was converted by Dean Smith.

Sat 28th April: **Mansfield Town (H)**
Won 1-0 **Attendance: 6,838**

A less than polished performance nevertheless brought about another win when, eventually, one of Doug Allder's crosses was nudged on by Jim McNichol for Steve Phillips to head into the back of the net to secure the victory.

Sat 5th May: **Blackpool (A)**
Won 1-0 **Attendance: 3,464**

A solid, well-organised display saw the midfield trio dominate proceedings – although goal-scoring chances were few and far between until the 74th minute, when Danis Salman's shot was parried by the keeper and Andy McCulloch followed up to ram the ball home to complete the double over the Seasiders.

Tue 8th May: **Swindon Town (H)**
Lost 1-2   **Attendance: 13,320**

The meeting of two in-form teams produced a vibrant, attacking game. The promotion-chasing visitors snatched the lead after 13 minutes with the equaliser coming 24 minutes later – Dave Carlton sent a low cross into the goalmouth, where the ball bobbed around with both John Fraser and Andy McCulloch missing the chance to net, before Dean Smith prodded home the goal. The match was settled in favour of Swindon 15 minutes into the second half with a stunning strike.

Tue 15th May: **Bury (A)**
Won 3-2   **Attendance: 2,512**

Ninety minutes of exciting end-to-end football produced a lively end of season showdown – the hosts took the lead after just 7 minutes and it took until the 40th minute for the equaliser to arrive. A long throw was headed on by Jim McNichol and Steve Phillips turned sharply to flick the ball home with his head. The scores were level for just two minutes, though, a misunderstanding between Pat Kruse and John Fraser presented Bury with a simple goal and the second, equalising strike came after 74 minutes when Andy McCulloch headed in from Doug Allder's corner. The winner, in the 83rd minute, was a carbon copy of the first goal as Steve Phillips repeated his earlier feat.

PRE-SEASON

Tommy Baldwin was appointed as player/coach to assist manager Bill Dodgin.

Len Bond was involved in a car crash, breaking two bones in his hand and facing at least two months out of action.

Graham Cox received a suspension for being sent off in a practice match in Guernsey at the end of last season and was banned for the first game of the new campaign.

Goalkeeper Trevor Porter was signed from Slough Town on a trial basis.

Steve Wilkins, brother of Ray, Dean and Graham, was given a one-month contract having been released by Chelsea.

Andy McCulloch spent the summer playing in the USA and returned for the first league game, but missed the entire pre-season programme and the League Cup ties.

John Fraser, who had been out with a groin injury since December, was expected to be fit for the start of the season.

OSGOOD'S BACK WITH THE BEES

AUGUST 1978

- 21-year old Trevor Porter was given a full contract at the end of his trial period.
- Steve Wilkins was released following his trial.
- A one-month trial was offered to freed Portsmouth striker, 20-year old Billy Eames.
- Nigel Smith was placed on the transfer list at his own request.
- John Fraser suffered a recurrence of his injury and both Paul Shrubb and Trevor Porter were stretchered off in the opening games.

Jim – you need hands

IMAGINE a fresh-faced youngster shivering and muddied in the rain between the posts of a Scottish municipal park football pitch.

Well, that was Brentford defender Jim McNichol in his early teens donning a goalkeeper's jersey for St. George's of Glasgow.

And when McNichol took over from a concussed Len Bond during the Tranmere victory on Saturday he had to recall those childhood memories to help him through the match which had his team-mates joking he should have kept the same position at Hull on Tuesday night.

"I hadn't played in goal since my schooldays," McNichol told me.

"Shrubby (Bees defender Paul Shrubb) was all set to take over from Len. He normally goes in goal when our goalkeeper is injured.

"But Tranmere had a lot of big lads and as Shrubby is fairly short I decided that it would be best if I went in, especially as I'd got at least some experience.

"I thought at first that Bondy was only going to be off for about 10 minutes, so we played as 10 men with Andy McCulloch coming back to fill my position in the middle of the defence. But

then I suddenly realised it was the whole game.

"It was a bit of a change! I didn't have all that much to do but the few crosses I had to do and didn't really have to deal with any direct shot. But I dropped the few crosses that came over."

"It was a great relief to win our first match away for 10 months. We played quite well and the result naturally cheered us."

Bees goalie 'lucky to be alive'

BRENTFORD goalkeeper Len Bond is lucky to be alive after a mystery car smash on Friday night.

Twenty-four-year-old Bond had been out for a drink and was returning to his home near Ilminster in Somerset when the car he'd only bought earlier that day went out of control and careered into a telegraph pole.

Yet he walked clear with only a couple of broken bones in his hand, concussion and bruising.

Len said: "I think I've got someone above to thank for the fact that I'm not in a wooden box by now.

"I also got a bang just above the eye and obviously that could have been a lot worse.

"But I can't remember anything about the crash — not even whether I was wearing my seat belt — and I just don't know what happened.

"It was just outside where my mum works and I must have driven past the spot thousands of times."

He passed a breathalyser test and police think the car burst a tyre before Len lost control.

He was taken to Taunton East Reach Hospital after the accident and was detained until Saturday evening with concussion and for X-rays.

SEPTEMBER 1978

• Bill Dodgin made a club record bid of £65,000 to Watford for striker Alan Mayes but the offer was rejected.
• A transfer bid was accepted by Millwall (£30,000) for defender Tony Hazell but the player failed to agree personal terms.
• Billy Eames was offered a second month's trial.
• Bob Booker was signed on a non-contract basis, having been playing for Hertfordshire county league side Bedmond.
• Dean Johns signed as an apprentice professional.
• Former Chelsea striker Peter Osgood was training with club on his return from the USA.
• Bill Dodgin was interested in offering a short-term deal to former QPR forward Mickey Leach, who was currently playing in America.

OCTOBER 1978

• 20-year old Scottish defender Jim McNichol was signed from Luton Town for a club record fee of £33,000.
• On the same day Dean Smith, a 19-year old striker arrived from Leicester City for £25,000.
• Striker Lee Frost aged 20 was signed on one month's loan from Chelsea.

Tana calls emergency meeting
Dodgin can go —Bees chief

By Colin Grant

BRENTFORD manager Bill Dodgin's future could be settled this week.

Chairman Dan Tana called an emergency board meeting for Tuesday night, just 24 hours after the shock news that Dodgin could be set to join West London rivals Chelsea as number two to boss Danny Blanchflower.

And the outcome of this meeting — attended by Dodgin — was likely to decide whether or not he stays at Griffin Park.

IMMEDIATE

A stunned Tana called for a board meeting immediately after returning from Italy where he first heard the news of Dodgin's possible move.

And whatever the outcome of Tuesday's meeting there was no hiding the disappointment of Tana who has seen previous managers leave the club in his six years at Griffin Park.

He said: "I am very disappointed indeed. Myself and the board have spent a lot of time trying to build something at the club and now this happens.

"I'd heard talks of rumours about Bill going to Chelsea but you hear that sort of talk all the time. Then I pick up a paper in Rome on Monday and read that my manager might be leaving.

"So we've called this meeting to find out just what the situation is.

"Obviously I would like Bill to stay and I like to feel I've always got on well with him. But personally I don't think we should try to keep anyone if they are not happy at the club.

"Even if Bill was under contract I wouldn't want to keep him here if he wasn't happy. And it's not a question of offering him more money either — just whether he wants to stay at Brentford."

FRIEND

Ironically it was Dodgin who first suggested to Chelsea chairman Brian Mears that he consider Blanchflower for the manager's job at Stamford Bridge.

And he is a long-time friend of Blanchflower who used to help coach Dodgin's teams at Fulham and QPR.

Dodgin, who has guided Brentford from the foot of Division Four to the middle of the third division in less than three years with the Bees, confirmed he'd had an initial approach from Blanchflower but said he'd heard nothing since.

He said: "I told Danny I might be interested. And it would be difficult to turn down a job like that.

"It would be a terrible wrench for me to leave Brentford — and particularly the players. It's given me a tremendous kick since I've been here to take the side from the bottom of the fourth to the middle of the third division.

"And Brentford could easily become at least a good second division side. But people can't expect miracles and it will take time. After years in the doldrums they've got to progress slowly.

"And I've got to think of myself as well. People might be saying I should stay but they're the same people who wanted me out after our bad start to the season.

"Things change quickly in football and I must think of what's best for myself."

Skipper Jackie Graham summed up the players feelings when he said: "I was terribly shocked when I heard the news. It would be a big blow to us if Bill went — he's been like a breath of fresh air at the club.

"All the lads would be really choked."

● Dodgin this week gave free transfers to long-serving full-back Mike Allen and to youngsters Gary Rolph and David Silman.

And 'keeper Len Bond has won the Players Player of the Year trophy.

● Sports View — P. 32

● A £30,000 bid for Andy McCulloch from Cambridge United was rejected.
● Bill Dodgin had a £25,000 bid for last season's loanee John Bain, turned down by Bristol City.
● 20-year old Bob Booker was signed on full professional terms.
● Billy Eames left the club following his trial period.
● Transfer-listed Nigel Smith had his contract cancelled by mutual consent and left the club.
● Graham Cox was freed to enable him to join Margate.

NOVEMBER 1978

● 28-year old midfielder Allan Glover, who was Bill Dodgin's first loan signing two years ago, returned to the club on a free transfer from Orient.
● Lee Frost returned to Chelsea at the end of his loan spell.
● Jim McNichol was selected for the Scotland international under-21 squad.

DECEMBER 1978

● John Murray, who failed to make an appearance during the season, had his contract cancelled and left the club.
● Mike Allen, who had been suffering from a viral infection for several months, underwent further hospital tests.
● Paul Shrubb was sent off in the match at Southend.

JANUARY 1979

● The matches against Sheffield Wednesday and Hull (both away) and Swindon (home) fell victim to the poor weather and were postponed.

Who says there's no sentiment in football?...

DODGIN STAYS AT BRENTFORD

FEBRUARY 1979

- The poor weather continued to see the cancellation of games and the matches at Lincoln and Bury were postponed.
- The home match with Watford was televised by ITV's *Big Match*.

MARCH 1979

- An unsuccessful bid was made to sign Southampton striker Tony Funnell.
- The proposed £10,000 transfer of Harrow Borough's highly-rated striker Peter Sharratt failed to materialise.
- Andy McCulloch was sent off at Lincoln.
- Len Bond was injured after 30 minutes in the game at Tranmere and Jim McNichol took over in goal for the remaining hour, keeping a clean sheet.
- Danis Salman was selected for the England under-21 squad, although the match was postponed.

Blanchflower wants Dodgin as his deputy at Chelsea

HE'LL be out of his mind if he leaves, was Brentford chairman Dan Tana's only comment this week when asked whether he thought Bill Dodgin was going to accept the offer from Danny Blanchflower to become the assistant manager at Chelsea.

The Brentford board had a special board meeting on Tuesday to discuss the offer to Dodgin. Dan Tana told the Chronicle:

"I'd be lying if I said I don't feel concerned. Bill Dodgin has done a marvellous job here at Griffin Park over the past 2½ years. I can't talk him into staying, its up to him. I saw him for about two hours during the week but its entirely his decision. It would be a great pity if Chelsea managed to lure him away. We have the foundation of great things here at Brentford."

193

Bees eye Euro stars

| EXCLUSIVE | By Colin Grant |

BRENTFORD are interested in bringing top Yugoslavian players to Griffin Park — and are prepared to smash the club transfer record to do so.

Leading the ambitious move is chairman Dan Tana, himself a former player in Yugoslavia for Red Star Belgrade.

Tana told me he has seen several players whom he is interested in signing out in Yugoslavia, in particular a big striker, and he's ready to pay £50,000 for a top Slav — that's double the club's record fee.

Tana will get another chance to run the rule over some of the players as he is currently in Yugoslavia.

Southampton have already signed a Yugoslavian — Marjan Golac — in the rush by British clubs to get foreign players.

Brentford boss Bill Dodgin said: "I know Dan's interested in getting a Yugoslavian player to Griffin Park and obviously I'm interested in getting good players here.

"However I can foresee problems and I'd be very wary of the situation. We'd have to pay a Yugoslav player more than our present lads are getting and that could cause trouble.

"Then there's the language barrier. Andy McCulloch's just come back from playing in America during the summer and he said that was one of the main problems out there with all the players of one nationality tending to play the ball to each other because they couldn't understand the others.

"But you can't dismiss the chance of getting players like this.

"And if Dan wants me to go out there and have a look at a player then I will."

Dodgin has made no secret of the fact that he needs to strengthen his squad after a poor start to their first season back in division three.

And a defender and midfielder are his top priorities after taking just one point from the opening three matches.

But the signing of a top Yugoslavian player would add class to the Bees side and boost interest at Griffin Park where the crowd was a disappointing 6,000 on Saturday in the face of competition from neighbours QPR and Fulham.

● **Dodgin set to swoop — Page 37.**

● Leading the chase ... Dan Tana

● Interested ... Bill Dodgin

APRIL 1979

● Bill Dodgin was offered the post of assistant manager at Chelsea. Not being under contract, he indicated that he would accept the job if terms could be agreed.
● Bradley Walsh was signed as a non-contract player.

MAY 1979

● Bill Dodgin announced that he had decided to remain with the club as he had unfinished work to complete and indicated that he felt he may have the basis of another promotion side.
● Free transfers were given to Mike Allen, Gary Rolph and Dave Silman.

Shape of things to come at Griffin Park

BRENTFORD FOOTBALL Club shook their fans at the end of last year when they announced plans to redevelop their Griffin Park stadium.

After years of speculation surrounding the future of the ground chairman Dan Tana told supporters at the annual meeting of their plans.

So with the ideas now in motion Gazette Sports Editor COLIN GRANT has been talking to the man in charge of the Stadium Committee, Colin Wheatley, and finding out just what is the likely shape of Griffin Park in the eighties.

Bees 'no' to all-seat stadium

● LOOKING TO the eighties . . . Brentford's Stadium Committee, left to right, Ronnie Blindell, Dan Tana, Colin Wheatley and Denis Piggott with architect John Guest.

IF you prefer watching Brentford from the terraces then relax, Griffin Park isn't likely to be turned into an all-seater stadium.

When the club announced its recent redevelopment plans one of the biggest fears of the average supporter was that he wouldn't be able to stand up and watch the Bees . . . being condemned, instead, to a life in the seats.

But after the latest meeting of the Stadium Committee last week, when architect John Guest was also present, they decided it would be better to keep some standing space at the ground.

MODERN

Director Colin Wheatley, the man in charge of the Stadium Committee, told me: "What we'd like in the end is a modern stadium that holds between 33 and 35,000 spectators and one that would be suitable for staging youth internationals and cup replays.

"But I think we would still have a fair measure of standing around the ground. We believe that is important on three counts.

"Firstly, some people prefer standing and we must consider the fans, while we can also get more people in the ground, standing up.

REPAIR

"And lastly there is the point that if you had seats in front of our present stand then people would still get wet as the roofing doesn't cover all the way down to the front — and that wouldn't be fair."

In fact the recent structural survey had on the ground shows that only one or two small sections are not economically worth repairing and that the rest of the ground — including the main stands — will need little work.

So just where do the Bees expect to make alterations to the ground?

Well, I understand that major development of the present site will involve one of the two covered sides of the ground — the first move probably being to put new seating in part of the present main stand.

But developing the present ground is only part of the Bees project. They also want to get the local people more involved with the club — that means possibly providing the fans with sports facilities of their own at the ground and making sure that Griffin Park is used as much as possible during the week.

IDEAS

"We want the local community and our fans to write to the club with their ideas for the future of the stadium.

"We want to know just what they want. Whether they'd prefer an all-seater stadium or lavish toilets, and if they'd like badminton or squash courts at the ground.

"It's a project to try to get the maximum use out of the stadium during the week and we want to hear the views of these people."

Meanwhile Mr. Wheatley will continue to look into all aspects of the redevelopment — and his next step will be a tour of Football League and Rugby League grounds to look at developments at other clubs.

SURVEY

He said: "We've got to see how other people have fared and what mistakes or improvements they've made."

At present the project is still very much at the drawing board stages. But the Stadium Committee have already spent £2,500 on the structural survey and have been allocated a further £10,000 to take the plans a stage further.

Committee meetings will continue, as will the planning and they hope that by next Autumn they'll be able to show a plan of a proposed new-look Griffin Park to their fans.

Then if everything goes according to plan work on the redevelopment plans should kick off during the close season before the 1980-81 campaign.

The fear of relegation . . .

RELEGATION straight back to the fourth division would see the Bees shelve their redevelopment plans.

Colin Wheatley said: "Loooking on the glomy side if we were to go straight back down to the fourth division then our plans would have to be kept in cold-storage. There would be no point in developing the ground with a fourth division side.

"But we're not thinking like that. We're looking to the side pushing for promotion to the second division next season and we must then have a ground to match the success on the field."

Promotion to division two would also mean the Bees coming under the regulations of the Safety of Grounds Act and the club would have to act then anyway to improve their ground so they're hoping to keep one step ahead off the field by redeveloping the stadium now.

GOOD PLAYERS

Mr. Wheatley said: "We don't want to get too ambitious and we agree we must concentrate on the team. But we must also strive to match their efforts off the field.

"At the moment we do the best we can but I feel the conditions our players work under are 30 years out of date.

"We have got to have the sort of facilities to attract good players and that's why manager Bill Dodgin will be fully involved discussing the redevelopment plans.

1979-80

The summer departure of star striker Andy McCulloch – to Sheffield Wednesday for a record £60,000 – being replaced by the unproven Lee Holmes, from non-League Enfield, looked to be a big gamble. The season started with three defeats in the opening four games, including a 4-1 hammering by Southend United in the League Cup and a 4-0 thrashing at Swindon Town.

The poor start was quickly brushed aside though, and just three defeats in the next 16 games, one of which produced a remarkable 5-4 loss at Blackpool, saw the team soar towards the top of the table, and a crowd of 13,764 turned up for the highly-charged and controversial top of the table visit of Sheffield United.

A run of three successive defeats, including a 4-1 FA Cup first round exit at Swindon Town, was ended with a stunning 7-2 home victory against Hull City, in which young striker, Bob Booker hit a hat-trick – but a dramatic decline in results thereafter produced a dreadful run of just one win in 18 games.

Heavy defeats at Grimsby Town (5-1) and Colchester United (6-1) accentuated the slide down the table and, despite the record transfer signing of Tony Funnell for £56,000 from Gillingham, four straight losses in March ended with Bill Dodgin being relieved of his managerial duties with seven games remaining to stave off the threat of relegation.

Dodgin's former assistant, Fred Callaghan, was drafted in from Woking, but two wins, two draws and two defeats left the team still facing a nail-biting climax in the final game at home to Millwall – where a late goal from Funnell ensured last day survival.

[Back Row] Dave Carlton, Lee Holmes, Terry Benning, Bob Booker, Trevor Porter, Pat Kruse, Len Bond, Jim McNichol, Dean Smith, John Fraser, Allan Glover **[Front Row]** Paul Walker, Dean Johns, Paul Shrubb, Steve Phillips, Jackie Graham, Barry Tucker, Doug Allder, Dave O'Mahoney, Willie Graham, Bradley Walsh

Football League	Division Three
Manager	Bill Dodgin / Fred Callaghan
Coach	Tommy Baldwin
Physio	Eddie Lyons
Captain	Jackie Graham
Final Position	19th
FA Cup	1st Round
League Cup	1st Round
Leading Goalscorer (all competitions)	Steve Phillips – 12 goals

[Previous page] Steve Phillips and Jackie Graham watch Billy Holmes in possession against Southend United at Griffin Park

BRENTFORD

v

SOUTHEND UNITED

Season 1979-80

**Football League Cup
1st Round, 2nd Leg**

Tuesday 21 August 1979

Kick off 7.30 pm

OFFICIAL MATCHDAY MAGAZINE 25p

		P	W	D	L	F	A	W	D	L	F	A	Pts
1	Grimsby	46	18	2	3	46	16	8	8	7	27	26	**62**
2	Blackburn	46	13	5	5	34	17	12	4	7	24	19	**59**
3	Sheff Wed	46	12	6	5	44	20	9	10	4	37	27	**58**
4	Chesterfield	46	16	5	2	46	16	7	6	10	25	30	**57**
5	Colchester	46	10	10	3	39	20	10	2	11	25	36	**52**
6	Carlisle	46	13	6	4	45	26	5	6	12	21	30	**48**
7	Reading	46	14	6	3	43	19	2	10	11	23	46	**48**
8	Exeter	46	14	5	4	38	22	5	5	13	22	46	**48**
9	Chester	46	14	6	3	29	18	3	7	13	20	39	**47**
10	Swindon	46	15	4	4	50	20	4	4	15	21	43	**46**
11	Barnsley	46	10	7	6	29	20	6	7	10	24	36	**46**
12	Sheffield	46	13	5	5	35	21	5	5	13	25	45	**46**
13	Rotherham	46	13	4	6	38	24	5	6	12	20	42	**46**
14	Millwall	46	14	6	3	49	23	2	7	14	16	36	**45**
15	Plymouth	46	13	7	3	39	17	3	5	15	20	38	**44**
16	Gillingham	46	8	9	6	26	18	6	5	12	23	33	**42**
17	Oxford	46	10	4	9	34	24	4	9	10	23	38	**41**
18	Blackpool	46	10	7	6	39	34	5	4	14	23	40	**41**
19	**Brentford**	**46**	**10**	**6**	**7**	**33**	**26**	**5**	**5**	**13**	**26**	**47**	**41**
20	Hull	46	11	7	5	29	21	1	9	13	22	48	**40**
21	Bury	46	10	4	9	30	23	6	3	14	15	36	**39**
22	Southend	46	11	6	6	33	23	3	4	16	14	35	**38**
23	Mansfield	46	9	9	5	31	24	1	7	15	16	34	**36**
24	Wimbledon	46	6	8	9	34	38	4	6	13	18	43	**34**

Total Home League Attendances **179,822**
Average Home League Attendance **7,818**
Highest Home League Attendance **13,764**
Lowest Home League Attendance **4,992**

League Position throughout the Season

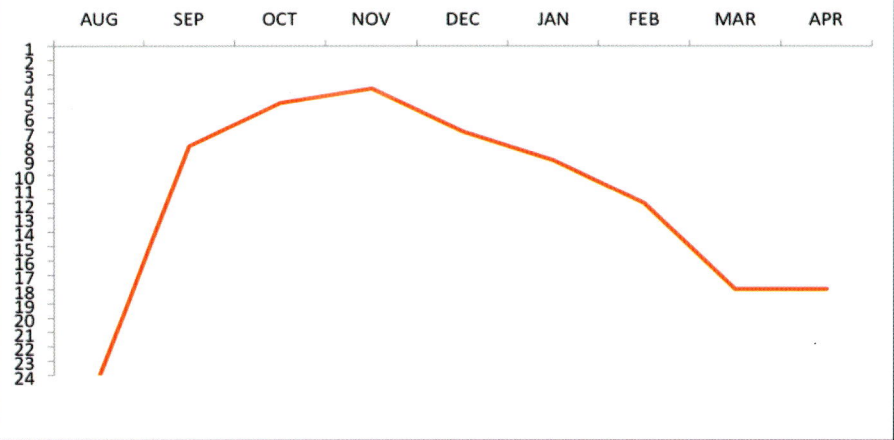

199

1979-80

Wed 15th August: **Southend (A) League Cup 1st Round**
Lost 1-2   **Attendance: 4,780**

Southend took the lead five minutes before the break and looked to have secured their passage to the second round when they doubled their advantage in the second half – but in the 85th minute, a cross from Doug Allder evaded Dean Smith, and debutant, Lee Holmes, calmly slotted the ball into the net to halve the deficit.

Sat 18th August: **Reading (A)**
Drew 2-2   **Attendance: 8,140**

A 29th minute goal ended a Football League defensive shut-out record for Reading, extending to 1,103 minutes, when Allan Glover's cross was inadvertently put into his own net by a home defender – but an equaliser arrived on the stroke of half-time. On the hour mark, John Fraser received a pass from Dean Smith and hit a cracking long range drive to secure the lead for a second time, but twelve minutes later, an identical, equalising goal ensured that the spoils were shared.

Tue 21st August: **Southend (H) League Cup 1st Round**
Lost 1-4   **Attendance: 7,818**

Despite a bright opening period, the visitor's goal, after 25 minutes, all but settled the tie – by the time the break arrived two further goals, the first following a Pat Kruse error, had killed all hopes of a revival. The aggregate score was extended to 6-1 ten minutes after half-time, before Doug Allder hit a late consolation with a fierce drive from the edge of the penalty box.

Sat 25th August: **Swindon Town (A)**
Lost 0-4   **Attendance: 7,204**

A heavy defeat was underway after 40 minutes when Jim McNichol's casual back-pass set up the opener and, just three minutes after the break, a second goal was conceded as Dave Carlton deflected a cross to present a lurking home striker with an easy chance. The game was ended as a contest, and the rout was completed, with further goals in the 68th and 74th minutes.

Sat 1st September: **Chesterfield (H)**
Won 3-1   **Attendance: 5,762**

A 9th minute goal was the inspiration for an impressive display, arriving courtesy of Dave Carlton, scoring after the keeper had parried a shot from Jackie Graham. But the lead lasted just three minutes before Carlton deflected a free-kick into his own net. Between the goals Steve Phillips missed a penalty, awarded for a foul on Jim McNichol, and it took until the 62nd minute for the crucial second goal to arrive – Jackie Graham, Doug Allder and Steve Phillips combined to set up John Fraser to score. In the 72nd minute Steve Phillips latched onto a pass from Doug Allder and laid the ball off to debutant Billy Holmes to seal the victory with a low drive.

Sat 8th September: **Sheffield Wednesday (A)**
Won 2-0   **Attendance: 11,778**

An eventful game produced a well-deserved victory that could have been even more comprehensive, as a 75th minute penalty was missed by Steve Phillips. The opening goal had arrived after 30 minutes when Phillips set up Lee Holmes to score – the decisive second goal came in the 51st minute, when the roles were reversed and Phillips netted from Holmes's pass.

Sat 15th September: **Grimsby Town (H)**
Won 1-0   **Attendance: 7,121**

The opening period produced entertaining, attacking football but, after taking the lead in the 21st minute, the performance deteriorated into a poor spectacle with the visitors threatening an equaliser

throughout. The goal was a freak effort – Danis Salman received the ball from Doug Allder and hit a hopeful 30-yard punt into the penalty box and the ball slipped through the keeper's hands and trickled between his legs into the net.

Mon 17th September: Exeter City (H)
Lost 0-2   Attendance: 7,809

Despite being dominated, and spending almost the entire game camped in their own half, Exeter found themselves two goals up before the break following two strikes in a five-minute period – the first of which came as a result of a Danis Salman misjudgement. A frustrating second half followed the same format, with the visiting goalkeeper in inspired form, Brentford enjoyed lots of possession without any reward.

Sat 22nd September: Wimbledon (A)
Drew 0-0   Attendance: 5,524

An obvious lack of fire power proved costly against the division's bottom team – even Wimbledon being reduced to ten men failed to improve the situation, despite a string of corners and overall domination during the game.

Sat 29th September: Southend United (H)
Won 2-0   Attendance: 6,928

After a bright start, the midfield battle was gradually lost, and it took two late goals to seal the win – the deadlock being broken in the 73rd minute as Jim McNichol powered home a corner from Jackie Graham. The second goal arrived in stoppage time when Steve Phillips nipped in to score after McNichol's free-kick had been parried by the keeper. The game attracted national press interest for the fact that Lee Holmes was raced across London by motorbike at the final whistle in order to get to his 5.30pm wedding in Barking – changing from his football kit into his wedding suit in a nearby pub car park on arrival.

Wed 3rd October: Exeter City (A)
Drew 0-0   Attendance: 3,297

The final whistle came as a relief to the crowd, who witnessed a dull draw played out in atrocious conditions, with rain pouring onto an already sodden pitch. The night was a washout in every sense of the word, even though The Bees held the upper hand.

Sat 6th October: Barnsley (H)
Won 3-1   Attendance: 7,292

The best performance of the season was acknowledged to be possibly the most impressive display of Bill Dodgin's reign as manager – two early goals provided the necessary impetus, the first of which, in the 14th minute, came when Pat Kruse rose highest to head home an overhead kick from Lee Holmes. Two minutes later Danis Salman crossed from the right, Dean Smith nodded on and Lee Holmes powered a header home. The game was settled after 42 minutes when Dean Smith slotted home after a flick-on by Billy Holmes from Jim McNichol's free-kick – although Barnsley grabbed a 50th minute penalty awarded for handball by McNichol.

Wed 10th October: Oxford United (A)
Won 2-0   Attendance: 6,362

A quality display brought an early reward when Jim McNichol hammered a 25-yard free-kick directly into the net in the 10th minute. The game was sewn up on 82 minutes with a piece of individual brilliance from Steve Phillips – latching onto a cross from Billy Holmes to drive the ball fiercely past the keeper.

Sat 13th October: Blackpool (A)
Lost 4-5   Attendance: 5,386

An extraordinary game came to life in the second half after a 15th minute 25-yard thunderbolt from Dave Carlton had been equalised on the stroke of half-time – Pat Kruse failed to clear the danger. Steve Phillips scored after 53 minutes from a Doug Allder cross, but the home side hit back with two goals in a minute, before Billy

Holmes restored parity with a text-book diving header from another Allder cross. Two more goals for the hosts, in the 82nd and 87th minutes, settled the game, but Jim McNichol blasted home an 89th minute free-kick to complete the goal feast.

Sat 20th October: **Blackburn Rovers (H)**
Won 2-0   **Attendance: 7,970**

Another early strike provided the platform for victory – a free-kick on the edge of the penalty box in the 7th minute was tapped by Jackie Graham to Jim McNichol, who cracked home a superb effort. The second goal arrived in the 52nd minute, when Danis Salman's pull-back was headed across goal by Doug Allder and the ball struck Steve Phillips on the shin and rolled into the net.

Mon 22nd October: **Sheffield United (H)**
Lost 1-2   **Attendance: 13,764**

A highly-charged match between the top two teams produced a pulsating, skilful, yet ill-tempered clash. The Blades took a 33rd minute lead, equalised in the second period when Dave Carlton's shot from Jim McNichol's cross, rebounded off the bar allowing Dean Smith to score. The lead lasted just two minutes and the winning goal came in controversial circumstances – FIFA referee, Alf Grey, ordered a penalty retake after Len Bond had saved the first attempt, adjudging the keeper had moved too soon. The tension boiled over when both sides were reduced to ten men, Doug Allder was sent off for his part in a touchline clash with Mickey Speight that escalated into a free for all involving players and officials.

Sat 27th October: **Plymouth Argyle (A)**
Won 1-0   **Attendance: 5,203**

A penalty save by Len Bond in the 10th minute, awarded for hand-ball against Pat Kruse, proved crucial in what ultimately proved to be a comfortable win after Jackie Graham scored in the 62nd minute, crashing the ball into an unguarded net having been set-up by Steve Phillips.

Sat 3rd November: **Reading (H)**
Drew 2-2   **Attendance: 10,011**

A hugely entertaining encounter saw Reading take a 43rd minute lead, which was cancelled out straight from the re-start when Jackie Graham back-headed Dave Carlton's cross into the path of Dean Smith, who hooked the ball into the net. Despite falling behind again in the 77th minute, another instant response secured a point – Danis Salman's cross was left by both Lee Holmes and Steve Phillips for Dean Smith to coolly slot home his second goal.

Tue 6th November: **Sheffield United (A)**
Won 2-0   **Attendance: 14,808**

Despite an attacking display, which brought its reward with victory, it was United who applied the most pressure throughout but failed to make the necessary breakthrough. In the 75th minute Steve Phillips cleverly beat the offside trap and, although his low cross was missed by both Billy Holmes and the keeper, the ball was turned into his own net by an on-rushing defender. The home side's attempted revival was thwarted three minutes from time when John Fraser's shot was deflected into the path of Dean Smith to volley into the roof of the net.

Sat 10th November: **Colchester United (H)**
Won 1-0   **Attendance: 9,070**

A goal in the 2nd minute from Jim McNichol, who powered home a header from the game's first corner by Dave Carlton, proved to be the match-winner. Although the visitors took control before the break, and dominated the game until the final whistle, Brentford's cause was not helped by Dave Carlton's 61st minute dismissal for a second booking.

Sat 17th November: **Rotherham United (A)**
Lost 2-4   **Attendance: 4,709**

Two first-half goals put the hosts in control, until Jim McNichol had a shot handled on the line just before the break and converted the

penalty-kick himself. Despite a third Rotherham goal, hope arrived in the 80th minute when Steve Phillips was fouled on the edge of the box and Jackie Graham's short free-kick was thumped low into the net by McNichol for his second goal. The killer strike came in injury-time to secure a flattering win for the home side.

Sat 24th November: **Swindon Town (A) FA Cup 1st Round**
Lost 1-4   **Attendance: 9,472**

A dreadful display saw Swindon go four up inside the first 35 minutes – the game was effectively a no contest after goals were conceded in the 5th, 20th, 25th and 35th minutes. Dean Smith scored a headed consolation after 58 minutes, but no further respectability could be added to the scoreline.

Sat 1st December: **Carlisle United (A)**
Lost 1-3   **Attendance: 4,275**

In a swirling wind the hosts took a 34th minute lead, but a deserved equaliser arrived in the 62nd minute, when a John Fraser cross resulted in a goalmouth scramble and Lee Holmes prodded the ball home. An unstoppable volley after 70 minutes all but settled the encounter, which was given an unrealistic scoreline when the home side snatched an injury-time third goal, on an afternoon compounded by Len Bond suffering a broken wrist.

Sat 8th December: **Hull City (H)**
Won 7-2   **Attendance: 6,793**

The scoring in a scintillating display was underway after 18 minutes, when Keith Fear's shot came back off the post for Steve Phillips to net and, seven minutes later, Phillips grabbed his second when he knocked the ball home after Bob Booker had flicked on Dave Carlton's cross. Booker snatched his first in the 35th minute – receiving a pass from Paul Shrubb, he turned smartly to place the ball low into the net. City pulled a goal back on the stroke of half-time, but

three goals in six minutes ended the game as a contest. Goals from Bob Booker, in the 53rd and 59th minutes, secured a hat-trick in only his third start, and sandwiched a splendid strike from Keith Fear who converted a Barry Tucker cross from the most acute of angles. In the 87th minute Keith Fear's cross was headed home by Pat Kruse – a last minute goal for the visitors ended the scoring exploits in a game that many Bees fans would always remember.

Sat 15th December: **Oxford United (H)**
Drew 1-1   **Attendance: 7,592**

Strong winds and biting, cold conditions did little to enthuse the crowd and the poor fare served up by the two teams did nothing to assist. Oxford took a 60th minute lead – taking advantage of a dreadful back-pass from Barry Tucker – but the equaliser came six minutes later, when Danis Salman headed home after a brilliant turn in the box by Keith Fear. But the win, which would have secured top spot, was not forthcoming.

Fri 21st December: **Bury (A)**
Lost 2-4   **Attendance: 2,443**

A poor first-half display ended with Bury in front after an 11th minute goal, and although a 25-yard screamer from John Fraser after the break drew the teams level, it was the home side who took advantage of poor defending to score twice more. Bob Booker's 86th minute goal provided a glimmer of hope, which was ended in the 90th minute, when the hosts completed the scoring.

Wed 26th December: **Chester (H)**
Drew 2-2   **Attendance: 10,139**

On an icy pitch, a mistake-ridden tussle produced a below-par performance. Jim McNichol opened the scoring when he netted from a rebound, after his own shot had been parried by the keeper. The visitors equalised in the 58th minute, but Keith Fear turned on a loose ball to drive home just 60 seconds later. An 88th minute second equaliser saw the points shared.

Sat 29th December: **Swindon Town (H)**
Lost 1-3   **Attendance: 12,122**

With Bill Dodgin stranded at his home as a result of flooding, a much-needed win looked on the cards when John Fraser smashed the opener after Danis Salman had created the chance in the 16th minute. But an equaliser after 35 minutes proved to be the game's turning point – the visitors dominated from that stage and 47th and 85th minute goals were scant reward for their superiority.

Sat 5th January: **Gillingham (H)**
Lost 0-2   **Attendance: 7,849**

A rough and tumble affair hardly looked like ending the poor run, and two goals for the Gills, the first of which coming after just nine minutes, never looked like being recovered despite lots of possession and a one man advantage for almost the entire second half.

Sat 12th January: **Chesterfield (A)**
Lost 0-1   **Attendance: 5,529**

A deserved point was not forthcoming after the encounter was decided by a 67th minute goal for Chesterfield – the 73rd minute sending-off of Pat Kruse for a second bookable offence simply compounded the disappointment of the day.

Sat 19th January: **Sheffield Wednesday (H)**
Drew 2-2   **Attendance: 8,389**

The ITV *Big Match* cameras witnessed a much improved performance in a superbly entertaining match. Wednesday took a 29th minute lead, before Steve Phillips equalised a minute after the break with a vicious half-volley from a Lee Holmes header. Despite falling behind for a second time, a point was earned when Bob Booker caused havoc amongst defenders, allowing Lee Holmes to tap the ball into an empty net.

[Right] Lee Holmes and Jackie Graham close in on the Sheffield Wednesday goalkeeper during the televised draw

Sat 2nd February: **Grimsby Town (A)**
Lost 1-5   **Attendance: 9,817**

Atrocious conditions turned the pitch into a muddy quagmire as overnight snow thawed – but the home side adapted better, taking the lead after 35 minutes and adding further goals in the 63rd and 75th minutes. Some bright play finally brought its reward in the 80th minute – Steve Phillips seized on a goalkeeping error to reduce the arrears, but two goals in the final two minutes, the last of which was an own goal by Danis Salman, rubbed salt into the wounds.

Sat 9th February: **Wimbledon (H)**
Lost 0-1   **Attendance: 7,383**

The terrible run of results reached rock-bottom with a dire display against opposition propping up the rest of the division – a first-half goal for the beleaguered visitors won the match as the worrying slide down the table continued.

Sat 16th February: **Southend United (A)**
Lost 2-3   **Attendance: 4,198**

Although an improved performance was evident, defensive frailties were shown up as early as the 5th minute when Pat Kruse steered the ball into his own net and, despite an excellent 28th minute equaliser from Paul Shrubb, blasting the ball home on the turn after good work from Steve Phillips, Willie Graham and Danis Salman, the hosts regained the lead just a minute later. Another defensive blunder after 70 minutes extended the advantage when Steve Phillips sent a long back-pass directly to a lurking home striker, although Phillips redeemed himself slightly when he converted the rebound after his own late penalty kick had been saved.

Sat 23rd February: **Blackpool (H)**
Won 2-1   **Attendance: 6,403**

The ten-match winless run finally ended, although it was the visitors who took the lead before the game was turned on its head by two goals in three second-half minutes. In the 73rd minute Bob Booker rose highest to guide home a header after a cross from Danis Salman and, with the crowd still celebrating, Salman raced forwards again to drive the ball into the net from a square ball laid on by Booker.

Sat 1st March: **Blackburn Rovers (A)**
Lost 0-3   **Attendance: 10,227**

Two goals down at half-time, confidence evaporated, and with no answer to wave after wave of home attacks, the third, inevitable strike came after 47 minutes to inflict another heavy and damaging defeat.

Sat 8th March: **Plymouth Argyle (H)**
Drew 0-0   **Attendance: 6,462**

Although Brentford looked the likelier of the two teams to score, clear-cut chances were few and far between – even the debut of club record signing Tony Funnell up front failed to inspire a tepid attack in a dull goal-less draw.

Mon 10th March: **Mansfield Town (A)**
Drew 0-0   **Attendance: 3,461**

With Noel Parkinson pulling the strings in an outstanding midfield display, a combination of poor finishing and good goalkeeping thwarted attempts to secure a desperately-needed away win – both teams failed to find the necessary breakthrough.

Sat 15th March: **Barnsley (A)**
Lost 0-1   **Attendance: 9,368**

In a game totally dominated by the home side, the single goal victory failed to reflect the balance of play. A series of goal-line clear-

[Right] Barry Tucker moves in to tackle a Mansfield Town forward during Brentford's 2-0 home win

ances and desperate defending restricted Barnsley to a solitary, 41st minute strike to earn the spoils.

Tue 18th March: **Millwall (A)**
Lost 1-3   **Attendance: 6,107**

A display of neat and enterprising approach play was not matched by finishing skills and, after the hosts had taken a 37th minute lead, the result was never in doubt. Two further Millwall goals followed, before an 88th minute consolation effort from Pat Kruse. The dramatic slide down the table from promotion contenders to relegation candidates in just three months showed no sign of ending.

Sat 22nd March: **Colchester United (A)**
Lost 1-6   **Attendance: 3,821**

A catastrophic error in the 6th minute gave the hosts the lead – Jim McNichol's back-pass gifted a goal, and although the rest of the half remained scoreless, the deficit was increased after 48 minutes. Tony Funnell pulled a goal back following some neat play from Steve Phillips, but just 10 minutes later came the decisive third goal, which signalled a total collapse. Three late goals gave the scoreline a look that did not flatter the home side.

Sat 29th March: **Rotherham United (H)**
Lost 0-1   **Attendance: 4,992**

A poor game saw the visitors score the all-important goal in the 56th minute and, when Steve Phillips missed a 78th minute spot-kick after Barry Tucker had been brought down, it signalled not only another defeat, to leave the team fighting a desperate struggle for survival, but also the end of the road for manager Bill Dodgin, who was given leave of absence days later.

Sat 5th April:	Chester (A)
Drew 1-1	Attendance: 2,930

Fred Callaghan's first game in charge produced a battling display, in which Steve Phillips grabbed a 12th minute goal when he latched onto a back-header from Doug Allder, after John Fraser's cross – his shot sneaking between the keeper's legs before rolling over the goal-line. The hosts equalised in the 76th minute, and the final ten minutes were played out with just ten men and Paul Shrubb in goal, after Len Bond was stretchered off.

Mon 7th April:	Mansfield Town (H)
Won 2-0	Attendance: 6,057

Showing more flight and flair than in recent months, a much-improved performance was marked by two second-half goals, – the first of which arrived on the hour when Noel Parkinson's corner was netted by Lee Holmes, and 14 minutes later, Steve Phillips made it two, deflecting Paul Shrubb's shot over the keeper's head following another Parkinson corner.

Tue 8th April:	Bury (H)
Drew 0-0	Attendance: 6,751

A second home match in just 24 hours provided another crucial point, gained despite a punchless performance against poor opposition – proceedings petered out into a bore draw as the encounter drifted towards an inevitable conclusion.

Sat 12th April:	Gillingham (A)
Won 1-0	Attendance: 5,889

After absorbing intense early pressure from the home side, confidence visibly grew, and five minutes before the half-time interval, a superb goal proved to be the match-winner – Bob Booker received a pass from Steve Phillips and curled a tremendous 20-yard effort beyond the keeper, a contender for the goal of the season.

Sat 19th April:	Carlisle United (H)
Lost 0-3	Attendance: 6,130

A poor display was highlighted by a series of defensive blunders, which started when 23rd minute errors by both John Fraser and Danis Salman led to the opening goal for the visitors. After the lead had been doubled on 47 minutes, another defensive slip, this time from Pat Kruse in the 71st minute, completed a heavy and costly defeat.

Sat 26th April:	Hull City (A)
Lost 1-2	Attendance: 5,382

Despite playing some attractive football in an overall disappointing game, a 23rd minute goal from Lee Holmes, who converted a cross from Barry Tucker, served only to equalise Hull's 16th minute opener. City then grabbed the winner in the 64th minute to leave the ultimate outcome of the season dependent on the final match.

Sat 3rd May:	Millwall (H)
Won 1-0	Attendance: 7,033

With just 12 minutes of a tense and nervous London derby encounter remaining, Tony Funnell raced clear and kept his composure to lash the ball high into the roof of the net for the game's only goal, thereby guaranteeing another season of Third Division football.

Allder: 'I never threw a punch'

'First thing I knew, the fellow pushed me . . .'
— Doug Allder

DOUG ALLDER spoke after the game about only the second sending off of his soccer career.

"I'm really upset about it. It all happened so quickly. The first thing I knew, the other fellow had hold of me up against the trainer's bench and everyone crowded round us.

"Then the ref told us not to come back on the pitch. I didn't throw any punches, I was amazed when the ref sent me off."

Brentford boss Bill Dodgin defended his winger, a constant source of torment to the United defence all evening.

"He couldn't punch his way out of a wet paper bag".

The last time Allder got his marching orders was as a Millwall player several years ago.

He has a reputation for conning referees and defenders — but his team-mate Barry Tucker said afterwards: "You should see Douggie's legs. He was really given some stick tonight."

United boss Harry Haslam said: "It is sad that something like this should happen, and people only remember the bad things. They will forget that there was some very good football played by both sides."

He wouldn't comment on Mr Grey's handling of the match, though. "I'll have to wait to see his report," he said.

Len Bond was "disgusted" at the decision that the penalty be re-taken. "No way did I move my feet before he kicked it.

"I swayed to my left and then the other way — but I didn't move my feet," he said.

Again, Dodgin backed his man: "I agree with Len. We were stupid to give away the penalty in the first place, though. But it shouldn't have been re-taken.

"I thought it was a fair save," he said. "But in any case, we should have had a penalty earlier instead of an indirect free-kick."

And on Mr Grey, Dodgin said: "What can you do? The result will stand, and you have to accept that with as much good grace as you can."

PRE-SEASON

Andy McCulloch rejected the offer of a new contract and was sold to Sheffield Wednesday for a club record sale fee of £60,000.

A £15,000 transfer was agreed with Plymouth Argyle for striker Keith Fear but the player decided that he did not wish to move to London and the deal collapsed.

23-year old striker Lee Holmes signed from Enfield on a one-year contract as a part-time player so that he could continue his career as a civil engineer.

Terry Benning aged 17 was given a one month contract having been released by Watford.

Danis Salman demanded a transfer, stating that he would not train with the team and would never kick another ball for the club.

AUGUST 1979

• Cup opponents Southend were hit by a bout of food poisoning and the matches were unable to be completed before the start of the season as scheduled. The opening home League game with Oxford was postponed to enable the cup ties to be re-arranged.
• Billy Holmes, a 28-year old striker, was signed from Hereford United for a reported fee of £10,000.
• Terry Benning was offered a one year contract.
• Danis Salman backed down in his dispute and signed a new one-year contract.

SEPTEMBER 1979

• Dave O'Mahoney was signed as an apprentice professional.
• Ken James was appointed as the new commercial manager, having previously held a similar post at Newport County.

● NICE TO see you . . . Brentford new boy Noel Parkinson, right, meets up again with former Ipswich clubmate Jim McNichol.

OCTOBER 1979

● Bob Booker was loaned to Barnet for a two-month period.
● Doug Allder was sent off in the top of the table clash with Sheffield United.

NOVEMBER 1979

● Former transfer target, 27-year old Keith Fear, having been released by Plymouth Argyle, signed a one-month contract.
● 19-year old Welsh defender, Iori Jenkins, was signed on a free transfer from Chelsea.
● Dave Carlton was sent off against Colchester.

● Denis Piggott confirmed that the club had once again enquired about the old Brentford Market land as a possible site for a new ground.

DECEMBER 1979

● Bob Booker was recalled from Barnet and scored a hat-trick in his first game back against Hull City.
● The board of directors announced that they had shelved plans to move to a new site and revealed proposals to redevelop Griffin Park, with a four-stage plan over a 10-year period. The first stage, to commence in the summer of 1981, would see the rebuilding of the New Road side to incorporate a new stand housing 5,250 seats, with standing for another 2,250. Future proposals included the rebuilding of the Brook Road and Ealing Road terraces.

JANUARY 1980

● The New Year's Day fixture at Mansfield Town was postponed as a result of bad weather, as was the end of month home game with Millwall.
● Steve Harding, a 23-year old centre-back, was signed on one month's loan from Bristol Rovers.
● Four players were placed on the transfer list as they did not figure in the manager's plans for the future – Paul Walker, Allan Glover, Willie Graham and Billy Holmes.
● Keith Fear was released at the end of his short-term contract.
● Barry Bowen was signed on a non-contract basis.
● Apprentice professional, Dean Johns, was not offered a professional contract and left the club.
● Bill Dodgin denied rumours that he had tried to re-sign 'unsettled' Andy McCulloch from Sheffield Wednesday.

THE BIG BRENTFORD BOOK OF THE SEVENTIES

Manager gets 'paid leave of absence'

DODGIN OUT IN BEES CRISIS

BRENTFORD yesterday smashed their transfer record by £23,000 when they signed unsettled Gillingham striker Tony Funnell.

Funnell, 22, signed for £56,000 after a medical in Toddington and should be in the Bees side which faces Plymouth Argyle at Griffin Park tomorrow.

Although Brentford may sign mid-fielder Noel Parkinson for £50,000 when his month's loan finishes in two weeks time, Funnell is easily the most expensive player Brentford have signed.

The previous record was £33,000 for Scottish Under-21 defender Jim McNichol.

Manager Bill Dodgin is anxious too that the Bees should score more goals and give a boost to their disappointing season which has seen them win only one of their last 12 games.

And he hopes Funnell will link up with Steve Phillips tomorrow.

He said: "I watched Tony at the end of last season and have been

HOPEFUL: Bill Dodgin.

keeping an eye on him ever since.

"He's able to score goals and should be a great asset. I've been looking for strikers all season because we badly need to score goals."

Funnell joined Gillingham from Southampton just under a year ago.

Scorer

He made an immediate impact in the Gillingham side that just missed promotion and finished as their third highest scorer

with seven goals in a dozen matches.

Injuries have restricted his performances this season and Gillingham have struggled to find last season's form.

Sussex born Funnell is five feet six inches tall and was signed from school by Southampton manager Lawrie McMenemy.

But £23,000 deal may well be beaten

- Pat Kruse was sent off in the match with Chesterfield.
- The ITV *Big Match* cameras covered the home clash with Sheffield Wednesday.
- Jim McNichol was suffering from knee ligament damage and faced a spell on the sidelines.
- Director, Bert Poyton, died at the age of 67.

FEBRUARY 1980

- 20-year old midfielder, Noel Parkinson, was signed on loan from Ipswich Town with a view to a permanent transfer for £50,000.
- Chairman, Dan Tana, was unhappy at criticism directed at him and his family at recent home games and indicated that he would stand down if it continued.

MARCH 1980

- After defeat at home to Rotherham, with the team in 18th position, the club announced that Bill Dodgin had been given paid leave of absence until the end of the season.
- Coach, Tommy Baldwin, was sacked
- Woking manager, Fred Callaghan, who assisted Bill Dodgin in 1977, was brought in to take charge of training and the running of all team affairs until the end of the season.
- Dan Tana withdrew his threat to resign as chairman of the board of directors.
- Bill Dodgin's last transfer activity was to pay a club record fee of £56,000 to Gillingham for 22-year old striker Tony Funnell.
- Noel Parkinson's loan period was extended until the end of the season.

CALLAGHAN SET TO GET VOTE

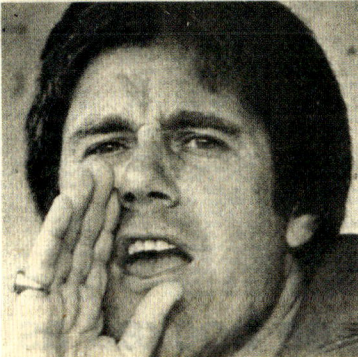

• Waiting and hoping . . . Fred Callaghan

FRED CALLAGHAN is set to be offered the Brentford manager's job tonight after a five-match trial.

Callaghan took charge of team affairs last month in place of Bill Dodgin, after a disastrous run had seen the Bees slide towards the fourth division.

Since then Brentford have taken six points from five games to ease those relegation fears.

And despite a 3-0 home defeat by Carlisle on Saturday, chairman Tana and his fellow directors seem certain to offer Callaghan a two-year contract when they meet at Griffin Park this evening.

By Colin Grant

Tana said today: "Fred Callaghan has performed miracles since taking charge.

"He's brought more discipline to the club and instilled the will to win in the players again.

"We had to take a gamble after our bad run — I think we should have done it a month earlier — but now it seems to have paid off.

"I'm sure we'd have gone down if we hadn't made the change but now we look certain to stay in the third division.

"And the credit must go to the manager. He's been like a breath of fresh air to the club and he'll certainly have my support at tonight's meeting."

Former Fulham player Callaghan is still officially boss of Isthmian League Woking.

However, before the board discuss his appointment they must first decide the future of Dodgin who has been on paid leave of absence since the managerial shake up last month.

And that seems just a question of tying up financial agreements between the manager and club before they part.

	Division 3							
Grimsby	44	25	9	10	69	42	59
Sheff Wed	43	20	15	8	79	43	55
Blackburn	42	23	9	10	53	31	55
Chester'd	42	21	11	10	66	43	53
Colchester	43	18	12	13	58	52	48
Reading	44	16	15	13	65	63	47
Exeter	44	18	10	16	59	65	46
Carlisle	44	17	11	16	64	56	45
Sheff Utd	43	17	10	16	58	64	44
Swindon	42	18	7	17	68	59	43
Rotherham	43	17	9	17	56	63	43
Millwall	42	15	12	15	61	55	42
Chester	43	15	12	16	46	54	42
Oxford	44	14	13	17	57	58	41
Barnsley	43	14	13	16	49	55	41
Plymouth	43	15	10	18	58	51	40
Gillingham	43	13	14	16	47	49	40
Brentford	44	14	11	19	57	71	39
Southend	43	14	9	20	46	55	37
Blackpool	43	13	10	20	59	74	36
Hull	42	10	16	16	47	64	36
Mansfield	44	10	15	19	45	55	35
Bury	42	14	6	22	41	56	34
Wimbledon	43	9	13	21	46	75	31

Too small to cope

BILL Dodgin's loyalty in turning down the Chelsea job last year was commendable but very foolish.

For you should never show loyalty to people who may not repay the compliment.

Unfortunately for Dodgin, as his track record shows, he showed a darn sight more loyalty than he was ever going to get back.

For the Brentford Board, full of big promises and little action, were simply too small to cope when the going got rough.

They had to find a scapegoat to take the blame off themselves — and, predictably, it had to be Dodgin and coach Tommy Baldwin.

They can issue statements saying Dodgin hasn't been dismissed and that he is only on a paid leave of absence.

But it looks certain that he will never pick another team at Griffin Park.

He deserved a lot more than he got from Brentford — even the dismissal was made behind cover of a phone from, of all places, Yugoslavia.

And if he wasn't such a nice bloke he could

WHAT WE SAY

By STEVE PITTS

certainly drag a few skeletons out of the cupboard. But he won't because, quite simply, he isn't that type of person.

Brentford have been in the doldrums for too long. But surely that is not the fault of the managers who have been in the hot seat at Griffin Park.

Dodgin won six promotions in 13 years and was coach at QPR when they won the League Cup. Former manager John Docherty is working wonders at little Cambridge while Frank Blunstone, among others, has proved himself.

Are they the reason why Brentford are still stuck in the lower regions of the Football League?

Of course not. Brentford is a club that has promised so much and produced so little.

If the Board really want to find the root of the trouble then let them look no further than those sitting around the boardroom table.

I'm not as nice as Bill Dodgin. If it wasn't for the supporters and players, I would be on my knees every night praying that those directors were given a team they rightly deserved . . . and that would be one that couldn't even make the local Sunday leagues.

• Although a fee of £4,000 was agreed with Wealdstone for the sale of Paul Walker, the transfer did not go through when the change of manager took place.

APRIL 1980

• 35-year old Fred Callaghan was appointed as the new team manager on a two-year contract. The former Fulham defender had previously managed Enfield and Woking.
• Bill Dodgin left the club with a payment of one year's salary as compensation.

• TIME TO REFLECT . . . Brentford's Paul Walker thinks over his future at Griffin Park

YES, IT'S FRED'S JOB!

FRED CALLAGHAN is the new team manager at Brentford.

He was given a two-year contract from May 1 at a board meeting last night after serving a successful five-match trial, and spoke excitedly today about his hopes at the club.

"I am very pleased, and now I just hope to bring success to Brentford," he said.

"I'm delighted to be back in the Football League — it's the only place to be — and the potential at Brentford is tremendous.

"I've always wanted to have a crack at being in charge at this particular club and it's just up to me to knock it into shape.

"However, my main priority at the moment is obviously to keep the club in the Third Division."

Callaghan, previously in charge of Isthmian League Woking, was drafted in to Griffin Park at the end of last month to replace Bill Dodgin. This followed just one win in 18 games which had seen the Bees sliding back towards Division 4.

Since then, they have managed six points from five games and although relegation is still a possibility, Callaghan's arrival looks to have ensured Third Division soccer again at Griffin Park next season.

"I've been very pleased with the team so far and the lads have given 100 per cent," went on Callaghan.

By Colin Grant

departing Dodgin officially leaves the club at the end of the month after coming to a financial agreement over compensation.

And ironically Callaghan becomes the first manager to have a contract at Griffin Park since Dodgin's father was in charge in the 50s.

WAKEMAN ON BOARD

Rock star Rick Wakeman is the new man on the Brentford board.

Wakeman, a life-long Bees fan, was co-opted on to the board at last night's meeting to replace Bert Pynton who died in January.

The former Hanwell schoolboy rocketed to fame as a member of the Yes pop group and has since established himself as one of the World's leading keyboard players.

He's now a tax exile, living in Switzerland, but watches the Bees when he is allowed in the country.

He and Bifran Lane, manager of the group Yes, were reported to be ready to put £1m into the club in the

ideas and a clear-out of players at Griffin Park now looks certain during the summer.

Callaghan is also expected to name an assistant in the next few weeks, with Alan Humphries, his No 2 at Woking, a leading candidate.

Callaghan had a successful spell in charge of Woking, guiding them to this season's FA Trophy semi-final.

He was previously boss at Enfield and played for Fulham in the 60s.

- Noel Parkinson returned to Ipswich before the end of his loan spell.
- Paul Shrubb took over in goal in the game at Chester after Len Bond was injured.
- Rock star Rick Wakeman (pictured above) joined the board to fill the vacancy created by Bert Poyton's death.
- The club announced that an application had been made to join the under-17 South East Counties League for the new season.

MAY 1980

- Tony Funnell's 78th minute goal against Millwall ensured survival by two points, with a 19th place finish in the table.
- Fred Callaghan announced that Chelsea's 35-year old defender, and captain, Ron Harris would join the club in the summer as player/assistant manager.
- Lee Holmes rejected the opportunity to become full-time and was placed on the transfer list.

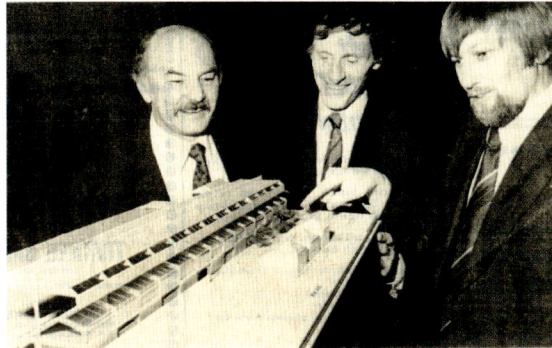

● This is the model of the new stand that we told you about in last week's Chronicle. It is planned for the New Road side of the ground with a seating capacity of 5,250 and standing room for 2,250. Club secretary Denis Piggott is shown here studying the model.

Building for the future

● Brentford FC . . . preparing for top class football.

● Denis Piggott . . . planning for the future.

Brentford put on show plans for new stand

BRENTFORD'S plans for a completely new stand at Griffin Park are to be unveiled at a public meeting tonight.

Fans and local residents are being given a golden opportunity to see the detailed proposals for a new stand on the New Road side of the ground.

Brentford are planning a stand that will have seating capacity of 5,250 and standing room for 2,250. They want to begin building it during the close season of 1981.

And club secretary Denis Piggott said: "This is only the first development of a four-stage plan that we hope will be completed within ten years."

The rest of the overall plan is to redevelop the Braemar Road stand and the Brook Road (Royal Oak) end and install squash courts and a restaurant behind the Ealing Road terraces.

Mr. Piggott said: "This will be the first major work carried out on the ground since 1930 and it makes our future very exciting and bright."

The proposed New Road stand—which will be brought a little closer to the pitch—will have facilities for extra programme stalls, sales kiosks and food and drink catering.

"We are preparing for football in the higher divisions," said Mr. Piggott. "It will not be long before we are in Division Two, I am certain of that, and we will then need a stadium that complies with the Safety of Sports Grounds Act.

"But we don't want to wait until we have to qualify for the certificate before we start improving the ground. At present only First and Second Division clubs need to comply with the Act but we want to be ready."

He added: "I hope this convinces the doubters who say we don't want Second Division football, that we really do.

"We are doing this for the supporters and the people who live in New Road because they all deserve it.

"I think the world of our supporters and they deserve this for supporting us during the bad years.

"It will also be a big improvement for the people of New Road because it will mean that we can build a big wall round the back of the stand that will block out any disturbance to them."

The cost of the new stand, and the complete redevelopment, has not been disclosed but Mr. Piggott said: "It is going to cost a lot of money."

He added: "We are very much aware of Chelsea's problems and the difficulty they have run into over their new stand but we have learned from the Chelsea experience.

"I can assure our fans that the money available for players will not be affected by these plans.

"After all, if we don't have a good enough team then there is little point in building new stands because we will have no one to fill them.

"I feel Chelsea's trouble was that while they were rebuilding the new stand they were doing well and didn't have the capacity to hold the crowds they could command.

"We will not run into that problem because our capacity is far greater than our crowds at the moment so we will not have to lock people out."

● The plans—including a scale model of the proposed stand—go on show at 7.45 pm tonight at the Methodist Church Hall, Clifden Road, Brentford.

217

MANAGERS

Frank Blunstone

Born: 17th October 1934
Blirthplace: Crewe
Appointed in December 1969
Resigned in July 1973

BACKGROUND

He initially joined his home-town team, Crewe Alexandra, on amateur terms at the age of 15 and, having progressed rapidly, made his first team bow a year later – scoring on his debut and attaining England Youth recognition. After making 48 League appearances, and scoring 12 goals, he attracted attention from the bigger clubs and, in February 1953, joined Chelsea for a £7,000 transfer fee. Frank played for the Army while doing his national service, and in November 1954, won the first of five full England international caps to add to the five under-23 appearances – Blunstone also won a First Division championship with the Blues in 1955. A flying left winger, Frank made 317 league appearances for Chelsea, scoring 47 goals, but he also suffered two broken legs – the second of which, in 1964, brought about a premature end to his playing career. He was appointed as youth team trainer/coach at Stamford Bridge in October 1964 and went on to discover, and nurture, many of the players who figured in the Chelsea teams of the late 60s and early 70s.

AS BRENTFORD MANAGER

Following the resignation of Jimmy Sirrell in November 1969, skipper Ron Fenton looked after team affairs as a caretaker until 35-year old Frank Blunstone was appointed as Brentford manager a month later. Blunstone immediately set about re-building the side on a shoe-string budget in the aftermath of the takeover crisis two years earlier. After almost winning promotion in 1969-70, the team made a dreadful start to the 1970-71 season, which opened with six straight defeats and produced just two wins in the first 16 games, although the team went on to reach the fifth round of the FA Cup. The following season,1971-72, saw promotion achieved with a squad of just 14 players and based on a philosophy of all-out attack at home, and deep defending away from home. Despite large home attendances, he was unable to obtain funding to strengthen his squad for the next season, and key players were allowed to leave without being replaced. The 1972/73 season, unsurprisingly, ended in relegation back to the bottom division after a dreadful run of 17 successive defeats away from Griffin Park.

Disillusioned by the lack of boardroom support, Blunstone resigned during the summer of 1973, stating that he had never been allowed to manage as he would have wished and took up the post of Youth Team coach at Manchester United, this despite suffering horrific injuries in a car crash, which prevented him from taking up his new position for several months.

Frank progressed to become assistant manager to Tommy Docherty at Old Trafford and then followed 'The Doc' to Derby County in a similar role, before leaving the English game and moving abroad for a couple of years to manage Greek sides Ethnikos and Aris Salonika. He returned to England in 1980 to coach at Sheffield Wednesday under Jack Charlton.

In October 1983, having left Hillsborough during the preceding summer, Blunstone applied for the post of assistant manager to Fred Callaghan back at Griffin Park, following the departure of Ron Harris. But his return, after an absence of ten years, saw him unable to arrest the decline in results, and when Callaghan was sacked in February 1984, Blunstone acted in a caretaker role for one game – a 3-2 home defeat to Gillingham. He lost his job days later when Frank McLintock and John Docherty were named as the new management team, a move that brought an end to Blunstone's involvement in the professional game.

Frank Blunstone's own thoughts regarding his time at Brentford appear on the following pages.

Record as Brentford Manager (not including one game as caretaker in 1984)   174 games   41% win ratio   61% unbeaten

	Games	Won	Drawn	Lost	F	A	Pts
League	162	66	35	61	219	196	167
FA Cup	8	4	1	3	11	9	-
FL Cup	4	1	0	3	2	6	-

The Brentford job was only the second manager's job that I'd put my name forward for. I'd had a nightmare interview for the Reading position once, when I was completely unprepared, but I did well enough to be given a chance at Griffin Park and I think I did well at the club. John Bond, who went on to take Norwich to the top flight, was also in the running for the Brentford job then.

When I took over in 1969 we were £69,000 in the red and everything was cut back to the bare bones. I remember for one game I had to name goalkeeper Gordon Phillips as sub, that was when you were only allowed one sub. But I simply didn't have any more outfield players to bring in, so I asked Gordon to sit on the bench.

The first two years were very good, we got promoted, but then got relegated again straight away – that was the chairman Les Davey's fault. The Cup run was good too, we went to Cardiff, who were top of the Second Division at the time, and beat them 2-0, before going out at Hull City in the Fifth Round. But we should have got something out of that game, one of their goals was a foul on the keeper and should have been disallowed.

We had some good crowds at Griffin Park then too including 18,000 against Crewe Alexandra during a season that we averaged almost 12,000 – that got the financial deficit right down. But the season we went down, I knew it was on the cards. The chairman didn't have a clue.

He came up to me once and asked why we didn't have better players, and when I told him why, because he wouldn't pay decent wages or transfers, he didn't like it. He wouldn't even give the players a rise when they won promotion.

Because of that, at the start of the following season, only six of the lads had signed a contract to play, so I had a major problem. I was always falling out with Davey, and we almost lost Stewart Houston because of the board – they just wouldn't pay out for anything.

Dave Sexton at Chelsea did me a massive favour by telling me about Houston.

John O'Mara had been banned for five games by the Football League because of his poor disciplinary record and we needed a replacement if we wanted to go up, but the chairman said we couldn't have one. Eric Radley-Smith, the old club doctor, gave me the money out of his own pocket to pay Houston's signing on fee in the end, that is the only reason we got the player and won promotion that season.

The best deal I did while I was at Brentford, though, was buying John O'Mara, I'd been watching him for ages. He was 6ft 3 inches tall, big built, but didn't have a clue about the game. But for £750 I knew I'd be able to do something with him. I put so much training in with O'Mara, coaching him myself and taught him the game and how to make good runs.

He got 30 goals for me, but he got booked almost as often as he scored! He was quick too, I entered him into the professional footballer's athletics meeting at Wimbledon Dog Track just after he arrived and he came through all the heats and came second in the 80 metres. For a big guy I thought that was fantastic.

But Brentford would sell anyone. Ken Furphy was manager at Blackburn at the time and straight after we'd beaten them 4-0 at Griffin Park he came up to me and asked if I'd sell John. I laughed and said knowing the chairman I expect so. He rang back on the Monday morning and offered £50,000 for John and he went, but he never scored a goal for them! But I knew how to deal with O'Mara, I knew how to wind him up to get the best out of him.

Ron Greenwood at West Ham did me a favour with Roger Cross, he let me have him for £10,000 because he didn't really need him, although he was a very good player, he still had Martin Peters and Geoff Hurst. Roger wasn't the bravest in the area, but he was good

on the ball and worked well with O'Mara and Little Doc - it was a lovely blend. Then one day Bill Dodgin rang me up and asked if I'd sell Roger Cross, so I had to say those words again, "I expect so, Brentford will sell anybody!" I wanted to sign Stan Bowles from Crewe too, I could have had him for £15,000 cash, but there's no way the chairman would have paid that, the same with Andy McCulloch who was at QPR at the time — we had the money from O'Mara and I thought he would have been the perfect replacement.

I loved Brentford, I had four enjoyable years there. I wouldn't have left – I had the chance of going to Everton, which I turned down, but in the end I decided to go to Old Trafford. I just couldn't continue working in those conditions and I simply couldn't get on with the chairman – everything was always a struggle. But I really liked the club and that was the reason I came back to Griffin Park to help Fred Callaghan when he was manager.

Frank Blunstone

223

Mike Everitt

Born: 16th January 1941
Birthplace: Clacton
Appointed in August 1973
Dismissed in January 1975

BACKGROUND

Highly rated as a schoolboy, the young Essex half-back opted to join Arsenal as a 15-year-old and, having signed professional terms, made his first-team debut in February 1958 aged 17 , marking Johnny Haynes. Following a club tour to Italy he was allowed to spend some time in the United States and, after nine League games at Highbury, during which he scored one goal, Everitt joined Northampton Town in February 1961 where, under Dave Bowen's management, the Cobblers underwent a meteoric and record-breaking run from the Fourth to the First Division. After 207 League appearances he was sold to Plymouth Argyle for £12,000 in March 1967, before moving on to Brighton and Hove Albion in the summer of 1968, where he saw out his professional playing days – ending with 272 league appearances and 17 goals to his name.

Everitt moved into coaching as player-manager at Western League Plymouth City and led them to third place in the division before financial difficulties caused the club to fold midway through the 1971-72 season. He was then handed a player-manager role at non-League Wimbledon.

AS BRENTFORD MANAGER

Following Frank Blunstone's resignation in the summer of 1973, and a week before the start of pre-season training, 32-year-old Mike Everitt was the surprise choice as the new team manager. His period of notice with Wimbledon meant that he was unable to take up his new role until seven days before the campaign kicked-off. Although officially appointed as a player-manager he indicated that he would only appear in the first-team in an emergency and, true to his word, he only ever played for the reserves.

Everitt's unavailability to participate in the bulk of the pre-season programme did not help with a difficult start to the season and, by the end of October, the team hit rock-bottom, sitting in 92nd place in the Football League. Considerable unrest had resulted in a host of established players being placed on the transfer list at their own request and, although the season ended strongly, with just two defeats in 15 matches, much of the credit went to senior professionals, Jimmy Gabriel and John Docherty, who were assisting with the coaching.

With the summer departure of the two acting coaches, the 1974/75 campaign proved to be another one of struggle and, mid-way through the season, just weeks after receiving a vote of confidence from the board, Everitt was sacked as manager in January 1975.

Everitt moved to Leicester City as a coach, then made a name for himself in Egyptian football by leading his team, Arab Contractors, to the African Cup Winners Cup in both 1982 and 1983, followed by the Egyptian League title in 1984. He also coached in both Kuwait and Morocco.

Living in retirement on the Isle of Man, Everitt was voted into Northampton Town's 'Team of the Century' in 2001.

Record as Brentford Manager   78 games   29% win ratio   58% unbeaten

	Games	Won	Drawn	Lost	F	A	Pts
League	72	21	22	29	75	78	64
FA Cup	3	1	0	2	5	4	-
FL Cup	3	1	0	2	5	4	-

Jess Willard

Born: 16th January 1924
Birthplace: Chichester
Caretaker Manager in January 1975

BACKGROUND

An old fashioned wing-half, Jess played for Chichester City and spent seven years at Brighton and Hove Albion before moving to Crystal Palace in 1953, where he made 47 appearances and scored five goals. Jess retired from the game because of injury at the age of 31 and moved into a coaching role working with the juniors at Selhurst Park.

He remained as a valued member of the backroom staff at Palace throughout the 1960s as the Eagles reached the top flight in 1969 – then extended his stay to almost 20 years by moving into the role of Chief Scout.

Having ended his long association with Crystal Palace, 49-year-old Cecil 'Jess' Willard joined up with the newly appointed manager Mike Everitt as trainer in the summer of 1973 and, when Everitt was dismissed in January 1975, took up the reins as caretaker for the 2-2 draw at home with Workington. Jess lost his job days later when John Docherty became manager and reinstated Eddie Lyons into the trainer's role.

Jess Willard died in 2005 at the age of 81.

Record as Brentford Manager

	Games	Won	Drawn	Lost	F	A	Pts
League	1	0	1	0	2	2	1

John Docherty

Born: 29th April 1940
Birthplace: Glasgow
Appointed in January 1975
Resigned in September 1976

BACKGROUND

John Docherty's long footballing career started at the Scottish junior club St Roch's, before he moved to London in July 1959 when he was signed by Brentford manager Malcolm MacDonald. Docherty made 17 appearances and scored two goals, before leaving Griffin Park to sign for Sheffield United (£17,500) in March 1961. Docherty played 41 games for The Blades, scoring 9 goals, but returned to Griffin Park in December 1965 when Tommy Cavanagh re-signed him for Brentford. Following 97 more League games, and another 31 goals, Docherty left again, this time to join Reading for a £12,000 fee in February 1968. In March 1970 he returned to Brentford for a third time as manager Frank Blunstone looked to build his new team.

A diminutive and speedy winger, with an excellent goal-scoring record, Docherty's final spell proved to be his most productive, scoring 34 goals in 141 league games, including 13 in the promotion winning campaign of 1971/72. He finally retired from playing when he was released by Mike Everitt in May 1974, and after assisting with the coaching and helping to develop the junior set-up at Griffin Park, he moved to Queens Park Rangers after being offered the role of youth team manager.

AS BRENTFORD MANAGER

Following the dismissal of Mike Everitt in January 1975, Bees chairman, Dan Tana, looked to John Docherty, then aged 34, to resurrect the team's fortunes. Although Docherty guided Brentford away from the relegation zone during the remainder of the 1974/75 campaign, he failed to maintain progress after a promising start to the following season, which saw a number of youngsters blooded but produced little in the way of entertainment or results. After another

poor start to the 1976/77 season, and an early season fall-out with Dan Tana, in which the chairman failed to satisfy Docherty's concerns that he was no longer wanted as manager, Docherty handed in his resignation.

He was then appointed as assistant manager to Ron Atkinson at Cambridge United and, after succeeding him as manager, helped them to a second successive promotion in 1977/78, and spent five full seasons successfully keeping them in the second tier of English football on a shoe-string budget.

In February 1984, two months after leaving the Abbey Stadium, he returned to Brentford for a fifth time when he was appointed as assistant manager to Frank McLintock and stayed until the summer of 1986, when he resigned, again, to take up the post of Millwall manager. Docherty led the Lions to the top flight for the first time in their history, and was re-joined by Frank McLintock in a reversal of their previous roles.

Following relegation back to the Second Division, he left The Den in March 1990, and had a brief spell as Bradford City boss before stints in non-League management at Halifax Town and Slough Town. Despite suffering a stroke in 1995, Docherty returned to Millwall to oversee all football playing affairs when the South London club were in administration in 1997, but the six-month arrangement proved to be his last appointment in the game.

Record as Brentford Manager   78 games   33% win ratio   63% unbeaten

	Games	Won	Drawn	Lost	F	A	Pts
League	69	23	20	26	82	81	66
FA Cup	4	2	1	1	4	2	-
FL Cup	5	1	2	2	5	7	-

Eddie Lyons

Born: 20th May 1920
Birthplace: Manchester
Caretaker Manager in September 1976

BACKGROUND

An uncompromising full-back, Eddie played two games for Bury, and six times for Millwall, in the immediate post-war years, then spent just over a year with Crewe Alexandra where he made 23 appearances. Lyons ended his League career with Rochdale, where he scored his solitary goal during a 19 match stay during the 1953/54 season. He moved into non-League football with Dartford, while also running a newsagents shop in Ealing and training at Griffin Park while assisting with the third team and then the Brentford reserves. He took up the role of first-team trainer under Frank Blunstone, a former playing colleague at Crewe, and subsequently qualified as a physiotherapist before resigning when Blunstone quit in the summer of 1973.

Eddie spent a short time assisting at Queens Park Rangers, before returning to Griffin Park with John Docherty in January 1975, and he remained as first-team trainer and physiotherapist under managers Bill Dodgin, Fred Callaghan and Frank McLintock. He retired in January 1985, although continuied to assist for a short time on a part-time basis and was awarded a testimonial match against Chelsea in May 1984, making a brief appearance as a substitute in the game which was played just six days short of his 64th birthday.

In September 1976, when John Docherty quit as manager, 56-year old Eddie Lyons took charge in a caretaker capacity for one game, a 1-1 draw at Aldershot and, although he also held the reins for the Final of the Kent County Challenge Cup against Luton Town four days later, he reverted to the role of trainer when Bill Dodgin moved into the manager's seat before the next match.

In October 1985 he suffered a heart attack and then in September 1992 he had a stroke before he died in November 1996 at the age of 76 following a lengthy battle with cancer.

Record as Brentford Manager

	Games	Won	Drawn	Lost	F	A	Pts
League	1	0	1	0	1	1	1

Bill Dodgin

Born: 4th November 1931
Birthplace: Gateshead
Appointed in September 1976
Dismissed in April 1980

BACKGROUND

Dodgin started his career as an amateur, before signing for Southampton who were managed by his father. Bill then followed Dodgin Senior to Fulham, where he made his debut in December 1951, and went on to make 35 League appearances before joining Arsenal two years later. He made his name at Highbury as a tall centre-half and became the regular incumbent of the number five shirt, playing in 191 League games.

Having captained England at under-23 level, Bill was eventually given a free transfer in March 1961 and returned to his former club Fulham, where he made a further 69 appearances before his playing days came an end when he suffered a broken leg. Although his career saw him make 295 appearances, he failed to register a single goal in League football.

Bill Dodgin Junior moved into coaching with Millwall and, in his first year at The Den, helped them win promotion from the Third Division and, 12 months later, was coach under Alec Stock at Loftus Road when Queens Park Rangers won the 1967 League Cup at Wembley as well as capturing the Division Three title. Rangers then achievied promotion to the top flight the following season.

Dodgin took over the managerial reins at Loftus Road for the first half of the 1968/69 season, but returned to Fulham as boss in December 1968 although he was unable to prevent a second successive relegation for the Cottagers. Bill led the club back to Division Two in 1970/71 with a brand of open, attacking football, but having lost his job in the summer of 1972, then took over at Northampton Town after a short spell coaching at Leicester City. Dodgin won another promotion in 1976, but quit the club straight afterwards having earned the highest win ratio of any manager in Northampton Town's history and the best ever points total for a second placed side.

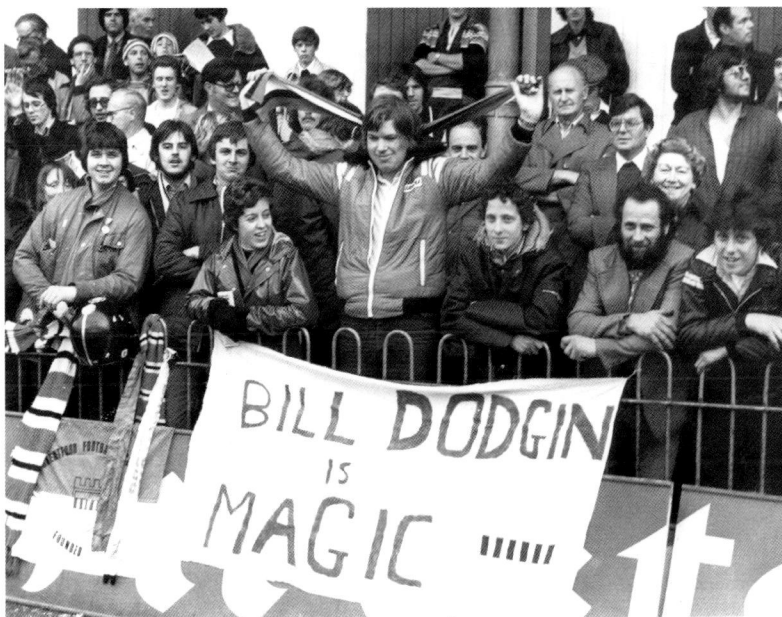

With Brentford in decline, and looking likely re-election candidates, Dodgin calmly re-built the team and, despite being seven points adrift of safety in February, the season ended in spectacular fashion, with an astonishing run of 11 wins and two draws in 15 games – 33 goals having been scored and some stunning attacking football being played along the way. Expectations for the new season were fully met and promotion was achieved with free-flowing football and goals aplenty, spear-headed by the 58-goal partnership of Andy McCulloch and Steve Phillips.

Despite a tricky start to the 1978/79 Third Division campaign, an excellent second half to the season raised hopes of further promotion. After rejecting the offer to join Chelsea as assistant manager, the 1979/80 season started in great fashion, but results declined after Christmas to such an extent that, in March 1980, with relegation looking distinctly likely, the board gave Dodgin leave of absence and dispensed with his services a few weeks later.

He returned to Northampton Town before taking over as manager at non-League Woking, after which he joined Brighton and Hove Albion as Chief Scout where he worked under his former player and captain, Barry Lloyd.

AS BRENTFORD MANAGER

Dodgin's appointment as Brentford manager, following John Docherty's departure in September 1976, saw the 44-year-old arrive at Griffin Park with an outstanding CV, which boasted five promotions in 11 seasons. Dodgin's appointment meant that he also took up the reins at the club that his father had managed between 1953 and 1957.

Bill's final job in football was a very brief stint as youth development officer at Fulham in 1994, but his 45 year involvement in the game ended as he fought a lengthy battle with Alzheimer's disease – he died, aged 68, in June 2000.

Record as Brentford Manager   184 games   40% win ratio   60% unbeaten

	Games	Won	Drawn	Lost	F	A	Pts
League	172	70	37	65	266	239	177
FA Cup	6	2	0	4	8	10	-
FL Cup	6	1	0	5	6	19	-

Fred Callaghan

Born: 19th December 1944
Birthplace: Fulham
Appointed in April 1980
Dismissed in February 1984

BACKGROUND

A genuine one club man, Fred had served his apprenticeship before signing as a professional with Fulham in the summer of 1962. Having made the first-team breakthrough during the 1963/64 campaign as a midfield replacement for Alan Mullery, he went on to make the left-back shirt his own during a stay that lasted 12 seasons. Callaghan totted up 295 League appearances, scoring 9 goals, as a tough-tackling defender who was not averse to crunching tackles and the occasional overlap down the flank. His playing career came to an end at a relatively early age when a serious back injury forced him into retirement at the end of the 1973/74 season.

Callaghan soon moved into coaching and was quickly marked down as someone with a bright future. He enjoyed a successful spell with Enfield, before moving to Griffin Park in February 1977 to assist Bill Dodgin with coaching duties – his three-month stay coinciding with an outstanding run of results and performances as the team soared up the table and, at the end of the campaign, he left to become manager at Woking.

AS BRENTFORD MANAGER

When Bill Dodgin was given 'leave of absence' in March 1980 after a disastrous sequence of results, Callaghan was offered the opportunity to return in a caretaker role and decided to leave Woking just days before their FA Trophy semi-final clash with Dagenham despite vigorous attempts to persuade him to stay. With three wins and two draws in the final seven matches, Fred steered the team away from the threat of relegation and safety was assured in the dying minutes of the last game against Millwall, by which time the board had offered him a two-year contract as manager.

[Above] Fred Callaghan, flanked by Gerry Potter, Ken James, Martin Lange and Eric White, welcoming Brentford legend, George Francis, back to Griffin Park

In readiness for the start of the 1980/81 season, Fred set about rebuilding the squad, and the shock sale of prolific goalscorer, Steve Phillips, enabled him to fund the signings of non-League recruits Terry Hurlock, David Crown and Gary Roberts, while a re-vamped backroom team saw the arrival of Chelsea legend Ron Harris as player/assistant manager and the re-formation of a youth set-up. Having established a solid defensive foundation Fred used the next season to work on his midfield, and although he put together the central trio of Hurlock, Stan Bowles and Chris Kamara, widely acknowledged as being one of the best outside the top two divisions, the team had a better record away than at home for the second successive year, which frustrated the supporters.

The signing of strikers Francis Joseph and Tony Mahoney for the 1982/83 season appeared to put in place the final pieces of Fred's jigsaw, but when Mahoney tragically broke his leg midway through the campaign, the team began to struggle and the decline continued into the following campaign. With Third Division status looking precarious, and the manager's self-acknowledged brusqueness towards supporters adding to his unpopularity, the board decided that a change was needed and, in February 1984, Callaghan was dismissed, ending his near-four-year tenure in the hot seat.

As the holder of a London black cab license, Fred returned to his primary occupation as a taxi driver although he continued to work for more than a decade in local non-league football as both a manager and coach with Kingstonian, Woking, Basingstoke, Wealdstone, Walton & Hersham and Carshalton – eventually returning to Fulham as a hospitality host in Craven Cottage's Riverside Restaurant.

Record as Brentford Manager   198 games   35% win ratio   64% unbeaten

	Games	Won	Drawn	Lost	F	A	Pts
League	170	59	50	61	236	227	210
FA Cup	13	5	4	4	27	20	-
FL Cup	15	5	3	7	17	26	-

BRENTFORD FIRST TEAM

PLAYERS

JOHN O"MARA

I don't remember many of my goals; I remember the ones I missed far more vividly. One in particular came during a match against Darlington – we were drawing 0-0 when the ball came to me off the woodwork about three yards out – I gave it the big time and tried to break the net from point blank range – but ended up putting it over the bar. They don't haunt me, but I remember the misses more than the goals, maybe that's part of the metabolism of being a good goal scorer. But that's where Frank Blunstone was so good, when I came off the pitch I said, "Sorry Frank, sorry pal…" And he replied; "Don't worry big man, you'll miss many, it's just cost us a point – it's fine." But I did worry about it.

And when we got into training the next day Frank asked if it was still bothering me, and he spent a lot of time crossing the ball and I'd put the ball in the back of the net until it was out of my system. That's how missing chances got to me back then and that's what made me the goal scorer I was.

Brentford went through a terrible spell while I was suspended and everything was building up for my return match – a big crowd turned up to see us beat Lincoln City. Everyone was thinking that as soon as 'the Big Man' was back that everything would be all right again, and it was. Everything went tickety-boo, I scored, punched the air and went "Yeah!" We were up and running again and I was seen as the hero. Everybody thought I'd get results back on track and that's how it transpired.

I never really got a buzz off that kind of attention, though, I got more of a buzz from the players' attitude towards me, knowing that they were lifted by me being back in the side. Terry Scales scored the second goal that night – he laced it with his left foot, one hell of a goal. I was more pleased for Terry as I think it was his first goal. I thought he had the makings of becoming a very good player.

The long suspension was handed out to me after I'd called the linesman a liar at the FA disciplinary hearing and stood up and confronted him when he said he hadn't seen the incident that had got

[Page 235] Brentford's new arrivals in the summer of 1976. Bobby Goldthorpe, Keith Pritchett, Gary Rolph [apprentice], Danis Salman [apprentice], Steve Russell [trialist] and John Fraser

[Left] O'Mara in devastating form, scoring one of his 27 goals for Brentford during the 1971-72 season

me into hot water. I told him to his face that he was lying through his back teeth and said; "And if God is watching, he will catch you… Beware!" The disciplinary panel obviously didn't take kindly to that, you're supposed to cower down to them and become a sycophant, but I let them know that they had no idea what football was all about in reality, sat there pontificating and dishing out punishments. I then told the FA that one day footballers would take over; "You mark my words!" They banned me for five weeks and, to make matters worse, Denis Piggott wanted to stop my wages for that period. Maybe it was the club's right to do that I don't know, but what I do know is that if you've got the goose that's laying golden eggs, you don't try and eat it for dinner do you?

Most of the referees back then were incompetent, they had no idea what was going on, and I'd let them know. And because I was such a big fella, and had some publicity, a lot of decisions went against me. I always spoke my mind and remember telling one referee after giving a foul against me that I hoped that when he got home he found his wife in bed with another bloke and his dinner was cold Funnily enough, I'm not sure I actually got booked for that.

But I did get sent off while being carried off on a stretcher once. A player had gone over the top of the ball in a tackle and I thought I'd broken my leg, in fact I've still got a red mark on my shin nearly 40 years later. Anyway, Eddie Lyons had come on to treat me, I was in agony, and I kept asking him if it was broken – I just needed

237

[Left] Jackie Graham jumps on O'Mara after the Big Man scores against Grimsby in 1972 [Right] O'Mara in action during the home win over Northampton in 1971

to know to help me deal with the pain. He said I'd be all right, but the stretcher still came for me and I started being carried off the pitch. At that point the player who'd clobbered me walked over to either apologise, or to see if I was all right, either way, I grabbed him, got in him in a headlock and punched him twice as hard as I could. So I was carried off and sent off at the same time. For whatever reason the referee couldn't have reported the incident after the game, because the suspension never came through. A bit of compassion perhaps?

Frank was a super fella; you simply couldn't dislike him. I wouldn't say that he wound me up to get the best out of me, but he knew what strings to pull and, just like me, he didn't entertain slackers or wasters. The fittest I've ever been was at Brentford – the training suited my size, structure and metabolism – there wasn't an ounce on me.

But what a job he did at Brentford, he was a tremendous coach – Frank had the sense to know that he was the strength behind the success at the club, despite being held back by the chairman. And Frank knew how to play to my strengths, which was where Ken Furphy at Blackburn failed when I went there.

I thought the deal was done for me to come back to Brentford a year later, everything had been agreed, but then, at the last moment, the Brentford chairman changed the terms and I walked away.

I loved playing with Jackie Graham and John Docherty, especially when they jumped on me when I scored – I remember in one game I didn't drop them and carried them both all the way back to the half-way line.

PETER GELSON

The FA Cup run was one of the highlights of the early 70s, and the two matches against Cardiff City and Hull City were really exciting to play in. It was a really great run and those two games were against the two leading teams in the Second Division. Apart from the goals, one of the memorable moments in that game at Cardiff was when City's Alan Warboys punched Dick Renwick. Although we didn't know it at the time, Dick had been hit so hard that he was playing while concussed and it was as if we were a man down. It's funny now, but I genuinely had to turn Dick around and point him in the right direction at the start of the second half because he didn't know where he was –you could almost see little birds circling his head like in the cartoons, he was so spaced out.

To get revenge I remember telling Alan Nelmes to give Warboys a dig back, although I thought Nelmesie would have understood that he needed to wait until the right moment and do it subtly. But no, he marched straight over and slapped him there and then! I went mad, what was he thinking of? Alan Nelmes weighed nine stone, soaking wet, but he was hard as nails. We held on and were through to the Fifth Round of the Cup. Hull City away was another tough game – things were looking good when we went 1-0 up and were playing well. Then Brian Turner hit a great shot, which beat the keeper all ends up, unfortunately the ball hit the inside of the post, quite how it didn't ricochet off the goalie and go into the net I'll never know.

When Hull equalised I didn't think it was a real problem, I thought we'd draw the match, then get them back to Griffin Park on the Tuesday night and finish them off in front of our own fans. But right at the end, Gordon Phillips got completely taken out while he was going up for a cross, a definite foul. But it wasn't to be, the referee played on and Hull scored the winner. I honestly thought we'd get them back to Brentford and win the replay because we were very hard to beat at home. I have to admit, losing that game is one of my biggest regrets.

When O'Mara first arrived at Brentford I thought to myself; "What the bloody hell has Frank [Blunstone] signed here?" But to give him his due, once John had got the pre-season training under his belt, there was no holding him back. Even after being suspended for five weeks 'Big Ted' was still our leading scorer and 'magic' is one of the few words that describe him that season. What surprised me was how quick he was, for a big bloke he was very fast and he certainly didn't muck about. Brentford played to his strengths that campaign – he was the big fish in our small pond. John loved the camaraderie and mixing with the players and it was a shame that he left.

As our record of 17 consecutive away defeats would suggest, we weren't great away from home in 1972-73 and were relegated at

[Right] Peter Gelson in relaxed mood at the training ground

the end of the season. To be fair, there were a lot of narrow defeats in that run and we were unlucky in some of the games, but at that time there were a few players who 'didn't play away from home'. At times, when you went up the country, you could look around the dressing room and know which lads would put in a performance and those who didn't fancy a scrap.

At some places up north you'd have to roll your sleeves up and fight, quite literally at times and, no names mentioned, there were some players who just weren't up for that. Sometimes you knew you'd get nothing out of the match before you even started. As soon as some players got a kick, that was that! Things are different now, the game isn't as physical and players can't be as easily intimidated, but I think the game was more enjoyable when we played – from a player's point of view in particular. I don't enjoy watching the game as much now, there's a lot more cheating that goes on – there's way too much 'falling over'.

It's not right that a player's first thought when he makes a run into the penalty area is to go down as soon as a tackle comes in, ahead of trying to get a shot on target. The likes of Jackie Graham would always try and stay on their feet and only go to ground if they were felled. Football is virtually a non-contact sport now, which is a real shame.

JACKIE GRAHAM

Frank Blunstone used to lay on some good training sessions I thought and he was a very good coach. If he'd got some more backing from the chairman he could have achieved a lot at Brentford. But ultimately, the lack of investment in the side obviously played a major part in what happened in the relegation season of 1972-73, but I thought we were really unlucky too. We played some great football that year in my view and it seemed as if we lost a lot of games just by the odd goal here and there, we seemed to get punished harshly for mistakes.

Peter Gelson and Alan Nelmes were also both hard men. Nelmesie is often thought of as being a more gentle player, but he would kick you as good as anyone, just more subtly and not get booked for it. Gelson was a great tackler, so strong in the air too, a marvellous player. At right-back was Alan Hawley, he was just class I thought, one of the best tacklers I ever played with.

But Dick Renwick is the hardest player I've ever seen. Dick knew everything about the game and he was a brilliant man to listen to, but Jesus was he tough. During a season some players count how many goals they've scored or helped set up... others count how many clean sheets they've helped keep... Dick used to count how many stitches he'd put into people. Seriously!

Bill Dodgin's arrival was a breath of fresh air. I once said that if Bill asked me to shoot somebody, I would. I meant it too, I just loved the man. I miss him today as much as I did when he first passed away, I really do. He was a player's manager, a real man's man, and under Dodgin it was nights out, red wine and golf-a-plenty! Some may say his ideas about the game were a bit old fashioned at the time, but I didn't see anything wrong with wanting to get the ball down and play.

I look back at my time at Brentford with a great deal of affection. I made some great friends at the club, friends I've remained close to after all these years, and the two promotion seasons I enjoyed at the club were truly special. We played some good stuff for the fans, and although there were a few moments when things weren't so good, they were happy days. Very happy days.

[Right] Captain, Jackie Graham, making a presentation to the Brentford Popular Front before a home game

ANDY McCULLOCH

The banter with the crowd at Brentford was different class and that rapport is something I've never forgotten. I was told that a lot of the lads who used to stand in a certain part of the ground were traders from the old Brentford Market and they used to come to the games straight from their stalls or via the pub.

Eddie Lyons, the physio, was a lovely man, a real character. Every morning, without fail, when we were arriving for training, he would come up to me and say, "Andy, what did you have for breakfast?" And before I'd had the chance to give him a reply, he'd say, "well I had three sausages, four rashers of bacon, two eggs, four tomatoes, three rounds of toast...." Every single morning he said that, to everyone. He was lovely, he used to play the spoons and do his tap dancing too, Eddie was a real one-off.

Bill Dodgin was such a lovely bloke too. His personality would win anyone over. Bill had a good philosophy on the game. He always had us training with the ball, letting the ball do the work. He was a real character away from football too.

They were happy, happy days at Brentford. The crowd was always good to me and I was part of a good team with great spirit. The social scene was the best I've known in the game. It was a great honour to be invited to the club's centenary celebrations in 1989. It was a very emotional night.

[Above] Andy McCulloch shows his displeasure as Brentord's last minute 'goal' against Bury is disallowed in 1978

[Right] McCulloch celebrates his goal against Hartlepool United in 1978 with Pat Kruse running in to join him

ALAN NELMES

We had an incredibly close team spirit at Brentford, which was essential. I'd joined the club from Chelsea where it was very much a case of them and us – the contrast at Brentford was incredible. We were all in it together and, because we had such a small squad, we all became very close.

The FA Cup run in 1970-71 was instrumental in promotion the following season – it gave us the extra confidence we needed as players and we were able to use our good experiences in the Cup to help us sustain a decent promotion challenge and it definitely gave us the lift we needed.

Stewart Houston was a very good player in that side – at Chelsea I'd always known him as a defender, yet initially, he played up front at Brentford. He was superb. He was quick and strong and he gave us a good outlet. When we used to go to away matches, a lot of times you would basically defend, but you'd give it to him and he used to go on the outside and hold the ball up superbly for us.

Having a player like that, who was so good yet was able to play in such a lot of positions, was a tremendous asset. Roger Cross was always impressive too. He would hold the ball up, shield it well, then lay it off. He did a very good job for us. Frank Blunstone was also an extremely knowledgeable manager. Mike Everitt was so different. He didn't have the technical expertise that Frank had got and you felt as if the club wasn't going anywhere with him.

When I was nearing the end of my career, John Docherty took over and it was clear that Danis Salman was going to be the future, and I didn't want to be just hanging on in there. I don't have any regrets, as I never really wanted to leave Brentford, but I would have perhaps liked to have had the chance of testing myself at a higher level. I mean, we went to Manchester United in the League Cup in 1975 and we lost 2-1 after going one up. I had a blinder up there against Sammy McIlroy, then you think, 'could I have done that week in, week out?' I enjoyed my Brentford career so much.

[Right] Alan Nelmes receives his testimonial cheque from Brentford's programme editor, Eric White

DOUG ALLDER

Jackie Graham was Brentford through and through. In training and on the pitch he never gave less than everything. He was really loyal to the club and probably should have made a move to see what he could have achieved.

Barry Tucker was another solid player, really reliable. Barry never used to do anything outstanding, but he was always there – there was nothing of him really – but he was a lovely bloke.

Steve Phillips's yellow t-shirt was a superstition to him and something he always had to put on before a game, but it seemed to work for him. I'm not sure if he used to wash it actually!

Dan Tana was the chairman at the time too and was a bit of a character, I remember him telling me once that he'd seen Marilyn Monroe the night she died and was one of the last people to see her alive!

I will always remember the day we beat Darlington and clinched promotion in 1978 – the crowd went mad. I can remember leaving the ground at about six o'clock and, as we walked towards The Griffin pub, it went really crazy, everyone was trying to get me to come in for a drink – it was brilliant!

That season I got a promotion medal with Watford and Brentford because they both went up and I'd played for both sides.

GORDON PHILLIPS

Charlie Brodie was a vastly experienced 'keeper and a very good one too. Other professional footballers don't enjoy the fact that a dog on the pitch at Layer Road ended his career, and I can remember Ian St. John saying just that on his TV show some years back. It was so out of order that the animal wasn't controlled sooner, it had been around the pitch for a little while before the incident happened. People say that the dog bit Charlie, but that's not what happened, as he bent down to collect the ball the dog smashed into his knee and damaged the ligaments. Today the damage could have been repaired I expect, but in those days knee operations weren't as advanced. It annoys me when I see it replayed and people joking about it to be honest.

I always think of Griffin Park as a lovely, compact ground. There always seemed to be a cracking atmosphere and more often than not there would be a good crowd. Even when things were going badly eight thousand fans still turned up, and when things were better, double that. A lot of our training was done in and around the ground and I remember every Friday morning we used to play five-a-side on what is now the Braemar Road forecourt. We used to call that area 'Little Hampden'. I always remember walking to the ground after getting off the bus and seeing gardens full of bikes and we used to go and get our lunch in the Bricklayer's Arms pub after training. Win or lose we'd always go out for the night locally after a game too. I used to love playing at Griffin Park.

PAT KRUSE

Brentford was a lovely, friendly club and it was a happy place to be. I jumped at the chance to join Brentford because I knew Bill Dodgin pretty well already. He used to stay in the same digs as me in Leicester and we often went out for a curry in the town in the evenings and talked about football. He was a lovely man, too nice perhaps at times.

Maybe it's not surprising that Bill was so well liked, he surrounded himself with decent, honest players, the sort who wanted to go out and play well for him, not because he'd screamed and shouted at them before a game, but because they simply didn't want to let the man down. More often than not the players at Brentford during that era gave all they could on the pitch, it didn't work all the time, but the way we played and the effort that was put in was down to Bill.

The squad I joined was a very good one, full of seasoned players who knew their trade. There were very few youngsters in that side, apart from Danis Salman. We had John Fraser at right-back, Mickey Allen at left-back, Jackie Graham in midfield, all committed, experienced players who had played a lot at that level.

As promotion became more and more of a reality every game was approached exactly the same, we weren't given any points targets, and even if a team was down the other end of the league Bill would treat them with respect. But we knew that if we played our normal brand of flowing football we would beat them over the 90 minutes if we stuck to our task.

I think the supporters seemed to appreciate that the players were giving it their all and when you see a packed ground, that in turn boosts the players, so it was a good combination. During that era fans could turn up at Griffin Park confident that they would probably see a home win. With Jackie Graham as captain Brentford were always going to give it everything, he was a whole-hearted player, a general, and the players responded to him. I couldn't say one word against Jackie Graham, he epitomised everything that was good about football at the time.

DANIS SALMAN

I have to admit that, as a kid, I'd never heard of Brentford and, between the ages of 11 and 15, I was training every night of the week with a different big London club. On Monday I'd be at Tottenham, Tuesday at West Ham, Wednesday at QPR and Thursday at Arsenal, who were emerging as the ones I'd chose to sign for when I was finally old enough to sign a contract. And, during the summer holidays I would go further afield, and train with West Bromwich Albion and Ipswich Town. At that time I had the pick of the best teams in the country after me.

After a trial session at Arsenal's London Colney training ground, where 280 other kids had been invited to attend, I was chosen as one of only six lads to be offered an apprenticeship – so everything pointed to me joining The Gunners. But then, completely out of the blue, I received a phone call from John Docherty, who I'd got to know from training at QPR with Bob Pearson, and he explained that he'd just been appointed as Brentford manager. He told me that he'd been really impressed with me during the training sessions, and asked if I'd be interested in playing for Brentford in a friendly match the next night. "Who the hell are Brentford I thought!"

Anyway, I agreed, as he'd always been friendly and had encouraged me, and I played at right full-back – I don't remember much about the game apart from feeling comfortable and having a shot from about 30 yards that the goalie tipped over the bar and, after the game, overhearing the trainer, Eddie Lyons, telling somebody that; "there's no way we'll get that kid here!" Then John Docherty came over and told me I'd done really well and that he really wanted me at Brentford and explained the added development potential at a smaller club. John Docherty spent a lot of time with me, and he became my first real mentor in the game.

I have to admit that all the players were really friendly, and I felt at home at The Bees straight away – as a Mediterranean I feel comfortable in family surroundings – and I was really being made to feel at home. Arsenal were far from happy, though, and they called my dad over from Cyprus and we both had to attend a board meeting at Highbury, where we were quizzed about Brentford's involvement and I felt there was a fair amount of pressure and I was scared stiff. That didn't do Arsenal any favours and things became clearer in my mind and, afterwards, dad said I should do what felt right in my heart. And that's why I chose Brentford – and I was pretty much drafted straight into the first team for a match at home to Watford.

In the build up to the match against Watford I was at home doing my homework when there was a knock at the door – it was a journalist from The Sun newspaper. This was all new to me, I was just a kid, and I had no idea of the significance of a 15-year-old making their Football League debut. I had a chat with the man and I had a photo taken holding my homework. Brentford arranged for a cab to pick me up on the day of the match and I walked into the changing room in my school uniform, and was met by the sight of big blokes walking around in their jock straps stinking of Whitehorse Oil – I remember thinking that they looked like gladiators preparing to go out to battle! I was nervous, but as soon as I was in my kit I was okay – that's how it was for me, I was still a kid, but felt totally confident as soon as I was on the football pitch.

I came on as centre-half that day, and the whole game was a total blur. I do remember going up for a challenge and accidentally butting one of the Watford strikers in the back of the head and he reacted aggressively – but I instinctively went face to face with him and just wanted a piece of him! Then Jackie Graham came steaming in, what an immense person he was to me. All the other players looked out for me too and Brentford won the game 1-0.

In one of my first away games for Brentford, away to Reading, I had a bit of a run-in with the legendary Robin Friday, who I was marking and had dished out one or two kicks too in the process. Finally he had enough and spat at my feet, telling me that if I fouled him again he'd kill me. He came over and said well done to me at the end of the game though – so I must have done alright!

Because I was still living at home in Barking, away games were always difficult for me, especially getting across London after the coach had dropped us back at Griffin Park. I don't know why I didn't let on that it was almost impossible for me to get home, as I'm sure I would have been put up for the night somewhere, but I lost count of the times I used to sneak into the treatment room after we'd been dropped off and would sleep the night in there. If it was cold, I'd turn on the heat lamps to try and warm the room up, then when I got up the next morning, I'd have to start unloading the dirty kit from the wicker hampers, then start soaking and washing everything. But I loved it, it was all I knew, and looking back, I wouldn't have had it any other way.

On the pages that follow, the totals next to each player's name show their overall appearances and goals for Brentford (all competitions). Details of Football League games for all the clubs during their career are shown at the end of their profile.

Every attempt has been made to ensure that the statistical data in the stats sections as accurate as possible. Endeavours have been made to provide records that are as complete as possible and where there are gaps, then no previously published information has been discovered.

John Docherty
29th April 1940 (Glasgow)
278 apps/78 goals

After signing from Scottish junior side St Roch's in July 1959 he left Brentford in March 1961 to sign for Sheffield United (£17,500) before returning in December 1965 and, after notching a goal in every three games, left again, this time to sign for Reading in March 1968 (£12,000). He re-signed from the Royals (for a third time) in March 1970 as manager Frank Blunstone built his new team. A diminutive and speedy winger, with an excellent goal-scoring record, he finally retired from playing in May 1974 after helping to develop the junior set-up, and joined Queens Park Rangers as youth team manager before returning yet again – this time as manager to replace Mike Everitt in January 1975. Following a relatively uneventful spell he resigned in September 1976 after a dispute with chairman Dan Tana then spent several successful years as manager of Cambridge United. In February 1984 he returned to Griffin Park, for a fifth time, as assistant manager to Frank McLintock and stayed until 1986, when he took over as Millwall manager and led them into the top flight for the first time in their history. He briefly managed Bradford City and Slough Town, before leaving the game after a final short-lived return to Millwall.

Brentford	17 appearances	2 goals
Sheffield United	41 appearances	9 goals
Brentford	97 appearances	31 goals
Reading	45+1 appearances	7 goals
Brentford	137+4 appearances	34 goals

Peter Gelson
18th October 1941 (Hammersmith)
516 apps/18 goals

A local boy from Chiswick, and recommended to the club by former winger Dennis Heath, Gelson initially signed on in 1959 as a part-timer whilst he pursued a career as a Post Office engineer. Although he didn't turn professional until 1964, Gelson went on to become the club's second highest appearance holder, playing 516 games as well as captaining the side for several seasons. He retired from the professional game in October 1974 – signing firstly for Hillingdon Borough, then seeing out his playing days at Hounslow and Walton & Hersham. A tough, no-nonsense centre-half, who many observers felt could have plied his trade at a higher level, Gelson was highly respected at the club and was given the rare distinction of being granted two testimonial matches – against West Ham in 1970 and Millwall in 1975.

Brentford	468+3 appearances	17 goals

Alan Hawley
7th June 1946 (Woking)
345 apps/4 goals

A hard-tackling, yet pacy right full-back, Hawley became an apprentice in June 1962 before signing professional forms a year later. He became the club's youngest-ever League performer at 16 years, three months and 21 days of age, after which he went

on to become a regular first-teamer for more than ten years. After requesting a transfer in 1971 Hawley was briefly loaned to Fulham, where he failed to make an appearance. He returned and was later appointed club captain when Bobby Ross left in 1972 – but was eventually released in the summer of 1974 and signed for Hillingdon Borough, where he had been on loan, and later became player-manager before a brief spell at Wimbledon. Hawley was awarded a well-earned testimonial match against Orient at the end of his professional career.

Brentford   315+3 appearances   4 goals

Gordon Phillips
17th January 1946 (Uxbridge)
227 apps/0 goals

After signing professional terms as a 17-year-old in 1963, Phillips went on to share the goalkeeper's jersey with Chic Brodie for the next seven seasons, although he made only occasional appearances until the 1966-67 season. When Brodie left in 1971, the promotion season that followed saw him as an ever-present and his magnificent performances, particularly away from home, were influential in the team's success. Whilst not the biggest in stature, his bravery was rarely in question and when he was released, at the end of the 1972-73 campaign, after over 200 games, he became one of a number of players who continued his career in non-League football with Hillingdon Borough, for whom he made more than 250 appearances. Phillips was awarded a testimonial match in 1973 to acknowledge ten years of loyal service and, almost 20 years later, he returned briefly as goalkeeping coach to assist manager Phil Holder.

Brentford   208 appearances   0 goals

Chic Brodie
22nd February 1937 (Duntocher)
224 apps/0 goals

Born on the outskirts of Glasgow, Chic had won Scottish junior and schoolboy honours before joining Manchester City, initially as an amateur and then a part-time professional in 1954. But he failed to break into the first-team and signed for Gillingham in 1957. One year later he joined Aldershot, while also carrying out his national service and, after almost 100 games he was transferred to First Division Wolverhampton Wanderers for a £9,000 fee. But one game, and seven months later, he moved again, this time to Northampton Town for £4,000. As an experienced goalkeeper, with a calming presence, and over 200 appearances to his name, Chic was signed by Brentford manager Malcolm MacDonald for £10,000 in November 1963 and spent the next eight years as the main custodian of the 'keeper's jersey, although often sharing the responsibilities with Gordon Phillips, who he eventually lost the shirt to. Chic retired from the professional game in May

1971, having played only five games after the infamous incident six months earlier, when a dog collided with him during a game at Colchester United and caused knee ligament damage. He completed his playing days at non-League Margate and then Wealdstone. Chic died in April 2000 aged 63 after a long battle with cancer.

Gillingham	18 appearances	0 goals
Aldershot	95 appearances	0 goals
Wolves	1 appearance	0 goals
Northampton Town	87 appearances	0 goals
Brentford	199 appearances	0 goals

Bobby Ross
18th May 1942 (Edinburgh)
323 apps/63 goals

Bobby started his career as an apprentice with his home-town club, Hearts, and broke into their first-team before moving south to join Shrewsbury Town in 1963 and, during his three year stay, he was their top scorer. After being signed by Tommy Cavanagh for £9,500 in March 1996 – in a double deal with John Regan – the Scottish midfielder went on to make more than 300 appearances over the next seven seasons, during which time he was a regular goal scorer and captained the team to promotion success in 1972. An inspirational skipper, and crowd favourite, Ross often played in a striking role and made 167 consecutive first-team starts between 1968 and 1972, following on from a previous run of 70 consecutive games. He was surprisingly released and signed for Cambridge United in October 1972 and, in his absence, the team suffered relegation back to Division Four, while he went on to take his total appearances close to the 500 mark. Ross retired in 1974, spending time as player/manager at non-League Hayes before coaching youngsters at both Queens Park Rangers and Millwall.

Shrewsbury Town	99 appearances	29 goals
Brentford	288+4 appearances	58 goals
Cambridge United	57+8 appearances	14 goals

Alan Nelmes
20th October 1948 (Hackney)
350 apps/2 goals

A defender who could play at full-back or in central defence he joined from Chelsea in the summer of 1967, where he had signed as a professional on his 17th birthday two years earlier. Nelmes went on to complete nine full seasons as a regular first-team player at Brentford, chalking up 350 appearances including over 100 consecutive games, although he managed only two goals and went seven years without getting on the score-sheet. After a difficult start Nelmes became the model of consistency, exemplified by his commitment and last-ditch tackles, until eventually being given a free transfer in the summer of 1976. Nelmes played for non-League Hillingdon Borough, then Hayes, before injury curtailed his career. His testimonial match against Chelsea, in May 1978, attracted a crowd of 7,400 and during the 8-2 defeat, he signed off with a trademark own goal.

Brentford	311+5 appearances	2 goals

Allan Mansley
31st August 1946 (Liverpool)
105 apps/30 goals

An immensely skilful left-winger, he began his career as a schoolboy at Everton but came to prominence with Skelmersdale United as one of the stars of their 1967 Amateur Cup run – after which he joined Blackpool. But before he managed an appearance at Bloomfield Road, Mansley was snapped up by Brentford's Jimmy Sirrell in January 1968 and looked set to fulfil his potential with a series of scintillating wing displays, but lost his form following the appointment of Frank Blunstone as manager and quickly fell out of favour. Mansley was allowed to join both Fulham and Notts County on loan, before making a free permanent move to Meadow Lane at the end of the 1970-71 season. After a few games for Lincoln City he drifted out of the game while still in his mid-20s and died of a heart attack in 2001 at the age of 54.

Brentford	93+2 appearances	24 goals
Fulham	1 appearance	0 goals
Notts County	11 appearances	2 goals
Lincoln City	3 appearances	0 goals

Gordon Neilson
28th May 1947 (Glasgow)
104 apps/15 goals

Having started his career as a winger with Arsenal, he was highly-regarded at Highbury and played a number of times for the first-team, scoring twice, before being signed by Brentford boss, Jimmy

Sirrell, for a £10,000 fee in October 1968. Speedy and with an eye for goal, Neilson enjoyed some early success, playing on the opposite flank to Allan Mansley, but the arrival of Frank Blunstone eventually saw him lose his place in a new playing formation and he spent much of his time on the substitute's bench. Frustrated by the situation, he requested a transfer after managing just eight starts during the promotion campaign of 1972-72 and was released at the end of the season. Neilson failed to resurrect his career in the professional game and joined Hillingdon Borough.

Arsenal	14 appearances	2 goals
Brentford	80+12 appearances	15 goals

Dick Renwick
27th November 1942 (Gilsland)
106 apps/5 goals

Renwick had been signed as a professional at Grimsby Town following his apprenticeship but failed to break into the first-team so, in 1963, moved south to join Aldershot where he established his reputation as an aggressive, tough-tackling left full-back. He played over 200 games for the Shots before being signed by Jimmy Sirrell for £1,500 in February 1969. He became the regular occupant of the number three shirt for the next couple of seasons, missing just a handful of matches and becoming renowned as the hardest of all 'hard-as-nails' defenders. In the summer of 1971 he rejected the offer of a new contract and was given a free transfer to enable him to return to his native north with Stockport County and then Rochdale. Renwick's career ended at Darlington with over 400 games to his name.

Aldershot	203+2 appearances	4 goals
Brentford	96 appearances	5 goals
Stockport County	30 appearances	1 goal
Rochdale	48+1 appearances	0 goals
Darlington	19 appearances	0 goals

Brian Turner
31st July 1949 (West Ham)
100 apps/7 goals

Having spent the majority of his early life in New Zealand after his family had emigrated, Turner returned to England to start his career at Chelsea, before making his breakthrough at Portsmouth, where he made four appearances. Brian became Frank Blunstone's first signing, arriving from Fratton Park in January 1970 and the hard-tackling midfielder was a main-stay of the team for the next two seasons. He picked up a number of cautions for his crunching play in the middle of the park. At the end of the 1971-72 promotion campaign he was released, enabling him to make a return to New Zealand where he joined Mount Wellington for eight seasons, after which he played for Blacktown FC, Wollongong Wolves (Australia), Gisborne City and Papatoetoe. Turner also had a remarkable international career that saw him earn his 100th cap for the "All-Whites"

when he came on as a substitute against Brazil in the 1982 World Cup Finals in Spain. He continued coaching in his adopted native country and was inducted into the New Zealand Soccer Hall of Fame, later working with the national team.

Portsmouth	3+1 appearances	0 goals
Brentford	88+5 appearances	7 goals

Brian Tawse
30th July 1945 (Ellon)
23 apps/1 goal

A small, slightly built winger, Tawse started his playing days with Arsenal, before moving to Brighton where he made over 100 appearances during a successful five-year stay. In February 1970 he became one of Frank Blunstone's early signings at Brentford. A skilful wide man, his diminutive 5'5" frame saw him sometimes struggle with the more physical side of the game and, having initially gained a regular place in the starting line-up, his career failed to develop and he became an almost permanent resident on the substitute's bench. Before the end of the 1970-71 season, after requesting a transfer, Tawse was allowed to move to Folkestone Town on loan, before being released and signing for Durban City in South Africa.

Arsenal	5 appearances	0 goals
Brighton and Hove Albion	97+5 appearances	14 goals
Brentford	20+2 appearances	1 goal

Roger Cross
20th October 1948 (East Ham)
228 apps/79 goals

Cross made seven appearances (scoring one goal) for his local side, West Ham United, where he had progressed from an apprentice. He'd also scored twice in six games on loan at Orient early in his Hammers career. The classy striker was signed by Frank Blunstone for £12,000 in March 1970 and, after contributing 14 goals in his first full season, the club kept their promise in allowing him to move on to a higher division team – Division Two Fulham signed him for £30,000 in September 1971. Despite scoring eight goals for the Cottagers, Cross failed to settle and returned to Griffin Park in January 1973 for a fee of £16,000, going on to score over 50 goals during the following few seasons, including hat-tricks in consecutive home matches in 1973. A powerful, elegant striker, who included a long-throw and a thunderbolt long-range left-footed shot in his armoury, Cross was surprisingly sold to Millwall by Bill Dodgin for £9,500 in January 1977. His career faded away with just a handful of further appearances. After a brief spell in the North American Soccer League he was appointed as youth team manager back at The Den and he went on to carve out a successful coaching career at Queens Park Rangers, Tottenham Hotspur then back at his original club, West Ham United.

West Ham United	5+2 appearances	1 goal
Orient	4+2 appearances	2 goals
Brentford	62 appearances	20 goals
Fulham	39+1 appearances	8 goals
Brentford	141+4 appearances	52 goals
Millwall	14+4 appearances	0 goals

Jackie Graham
16th July 1946 (Glasgow)
409 apps/40 goals

The hard-working Scottish midfielder became a hugely popular player at Brentford after being signed by Frank Blunstone from non-League Guildford City in the summer of 1970 for a £2,500 fee. He had previously appeared in the Scottish League, starting out at Morton, then signing for Dundee United in 1966 for £15,000. A consistent performer in the heart of the midfield, Bill Dodgin built his team around Graham in 1976, appointing him as captain and describing him on his arrival as being "half of the team". After making 409 first team appearances – the fourth highest in the club's history at the time – he was released by Fred Callaghan in May 1980 and joined Addlestone and Weybridge, making an emotional return to Griffin Park the following season when the two teams were drawn together in the FA Cup first round. He was rewarded for his loyal service with a testimonial match against Watford in 1982 and he saw out his playing days with spells at Hounslow Town, Woking, Burnham & Hillingdon, Farnborough Town and Staines Town – where he also had spells as manager and coach.

Brentford	371+3 appearances	38 goals

Paul Bence
21st December 1948 (Littlehampton)
268 apps/6 goals

Following an apprenticeship he signed professional forms for his local club Brighton in 1967 but, after making just one substitute appearance, he was released and signed for Reading in the 1968 close season. After two years and just a handful of games, he was given another free transfer, but was picked up by Frank Blunstone in the summer of 1970. The flame-haired midfielder was a steady and regular performer for a number of seasons and was appointed captain by John Docherty, developing into an excellent over-lapping right full-back. After playing in 99 consecutive games, he lost his place and fell out of favour with newly-appointed manager Bill Dodgin. Bence made only a couple of further appearances before joining Torquay United on loan, then was released from his contract in March 1977. He had qualified as an FA Coach in his early twenties and he became player/coach at Wokingham Town and also had a spell as a youth coach with Queens Park Rangers, before managing non-League Wycombe Wanderers between 1984 and 1986.

Brighton and Hove Albion	0+1 appearance	0 goals
Reading	12+2 appearances	2 goals
Brentford	238+6 appearances	6 goals
Torquay United	5 appearances	0 goals

Michael Maskell
25th January 1952 (Eynsham)
1 app/0 goals

A sturdy, well built left full-back, the 18-year-old was signed from Chelsea in the summer of 1970, where he had previously been coached by Frank Blunstone but, after missing the start of the season through injury, he made what transpired to be his only appearance in a heavy defeat at Oldham. A month later he had his contract cancelled for an alleged serious breach of discipline and he never re-emerged in the game again.

Brentford	1 appearance	0 goals

Alex Dawson
21st February 1940 (Aberdeen)
11 apps/7 goals

A former 'Busby Babe' who had signed as an apprentice at Manchester United in 1956 and as a professional a year later. Dawson had been thrust into first-team action at the age of 18 following the fateful Munich air crash in 1958, and went on to play in the FA Cup Final at the end of that season. After 45 goals in 80 games for the Red Devils he joined Preston North End in 1961 and stayed for five years, during which time he hit 114 goals in 197 matches and made another FA Cup Final appearance. A further move to Bury in 1967 saw his goal-scoring exploits continue with 21 goals in 50 games before moving to Brighton. He was signed, on loan, by Frank Blunstone, in September 1970 as the club tried to recover from a disastrous start to the season and the 'battering ram' centre-forward was an instant success with seven goals in 11 appearances. Attempts to try and make the move a permanent one proved unsuccessful as the player's personal terms could not be met, despite the board agreeing to meet the £7,000 transfer fee and, after two months, the Scotsman returned to Brighton where he failed to make another appearance and left the professional game to join Corby Town.

Manchester United	80 appearances	45 goals
Preston North End	197 appearances	114 goals
Bury	49+1 appearances	21 goals
Brighton and Hove Albion	53+4 appearances	26 goals
Brentford	10 appearances	6 goals

John O'Mara
19th March 1947 (Farnworth)
57 apps/30 goals

Born in Lancashire, O'Mara's career began in Gillingham's reserve team before he signed for non-League Wimbledon, where he began to find the net on a regular basis. The 6'4" striker made an unimpressive start to his Brentford career, having been signed by Frank Blunstone for £750 in March 1971, but he went on to attain cult status the following season as he hit 27 goals to spear-head a successful promotion campaign – despite incur-

ring a five-week suspension after accumulating a succession of bookings. A fiery temperament complemented a fine touch for a man built like a tank, but it was in the air where he proved lethal, netting a host of bullet-like headers. Just weeks into the start of the 1972-73 season he was astonishingly sold to fellow Division Three side Blackburn Rovers, for a club record fee of £50,000. His loss saw the team relegated back to Division Four, while the player's own career failed to hit the expected heights and his professional days ended in 1974 when he was released, having notched only 12 goals in two seasons. After a return move to Brentford fell through, O'Mara dropped back into non-League football with Chelmsford City - although he did have a brief three-match trial with Bradford City - before playing in South Africa for three seasons. O'Mara finally returned to see out his playing days with Dover and Margate, retiring in 1980 and taking up a mining job.

Brentford	53 appearances	28 goals
Blackburn Rovers	30+5 appearances	10 goals
Bradford City	3 appearances	1 goal

Mickey Heath
9th January 1953 (Hillingdon)
1 app/0 goals

A local boy who was a member of the junior set-up, Heath had originally been recommended to the club by the Fulham manager Bill Dodgin. His early promise with the juniors led to him being registered as an amateur. He played in the final game of the 1970-71 season in a midfield role, but his career failed to develop, and although he made further appearances in the club's London Challenge Cup games during the following two seasons, he continued his playing days with Walton & Hersham.

Brentford	1 appearance	0 goals

Terry Scales
18th November 1951 (Stratford)
234 apps/6 goals

Signed as a 19-year-old in the summer of 1971, as a left-back from West Ham United on the recommendation of Roger Cross. Scales's only appearance for the Hammers had come at Griffin Park in the testimonial match for Peter Gelson. He was immediately plunged into the first team by Frank Blunstone and made the position his own in the next couple of seasons, before being converted into an impressive central midfielder by Mike Everitt. Scales continued to retain a regular place in the first team playing well over 200 games as a steady, if unspectacular, performer. His career ended when he lost his place with the arrival of Bill Dodgin and, following his subsequent release in March 1977, he joined Dagenham, where he notched up a further 358 games in non-League football. He completed his career with a brief stint at Heybridge Swifts and as player/manager at Hoddesden Town.

| Brentford | 212 appearances | 5 goals |

Steve Tom
5th February 1951 (Cheshunt)
21 apps/1 goal

Tom was a 1971 summer signing from Queens Park Rangers, where he had failed to break into the first-team. The versatile midfielder scored on his debut at Bury in the opening match of the season. Largely used as a squad player, Tom also filled in at

centre-back, but he never managed to secure a regular spot and was given a free transfer at the end of the promotion-winning campaign. He joined non-League Barnet where he played more than 100 games in the Southern League and then joined Ilford.

| Brentford | 13+5 appearances 1 goal |

Trevor Dawkins
7th October 1945 (Southend)
4 apps/0 goals

A member of West Ham United's 1963 FA Youth Cup winning side, Dawkins had also won England schoolboy and Youth international honours but the young midfielder's career failed to develop as expected – although he did experience top flight football with the Hammers and then with Crystal Palace. In September 1971 he was taken on loan from Selhurst Park by Frank Blunstone, but failed to impress in four appearances and returned to Crystal Palace where he quickly dropped out of League football, re-emerging in American Major Indoor Soccer, where he played until he was 40.

West Ham United	5+1 appearances	0 goals
Crystal Palace	24+1 appearances	3 goals
Brentford	3+1 appearances	0 goals

Mike Allen
30th March 1949 (South Shields)
255 apps/13 goals

He was signed by Frank Blunstone for an £8,000 fee from Division Two Middlesbrough having made only 34 appearances in four years for his home-town club. Allen immediately assumed a midfield role as a solid and hard-working performer. However, his switch to the left full-back position by Mike Everitt two years later was a master-stroke and Allen went on to become one of the club's most consistent players during an eight year stay – making more than 250 appearances. A reliable and unspectacular defender, who probably failed to receive the plaudits he deserved, Allen was eventually released by Bill Dodgin at the end of the 1978-79 season and, despite being only 30 years of age, he made a return to the north and moved into non-League football as player/coach at Whitby Town.

Middlesbrough	32+2 appearances	1 goal
Brentford	223+10 appearances	11 goals

Ken Wallace
8th June 1952 (Islington)
3 apps/0 goals

In a bid to compensate for John O'Mara's suspension in February 1972, the 19-year old striker was signed on a month's loan from West Ham United and, although he had made no previous League appearances, he'd spent some time playing in Canada. The challenge at Brentford was not helped by the team being on a win-less run and he struggled, returning to Upton Park at the end of the month. He spent the next two summers playing in the North American Soccer League with Montreal before joining Hereford United on their elevation into the Football League. Wallace also played for Exeter City briefly and, with his career winding down, at non-League Dover, Maidstone United and Crawley Town.

Brentford	3 appearances	0 goals
Hereford United	26+6 appearances	4 goals
Exeter City	8+2 appearances	1 goal

Stewart Houston
20th August 1949 (Dunoon)
82 apps/9 goals

Frank Blunstone had known the young Scotsman from his time at Chelsea, where Houston had started as an apprentice. Having taken him on loan in March 1972 to bolster the promotion bid, Houston made such an impact that a fee of £15,000 was paid to secure his services in the summer. Initially signed to play as a striker, he quickly settled as a classy central defender, but after requesting a transfer under Mike Everitt, was signed by Manchester United for a club record £50,000 fee in December 1973. He went on to play more than 200 games for the Old Trafford giants, mainly at left-back, and earned under-23 and full Scottish international honours before moving to Sheffield United and then Colchester

United, where he ended his career as player/coach with over 500 games to his name. Houston coached at Plymouth Argyle, then became George Graham's assistant during Arsenal's golden spell in the early 1990s and twice held the caretaker reins at Highbury before being appointed as manager at Queens Park Rangers in 1996, after which he had further spells coaching at Ipswich Town, Tottenham Hotspur (back with George Graham) and Walsall.

Chelsea	6+3 appearances	0 goals
Brentford	77 appearances	9 goals
Manchester United	204+1 appearances	13 goals
Sheffield United	93+1 appearances	1 goal
Colchester United	106+1 appearances	5 goals

Paul Priddy
11th July 1953 (Isleworth)
134 apps/0 goals

Priddy originally signed as an amateur to provide goalkeeping cover while playing for Hayes and Maidenhead United before he was called on by Frank Blunstone to keep goal when Gordon Phillips was injured on the eve of the 1972-73 season, and signed professional forms in October 1972 after successfully establishing himself in the team. Having lost his place to loanee Steve Sherwood, Priddy left in October 1974 to play for non-League Wimbledon, but joined Walton & Hersham in the summer of 1975

and, following a pre-season friendly against Brentford, he was brought back to Griffin Park by manager John Docherty, taking over from Bill Glazier as first-team 'keeper early in the season. Surprisingly, Bill Dodgin deemed him as surplus to requirements, and he was released in May 1977 to sign for Tooting and Mitcham before having a solitary League game for Wimbledon. Spells at Wealdstone and Oxford City followed, before he returned to Brentford for a third time in 1981, to assist on a part-time basis, making one final League appearance. Priddy's career came to an end when he suffered a ruptured spleen playing for Hampton and, after a spell living in New Zealand, he returned to take up the role of goalkeeping coach at Aldershot Town – a position he held from 1994 until 2009. He also made an appearance in goal for the Shots at the age of 45.

Brentford	121 appearances	0 goals
Wimbledon	1 appearance	0 goals
Brentford	1 appearance	0 goals

Alan Murray
5th December 1949 (Newcastle)
48 apps/7 goals

An energetic midfielder with an eye for goal, Murray was signed from Middlesbrough by Frank Blunstone on a free transfer in the summer of 1972. Having first joined the Ayresome Park club as a schoolboy Murray had had a spell on loan at York City. At Brentford he missed just one game during the 1972-73 season and also finished as joint leading goalscorer with seven goals. He was surprisingly released at the end of the campaign and moved to

Doncaster Rovers, where he ended his professional playing career after more than 200 games. Having already become a qualified coach at the age of 22, Murray became player/manager at Willington in the Northern League, before a stint as commercial manager back at Middlesbrough. A role back in football management followed with Hartlepool – where he replaced the illness-stricken Cyril Knowles - then Darlington and, finally, as assistant manager to Graeme Souness at Newcastle United.

Middlesbrough	6+4 appearances	1 goal
York City	4 appearances	0 goals
Brentford	42+3 appearances	7 goals
Doncaster Rovers	133+13 appearances	21 goals

David Jenkins
2nd September 1946 (Bristol)
19 apps/1 goal

A winger who started his career at Arsenal as an apprentice in 1962, Jenkins played for the Gunners in the 1968 League Cup Final against Leeds United and had become one of the few players to switch allegiance to north London rivals Tottenham Hotspur – in a £55,000 move that took Jimmy Robertson to Highbury. Much was expected of Jenkins but he failed to live up to expectations and struggled to settle at White Hart Lane, making just 17 appearances in four seasons. In the summer of 1972 he was signed by Frank Blunstone on a free transfer in a bid to kick-start his ailing career, but he failed to maintain his form after some decent early performances and, after just eight months, he joined Hereford

United on loan. The move was made permanent, although he later had spells with Newport County, Shrewsbury Town and Workington – eventually joining Durban City in South Africa.

Arsenal	16+1 appearances	3 goals
Tottenham Hotspur	11+3 appearances	2 goals
Brentford	13+5 appearances	1 goal
Hereford United	18+4 appearances	3 goals
Newport County	6 appearances	1 goal
Shrewsbury Town	2 appearances	1 goal
Workington	6 appearances	0 goals

David Court
1st March 1944 (Mitcham)
13 apps/1 goal

Court joined Arsenal as a schoolboy in 1959 and made his first team debut three years later, which set him off on an 11-year stay at Highbury, in which he played almost 200 games in a variety of roles ranging from centre-forward to inside-forward to right-winger and eventually right full-back. In the summer of 1970 he joined Luton Town for a £30,000 fee and spent two seasons at Kenilworth Road, making more than 50 appearances, before he was freed and was signed by Frank Blunstone in the summer of 1972. By this stage Court had become a central midfield player but, although only 28 years of age, the stocky play-maker seemed lethargic and past his best. He made just eight starts in a disappointing one-year stay, before being released to join non-League Barnet. Having left the game Court carved out a career for himself in the financial sector but he returned to football in 1996 when he was appointed as Assistant Academy Director and Assistant Head of Youth Development back at Arsenal.

Arsenal	168+7 appearances	17 goals
Luton Town	50+2 appearances	0 goals
Brentford	8+4 appearances	1 goal

Stan Webb
6th December 1947 (Middlesbrough)
41 apps/9 goals

A native of the north-east this tall striker, had started his career with Middlesbrough, and had long been a transfer target for manager Frank Blunstone. After previous attempts to secure his signature had been unsuccessful, the manager finally got his man in October 1972, when he signed him from Carlisle United for a fee of £10,000. Webb was seen as the replacement for the recently-sold John O'Mara, but a totally different type of player, he struggled to make any sort of impact and failed to win over the majority of supporters, enduring a miserable stay in which he managed only eight League goals in just under two seasons. He was released by Mike Everitt at the end of the 1973-74 campaign and returned to the north-east where he joined Darlington and re-discovered his scoring touch. He finished the following season as the their leading goalscorer and player-of-the-season, although his career ended just over a year later.

Middlesbrough	20+8 appearances	6 goals

Carlisle United	16+10 appearances	5 goals
Brentford	37+2 appearances	8 goals
Darlington	69+5 appearances	21 goals

Andy Woon
26th June 1952 (Bognor Regis)
56 apps/15 goals

A tall striker, Woon was signed as an amateur from non-League Bognor Regis on trial by Frank Blunstone in October 1972 and impressed enough to be awarded a professional contract. He had been top scorer for the Sussex County League team in the previous two seasons and he quickly wrote himself into the Griffin Park Hall of Fame when he became the first player to score a hat-trick on his full debut – in a 5-0 win against Port Vale. Woon failed to live up to that early promise and, although he had some lengthy runs in the team, was eventually released by John Docherty in May 1975, which signalled the end of his League career. He joined Maidstone United, then Gravesend, before ending his days through injury at Hastings United.

Brentford	42+8 appearances	12 goals

Barry Salvage
21st December 1946 (Bristol)
92 apps/8 goals

A pacey, out-and-out left winger who rarely missed the chance for a shot on goal, Salvage started his professional career with Fulham before moving onto Millwall, then Queens Park Rangers, from where Frank Blunstone paid a £9,000 fee in February 1973. He scored on his debut and, in the same month, was also credited with one of the fastest goals in the club's history, scoring after just 24 seconds against Charlton Athletic. He maintained a regular place in the team in the following two seasons under the management of Mike Everitt and John Docherty, before asking to be released from his contract in the summer of 1975. He returned to Millwall where he ended his League playing days, before going to the North American Soccer League and featuring for St Louis All Stars. A move to Norway saw him represent Kopervik, Accra and Hauger where he was player/coach. Barry died at the age of 39 in 1986 after collapsing during a marathon run in his home town of Eastbourne.

Fulham	7 appearances	0 goals
Millwall	1+1 appearances	0 goals
Queens Park Rangers	16+5 appearances	1 goal
Brentford	87 appearances	8 goals
Millwall	43+12 appearances	9 goals

Kieron Baker
29th October 1949 (Isle of Wight)
6 apps/0 goals

One of the few footballers to be born on the Isle of Wight, Baker started his career at Fulham, and also had a spell on loan at Mansfield Town, before he finally made his League debut for Bourne-mouth, having signed for the south coast club in the summer of 1967. He was largely used as a back-up goalkeeper and had spent some time playing for Montreal Olympic in the North American Soccer League before he was signed on loan in February 1973 for the rest of the season by Frank Blunstone to assist in the battle against relegation. Baker was recalled by the Cherries after just six appearances, though, and went on to establish himself as the number one keeper at Dean Court. In the summer of 1978 he signed for Ipswich Town but suffered an injury and was forced to retire without making a first-team appearance.

| Bournemouth | 217 appearances | 0 goals |
| Brentford | 6 appearances | 0 goals |

Garry Towse
14th May 1952 (Dover)
5 apps/0 goals

A goalkeeper on the books of Crystal Palace, he'd joined the Eagles in January 1972 from Folkestone, but having failed to make a breakthrough to the first-team, moved to Griffin Park in the summer of 1973 to act as back-up to Paul Priddy. Unfortunately he suffered a fractured finger which prevented him from taking part in the pre-season programme and made just five first-team appearances – the last of which was a 4-1 defeat, which left the team in 92nd place in the Football League. Towse generally failed to impress and was released from his contract in the December and he pursued his career in South Africa.

| Brentford | 5 appearances | 0 goals |

Mick Brown
27th September 1951 (Swansea)
3 apps/0 goals

The rugged central defender, and former Welsh schoolboy international, started his career at Crystal Palace before moving on to Brighton and Hove Albion. Brown became Mike Everitt's first arrival on loan in September 1973. Initially, his no-nonsense, aggressive style paid dividends and The Bees won 5-1 on his debut, but he was recalled by the Seagulls after just three starts and, having failed to establish himself back at the Goldstone Ground, Brown disappeared from the professional game at the end of the season.

Brighton & Hove Albion	5+3 appearances	1 goal
Brentford	3 appearances	0 goals

playing in the North American Soccer League, enjoying spells at Atlanta Chiefs, Miami Gatos and Atlanta Apollos. In September 1973 he became one of Mike Everitt's first signings, initially on a 28-day trial period, which was made permanent a month later. The neat and tidy midfielder became a regular performer in the heart of the team during much of the next two seasons. He was given a free transfer in the summer of 1975 and flitted around the non-League scene thereafter with Barnet, Hendon, Hillingdon Borough, Woking and Weymouth. In early 1978 he returned to Griffin Park on a non-contract basis to assist the reserve team.

Fulham	47 appearances	9 goals
Orient	75 appearances	15 goals
Peterborough United	38 appearances	6 goals
Queens Park Rangers	0+3 appearances	1 goal
Brentford	57+4 appearances	4 goals

Dave Metchick
14th August 1943 (Bakewell)
65 apps/4 goals

Metchick, a former England schoolboy international, served an apprenticeship with Fulham, before signing professional terms in the summer of 1961 – he made more than 50 first-team appearances for The Cottagers before joining Orient in December 1964. Metchick moved on to Peterborough United in March 1967, then Queens Park Rangers in readiness for the 1968-69 season and, a year later, he joined Arsenal but failed to make a first team appearance. One of only a few Jewish players in League football at the time, he moved to the United States in 1970 and spent four years

Hugh Reed
23rd August 1950 (Dumbarton)
4 apps/0 goals

Born in Aberdeen, this tiny, 5'4" winger joined West Bromwich Albion as an apprentice on leaving school and, having made a few Division One appearances, he was sold to Plymouth Argyle for £12,000 in November 1971, from where Mike Everitt signed him for a brief loan spell in October 1973. Reed failed to make any impression in a struggling team and later spent two seasons at Crewe Alexandra. His career ended in 1976 with trial periods at Huddersfield Town and Hartlepool United. He saw out his final playing days with a couple of seasons at Stafford Rangers in the Northern Premier League. In 1992, he was found dead at his home aged just 42.

West Bromwich Albion	5+3 appearances	2 goals
Plymouth Argyle	44+12 appearances	9 goals
Brentford	3+1 appearances	0 goals
Crewe Alexandra	38+9 appearances	9 goals
Hartlepool United	6 appearances	1 goal

Gordon Riddick
6th November 1943 (Watford)
120 apps/5 goals

A veteran of over 300 games, Riddick had originally joined Luton Town as a 15-year-old. After eight years at Kennilworth Road he signed for Gillingham on transfer deadline day, 1966, for £15,000. A striker at that stage, he hit 20 goals in just 15 games and remained at Priestfield for three years, joining Charlton Athletic for £25,000 In November 1969, where a two-year stay was followed by a two-season stint at Orient, then a year at Northampton Town. Brentford manager, Mike Everitt, brought Riddick to Griffin Park in October 1973 after he had been the target of several unsuccessful bids by the new Bees boss in the preceding months. A vastly experienced and steady midfielder, he was appointed team captain soon after his arrival, but failed to win over supporters until he was converted to a very effective central defender by John Docherty and he became a main-stay of the back four. After suffering an ankle injury early in the 1976-77 season, Riddick announced his retirement, however, new manager, Bill Dodgin, persuaded him to re-consider and he made a surprise return on a non-contract basis and played a crucial short-term role, before finally leaving the game in February 1977. An accomplished cricketer, Riddick also represented Hertfordshire in the Minor Counties Championship.

Luton Town	101+1 appearances	16 goals
Gillingham	114 appearances	24 goals
Charlton Athletic	26+3 appearances	5 goals
Orient	13+8 appearances	3 goals
Northampton Town	28 appearances	3 goals
Brentford	106+4 appearances	5 goals

Roy Cotton
14th November 1955 (Hammersmith)
2 apps/0goals

Cotton graduated from Tottenham Hotspur before moving to Griffin Park and was a member of the successful junior set-up that won an international tournament in Frankfurt. He continued his career as an amateur, before signing professional terms and making his first team debut as an 18-year old in December 1973. A talented young striker/winger he failed to progress and left at the end of that season to join Orient, where he was top scorer in their reserve team during a two-year stay, signing for Aldershot in the summer of 1976. His progress was stunted by a badly broken leg and he moved to Australia to continue his career with St George and Sydney Olympic.

Brentford	1+1 appearances	0 goals
Orient	0+3 appearances	0 goals
Aldershot	5 appearances	0 goals

Steve Sherwood
10th December 1953 (Selby)
66 apps/0 goals

A tall, commanding goalkeeper, Sherwood made his League debut for Chelsea in front of a 43,000 crowd as a 17-year-old, which was the start of a career that would see him make well over 500 appearances and play professional football past his 40th birthday. Having already had a brief loan spell at Millwall, he was signed on loan by Mike Everitt in January 1974, and had the unusual experience of playing 66 games whilst on loan for a season and a half, during which he was voted the club's player of the year. His performances prompted an attempt to retain his services but the £30,000 asking price was not met and he was eventually sold by Chelsea to Watford. During an 11-year stay at Vicarage Road he played in every division during their meteoric rise, as well as appearing in an FA Cup Final and playing European football. He then moved to Grimsby Town, where he made a further 200 appearances. After a short spell at Northampton Town he played part-time for Immingham Town in the Northern League before he was called to assist at Lincoln City aged 41. His career finally came to an end with Gainsborough Trinity.

Chelsea	16 appearances	0 goals
Millwall	1 appearance	0 goals
Brentford	62 appearances	0 goals
Watford	211 appearances	1 goal
Grimsby Town	183 appearances	0 goals
Northampton Town	15+1 appearances	0 goals
Lincoln City	6+1 appearances	0 goals

Jimmy Gabriel
16th October 1940 (Dundee)
9 apps/0 goals

Having earned Scottish schoolboy honours Gabriel became one of the most expensive teenagers in the game when he signed for Everton from Dundee for £30,000 in March 1960. He played over 250 games at Goodison Park, winning the League Championship, the FA Cup and earning two full international caps, before being sold to Southampton in the summer of 1967. After five seasons at The Dell he joined Bournemouth in July 1972 and, following a loan spell at Swindon Town, he was signed by Mike Everitt on a short-term contract in March 1974. As a gritty midfielder his influence on the pitch was crucial in steering the team away from the bottom of the division – he also played a key coaching role and his end of season departure to the USA was a major loss. Gabriel captained Seattle Sounders and spent a further 13 years coaching in the States, as well as having a brief spell in Argentina. He returned to England as Harry Redknapp's assistant at Bournemouth in 1987 and, three years later, returned to Goodison Park and assisted in various coaching roles until 1997, when he returned to the United States.

Everton	255+1 appearances	33 goals
Southampton	190+1 appearances	25 goals
Bournemouth	53 appearances	4 goals
Swindon Town	6 appearances	0 goals
Brentford	9 appearances	0 goals

Richard Poole
3rd July 1957 (Heston)
21 apps/1 goal

A tall, gangly striker, Poole became the first of the newly-formed juniors to make the step up to the first team when he was given his debut by Mike Everitt in February 1974 – becoming the second youngest player in the club's history at the age of 16 years and five months. Having already made 14 appearances, he signed professional terms in the summer of 1975, but was released after just one season and briefly moved to Watford which proved to be his only other foray into League football.

Brentford	12+9 appearances	1 goal
Watford	3+4 appearances	1 goal

Kevin Harding
19th March 1957 (Isleworth)
8 apps/0 goals

Along with Richard Poole, Harding became the first youngster to be signed on junior terms in 1972, following the reformation of the youth set-up and the young defender/midfielder enjoyed a promising start – captaining the junior team as a 15-year-old while also playing for the first team in the London Challenge Cup in September 1972. He made his League debut just before his 17th birthday in March 1974, but made only limited appearances during his apprenticeship and failed to do enough to earn a full professional contract. Harding left Brentford in March 1975.

Brentford	8 appearances	0 goals

Dave Simmons
24th October 1948 (Isle of Wight)
58 apps/18 goals

Simmons was initially a member of Arsenal's FA Youth Cup winning side in 1966, but he failed to progress further at Highbury and, after a loan spell at Bournemouth, he became a journeyman striker, moving to Aston Villa in February 1969, followed by spells at Walsall (loan), Colchester United – where he made national headlines as one of the scorers in the famous FA Cup win against Leeds United – and Cambridge United. He was signed by Mike Everitt for a £12,000 fee on transfer deadline day in March 1974 and the bustling front-man, never afraid to throw himself into the thick of the action, had the most prolific season of his career the following year with 12 goals in 25 appearances. He lost his touch soon after and briefly returned to Cambridge United in November 1975, where he ended his professional days, being forced to retire as a result of arthritis. He remained in non-League football with Cambridge City, Bishops Stortford, Newmarket Town, Soham Town and Ely City. Simmons died in June 2007, following a lengthy battle with cancer, at the age of 58.

Bournemouth	7 appearances	3 goals
Aston Villa	13+4 appearances	7 goals
Walsall	5 appearances	2 goals
Colchester United	52+5 appearances	11 goals
Cambridge United	19+5 appearances	3 goals
Brentford	47+5 appearances	17 goals
Cambridge United	16+1 appearances	5 goals

Keith Lawrence
26th March 1954 (Sidcup)
89 apps/2 goals

Signed as a 20-year-old by Mike Everitt in the summer of 1974, having been released by Chelsea – although he had also spent four months on loan at West Bromwich Albion without making an appearance – the young centre-half became a giant figure in the back four at Brentford. Despite managing to maintain a regular place in the line-up throughout his two seasons at Griffin Park, he was surprisingly given a free transfer by John Docherty at the end of the 1975-76 season. Strong and powerful in the air, the highlight of his brief career was scoring at Old Trafford in the League Cup defeat by Manchester United in 1975. He never resurfaced in the professional game again and played for Wealdstone, Bromley, Tonbridge and Brading Town before embarking on a career with the police force.

Brentford	78 appearances	1 goal

Ian Filby
9th October 1954 (Woodford)
3 apps/0 goals

A young midfielder, Filby signed for his local club Orient as a professional on his 18th birthday in October 1972, after he had been a member of the O's team that won the London Challenge Cup earlier that year. Despite having no first-team experience he was signed on a one-month loan by Mike Everitt in September 1974, but started just one game and returned to Orient at the end of his stay. He was released at the end of the season without making another appearance. Although he disappeared from the Football League, he continued his career playing professionally in South Africa (Durban City and Lusitano FC) and North America (Sacramento Gold, Pennsylvania Stoners and California Surf). His brief stay at Griffin Park was best remembered for an incident as the named substitute in a home game against Crewe Alexandra when he got himself locked in the dressing room at half time and was only released in the second half when his absence from the bench was eventually noticed.

Brentford	1+2 appearances	0 goals

Billy Stagg
17th October 1957 (Ealing)
4 apps/0 goals

At 5'4" Stagg is one of the smallest players to appear for the club – the tiny midfield/winger made his debut in September 1974 as an apprentice, having progressed through the schoolboy ranks. Although he maintained his place in the team for a run of four matches his stature made it difficult for him to compete and he was never offered a full professional contract. He left Brentford at the end of the 1974-75 season but went on to play for a host of non-League teams, as well as enjoying spells playing in Denmark and the United States.

Brentford	4 appearances	0 goals

Graham Smith
7th August 1951 (Wimbledon)
7 apps/0 goals

A little-known midfielder, Smith was signed from manager Mike Everitt's previous club Wimbledon for a trial period in August 1974 and he made an early breakthrough into the first team and signed a contract until the end of the season. However, Smith lost his place soon afterwards and disappeared as quickly as he'd arrived and returned to Plough Lane in February 1975 on loan, before re-joining on a permanent basis at the end of the season. Smith later joined Hillingdon Borough and was a member of their team that earned FA Cup headlines by beating Torquay United in 1976.

Brentford	7 appearances	0 goals

Terry Johnson
30th August 1949 (Newcastle)
111 apps/30 goals

Originally from the north-east of England, Johnson spent his early years as an apprentice, and then a professional, with Newcastle United. After a loan spell with Darlington he failed to break into the Magpies first-team and was eventually signed by Southend United on a free transfer in January 1971, where he became a regular member of the team. In November 1974 he was signed by Mike Everitt for a fee of £15,000 and, as an energetic right winger with an excellent goal-scoring record, he quickly established himself as a consistent key performer and was popular with supporters. He asked to be released from his contract in the summer of 1977 to enable him to return to his native north-east and signed for non-League Blyth Spartans where he attained legendary status for his role in the club's FA Cup run to the fifth round.

Darlington	4 appearances	1 goal
Southend United	155+2 appearances	35 goals
Brentford	98+3 appearances	27 goals

Willie Brown
5th February 1950 (Falkirk)
17 apps/9 goals

A prolific goalscorer in the lower leagues, the little Scotsman had enjoyed striking success at all of his previous clubs. Having started out at Burnley, where he won an FA Youth Cup winners medal, Brown joined Carlisle United in July 1969 and, after a loan spell at Barrow, he moved to Newport County for £1,500 in the summer of 1970, and was the leading goalscorer in three out of four seasons. Following a loan stint at Hereford United Brown was signed by Mike Everitt in November 1974 for £4,000 and his arrival was seen as an astute move based on his previous exploits. Small in stature, but lethal in front of goal, he did not disappoint and continued to score at will. But the change of manager proved fatal for his fortunes and John Docherty sold him to Torquay United for £5,000 just weeks after his appointment. Brown continued to find the net on a regular basis for the Gulls, with another 50 goals in the next three seasons. He left the Football League scene in 1978 and settled in Minehead, where he initially became player/coach and then took on a role as commercial manager before running a newsagent's business.

Burnley	0+1 appearance	0 goals
Carlisle United	16+3 appearances	8 goals
Barrow	6 appearances	1 goal
Newport County	166+2 appearances	50 goals
Hereford United	9 appearances	6 goals
Brentford	16 appearances	9 goals
Torquay United	137+2 appearances	46 goals

Gary Smith
4th November 1955 (Greenford)
3 apps/0 goals

A local lad from Greenford, the tall centre-back came through the junior ranks before signing a professional contract in December 1973, just after his 18th birthday. Although he was predicted to have a promising future, Smith had to wait a year before making his debut, replacing Keith Lawrence at the turn of the year in the 1974-75 season. Mike Everitt's sacking as manager failed to help his cause – he did not prosper under John Docherty, being loaned to Wimbledon, then signing permanently at Plough Lane in the summer of 1975 following his release. He later played for Clacton Town and Wivenhoe Town, as well as having a non-contract spell with Colchester United.

Brentford	3 appearances	0 goals

Mickey French
7th May 1955 (Eastbourne)
73 apps/17 goals

A former West Ham United apprentice, and an England under-18 international, the young striker had become known to manager John Docherty during his brief spell working with the Queens Park Rangers reserve team. In February 1975 he became Docherty's first signing for a £2,000 fee. The 19-year-old made an instant impact with a spectacular overhead kick debut goal but, despite his powerful physique and silky skills, French never really delivered the promise he showed and Bill Dodgin deemed him surplus to requirements in February 1977 when he was sold to Swindon Town for £7,000. He moved on to Doncaster Rovers in the summer of 1978, and to Aldershot a year later, where he enjoyed a successful spell before ending his professional career with a one-season stint at Rochdale in 1982-83. French returned to his birthplace and had spells with Lewes and Hailsham, where he moved into coaching and later held a similar role with Eastbourne Borough.

Brentford	56+9 appearances	16 goals
Swindon Town	5+5 appearances	1 goal
Doncaster Rovers	36 appearances	5 goals
Aldershot	70+4 appearances	16 goals
Rochdale	35+1 appearances	11 goals

Nigel Smith
3rd January 1958 (Banstead)
94 apps/0 goals

Following a spell as a schoolboy at Queens Park Rangers, Smith made nearly 20 appearances for their reserve team while still studying for his 'A' levels before following his mentor, John Docherty, to Griffin Park and signing a professional contract on leaving school in April 1975. He was immediately given his opportunity in the first-team in the final two matches of the season and showed tremendous maturity and ability as a 17-year old at the heart of the defence. He retained his place during the following season, being called up for training with the England under 18 squad and he had clocked up 70 games before his 20th birthday. His calmness belied his tender years and Smith seemed destined for the top echelons of the game – but his career stuttered under the management of Bill Dodgin and, having fallen out of favour, he was transfer-listed at the start of the 1978-79 season and had his contract cancelled in October, whereupon he linked up with John Docherty yet again, this time at Cambridge United. However, he failed to start a League game at the Abbey Stadium and, shortly after, quit at the age of 21 to join the police, representing the Metropolitan Police in the Isthmian League and also the England Police team, while also having a few games for Woking.

Brentford	81+4 appearances	0 goals
Cambridge United	0+1 appearance	0 goals

Bill Glazier
2nd August 1943 (Nottingham)
12 apps/0 goals

A goalkeeper who attained a reputation at the highest level, Glazier had started out at Crystal Palace and signed professionally in October 1961. He was subject of a, then, record transfer fee for a goalkeeper, when Jimmy Hill signed him for Coventry City for £35,000 where he made almost 400 appearances for the Sky Blues and earned England under-23 honours. Only a broken leg prevented him from staking a claim for inclusion in the 1966 England World Cup winning squad – who later provided the opposition for his testimonial game. His £4,000 signing by John Docherty in the summer of 1975 was seen as a major coup, but despite being only 32 years of age, his disastrous short stay was littered with blunders and, after just 12 appearances, he asked to be released to concentrate on running his hotel on the south coast. Glazier's contract was cancelled, although his registration was retained. He later had a few games for the St Louis All-Stars in the USA.

Crystal Palace	106 appearances	0 goals
Coventry City	346 appearances	0 goals
Brentford	9 appearances	0 goals

Gordon Sweetzer
27th January 1957 (Canada)
88 apps/45 goals

Another former Queens Park Rangers junior to follow John Docherty from Loftus Road to Griffin Park, the young Canadian striker signed professional terms in September 1975 and was soon given an extended run in the first-team where he showed promise without giving an indication of what was to follow. Despite niggling injuries wrecking the start of the 1976-77 campaign, his season burst into life and Sweetzer scored 23 goals in just 25 starts, as the team rose dramatically up the table. An aggressive, all-action, bustling striker with little finesse about his game, he continued in the same vein the following season, with 12 goals in 18 League games, before Bill Dodgin stunned supporters by selling him to Cambridge United for £30,000. The team went on to gain promotion in his absence, but his own career fell to pieces – injuries restricting him to just nine starts in two-and-a-half years and he quit to join Toronto Blizzard in his native Canada. He made a short, but unsuccessful, return to Griffin Park under Fred Callaghan's management in 1982, before going back to his homeland to play for Edmonton Drillers and was a member of the Canadian side which narrowly failed to qualify for the World Cup Finals.

Brentford	68+4 appearances	40 goals
Cambridge United	9 appearances	3 goals
Brentford	8+1 appearances	1 goals

Graham Horn
23rd August 1954 (Westminster)
3 apps/0 goals

A member of Arsenal's FA Youth Cup winning team in 1970, the goalkeeper failed to make a first-team appearance at Highbury and made his League debut during a long-term loan spell with Portsmouth, before signing for Luton Town in February 1973. He was signed on loan by John Docherty in November 1975 after first-choice Paul Priddy was injured, but his first game at Tranmere Rovers resulted in a 5-1 defeat, in which he had his ear partly severed in a collision. A spell playing for Los Angeles Aztecs was followed by short stays at Charlton Athletic, Kettering, Southend United and Aldershot, before his career came to an end with two years at Torquay United and at non-League Barnstaple Town.

Portsmouth	22 appearances	0 goals
Luton Town	58 appearances	0 goals
Brentford	3 appearances	0 goals
Southend United	9 appearances	0 goals
Aldershot	9 appearances	0 goals
Torquay United	47 appearances	0 goals

Danis Salman
12th March 1960 (Cyprus)
371 apps/8 goals

Cypriot-born, and of Turkish origin, Danis came to England as a very small child. He spent varying amounts of time training as a youngster with Arsenal, Tottenham and Queens Park Rangers, from where he followed John Docherty to Griffin Park and signed schoolboy terms. In November 1975 he was named as substitute for the home game with Watford and his appearance at the

age of fifteen years, eight months and three days made him the club's youngest ever League player. A stylish and speedy defender, comfortable at either full-back or in central defence, Danis went on to complete more than ten years service, despite twice walking out in dispute and threatening never to play for the club again. He earned a testimonial match against Tottenham Hotspur (raising £5,552) in 1986 and made over 350 appearances, as well as earning five England Youth International caps. In the summer of 1986 he moved across London to join former boss, John Docherty, at Millwall for a tribunal-fixed fee of £20,000 and played in the top flight with the Lions, before a £50,000 move to Plymouth Argyle in 1990. He completed an eighteen-year playing career with spells at Peterborough United (loan) and Torquay United, before moving into a commercial role with Torquay.

Brentford	316+9 appearances	8 goals
Millwall	85+8 appearances	4 goals
Plymouth Argyle	71+3 appearances	4 goals
Peterborough United	1 appearance	0 goals
Torquay United	20 appearances	0 goals

Tom Sharp
30th July 1957 (Newmains)
17 apps/1 goal

Previously the captain of a successful Everton youth team, Sharp was signed on full professional terms at Goodison Park in the summer of 1975 but, six months later, the Scottish centre-half was taken on loan by John Docherty and impressed enough to be offered a permanent move and was signed on a free transfer in March 1976. Sharp only made sporadic appearances throughout his stay and was released by Bill Dodgin at the end of the 1976-77 season, failing to re-emerge in the professional game.

Brentford   4+12 appearances
1 goal

Andy McCulloch
3rd January 1950 (Northampton)
122 apps/49 goals

The 'fearless target-man' tag did little justice to the abilities of the 6'2" striker who possessed bravery in abundance, but also showed immense talent both on the ground and in the air to complement his lethal finishing in the penalty box. He'd started his career in non-League with Fleet Town, Alton and Walton & Hersham after his family returned from a spell living in Australia and, at the age of 20, he was offered a trial by Queens Park Rangers which led to a permanent contract. A £45,000 move to Cardiff City in October 1972, where he won a Scottish under-23 international cap, was followed by a £75,000 transfer to Oxford United in the summer of 1974, before he was captured by John Docherty in March 1976 for a then club record fee of £25,000. The money paid out proved to be a massive bargain, after an injury stricken first season, he was crucial to the promotion campaign of 1977-78, forming a deadly partnership with Steve Phillips and notching 22 goals of his own. Following another successful season in Division Three, he was sold to Sheffield Wednesday for £60,000, where he netted 50 goals in four seasons, before completing his career with short stays at Crystal Palace and Aldershot.

Queens Park Rangers	30+12 appearances	10 goals
Cardiff City	58 appearances	24 goals
Oxford United	41 appearances	9 goals
Brentford	115+2 appearances	49 goals
Sheffield Wednesday	122+3 appearances	44 goals
Crystal Palace	25 appearances	3 goals
Aldershot	16 appearances	2 goals

Paul Walker
17th December 1960 (Wood Green)
79 apps/6 goals

A great future was widely predicted for the young midfielder, who captained the England schoolboy team and made his debut for the first-team in a League Cup tie at Watford while still at school – aged 15 years, seven months and 28 days – thereby becoming the youngest ever Bees player in all competitions. Despite so much early promise, Walker's career failed to reach the expected heights and, after signing as a professional in January 1978, he struggled to make a breakthrough into the squad during the next couple of seasons. Having finally secured a regular midfield berth under Fred Callaghan's management in 1980-81, his performances prompted the club to sign him on a four-year contract, but he failed

to maintain his progress and, after two ineffective seasons, in the summer of 1983, he left on a free transfer to try his luck with South African side PG Rangers in Johannesburg. He proved a revelation there and was looking to return to England when he suffered a badly broken leg and his playing career was all but finished. Walker had a few stints with a number of non-League clubs and coached/managed at Yeading, Chertsey Town and Egham Town.

Brentford	53+18 appearances	5 goals

John Fraser
12th July 1953 (Hammersmith)
132 apps/7 goals

A full-back who had signed for Fulham in the summer of 1971 on completion of his apprenticeship. Fraser spent five years at Craven Cottage and played in the 1975 FA Cup Final against West Ham United. He was signed by John Docherty on a free transfer in the 1976 close season and quickly established himself as a first-team regular under new manager Bill Dodgin, a position he retained until midway through the following season, when he suffered a severe groin injury, which necessitated missing the second half of the promotion campaign. He recovered sufficiently to re-establish himself as a hard working, reliable midfielder until he refused the new contract offered when Fred Callaghan was appointed as manager and was given a free transfer just weeks into the 1980-81 season. That signalled the end of his professional career as he dropped into non-League football with Oxford City.

Fulham	55+1 appearances	1 goal
Brentford	121+2 appearances	6 goals

Keith Pritchett
8th November 1953 (Glasgow)
13 apps/1 goal

The Scottish schoolboy international started his career with Wolverhampton Wanderers but only made his first League start when he joined Doncaster Rovers in the summer of 1973. Less than a year later he moved on to Queens Park Rangers, then became one of John Docherty's quartet of summer Brentford signings in 1976. He impressed in his performances at left-back in the opening matches, but Bill Dodgin's arrival saw him quickly sold on to Watford for a £4,000 fee, where he played a leading role in the Hornets' rise through the divisions to the top flight. He joined Blackpool in November 1982 for a final two-year stint in England, later emerging in New Zealand, where he managed Auckland club Waitakere City, before becoming manager of the New Zealand national team between 1996 and 1997. Pritchett was later appointed as director of football with United Soccer 1, the country's northern-most football federation.

Doncaster Rovers	6 appearances	0 goals
Queens Park Rangers	4 appearances	0 goals
Brentford	11 appearances	1 goal
Watford	133+7 appearances	9 goals
Blackpool	36+1 appearances	1 goal

Bobby Goldthorpe
6th December 1950 (Osterley)
23 apps/2 goals

When Bobby was signed by John Docherty in the 1976 close season, it was a case of second time lucky for the giant centre-half, who had been a victim of the 1967 financial crisis when the junior set-up was disbanded and he was forced to leave his local club. He continued with his junior career at Crystal Palace where he signed professionally in the summer of 1968, staying for more than four years, but managing just one first-team appearance before joining Charlton Athletic in December 1972, initially on loan and then permanently. After a loan period at Aldershot the lanky, blond-haired defender returned to Griffin Park on a free transfer as first choice centre-back, but he failed to impress new boss Bill Dodgin and was quickly told that he did not figure in future plans before being released at the end of the season.

Crystal Palace	1 appearance	0 goals
Charlton Athletic	70+8 appearances	6 goals
Aldershot	16 appearances	0 goals
Brentford	19 appearances	2 goals

Steve Aylott
3rd September 1951 (Ilford)
7 apps/0 goals

A junior centre-half with West Ham United, Aylott signed professional terms in the summer of 1969 but was unable to get close to first team action and, two years later, he joined Oxford United, where he was converted into a defensive midfielder and groomed to replace the ageing Ron Atkinson. He remained at the Manor Ground for five seasons, making more than 150 appearances before the financial implications of relegation saw him released and he was

signed by John Docherty in the summer of 1976. He was immediately plagued with injury problems, which blighted his entire season – he managed just five games, and although he was offered a free transfer by Bill Dodgin at the end of the campaign, he opted to see out the second year of his contract, making just two more appearances and leaving the professional game in May 1978.

| Oxford United | 143+11 appearances | 8 goals |
| Brentford | 6+1 appearances | 0 goals |

Harry Redknapp
2nd March 1947 (Poplar)
1 app/0 goals

Redknapp, later to become one of the best known names in English football, was a skilful winger who started his career as an apprentice at West Ham United, spending seven seasons at Upton Park as well as being a member of the England team that won the Little World Cup in 1964. He was transferred to Bournemouth for a club record £31,000 in the summer of 1972 but, after four seasons, was lured by the soccer boom in the USA and joined Seattle Sounders. On his return he became John Docherty's last signing, on a trial basis, in September 1976, but he was injured and substituted just 38 minutes into his debut game at Aldershot. Following the arrival of Bill Dodgin as manager days later,

Redknapp's trial ended as he left with one of the shortest Brentford careers on record, to return to the United States. He made one final League appearance six years later, when he was coach at Bournemouth, where he was later appointed as manager and, despite being badly injured in an horrific car crash in Italy in 1990, he went on to attain a reputation as one of the country's top managers with tenures at West Ham, Portsmouth (twice), Southampton and Tottenham Hotspur.

West Ham United	146+3 appearances	7 goals
Bournemouth	96+5 appearances	5 goals
Brentford	1 appearance	0 goals
Bournemouth	1 appearance	0 goals

Allan Glover
21st October 1950 (Staines)
32 apps/2 goals

Glover's early career at Queens Park Rangers saw him make just a handful of appearances after progressing from the junior ranks and he was still only 18 years of age when West Bromwich Albion signed him in a swap deal, which valued him at £70,000. He spent seven years at the Hawthorns before an ill-fated loan to Southend United, in which he got injured after just 30 seconds of his only appearance, preceded another loan move in October 1976, when he became Bill Dodgin's first signing. A bid to make the move permanent proved unsuccessful when personal terms could not be agreed and the busy, elegant midfielder signed for Orient but, in November 1978, Dodgin finally got his man when he was signed on a free transfer. His second spell was far less effective and Glover was released at the end of the 1979-80 season.

280

Queens Park Rangers	5+1 appearances	0 goals
West Bromwich Albion	84+8 appearances	9 goals
Southend United	0+1 appearance	0 goals
Brentford	6 appearances	0 goals
Orient	37 appearances	5 goals
Brentford	21+2 appearances	2 goals

Dave Carlton
21st November 1952 (Stepney)
148 apps/7 goals

A gritty, hard-working and tough midfielder, whose aggressive approach sometimes overshadowed his superb passing ability, Carlton had struggled against injury in his early days – making just a handful of appearances in a four-year spell at Fulham after completing his apprenticeship in December 1969. Following a loan spell at Dallas Tornado in the North American Soccer League he joined Northampton Town in October 1973, where his career and reputation blossomed under the management of Bill Dodgin and, three years later, he followed Dodgin to West London when he signed in October 1976 for a £3,000 fee. Carlton became an integral part of the midfield for the next four seasons, enhancing his reputation as a first-class passer, but following the change of manager in 1980, became one of the 'contract rebels' and returned to Northampton Town, where he took his tally of appearances to over 350 games in a final two-year stay.

Fulham	5+4 appearances	0 goals
Northampton Town	99+5 appearances	6 goals
Brentford	138+2 appearances	7 goals
Northampton Town	76 appearances	1 goal

Gary Rolph
24th February 1960 (Stepney)
15 apps/3 goals

Having broken into Bill Dodgin's first-team as a 16-year-old in December 1976, the tall, young apprentice striker became the club's youngest ever goalscorer in the FA Cup, when he netted in a tie at Colchester – he went on to sign professional terms shortly after his 18th birthday in March 1978. Although Rolph looked impressive in his early games, his progress was limited, making just one further appearance in the 1978-79 season and he was released at the end of the campaign. He failed to find another professional club and played for Woking, Billericay and Leytonstone and Ilford amongst others.

Brentford	8+4 appearances	1 goal

Steve Scrivens
11th March 1957 (Ewell)
5 apps/0 goals

Scrivens had made a few starts for Fulham, where he had signed professional terms on his 18th birthday in March 1975, but with opportunities limited at Craven Cottage, he was taken on loan by Bill Dodgin in December 1976. A slightly-built, speedy and exciting left-winger, he impressed during his stay, despite the team struggling and Dodgin attempted to make the move permanent.

But Fulham refused to accept the request although, strangely, he failed to add to his appearances tally back at Craven Cottage and subsequently drifted out of the game.

| Fulham | 3+1 appearances | 1 goal |
| Brentford | 5 appearances | 0 goals |

Graham Cox
30th April 1959 (Willesden)
4 apps/0 goals

After impressing in a 1975 pre-season friendly at Hayes, the young goalkeeper was signed as an apprentice, making his first-team bow in December 1976 in the midst of Bill Dodgin's team-building revamp. But the opportunity came too early – ten goals conceded in three games dented his confidence badly. He signed professional terms in April 1977 but made just one further first team appearance and was released in October 1978 to join Margate, marking his final game for the club by coming on as an outfield player in a reserve match and scoring a goal. In January 1985, he re-emerged in league football when he left Hillingdon Borough to join Aldershot and played thirteen league games for the Shots.

| Brentford | 4 appearances | 0 goals |
| Aldershot | 13 appearances | 0 goals |

Tony Burns
27th March 1944 (Edenbridge)

6 apps/0 goals

A vastly experienced goalkeeper, Burns was signed by Bill Dodgin in January 1977 on loan from Crystal Palace with a view to the 32-year-old staying permanently, but after just six games, his parent club had a change of heart and he was recalled. A calm, reliable keeper with a monumental throw, Burns had broken into League football from Southern League Tonbridge Angels – in March 1963 he was then snapped up by Arsenal and, having made his debut two seasons later, had 24 consecutive games in goal for the Gunners. He moved to Brighton in the summer of 1966, and onto Charlton Athletic three years later, before a spell with Durban City in South Africa, then on to Crystal Palace in October 1973. Following his loan at Griffin Park, Burns had brief spells at Memphis (USA) and Plymouth Argyle before hanging up his gloves – his post-playing career included three separate stints as manager at Tonbridge, a managerial post at Gravesend and Northfleet and 14 years as goalkeeping coach at Millwall, before taking up a similar role at Crystal Palace, then returning to the New Den.

Arsenal	31 appearances	0 goals
Brighton	54 appearances	0 goals
Charlton Athletic	10 appearances	0 goals
Crystal Palace	90 appearances	0 goals
Brentford	6 appearances	0 goals
Plymouth Argyle	8 appearances	0 goals

Neil Smillie
19th July 1958 (Barnsley)
227 apps/22 goals

The son of a former Barnsley player, Smillie signed on with Crystal Palace in October 1975, making almost 100 appearances in a seven-year spell. It was during this time that he first arrived at Griffin Park, signed for a brief three-match loan as an 18-year old by Bill Dodgin. He eventually moved on to Brighton at the start of the 1982-83 season and played in that year's FA Cup Final games against Manchester United, before being sold on to Watford 12 months later for a £100,000 fee – then joining Reading in March 1987 following a loan spell there. In the summer of 1988 Smillie was signed by Steve Perryman and, in a five-year stay, he enjoyed the best period of his career as a traditional style , two-footed winger able to play on either flank. He was an automatic choice, the creator of numerous goals and a hugely popular player – a crucial member of the 1992 championship-winning team. Smillie's release, following David Webb's arrival in 1993, disappointed many supporters. He saw out his playing days with a two-year stint at Gillingham as player/coach, including a lengthy spell as caretaker manager, before moving on to Wycombe Wanderers as youth team coach and later becoming first-team manager.

Crystal Palace	71+12 appearances	7 goals
Brentford	3 appearances	0 goals
Brighton and Hove Albion	62+13 appearances	2 goals
Watford	10+6 appearances	3 goals
Reading	38+1 appearances	0 goals

Brentford	163+9 appearances	18 goals
Gillingham	53 appearances	3 goals

John Bain
23rd June 1957 (Falkirk)
18 apps/1 goal

As an inexperienced 19-year-old, with only two first games under his belt, Bain was signed on loan from Bristol City by Bill Dodgin in February 1977 and his presence and form were major factors in the magnificent end to the season as the threat of re-election was staved off. The exciting midfield talent oozed quality, and his outstanding displays belied his youthfulness – strenuous efforts were made to make the move permanent at the end of the campaign but no agreement was reached with his parent club. He returned to Ashton Gate, but spent the whole of the following year in the reserves and was eventually released in February 1979 after adding just another three starts to his tally – despite earning Scottish under-21 honours. He moved to the USA to play both outdoor and indoor soccer, becoming one of the all-time great players for Portland Timber. He made a name for himself with a number of other clubs and when his 20-year playing career came to an end, Bain remained in the States to coach at professional, youth club and high school levels.

Bristol City	5+1 appearances	0 goals
Brentford	17+1 appearances	1 goal

Steve Phillips
4th August 1954 (Edmonton)
167 apps/69 goals

A diminutive, 5'4" midfielder, Phillips had enjoyed a relatively uneventful few seasons with Birmingham City – where he had served an apprenticeship and had a loan spell at Torquay United – although he came off the bench to score the winning goal for the England under-19 team in the 1973 European Nations tournament ('Little World Cup') success. Northampton Town signed him for £5,000 in October 1975, he then followed Bill Dodgin to Griffin Park for a £4,000 fee in February 1977 – the move proving to be a masterstroke as the little man showed tremendous ability and skill to start 157 consecutive League games. He netted 36 goals in the 1977-78 promotion campaign, just falling short of the club's all-time record. His move up front formed a lethal strike partnership with Andy McCulloch and he earned the Adidas Golden Boot as the country's top goalscorer. Phillips led the scoring charts for the next two seasons and remained ever-present in the number 11 shirt until new manager, Fred Callaghan, ended the run when he relegated him to the substitute's bench for the final game of the 1979-80 season, then sold him back to Northampton Town in the close season for £40,000. Phillips continued to be a prolific scorer for the Cobblers and Southend United before seeing out his career with spells at Torquay United, Peterborough United, Exeter City (loan) and Chesterfield (loan) – ending his days with over 200 goals to his name.

Birmingham City	15+5 appearances	1 goal
Torquay United	6 appearances	0 goals
Northampton Town	50+1 appearances	9 goals
Brentford	156+1 appearances	65 goals
Northampton Town	75 appearances	29 goals
Southend United	157+1 appearances	66 goals
Torquay United	32 appearances	11 goals
Peterborough United	46+2 appearances	16 goals
Exeter City	5+1 appearances	1 goal
Chesterfield	9 appearances	2 goals

Paul Shrubb
1st August 1955 (Guildford)
198 apps/8 goals

Having made just one start for Fulham, where he had signed as a professional at the age of 17, the busy, little midfielder left to play in South Africa and returned from two years with Hellenic FC to sign for manager Bill Dodgin in February 1977. Shrubb gained an immediate first team place and became a regular, versatile performer for the next five seasons. Slotting into midfield or central defence with equal comfort, and captaining the team on a number of occasions, Shrubb eventually lost his first-team berth under Fred Callaghan following almost 200 games and, after a disappointing campaign in 1982-83, in which he started only four games, he joined Aldershot, where he spent another five years. When his League days were over Shrubb joined Woking as player/coach and also had spells coaching at Dorking, Cove, Hampton and Kingstonian, but returned to the newly-formed Aldershot Town and was instrumental in their rise through the non-League divisions as coach and assistant manager, before taking on a scouting role with Charlton Athletic. In 2007, Aldershot and Charlton staged a benefit match for him after he was diagnosed with motor neurone disease at the age of 51.

Fulham	1 appearance	0 goals
Brentford	170+12 appearances	8 goals
Aldershot	165+9 appearances	5 goals

Pat Kruse
30th November 1953 (Biggleswade)
201 apps/12 goals

Kruse started out as an apprentice with Leicester City, making just two first team appearances after signing professionally at the age of 18 and had had a loan spell with Mansfield Town before joining Torquay United in March 1975. Shortly after entering the record books, when he scored what was deemed to be the quickest own goal in football history, six seconds after kick-off, Kruse was signed by Bill Dodgin in March 1977 days after Gordon Sweetzer had scored a hat-trick against him in a match at Griffin Park. The £20,000 transfer fee was a club record for a defender, but the money proved to be a steal as he became an outstanding centre-back. Short in size for a centre-half, his exceptional qualities made him one of the best defenders in the lower divisions and he dominated at the heart of the back four during the next four seasons. In the summer of 1981 Fred Callaghan surprisingly signed Alan Whitehead to replace Kruse who eventually departed to join Northampton Town in April 1982. His League career ended at the conclusion of the season and he finished his playing days with a brief spell at non-League Barnet.

Leicester City	2 appearances	0 goals
Mansfield Town	6 appearances	1 goal
Torquay United	79 appearances	4 goals
Brentford	186 appearances	12 goals
Northampton Town	18 appearances	0 goals

Terry Glynn
17th December 1958 (Hackney)
1 app/0 goals

Just six months and two games after completing his apprenticeship in August 1977, the gangly, young striker had been freed by Orient and was offered a two-month trial by Bill Dodgin. But he failed to make a League appearance and had just a brief stint as a second half substitute in a first round second leg League Cup tie at Crystal Palace before being released. Glynn moved into non-League football with Ilford, then hit 90 goals in 186 games for Wycombe Wanderers before moving on to Dartford.

Orient	1+1 appearances	0 goals

Len Bond
12th February 1954 (Ilminster)
130 apps/0 goals

The signing of the 23-year-old goalkeeper from Bristol City in August 1977 ended Bill Dodgin's long search for a new custodian and the West Country stopper did not let him down. Although he had made over 30 appearances at Aston Gate, where he had played his first game whilst still an apprentice, Bond had also spent loan periods with Exeter City, Torquay United, Scunthorpe United and Colchester United, as well as spending the summer of 1976 play-

ing for St Louis All-Stars in the USA. After his £8,000 arrival at Griffin Park he had three very successful seasons, in which his bravery and commanding displays helped him become a crowd favourite – but following the arrival of Fred Callaghan as manager Bond was involved in a contractual dispute and was sold to Exeter City for £12,000 in the summer of 1980, where he had four further years in goal. Spells with Weymouth, Bath City, Yeovil Town and Gloucester City completed his playing days – he then embarked on a coaching career taking in three of his former clubs – Exeter, Bristol City and Yeovil – as well as spells at Torquay, in the USA and with the FA Youth Academy.

Bristol City	30 appearances	0 goals
Exeter City	30 appearances	0 goals
Torquay United	3 appearances	0 goals
Scunthorpe United	8 appearances	0 goals
Colchester United	3 appearances	0 goals
Brentford	122 appearances	0 goals
Exeter City	138 appearances	0 goals

Barry Lloyd
19th February 1949 (Uxbridge)
35 apps/4 goals

Almost three years as a professional at Stamford Bridge with Chelsea – with whom he completed an apprenticeship in February 1966 – yielded just a handful of games and he moved the short distance to Fulham in December 1968. Lloyd went on to enjoy a successful eight-year stay at Craven Cottage, in which time he played over 250 games and led the team to promotion as captain. Having been

released in 1976, he spent a disappointing season with Hereford United before being signed by Bill Dodgin on a free transfer in the summer of 1977. Although he initially gained a regular central midfield spot, his style of play alienated him with supporters and he became the target of much, largely unwarranted, abuse from the terraces and lost his place soon after the turn of the year. He was released at the end of the promotion-winning campaign and moved to the USA with Houston Hurricanes, returning to take up the role of assistant manager at non-League Yeovil Town. He later managed Yeovil, Worthing and Brighton, where he achieved promotion and a play-off place and ,14 years after resigning, he returned to the club as chief scout.

Chelsea	8+2 appearances	0 goals
Fulham	249+8 appearances	29 goals
Hereford United	12+2 appearances	0 goals
Brentford	26+5 appearances	4 goals

Willie Graham
14th February 1959 (Armagh)
51 apps/3 goals

An apprenticeship and professional contract at Northampton Town yielded no first team appearances for the young, Irish midfielder and, as he was about to embark on a non-League career, Graham was offered a trial by Bill Dodgin in August 1977. A permanent contract quickly materialised and he proved a revelation with a series of outstanding displays in central midfield, alongside his namesake, Jackie. After the start of the following season he seemed to lose his spark, along with his place, and despite signing a long-term

deal, he never re-asserted himself again, making only 14 starts in the following three campaigns. Having been transfer-listed, Willie was eventually freed by Fred Callaghan at the end of 1980/81 and he subsequently left the professional game for the lower echelons of non-League with Bracknell Town, Camberley Town and Sandhurst Town.

Brentford	42+6 appearances	3 goals

Tommy Baldwin
10th June 1945 (Gateshead)
5 apps/1 goal

Gateshead-born Baldwin turned professional at Arsenal in December 1962, but had to wait more than two years for his first team debut. In September 1966 he was transferred to Chelsea in a player-exchange deal involving George Graham. Baldwin became a prolific striker at Stamford Bridge, playing in two FA Cup Finals as well as the 1971 European Cup Winners Cup Final, but after suffering a succession of injuries, and fall-outs with manager Dave Sexton, he was loaned out – firstly to Millwall in November 1974, then to Manchester United two months later. He drifted into non-League football with Gravesend and Northfleet, as well as having a spell in the USA with Seattle Sounders. In October 1977, at the age of 32, Baldwin was signed by Bill Dodgin on a non-contract basis, and although he managed just four first team appearances, his experience was used to assist off-the-pitch, and in the summer of 1978, he was appointed as coach – a position he held until April 1980, when he was sacked along with Dodgin.

Arsenal	17 appearances	7 goals
Chelsea	182+5 appearances	74 goals
Millwall	6 appearances	1 goal
Manchester United	2 appearances	0 goals
Brentford	4 appearances	1 goal

Doug Allder
30th December 1951 (Hammersmith)
95 apps/3 goals

After more than 200 games for Millwall, a club he debuted for as a 17-year-old in 1969, and where he was later inducted into the club's Hall of Fame, the elegant, pacy left-winger joined Orient in a player-exchange deal in the summer of 1975. But two disappointing seasons followed and he started the following campaign with unsuccessful trial periods at both Torquay United and Watford. In October 1977 Allder was offered a further trial by Bill Dodgin and his displays prompted the offer of a full contract – he went on to play an instrumental role in the promotion campaign, providing many of the 58 goals scored by the McCulloch/Phillips striking partnership. Although he spent a further two seasons at Brentford, Allder didn't really re-capture the same form and he was finally released at the end of the 1979-80 campaign – moving into non-League football with Tooting and Mitcham, Staines Town and Walton and Hersham.

Millwall	191+11 appearances	10 goals
Orient	34+7 appearances	0 goals
Watford	1 appearance	0 goals
Brentford	68+20 appearances	2 goals

Barry Tucker
28th August 1952 (Swansea)
181 apps/5 goals

A Welshman by birth, Tucker started his career at Northampton Town and, having progressed through an apprenticeship, he went on to play more than 200 games before he followed Bill Dodgin from the County Ground – signing for £10,000 in February 1978. A stocky, reliable full-back, capable of playing on either side of the defence, he steadied the ship and his arrival was viewed by many as being the catalyst for the final promotion push. Apart from the first half of the 1980-81 season, when he was involved in a contractual dispute, Tucker was virtually ever-present for the next four years until he eventually lost his place at the start of the 1982/83 campaign, returning to Northampton Town to see out the remainder of his career.

Northampton Town	209+5 appearances	3 goals
Brentford	168+1 appearances	5 goals
Northampton Town	62+1 appearances	5 goals

John Murray
2nd March 1948 (Newcastle)
5 apps/1 goal

The Geordie striker had an impressive scoring record after starting out at Burnley in March 1965. Five years later he moved to Blackpool, followed by a spell at Bury. He was transferred to Reading in the summer of 1974 and enjoyed a prolific four-year spell at Elm Park, until being signed by Bill Dodgin for a £3,000 fee in February 1978, primarily to provide striking cover for the run-in, Murray was seen as a 'lucky charm' with three of his previous clubs securing promotion. He played his part in the 1977-78 successful campaign, although managing just five appearances, all away from home. He was released a few months after the start of the following season without having added to his tally and was later player/manager at both Newbury Town and Wallington, before becoming youth team coach at Northampton Town.

Burnley	20+2 appearances	6 goals
Blackpool	5+3 appearances	1 goal
Bury	117+9 appearances	37 goals
Reading	123+8 appearances	44 goals
Brentford	2+3 appearances	1 goal

Steve Wilkins
31st August 1959 (Hillingdon)
1 app/0 goals

Despite being the brother of Chelsea's Ray and Graham this little-known midfielder had also spent some time at Stamford Bridge before being given a pre-season trial by Bill Dodgin in 1978. Wilkins played a full role in the warm-up programme, but his only first-team involvement was as a substitute against Watford in a first round second leg League Cup tie. Following the unsuccessful trial, he made no further progress in the professional game, although he moved to Dagenham and had a non-contract spell at Peterborough United as well as drifting around the non-League scene and playing football in New Zealand.

Trevor Porter
16th October 1956 (Guildford)
17 apps/0 goals

Porter first became known to Bill Dodgin when he was an apprentice goalkeeper at Fulham, he'd signed professionally at Craven Cottage in May 1974 but his career progressed no further. Prior to the start of the 1978-79 season, with regular keeper Len Bond injured, Dodgin paid Slough Town £750 for Porter's services and he held the number one position for the opening two months of the campaign. He remained as back-up for two seasons, combining playing with his window cleaning job – a dual role he continued when he later moved into coaching.

Brentford	15 appearances	0 goals

Billy Eames
20th September 1957 (Malta)
2 apps/1 goal

Eames had signed as an apprentice with his local club Portsmouth on leaving school at the age of 17 in the summer of 1974, making his first-team debut a year later under the guidance of manager Ian St John. He scored within three minutes on his debut, but the young striker added just one game to his tally during the following campaign, before being released to join Waterlooville for a brief period. He was then offered a trial by Bill Dodgin at the start of the 1978-79 season. Despite impressing in two first team run outs and scoring a goal, he was not offered a contract and left Brentford in October, deciding not to pursue his football career any further and he moved into teaching

Portsmouth	9+3 appearances	1 goal
Brentford	2 appearances	1 goal

Lee Frost
4th December 1957 (Woking)
21 apps/3 goals

A promising young forward who had become a professional at Chelsea in the summer of 1976, Frost had broken into the Blues' first-team before he was signed by Bill Dodgin for a succesful one month loan spell in October 1978. On his return to Stamford Bridge he hit a rich vein of form with five goals in eight starts, but in December 1980 he switched back again to Griffin Park on a short-term contract until the end of the season, as part of a deal that saw Fred Callaghan sign Gary Johnson. There were no signs of the speedy, direct play that had marked his earlier stint, and a string of disappointing displays made Frost the target of terrace criticism before he left the club, and the game, at the end of his contract in May 1981.

Chelsea	11+3 appearances	5 goals
Brentford	5+1 appearances	0 goals
Brentford	15 appearances	3 goals

Bob Booker
25th January 1958 (Watford)
320 apps/48 goals

One of the cult names associated with Brentford Football Club, Booker was first spotted playing as a striker in the Hertford-shire County League and, having been offered a trial by Bill Dodgin, he signed a contract in October 1978. A slow start to his career was blown away when he returned from a loan spell at non-League Barnet and hit a hat-trick in his first match back and become a versatile performer, wearing every shirt bar the goalkeeper's and winning over supporters after a difficult few seasons to become their player of the year. His 'never-say-die' approach endeared him to fans and managers alike, but with almost 300 games to his name he suffered a career-threatening knee injury in August 1986, which sidelined him for a whole year. After failing to re-establish himself as a first-team regular Booker made a surprise move when he joined Sheffield United on a free transfer in November 1988. Remarkably, he attained legendary status at Bramall Lane as they rose to the top flight, captaining the side along the way and becoming one of their most popular players. In November 1991, and approaching 34 years of age, Booker made a return to Griffin Park when Phil Holder signed him, and although he played a role in the champion-ship-winning squad, he failed to recapture previous heights and eventually retired through injury in the summer of 1993. A short spell at Harrow Borough preceded a third return, as youth team

manager under David Webb, before leaving in October 2000 to become assistant manager at Brighton – a club he continued to serve on and off in a variety of roles throughout a ten-year period.

Brentford	207+44 appearances	41 goals
Sheffield United	91+18 appearances	13 goals
Brentford	15+4 appearances	2 goals

Jim McNichol
9th June 1958 (Glasgow)
176 apps/23 goals

A Scottish under-21 international who earned seven caps during his stay at Grif-fin Park, McNichol had started his career as an apprentice at Ipswich Town before joining Luton Town in the summer of 1976 at the age of 18. He made 15 appear-ances for the Hatters before being signed by Bill Dodgin for a then club record fee of £33,000 in October 1978. His hugely influential presence helped transform the team's fortunes and, during the next five seasons, he became a very popular centre-back, gaining notoriety for his powerful long-range shots from free-kicks, which brought him a number of goals. A series of disagreements with the man-agement preceded his eventual release by Frank McLintock in the summer of 1984, and he moved on to conclude his career in the West Country with spells at Exeter City (twice) and Torquay United (twice) where he became known for a well-documented incident in which he was bitten by a police dog and, in the subsequent injury time at the end of the game, Torquay scored the goal to retain their Football League status. His footballing days came to an end with a stint as player/coach at Western League Torrington.

Luton Town	13+2 appearances	0 goals
Brentford	151+4 appearances	22 goals
Exeter City	87 appearances	10 goals
Torquay United	124 appearances	13 goals
Exeter City	42 appearances	8 goals
Torquay United	2 appearances	0 goals

Dean Smith
28th November 1958 (Leicester)
61 apps/17 goals

Smith had initially caught the eye as a young Leicester City striker, signing professionally in December 1976 and making the first-team before his 18th birthday but, before the end of the 1977-78 season, he jetted across the Atlantic for a loan spell with Houston Hurricanes. On his return to the reserves at Filbert Street he was spotted by Bill Dodgin and signed for a £25,000 fee in October 1978. A talented, skilful, ball-playing striker, he seemed destined for a bright future, but early expectations failed to materialise and Smith made only a minimal impact in the next few years before falling out of favour with manager Fred Callaghan. A club suspension for a breach of discipline led to his release in February 1981, which signalled the end of his professional career. After a year's absence from the game he went on to do the rounds in lower non-League circles with spells at Nuneaton Borough, Enderby, Corby Town, Shepshed Charterhouse, St Andrews and Oadby Town. After battling throat cancer and a stroke, Dean died in April 2009 at the age of 50.

| Leicester City | 8+2 appearances | 1 goal |
| Brentford | 48+6 appearances | 15 goals |

David Silman
28th October 1959 (Hampstead)
1 app/0 goals

A giant centre-back, Silman had made little impression during his time at Wolverhampton Wanderers and, having been released at the age of 18, was signed on trial by Bill Dodgin in February 1978, then offered a one-year contract at the end of the season. He made just one solitary appearance during the following campaign and was given a free transfer in May 1979, Brentford proving to be his only foray into the professional game. He subsequently played for Walthamstow, Harrow Borough, Hayes, Hounslow Town and Staines Town.

| Brentford | 1 appearance | 0 goals |

Lee Holmes
28th September 1955 (Aveley)
30 apps/7 goals

Holmes, initially a West Ham United apprentice, had drifted into non-League football and was spotted playing as a striker for Haringey Borough and, after playing a few reserve team games during the 1978-79 season, he was awarded a one-year contract by Bill Dodgin in the summer of 1979, albeit on a part-time basis as he wished to continue his academic studies. A tall, front man, not afraid to make his presence felt,

Holmes enjoyed a reasonable campaign, but incoming manager, Fred Callaghan, insisted that any new deal should be on a full-time basis and the player rejected the offer. He returned to non-League football and his civil engineering studies after being sold to Enfield for £5,000 in June 1980. He had further spells with Dartford, Wealdstone, Dagenham and Leyton Wingate, before his playing career ended. In September 1979 he made the national press when his marriage ceremony took place in East London 45 minutes after a home game – a pillion passenger dash across London on a motorbike ensued, followed by a car park change into his wedding suit, but he got to his wedding ceremony as planned.

Brentford	26+2 appearances	6 goals

Billy Holmes
4th February 1951 (Balham)
15 apps/2 goals

His early career was uneventful and, after joining Millwall from Woking in the summer of 1970, he played just one League game as a substitute in three seasons before moving to Luton Town, where he also managed a solitary substitute appearance. He then dropped back out of the league to join Barnet. In the summer of 1975 Holmes moved to Wimbledon for a £2,000 fee and made a big impact with 20 goals as the Dons achieved League football status. Three months into the 1977-78 campaign he moved on again, to Hereford United, from where Bill Dodgin signed him for £10,000 in August 1979 and, although Holmes scored on his debut after coming on as a substitute, he didn't look entirely comfortable at the higher level and played only a handful of games in either a midfield or striking role. He was freed at the end of the season, disappearing from the game completely after making only 44 League starts in ten years. In 1988 it was announced that he had died at the age of 36.

Millwall	0+1 appearance	0 goals
Luton Town	0+1 appearance	0 goals
Wimbledon	15 appearances	5 goals
Hereford United	21+10 appearances	5 goals
Brentford	8+7 appearances	2 goals

Keith Fear
8th May 1952 (Bristol)
8 apps/2 goals

A successful youth player who progressed through the ranks with Bristol City and captained the youth team, Fear made more than 150 appearances at Ashton Gate and was twice leading goalscorer. But he played only a handful of games as the club hit the heights of Division One and had loan spells at both Hereford United and Blackburn Rovers before signing for Plymouth Argyle for £20,000 in February 1978. Bill Dodgin originally attempted to sign the diminutive midfielder on trial a year before he finally secured his target after Fear had been released by the Pilgrims. Clearly an intelligent and skilful front man, with an eye for goal and an ability to create chances for others, his trial was successful enough for him to be offered a contract, but personal terms could not be agreed and he moved on to Chester City to see out his League days. Further spells followed at Bangor City and Scarborough, before he returned to his native West County and managed Mangotsfield Town.

Bristol City	126+25 appearances	32 goals
Hereford United	6 appearances	0 goals
Blackburn Rovers	5 appearances	2 goals
Plymouth Argyle	40+5 appearances	9 goals
Brentford	7+1 appearances	2 goals
Chester City	41+3 appearances	3 goals

Iori Jenkins
11th December 1959 (Neath)
17 apps/1 goal

A promising youngster who attained Welsh international honours at schoolboy level, Jenkins completed an apprenticeship with Chelsea before signing professional terms in the summer of 1978. He was released a year later without making a first-team appearance, then signed by Bill Dodgin in November 1979, and although he played only two games, they provided enough evidence to show that he was a good ball-playing centre-back with skill to match. Jenkins made his first-team breakthrough the following season under Fred Callaghan's management but, before the campaign ended, he asked to be released from his contract to enable him to take up a new career with the Metropolitan Police. He left Brentford in February 1981.

| Brentford | 12+3 appearances | 1 goal |

Steve Harding
23rd July 1956 (Bristol)
4 apps/1 goal

Big, uncompromising and rugged, the tall centre-back had come up through the ranks at Bristol City and spent three years as a professional having completed his apprenticeship in the summer of 1974. Harding failed to establish himself in the first-team at Ashton Gate and he had brief loan spells with both Southend United and Grimsby Town. In the summer of 1977 he switched allegiances and joined Bristol Rovers from where Bill Dodgin signed him on a month's loan in January 1980 to cover for suspensions and injuries. But with the team in the midst of a losing run he failed to impress sufficiently and the end of the loan signalled the end of his playing days.

Bristol City	2 appearances	0 goals
Southend United	2 appearances	0 goals
Grimsby Town	8 appearances	0 goals
Bristol Rovers	37+1 appearances	1 goal
Brentford	3+1 appearances	0 goals

Noel Parkinson
16th November 1959 (Hull)
10 apps/0 goals

The classy, highly-rated midfielder arrived from Ipswich Town in February 1980, signed on loan for one month by Bill Dodgin with a view to a permanent transfer. A reported £75,000 fee was agreed to secure his services, although the 20-year-old had never made a League appearance at Portman Road, despite playing in two European Cup ties. He had signed as a professional in December 1976, before having loan spells at Peterborough United and Bristol Rovers. A change of management midway into his Brentford

loan saw the temporary move extended until the end of the season, after which Fred Callaghan decided not to pursue matters and Ipswich eventually sold him to Mansfield Town for £35,000. During the next six seasons he also had spells with Scunthorpe United and Colchester United, but Parkinson's career never hit the heights expected of him and his playing days ended when he was just 26 after he suffered a serious pelvic injury and he became a successful businessman.

Bristol Rovers	5 appearances	1 goal
Brentford	9+1 appearances	0 goals
Mansfield Town	66+4 appearances	13 goals
Scunthorpe United	39+2 appearances	7 goals
Colchester United	79 appearances	13 goals

Tony Funnell
20th August 1957 (Eastbourne)
35 apps/10 goals

The tiny striker started his career at Newhaven Town and Eastbourne before joining Southampton for £250 in January 1977. He appeared in the Saints' first-team as a 19-year-old, before going for a spell on loan in Vancouver. On his return Funnell hit the headlines with eight goals in 12 games to secure the Saints' return to the top flight but, in March 1979, he moved to Gillingham for £50,000 despite being a target for Bill Dodgin. A year later the manager got his man when a March 1980 transfer set a new club record of £56,000, however, Fred Callaghan took over the Brentford hot seat just weeks later and, despite six goals in the opening eight games of the new season, the busy little front-man found himself out of favour. He remained popular with supporters though, but in

September 1981 he was sold to Bournemouth for just £5,000. Funnell re-gained his scoring touch at Dean Court, ending the campaign with 18 goals, but a serious back injury finished his professional career early and he dropped into non-League football with Poole Town, where a tremendous run saw him virtually ever-present for the next six seasons, hitting 127 goals in 308 games and being rewarded with a testimonial against Southampton.

Southampton	13+4 appearances	8 goals
Gillingham	27+6 appearances	10 goals
Brentford	29+3 appearances	8 goals
Bournemouth	59+5 appearances	22 goals

Alan Gane
11th June 1950 (Chiswick)
0 apps/0 goals

During the 1970s, only one player was named as substitute for a first-team match without ever making an appearance. For the 1-0 home defeat by Scunthorpe United on 10th April 1971 (Easter Saturday), midfielder Alan Gane was named as substitute but remained on the bench for the duration of the match. Alan spent three years as an amateur with Brentford, playing in a number of London Challenge Cup matches as well as turning out for Sutton United, Slough Town and Wycombe Wanderers, before being offered a trial at the start of the 1973-74 campaign and appearing in the friendly warm-up matches. He rejected the offer of a further trial period and made his only foray into League football when he joined Hereford United, making nine appearances while at Edgar Street, scoring one goal.

OTHER FIXTURES

FRIENDLIES, TESTIMONIALS AND NON-COMPETITIVE MATCHES

GRIFFIN PARK
BRENTFORD

PETER GELSON
TESTIMONIAL MATCH

BRENTFORD
v
WEST HAM UNITED

1970-71 PRE-SEASON FRIENDLIES AND OTHER NON-COMPETITIVE MATCHES

Friendly: **Sat 1 August**
Plymouth Argyle (A)   **Lost 0-2**

Chic Brodie, Alan Hawley, Dick Renwick, Bobby Ross, Peter Gelson, Alan Nelmes, Gordon Neilson, John Docherty, Roger Cross, Jackie Graham, Allan Mansley Sub: Brian Turner

Friendly: **Mon 3 August**
Yeovil Town (A)   **Drew 2-2**
Scorers: Docherty, Hawley

Gordon Phillips, Alan Hawley, Dick Renwick, Alan Nelmes, Peter Gelson, Brian Turner, Brian Tawse, John Docherty, Roger Cross, Jackie Graham, Allan Mansley Sub: Bobby Ross

Friendly: **Sat 8 August**
Hillingdon Borough (A)   **Drew 1-1**
Scorer: Cross

Gordon Phillips, Alan Hawley, Dick Renwick, Bobby Ross, Peter Gelson, Alan Nelmes, Brian Tawse, John Docherty, Roger Cross, Jackie Graham, Allan Mansley Subs: Gordon Neilson, Michael Maskell

Friendly: **Mon 10 August**
Bristol Rovers (H)   **Drew 1-1**
Scorer: Docherty   **Attendance: 3,900**

Chic Brodie, Alan Hawley, Michael Maskell, Bobby Ross, Peter Gelson, Alan Nelmes, Gordon Neilson, John Docherty, Roger Cross, Jackie Graham, Allan Mansley Sub: Brian Tawse

London Challenge Cup: **Wed 30 September**
Barnet (H)   **Lost 1-2**
Scorer: Gelson

Gordon Phillips, Danny Pipe, Barry Futerill, Paul Bence, Peter Gelson, Alan Nelmes, Brian Tawse, Gordon Neilson, Bobby Ross, John Docherty, Allan Mansley Sub: Brian Turner

Peter Gelson Testimonial: **Wed 11 November**
West Ham United (H)   **Lost 0-3**
Attendance: 5,950

Gordon Phillips, Paul Bence, Dick Renwick, Brian Turner, Peter Gelson, Alan Nelmes, John Docherty, Bobby Ross, Alex Dawson, Roger Cross, Jackie Graham Subs: Allan Mansley, Gordon Neilson, Brian Tawse

An attendance of 5,950 saw former player Ron Greenwood bring his First Division team to Griffin Park and despite being unable to field star performers Bobby Moore and Jimmy Greaves through injury, the visitors proved strong opposition and scored three late goals to record a comprehensive victory. The gate receipts of £1,670 incorporated matchday expenses of £100 which were borne by the club to provide Peter Gelson with a final total benefit fund exceeding £2,000.

Benefit Match (Moore)   **Wednesday 21 April**
Guildford City (A)   **Won 1-0**
Scorer: Graham

Team not known

1971-72 PRE-SEASON FRIENDLIES AND OTHER NON-COMPETITIVE MATCHES

Friendly: **Sat 31 July**
Southampton (H)   **Lost 1-3**
Scorer: OG

Gordon Phillips, Paul Bence, Alan Nelmes, Peter Gelson, Terry Scales, Brian Turner, Bobby Ross, Jackie Graham, John O'Mara, Roger Cross, John Docherty Subs: Gordon Neilson, Dave Collyer

Friendly: **Wed 4 August**
Hillingdon Borough (A)   **Won 2-1**
Scorers: O'Mara, Scales

Gordon Phillips, Paul Bence, Nigel Saywood, Alan Nelmes, Clinch, McKay, Bobby Ross, Jackie Graham, John O'Mara, Roger Cross, Gordon Neilson Subs: Terry Scales, Dave Collyer

Friendly: **Sat 7 August**
Oxford United (H)   **Lost 2-4**
Scorers: O'Mara, Cross

Gordon Phillips, Paul Bence, Alan Nelmes, Peter Gelson, Terry Scales, Bobby Ross, Steve Tom, Jackie Graham, John Docherty, Roger Cross, John O'Mara Subs: Gordon Neilson, Nigel Saywood

London Challenge Cup: **Mon 20 September**
Millwall (H)   **Drew 0-0**

Paul Priddy, Gordon Neilson, Cole, Steve Tom, Olrog, Gavin Fraser, Mickey Heath, Brian Carnaby, Chatterton, Henderson, Paul Devis

London Challenge Cup: **Mon 11 October**
Millwall (A)   **Lost 0-3**
Attendance: 278

Paul Priddy, Gordon Neilson, Steve Tom, Cole, Danny Pipe, Baker, Mickey Heath, Alan Gane, Tottman, Ward, Woozley Sub: Phil Jarratt

Friendly (Tour Match):   **Tue 2 May**
Guernsey XI (A)   **Won 6-0**
Scorers: O'Mara (4), Houston, Bence

Gordon Phillips, Alan Hawley, Peter Gelson, Alan Nelmes, Terry Scales, Bobby Ross, Paul Bence, Jackie Graham, John O'Mara, Stewart Houston, John Docherty Sub: Brian Turner

Friendly (Tour Match):   **Thu 4 May**
Guernsey XI (A)   **Won 7-1**
Scorers: O'Mara (2), Houston (2), Ross, Graham, Docherty

Gordon Phillips, Alan Hawley, Steve Tom, Alan Nelmes, Terry Scales, Bobby Ross, Paul Bence, Jackie Graham, John O'Mara, Stewart Houston, John Docherty

Benefit Match (Collins and Guy)   **Tue 9 May**
Wimbledon (A)   **Drew 2-2**
Scorers: Docherty, Graham

Paul Priddy, Alan Hawley, Alan Nelmes, Steve Tom, Terry Scales, Brian Turner, Paul Bence, Jackie Graham, John O'Mara, John Docherty, Gordon Neilson

1972-73 PRE-SEASON FRIENDLIES AND OTHER NON-COMPETITIVE MATCHES

Friendly: **Sat 29 July**
Portsmouth (H)   **Lost 0-1**

Paul Priddy, Alan Hawley, Alan Nelmes, Peter Gelson, Terry Scales, Paul Bence, Mike Allen, Jackie Graham, John O'Mara, Stewart Houston, David Jenkins Sub: Alan Murray

Friendly: **Tue 1 August**
Hillingdon Borough (A)   **Won 2-1**
Scorers: Allen, Murray (pen)

Paul Priddy, Alan Hawley, Alan Nelmes, Peter Gelson, Terry Scales, Alan Murray, Mike Allen, Jackie Graham, John O'Mara, Stewart Houston, David Jenkins Subs: Paul Bence, Bobby Ross

Friendly: **Sat 5 August**
Aldershot (A)   **Drew 1-1**
Scorer: Allen   **Attendance: 2,730**

Paul Priddy, Alan Hawley, Alan Nelmes, Peter Gelson, Terry Scales, David Court, Mike Allen, Jackie Graham, John O'Mara, Stewart Houston, Bobby Ross Subs: Paul Bence, Alan Murray

Friendly: **Tue 8 August**
Ashford (A)   **Lost 1-4**
Scorer: Murray (pen)

Gordon Phillips, Paul Bence, Alan Nelmes, Peter Gelson, Terry Scales, Alan Murray, David Court, David Jenkins, David Proctor, John O'Mara, John Docherty

[Right] Peter Gelson jumps with a Portsmouth forward during the friendly match at Griffin Park in July 1972

London Challenge Cup: **Mon 18 September**
Tottenham Hotspur (A)   **Lost 1-2**
Scorer: Bence

Gordon Phillips, Alan Gane, Paul Bence, Kevin Harding, Gary Huxley, Mickey Heath, David Court, Woozley, John Docherty, David Proctor, Andy Woon

Friendly: **Wed 18 October**
Hampton (A)   **Lost 2-3**
Scorers: Murray, Proctor

Gordon Phillips, Alan Hawley, Alan Nelmes, Peter Gelson, Terry Scales, David Court, Mike Allen, Alan Murray, David Jenkins, David Proctor, John Docherty Subs: Paul Bence, Andy Woon

Friendly: **Sat 9 December**
Exeter City (A)   **Lost 0-1**

Gordon Phillips, Paul Bence, Alan Nelmes, Stewart Houston, Terry Scales, Alan Murray, David Court, Jackie Graham, David Jenkins, Stan Webb, Andy Woon Sub: Roy Cotton

Denis Piggott Testimonial: **Fri 4 May**
Everton (H)   **Won 3-0**
Scorers: Salvage, Woon, Bence Attendance: 3,035

Paul Priddy, Alan Hawley, Peter Gelson, Alan Nelmes, Terry Scales, Alan Murray, Paul Bence, Stewart Houston, Andy Woon, Roger Cross, Barry Salvage Sub: Stan Webb

Despite the disappointment of relegation, a crowd of 3,035 paid £1,124 to reward General Manager Piggott for more than 25 years service, while Harry Catterick's last match as manager of the First Division giants, saw him field eight first-team regulars. In the 19th minute Barry Salvage surged in from the left wing to fire in a low drive, before Andy Woon doubled the lead, slamming home a cross from Alan Murray. Paul Bence headed the third from a left-wing centre by Roger Cross early in the second half.

[Above] Long serving general manager, Denis Piggott, poses with the poster advertising his testimonial match

[Right] Peter Gelson takes on an Everton defender, while Alan Nelmes offers some support

1973-74 PRE-SEASON FRIENDLIES AND OTHER NON-COMPETITIVE MATCHES

Friendly: **Sat 11 August**
Hereford United (H)   **Drew 2-2**
Scorers: Webb, Graham   **Attendance: 3,330**

Paul Priddy, Alan Hawley, Terry Scales, Paul Bence, Peter Gelson, Stewart Houston, Mike Allen, Jackie Graham, Stan Webb, Roger Cross, Barry Salvage Sub: Alan Gane

Friendly: **Sat 18 August**
Aldershot (A)   **Lost 0-1**
Attendance: 2,363

Paul Priddy, Alan Nelmes, Terry Scales, Paul Bence, Peter Gelson, Stewart Houston, Mike Allen, Jackie Graham, Stan Webb, Roger Cross, Barry Salvage Subs: Alan Gane, Alan Hawley, John Docherty, Andy Woon

Friendly: **Mon 20 August**
Luton Town (H)   **Drew 1-1**
Scorer: Cross   **Attendance: 2,320**

Paul Priddy, Alan Hawley, Terry Scales, Paul Bence, Peter Gelson, Stewart Houston, Mike Allen, John Docherty, Stan Webb, Roger Cross, Barry Salvage Subs: Jackie Graham, Alan Nelmes, Andy Woon

London Challenge Cup: **Mon 8 October**
Enfield (A)   **Won 2-0**
Scorers: Allen, Palfrey

Garry Towse, Alan Nelmes, Terry Scales, Paul Bence, Kevin Harding, Gary Smith, Stan Webb, Terry Palfrey, John Docherty, Jackie Graham, Mike Allen Sub: Richard Poole

Gordon Phillips Testimonial

THREE MUSKETEERS (by courtesy Brentford & Chiswick Times)

BRENTFORD
versus
EX-BRENTFORD

GRIFFIN PARK, BRAEMAR RD., BRENTFORD

Monday, 29th October, 1973
Kick-off 7.30 p.m.

Official Programme Price 7p

London Challenge Cup:　　　　**Mon 15 October**
Queens Park Rangers (H)　　　　**Drew 0-0**

Garry Towse, Kevin Harding, Terry Scales, Gary Smith, Alan Nelmes, Roy Cotton, Les Wicks, Richard Poole, Stan Webb, Jackie Graham, Mike Allen Sub: Stephen Murphy

London Challenge Cup:　　　　**Wed 31 October**
Queens Park Rangers (A)　　　　**Lost 1-2**
Scorer: Riddick

Paul Priddy, Alan Hawley, Terry Scales, Gary Smith, Peter Gelson, Gordon Riddick, Paul Bence, Roger Cross, Andy Woon, Dave Metchick, Barry Salvage Sub: Alan Nelmes

Gordon Phillips Testimonial:　　　**Mon 29 October**
Ex-Bees XI (H)　　　　　　　　**Lost 3-4**
Scorers: Woon, Salvage, Metchick　　**Attendance: 1,461**

Paul Priddy, Alan Hawley, Terry Scales, Paul Bence, Peter Gelson, Alan Nelmes, Jackie Graham, Mike Allen, Andy Woon, Dave Metchick, Barry Salvage Sub: Roger Cross

In front of a small crowd numbering just 1,461, Andy Woon converted an eighth minute centre from Barry Salvage, before John O'Mara raced onto a through-ball from Richard Poole to equalise for the Ex's eleven minutes later. On the half-hour mark Barry Salvage curled the ball beyond Gordon Phillips to regain the lead, but John O'Mara headed home a David Jenkins corner within 60 seconds and, three minutes later, Steve Tom powered in a header from a Stan Webb cross. The Ex-Bees took a 4-2 lead in the 70th minute when Cliff Myers' 25-yard effort went in off a post and the scoring was completed in the 85th minute by Dave Metchick with a diving header from a Paul Bence centre. Gate receipts of £595 contributed towards a final pay-out of £825. Ex-Bees: Phillips, Harding, Renwick, Higginson, Tom, Richardson, Webb, Poole, O'Mara, Myers, Jenkins

Alan Hawley Testimonial:　　　**Mon 6 May**
Orient (H)　　　　　　　　　**Drew 2-2**
Scorers: O'Mara, Docherty　　　**Attendance: 2,550**

Paul Priddy, Alan Hawley, Terry Scales, Kevin Harding, Peter Gelson, Gordon Riddick, John Docherty, Dave Simmons, John O'Mara, Dave Metchick, Barry Salvage Subs: Richard Poole, Gary Smith, Terry Palfrey, Parry

On a cold, wintery spring evening, the game came to life two minutes after the break when the visitors took the lead. They added a second shortly afterwards but the 'guesting' John O'Mara leapt high to head a trademark goal from a Dave Metchick free-kick before being helped from the pitch with a damaged collarbone. In the dying seconds of the match, a through-ball from Dave Metchick enabled the on-rushing John Docherty to head an equaliser and complete his playing career with a goal. The 2,550 attendance boosted Alan Hawley's final windfall to £1,732.

1974-75 PRE-SEASON FRIENDLIES AND OTHER NON-COMPETITIVE MATCHES

Friendly: Sat 3 August
Portsmouth (H) Lost 0-4
Attendance: 1,790

Paul Priddy, Paul Bence, Mike Allen, Gordon Riddick, Keith Lawrence, Alan Nelmes, Jackie Graham, Roger Cross, Dave Simmons, Dave Metchick, Barry Salvage Subs: Peter Gelson, Terry Scales, Andy Woon, Richard Poole, Graham Smith, Gary Smith

Friendly: Tue 6 August
Aldershot (H) Lost 1-3
Scorer: Simmons Attendance: 1,440

Steve Sherwood, Paul Bence, Mike Allen, Gordon Riddick, Keith Lawrence, Alan Nelmes, Jackie Graham, Roger Cross, Dave Simmons, Dave Metchick, Barry Salvage Sub: Graham Smith

Friendly: Fri 9 August
Millwall (H) Won 2-0
Scorers: Woon, OG Attendance: 1,190

Steve Sherwood, Paul Bence, Mike Allen, Terry Scales, Keith Lawrence, Gordon Riddick, Jackie Graham, Roger Cross, Andy Woon, Dave Metchick, Barry Salvage

Friendly: Mon 12 August
Stevenage (A) Won 3-0
Scorers: Woon (2), Cross

Steve Sherwood, Paul Bence, Mike Allen, Terry Scales, Keith Lawrence, Gordon Riddick, Jackie Graham, Roger Cross, Andy Woon, Kevin Harding, Barry Salvage

Friendly: Sun 16 March
Guernsey XI (A) Won 1-0
Scorer: Lawrence

Steve Sherwood, Paul Bence, Alan Nelmes, Terry Johnson, Keith Lawrence, Gordon Riddick, Jackie Graham, Mickey French, Roger Cross, Terry Scales, Barry Salvage Sub: John Docherty

Peter Gelson Testimonial
Mon 28 April
Millwall (H)
Drew 0-0
Attendance: 2,262

Steve Sherwood, Alan Nelmes, Dave Metchick, Paul Bence, Peter Gelson, Nigel Smith, Jackie Graham, Terry Scales, Roger Cross, Dave Simmons, Terry Johnson Subs: Richard Poole, John Docherty

A second benefit match was arranged for Peter Gelson who, by that stage, was playing for Hillingdon-Borough and produced another £2,000 plus cheque as a reward for 15 years service. Despite the goal-less scoreline, the crowd of 2,262 witnessed an entertaining affair on a fine spring evening – Terry Johnson coming closest to breaking the deadlock on more than one occasion against the newly-relegated visitors.

[Right] Peter Gelson with the team before his first Brentford testimonial in November 1970

1975-76 PRE-SEASON FRIENDLIES AND OTHER NON-COMPETITIVE MATCHES

Friendly: **Sat 2 August**
Oxford United (H)   **Lost 1-5**
Scorer: Lawrence   **Attendance: 1,420**
Bill Glazier, Alan Nelmes, Mike Allen, Paul Bence, Keith Lawrence, Gordon Riddick, Jackie Graham, Terry Scales, Roger Cross, Mickey French, Terry Johnson Subs: Dave Simmons, Gordon Sweetzer, Nigel Smith, Ken Foggo

Friendly: **Mon 4 August**
Walton (A)   **Drew 0-0**
Bill Glazier, Alan Nelmes, Mike Allen, Ken Foggo, Keith Lawrence, Nigel Smith, Jackie Graham, Terry Scales, Dave Simmons, Mickey French, Gordon Sweetzer Subs: Gordon Riddick, Richard Poole

Friendly: **Wed 6 August**
Portsmouth (H)   **Lost 0-1**
Attendance: 955
Bill Glazier, Alan Nelmes, Mike Allen, Ken Foggo, Keith Lawrence, Nigel Smith, Jackie Graham, Terry Scales, Dave Simmons, Roger Cross, Terry Johnson Subs: Mickey French, Gordon Sweetzer

Friendly: **Thu 7 August**
Hayes (A)   **Won 2-1**
Scorers: Graham, Bartlett
Bill Glazier, Alan Nelmes, Mike Allen, Ken Foggo, Keith Lawrence, Nigel Smith, Jackie Graham, Terry Scales, Mickey French, Roger Cross, Gordon Bartlett Subs: Graham Cox, Mickey Tripp, Paul Bence, Paul Kerr, John Fielding, Richard Poole

Friendly: **Sat 9 August**
Aldershot (H)   **Drew 1-1**
Scorer: Cross   **Attendance: 1,490**
Bill Glazier, Alan Nelmes, Mike Allen, Paul Bence, Keith Lawrence, Nigel Smith, Jackie Graham, Terry Scales, Dave Simmons, Mickey French, Gordon Sweetzer Subs: Terry Johnson, Roger Cross, Gordon Riddick

Friendly: **Mon 11 August**
Bexley (A)   **Won 5-0**
Scorers: Cross (2), Simmons, French, OG
Bill Glazier, Mickey Tripp, Mike Allen, Paul Bence, Keith Lawrence, Nigel Smith, Jackie Graham, Terry Scales, Dave Simmons, Roger Cross, Terry Johnson Subs: Gordon Sweetzer, Mickey French, Gordon Bartlett

Benefit Match (Bishop)   **Thu 29 April**
Hillingdon Borough (A)   **Won 4-2**
Scorers: Scales, Lawrence, Sweetzer, Poole
Attendance: 513
Paul Priddy, Alan Nelmes, Mickey Tripp, Paul Bence, John Docherty, Keith Lawrence, Terry Johnson, Terry Scales, Roger Cross, Richard Poole, Mickey French Subs: Gordon Sweetzer, Larry McGettigan, Tom Sharp

Friendly: **Mon 3 May**
Hounslow (A)   **Won 3-1**
Scorers: Russell, Malcolm, Sweetzer
Paul Priddy, Danis Salman, Keith Pritchett, Steve Russell, John Docherty, Keith Lawrence, Terry Scales, Alex Malcolm, Andy McCulloch, Roger Cross, Terry Johnson Subs: Mickey French, Gordon Sweetzer, Graham Cox

[Right] The Bees in training for the 1976-77 season

1976-77 PRE-SEASON FRIENDLIES AND OTHER NON-COMPETITIVE MATCHES

[Right] Brentford's 15-year-old, Paul Walker, tackles Millwall forward, Trevor Lee, while Paul Bence, Bobby Goldthorpe and Paul Priddy await the outcome during the 4-2 Kent Cup win

Friendly: **Mon 2 August**
Walton (A)   **Drew 1-1**
Scorer: Sweetzer
Team not known

Friendly: **Mon 9 August**
Hayes (A)   **Lost 1-3**
Scorer: Cross
Paul Priddy, Steve Aylott, Nigel Smith, Bobby Goldthorpe, Danis Salman, Paul Bence, Terry Scales, Gary Rolph, Jackie Graham, Roger Cross, Mickey French Subs: Graham Cox, Tom Sharp

Friendly: **Thu 12 August**
Addlestone (A)   **Lost 2-4**
Scorers: Cross, Walker
Team not known

The Kent Challenge Cup was played as a pre-season competition with the two section winners meeting in the Final in the early part of the season. Section A: Luton Town, Oxford United, Portsmouth and Watford. Section B: Aldershot, Brentford, Gillingham and Millwall

Kent Challenge Cup: **Sat 31 July**
Millwall (H)   **Won 4-2**
Scorers: Allen, McCulloch, Walker, Aylott (pen)
Attendance: 2,700
Paul Priddy, Steve Aylott, Keith Pritchett, Paul Bence, Bobby Goldthorpe, Gordon Riddick, Terry Scales, Mike Allen, Mickey French, Andy McCulloch, Jackie Graham Subs: Paul Walker, Roger Cross

Kent Challenge Cup: **Wed 4 August**
Gillingham (H)   **Won 1-0**
Scorer: French
Attendance: 2,280
Paul Priddy, Steve Aylott, Keith Pritchett, Paul Bence, Bobby Goldthorpe, Nigel Smith, Terry Scales, Mike Allen, Mickey French, Roger Cross, Jackie Graham Sub: John Fraser

Kent Challenge Cup: **Sat 7 August**
Aldershot (A)   **Lost 1-2**
Scorer: OG
Attendance: 1,421
Paul Priddy, John Fraser, Keith Pritchett, Paul Bence, Bobby Goldthorpe, Gordon Riddick, Terry Scales, Steve Aylott, Gordon Sweetzer, Andy McCulloch, Jackie Graham Subs: Tom Sharp, Roger Cross

Kent Challenge Cup Final: **Tue 14 September**
Luton Town (H)   **Lost 0-1**
Attendance: 3,030
Paul Priddy, Danis Salman, John Fraser, Paul Bence, Bobby Goldthorpe, Nigel Smith, Terry Scales, Terry Johnson, Mickey French, Roger Cross, Keith Pritchett

With Eddie Lyons taking charge of the managerless team, a creditable effort produced little to match the higher division opposition whose dominance meant the outcome was rarely in doubt. Despite the margin of victory being restricted to a solitary goal, scored in the 55th minute, it was sufficient to secure the trophy for the Bedfordshire team in the pouring rain.

1977-78 PRE-SEASON FRIENDLIES AND OTHER NON-COMPETITIVE MATCHES

Friendly: **Tue 2 August**
Brighton (H)   **Lost 2-3**
Scorers: Sweetzer, Phillips   **Attendance: 2,501**

Graham Cox, John Fraser, Mike Allen, Nigel Smith, Pat Kruse, Paul Shrubb, Dave Carlton, Jackie Graham, Gordon Sweetzer, Terry Glynn, Steve Phillips Sub: Paul Walker

Friendly: **Mon 8 August**
Charlton Athletic (H)   **Drew 2-2**
Scorers: Sweetzer (2)   **Attendance: 2,260**

Len Bond, John Fraser, Mike Allen, Barry Lloyd, Pat Kruse, Paul Shrubb, Dave Carlton, Jackie Graham, Gordon Sweetzer, Andy McCulloch, Steve Phillips Sub: Terry Glynn

Friendly: **Wed 10 August**
Barnet (A)   **Won 4-1**
Scorers: Glynn (2), McCulloch, Phillips

Len Bond, Steve Aylott, Mike Allen, Nigel Smith, Danis Salman, Barry Lloyd, Gary Rolph, Paul Walker, Terry Glynn, Andy McCulloch, Steve Phillips Subs: Graham Cox, Jackie Graham, Willie Graham

Friendly: **Tue 30 August**
Kuwait (H)   **Lost 0-2**

Graham Cox, Steve Aylott, Danis Salman, Paul Shrubb, Nigel Smith, Barry Lloyd, Johnny Ayris, Willie Graham, Andy McCulloch, Terry Glynn, Steve Phillips Subs: John Fraser, Paul Walker, Gary Rolph

[Right] Jackie Graham evades a tackle from Brighton's Brian Horton during the pre-season friendly at Griffin Park

Benefit Match (Watmore/Talbot)   **Tue 2 May**
Staines Town (A)   **Won 2-1**
Scorers: Rolph, Walker

Team not known

Benefit Match (Tredwell)   **Wed 3 May**
Folkestone (A)   **Drew 0-0**

Team not known

Alan Nelmes Testimonial   **Tue 9 May**
Chelsea (H)   **Lost 2-8**
Scorers: Allder, Kruse   **Attendance: 7,400**

Graham Cox, Alan Nelmes, Barry Tucker, Paul Shrubb, Pat Kruse, Willie Graham, Dave Carlton, Barry Lloyd, Doug Allder, Tommy Baldwin, Steve Phillips Sub: Gary Rolph

In the wake of promotion to the Third Division, a bumper crowd of 7,400 (paying £6,800) greeted Alan Nelmes and the illustrious First Division visitors with Nelmes scoring a superbly-placed, trademark own-goal after 12 minutes to open the scoring. Doug Allder equalised in the 23rd minute before a Ron Harris penalty for the Blues completed an evenly matched first-half. The visitors turned on the style after the break, and although a 3-1 lead was pegged back when a bullet header from Pat Kruse beat Peter Bonetti, a further five goals ensured a thumping final scoreline with Nelmes final payout amounting to a record £7,193.

A warm-up for the main event saw the 1972-promotion-winning team beat a Rick Wakeman celebrity XI 2-1 with John O'Mara tapping home the opener and Bobby Ross scoring from the penalty spot – Paul Walker netted for the celebrities.

Team: Phillips, Hawley, Scales, Tom, Gelson, Jackie Graham, Allen, Ross, O'Mara, Cross, Higginson

1978-79 PRE-SEASON FRIENDLIES AND OTHER NON-COMPETITIVE MATCHES

Friendly: **Tue 1 August**
Charlton Athletic (H)   **Drew 1-1**
Scorer: Phillips   **Attendance: 2,500**

Graham Cox, John Fraser, Barry Tucker, Danis Salman, Pat Kruse, Jackie Graham, Willie Graham, Steve Wilkins, Doug Allder, John Murray, Steve Phillips Subs: Mike Allen, Paul Walker

Friendly: **Thu 3 August**
Chesham (A)   **Drew 0-0**

Trevor Porter, John Fraser, Mike Allen, Nigel Smith, David Silman, Paul Walker, Steve Wilkins, Dave Carlton, Bob Booker, Billy Eames, Steve Phillips Subs: Graham Cox, Gary Rolph

Friendly: **Mon 7 August**
Brighton (H)   **Lost 1-4**
Scorer: J.Graham   **Attendance: 2,800**

Graham Cox, John Fraser, Barry Tucker, Danis Salman, Pat Kruse, Jackie Graham, Willie Graham, Dave Carlton, Doug Allder, John Murray, Steve Phillips Subs: Steve Wilkins, Paul Walker, Billy Eames, Paul Shrubb

Friendly: **Tue 8 August**
Woking (A)   **Lost 0-3**

Graham Cox, Nigel Smith, Mike Allen, Danis Salman, David Silman, Paul Walker, Paul Shrubb, Dave Carlton, Gary Rolph, Tommy Baldwin, Billy Eames Subs: John Fraser, Steve Wilkins, Steve Phillips

Friendly: **Wed 9 August**
Aldershot (A)   **Won 2-1**
Scorers: Phillips, Kruse

Trevor Porter, Danis Salman, Barry Tucker, Paul Shrubb, Pat Kruse, Jackie Graham, Willie Graham, Dave Carlton, Doug Allder, Tommy Baldwin, Steve Phillips Subs: John Fraser, Steve Wilkins, John Murray

Friendly: **Fri 15 December**
Northampton Town (A)   **Lost 0-3**

Team not known

1979-80 PRE-SEASON FRIENDLIES AND OTHER NON-COMPETITIVE MATCHES

Friendly: **Tue 31 July**
Wrexham (H)   **Won 5-1**
Scorers: Phillips (3), Shrubb, Fraser

Len Bond, Paul Shrubb, Barry Tucker, Jim McNichol, Pat Kruse, John Fraser, Allan Glover, Jackie Graham, Dean Smith, Doug Allder, Steve Phillips Subs: Paul Walker, Willie Graham, Lee Holmes

Friendly: **Fri 3 August**
Charlton Athletic (H)   **Won 2-1**
Scorers: McNichol. Holmes

Len Bond, Paul Shrubb, Barry Tucker, Jim McNichol, Pat Kruse, John Fraser, Allan Glover, Jackie Graham, Dean Smith, Lee Holmes, Steve Phillips Subs: Trevor Porter, Willie Graham, Doug Allder

Friendly: **Tue 7 August**
St Albans (A)   **Won 1-0**
Scorer: McNichol

Len Bond, Danis Salman, Barry Tucker, Jim McNichol, Pat Kruse, Willie Graham, Dave Carlton, Jackie Graham, Lee Holmes, Dean Smith, Steve Phillips Subs: Paul Walker, Bob Booker, Dean Johns, Terry Benning, Dave O'Mahoney

Friendly: **Wed 8 August**
Epsom (A)   **Won 2-0**
Scorers: Holmes, Glover

Trevor Porter, Dean Johns, Doug Allder, Paul Shrubb, John Fraser, Paul Walker, Allan Glover, Willie Graham, Lee Holmes, Bob Booker, Terry Benning

Friendly: **Mon 14 April**
Slough Town (A)   **Won 2-1**
Scorer: Booker (2)

Trevor Porter, Allan Glover, Jackie Graham, Danis Salman, Iori Jenkins, Paul Walker, Willie Graham, Noel Parkinson, Bob Booker, Tony Funnell, Billy Holmes Subs: Dave O'Mahoney, Terry Benning

Benefit Match (Berrecloth)   **Tue 6 May**
Tooting (A)   **Lost 1-2**
Scorer: Phillips

Len Bond, John Fraser, Barry Tucker, Danis Salman, Pat Kruse, Ron Harris, Steve Phillips, Paul Walker, Dean Smith, Dave Carlton, Tony Funnell Subs: Paul Shrubb, Jim McNichol, Pearce

APPEARANCES

FIRST TEAM INFORMATION AND VARIOUS STATISTICS

SEASON 1970-1971

	League Apps	League Goals	FAC Apps	FAC Goals	FLC Apps	FLC Goals	Total Apps	Total Goals
Roger Cross	46	14	5	1	1		52	15
Alan Nelmes	46		5		1		52	
Bobby Ross	46	15	5	1	1		52	16
Peter Gelson	45		5		1		51	
Paul Bence	44	4	5		1		50	4
Jackie Graham	42	6	5	1	1		48	7
Brian Turner	40+2	2	4				44+2	2
Dick Renwick	40	1	5				45	1
John Docherty	35+1	10	5	3	1		41+1	13
Gordon Phillips	29		4				33	
Alan Hawley	25+1		3		1		29+1	
Chic Brodie	17		1		1		19	
Gordon Neilson	16+3	4	2+1		1		19+4	4
Alex Dawson	10	6	1	1			11	7
John O'Mara	9	2					9	2
Allan Mansley	7+2						7+2	
Brian Tawse	7+2	1			1		8+2	1
Michael Maskell	1						1	
Mickey Heath	1						1	

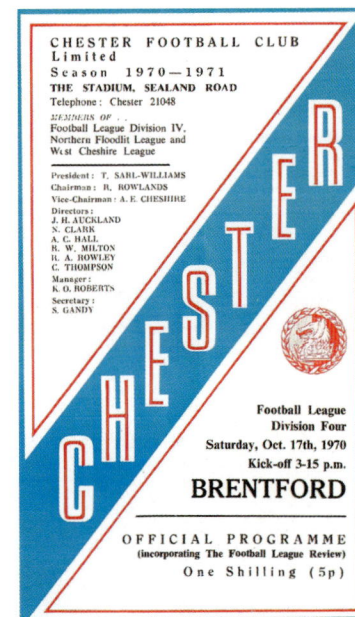

Alex Dawson scored his first goal for the Bees during the away fixture at Chester in October 1970.

Unused as a substitute

21 occasions	Brian Tawse
7 occasions	Gordon Neilson
4 occasions	Brian Turner
2 occasions	Alan Hawley, Gordon Neilson
1 occasion	Alan Gane, Jackie Graham, John O'Mara, Gordon Phillips

Total number of players used during the season 19

Number of goalscorers 11

SEASON 1971-1972

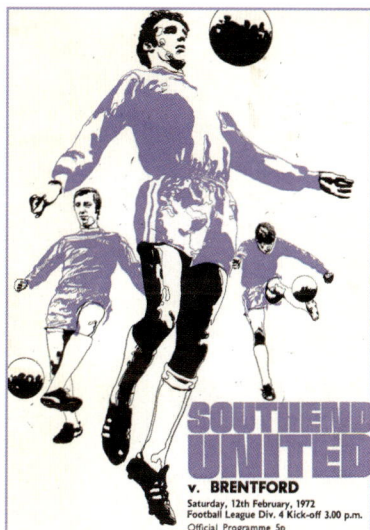

Bobby Ross made the last of his 167 consecutive starts for Brentford at Roots Hall in February 1972.

	League Apps	League Goals	FAC Apps	FAC Goals	FLC Apps	FLC Goals	Total Apps	Total Goals
Alan Nelmes	46		2		1		49	
Gordon Phillips	46		2		1		49	
Jackie Graham	45	7	2		1		48	7
Bobby Ross	44+1	13	2	1	1	1	47+1	15
John Docherty	44	13	2				46	13
Terry Scales	43	1	2		1		46	1
John O'Mara	40	25	2	2	1		43	27
Peter Gelson	36+1	2			1		37+1	2
Brian Turner	34+1	4	2		1		37+1	4
Paul Bence	32+2		2		1		35+2	
Mike Allen	29+1	3	2				31+1	3
Alan Hawley	20						20	
Stewart Houston	15	2					15	2
Steve Tom	13+5	1	2		1		16+5	1
Gordon Neilson	8+4	2			0+1		8+5	2
Roger Cross	5	2			1		6	2
Trevor Dawkins	3+1						3+1	
Ken Wallace	3						3	

Total number of players used during the season 18

Number of goalscorers 11

Unused as a substitute

14 occasions	Steve Tom
13 occasions	Gordon Neilson
3 occasions	Peter Gelson
1 occasion	Paul Bence, Brian Turner

SEASON 1972-1973

	League Apps	League Goals	FAC Apps	FAC Goals	FLC Apps	FLC Goals	Total Apps	Total Goals
Alan Hawley	43				2		45	
Alan Murray	42+3	7	1		2		45+3	7
Peter Gelson	41+1		1		2		44+1	
Terry Scales	41		1		2		44	
Stewart Houston	39	6	1		2		42	6
Alan Nelmes	35+1		1		2		38+1	
John Docherty	34+2	6	1		1	1	36+2	7
Paul Bence	33+3		1				34+1	
Jackie Graham	30+1	6	1		2		33+1	6
Mike Allen	26	4	1	1	1		28	5
Paul Priddy	25				2		27	
Stan Webb	24	6	1				25	6
Roger Cross	19	4					19	4
Barry Salvage	16	3					16	3
Gordon Phillips	15		1				16	
David Jenkins	13+5	1			1		14+5	1
David Court	8+4	1			1		9+4	1
Bobby Ross	7				1+1		8+1	
Keiron Baker	6						6	
Andy Woon	5+1	3					5+1	3
John O'Mara	4	1			1		5	1

Jackie Graham scored at Ewood Park during Brentford's record-equalling 13th consecutive away defeat.

Unused as a substitute

9 occasions	David Court
5 occasions	David Jenkins
4 occasions	Alan Nelmes
3 occasions	Mike Allen
2 occasions	Paul Bence, Peter Gelson
1 occasion	Alan Murray, Andy Woon

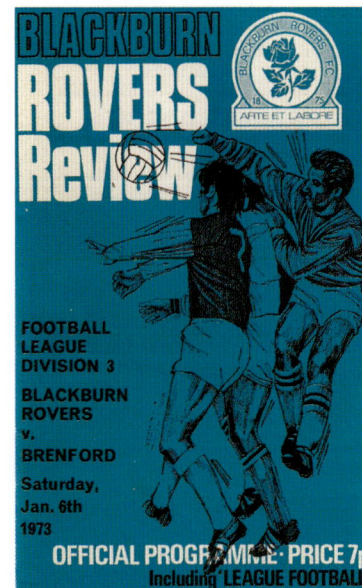

Total number of players used during the season   21

Number of goalscorers   12

SEASON 1973-1974

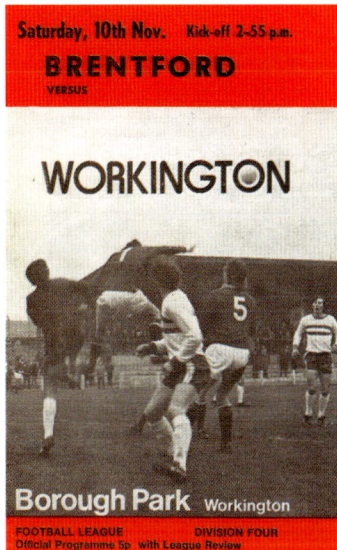

Gordon Riddick scored his first goal in a Brentford shirt during the away trip to Borough Park, Workington in November 1973.

	League Apps	League Goals	FAC Apps	FAC Goals	FLC Apps	FLC Goals	Total Apps	Total Goals
Peter Gelson	40		1		1		42	
Roger Cross	39+2	17	1		1		41+2	17
Barry Salvage	37	5			1		38	5
Dave Metchick	33+1	3	1				34+1	3
Alan Nelmes	33		1		1		35	
Terry Scales	33		1		1		35	
Jackie Graham	31	2	1				32	2
Paul Bence	30				1		31	
Gordon Riddick	26+1	2	1				27+1	2
Mike Allen	25+7	2	0+1	1	1		26+8	3
Paul Priddy	25		1		1		27	
Andy Woon	24+3	7	1		0+1		25+4	7
Stewart Houston	23	1	1		1		25	1
Alan Hawley	22				1		23	
Steve Sherwood	16						16	
Stan Webb	13+2	2			1	1	14+2	3
John Docherty	13+1	1	1				14+1	1
Dave Simmons	12	4					12	4
Jimmy Gabriel	9						9	
Richard Poole	5+1	1					5+1	1
Kevin Harding	5						5	
Garry Towse	5						5	
Hugh Reed	3+1						3+1	
Mick Brown	3						3	
Roy Cotton	1+1						1+1	

Total number of players used during the season 25

Number of goalscorers 12

Unused as a substitute

6 occasions	Gordon Riddick
4 occasions	Mike Allen, Stan Webb
3 occasions	Andy Woon
2 occasions	Jackie Graham
1 occasion	John Docherty, Jimmy Gabriel, Kevin Harding, Alan Nelmes, Richard Poole, Barry Salvage, Gary Smith

SEASON 1974-1975

	League Apps	League Goals	FAC Apps	FAC Goals	FLC Apps	FLC Goals	Total Apps	Total Goals
Steve Sherwood	46		2		2		50	
Paul Bence	43	1	2		2		47	1
Keith Lawrence	43	1	2		2		47	1
Jackie Graham	43	4	2	1	1		46	5
Gordon Riddick	42	1	2		2		46	1
Terry Scales	40	1	2		2	1	44	2
Barry Salvage	34		2		2		38	
Mike Allen	32		1		2		35	
Terry Johnson	28	8	2				30	8
Dave Simmons	25+5	12	1+1	1	1		27+6	13
Roger Cross	25+2	8			2	2	27+2	10
Dave Metchick	24+3	1	1		2		27+3	1
Willie Brown	16	9	1				17	9
Mickey French	14+1	4					14+1	4
Andy Woon	13+4	2	2	2	1+1	1	16+5	5
Alan Nelmes	10+3						10+3	
Graham Smith	7						7	
Richard Poole	5+3						5+3	
Billy Stagg	4						4	
Peter Gelson	3				1		4	
Kevin Harding	3						3	
Gary Smith	3						3	
Nigel Smith	2						2	
Ian Filby	1+2						1+2	

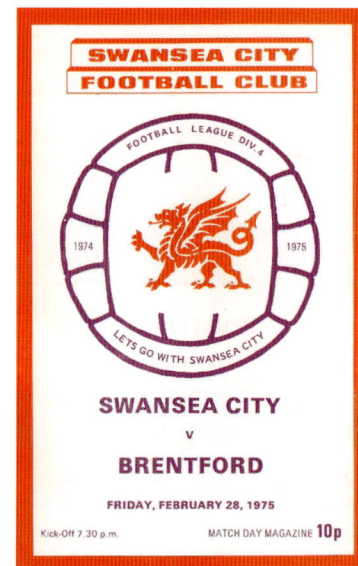

Willie Brown's last goal and last game for Brentford coincided with the trip to Swansea in February 1975.

Unused as a substitute

5 occasions	Alan Nelmes, Andy Woon
3 occasions	Roger Cross, Ian Filby, Richard Poole
2 occasions	Dave Metchick, Dave Simmons
1 occasion	Terry Scales, Graham Smith

Total number of players used during the season 24

Number of goalscorers 12

SEASON 1975-1976

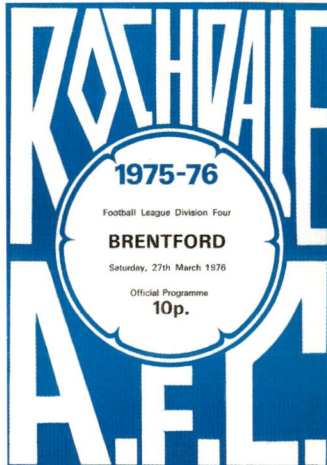

Andy McCulloch scored his first goal for the Bees in the away match at Rochdale in March 1976.

	League Apps	League Goals	FAC Apps	FAC Goals	FLC Apps	FLC Goals	Total Apps	Total Goals
Paul Bence	46	1	4		3		53	1
Terry Johnson	46	11	4	2	3	1	53	14
Mike Allen	45	1	4		3		52	1
Terry Scales	43	3	4		3		50	3
Jackie Graham	38	5	4		3		45	5
Roger Cross	37	14	3		2+1	2	42+1	16
Nigel Smith	37		4		3		44	
Keith Lawrence	35		4		3	1	42	1
Paul Priddy	34		4				38	
Alan Nelmes	28+1		3+1		3		34+2	
Mickey French	27+4	8	1+1		2		30+5	8
Gordon Sweetzer	25+2	5	4	2			29+2	7
Gordon Riddick	23+3	2	1+1		0+1		24+5	2
Andy McCulloch	13	3					13	3
Dave Simmons	10	1			2+1		12+1	1
Bill Glazier	9				3		12	
Danis Salman	3+3						3+3	
Graham Horn	3						3	
Tom Sharp	2+10	1					2+10	1
Richard Poole	2+5						2+5	

Unused as a substitute

8 occasions	Gordon Riddick
3 occasions	Tom Sharp
2 occasions	Mickey French, Keith Lawrence
1 occasion	Alan Nelmes, Richard Poole, Nigel Smith, Gordon Sweetzer

Total number of players used during the season 20

Number of goalscorers 13

SEASON 1976-1977

	League Apps	League Goals	FAC Apps	FAC Goals	FLC Apps	FLC Goals	Total Apps	Total Goals
Jackie Graham	42	4	2		2		46	4
Mike Allen	40	1	2				42	1
John Fraser	39	2	2	1			41	3
Paul Priddy	37		2		2		41	
Nigel Smith	32+2				2		34+2	
Dave Carlton	31+1		2				33+1	
Gordon Sweetzer	25+2	23	1				26+2	23
Terry Johnson	24+3	8	1				25+3	8
Roger Cross	21	9	2	1	2	1	25	11
Bobby Goldthorpe	19	2	1+1		2		22+1	2
Steve Phillips	19	7					19	7
Andy McCulloch	18+2	10					18+2	10
John Bain	17+1	1					17+1	1
Danis Salman	16+2	1	1+1		2		19+3	1
Mickey French	15+4	4	2	1	2		19+4	5
Pat Kruse	15	2					15	2
Gordon Riddick	15		2				17	
Terry Scales	12		1		2		15	
Keith Pritchett	11	1			2		13	1
Paul Shrubb	10+3	2					10+3	2
Paul Bence	10+1				2		12+1	
Gary Rolph	6+1		1	1			7+1	1
Tony Burns	6						6	
Allan Glover	6						6	
Steve Aylott	5						5	
Steve Scrivens	5						5	
Graham Cox	3						3	
Neil Smillie	3						3	
Tom Sharp	2+2				0+1		2+3	
Paul Walker	1+1				2		3+1	
Harry Redknapp	1						1	

Brentford goalkeeper Paul Priddy made two penalty saves during the away match at Watford in April 1977.

Unused as a substitute

3 occasions	Mickey French, Danis Salman, Paul Shrubb
2 occasions	Terry Johnson, Gary Rolph, Paul Walker
1 occasion	Mike Allen, John Fraser, Bobby Goldthorpe, Terry Scales, Tom Sharp, Neil Smillie, Nigel Smith

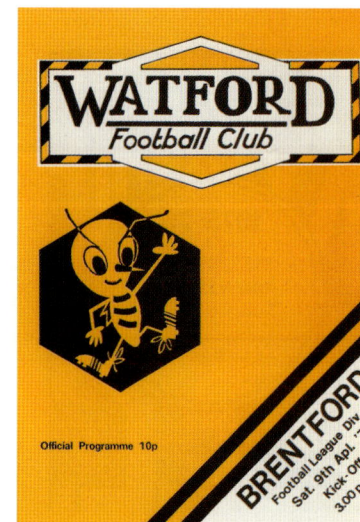

Total number of players used during the season **31**

Number of goalscorers **16**

SEASON 1977-1978

	League Apps	League Goals	FAC Apps	FAC Goals	FLC Apps	FLC Goals	Total Apps	Total Goals
Steve Phillips	46	32	2	3	2	1	50	36
Len Bond	45		2		2		49	
Andy McCulloch	45	22	2		2		49	22
Paul Shrubb	45	1	2		2		49	1
Pat Kruse	40	1	2		2		44	1
Danis Salman	36+1		2		2		40+1	
Jackie Graham	35+1	2	2		2		39+1	2
Dave Carlton	33	3					33	3
Doug Allder	31	2	2				33	2
Willie Graham	28+3	2	1				29+3	2
Barry Lloyd	26+5	4	2		2		30+5	4
Mike Allen	21		2		2		25	
John Fraser	19		1		2		22	
Gordon Sweetzer	18	12			2	2	20	14
Barry Tucker	18						18	
Nigel Smith	8+1						8+1	
Tommy Baldwin	4	1					4	1
Paul Walker	3+2						3+2	
John Murray	2+3	1					2+3	1
Gary Rolph	1+3	1	0+1				1+4	1
Steve Aylott	1+1						1+1	
Graham Cox	1						1	
Terry Glynn					0+1		0+1	

Unused as a substitute

6 occasions	Barry Lloyd
4 occasions	Steve Aylott, Willie Graham, Gary Rolph, Danis Salman
3 occasions	Paul Walker
1 occasion	Mike Allen, Tommy Baldwin, John Murray

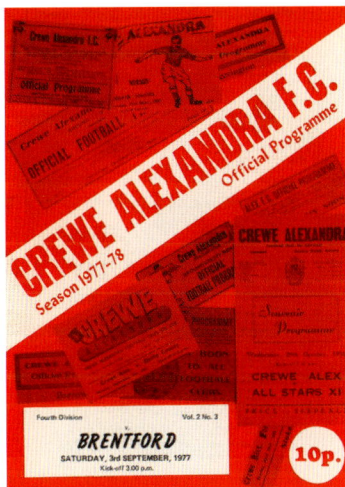

Gordon Sweetzer grabbed a hat-trick, and Dave Carlton scored two, in the remarkable 6-4 win against Crewe Alexandra at Gresty Road.

Total number of players used during the season 23

Number of goalscorers 13

SEASON 1978-1979

	League Apps	League Goals	FAC Apps	FAC Goals	FLC Apps	FLC Goals	Total Apps	Total Goals
Steve Phillips	46	14	1		2		49	14
Pat Kruse	44	4	1		2		47	4
Barry Tucker	43		1		2		46	
Danis Salman	39+1	1	1		2		42+1	1
Paul Shrubb	39	2	1		2		42	2
Andy McCulloch	39	14	1				40	14
Dave Carlton	36+1	2	1		2		39+1	2
Jackie Graham	35	1	1		2		38	1
Len Bond	35		1				36	
Jim McNichol	32	4	1				33	4
Dean Smith	22+3	8	0+1				22+4	8
John Fraser	21+2				0+1		21+3	
Doug Allder	18+12				2		20+12	
Allan Glover	18+1	2	1				19+1	2
Trevor Porter	11				2		13	
Willie Graham	8+3				2		10+3	
Mike Allen	5+2						5+2	
Lee Frost	5+1						5+1	
Paul Walker	2+5						2+5	
Bob Booker	2+1						2+1	
Nigel Smith	2+1						2+1	
Billy Eames	2	1					2	1
Gary Rolph	1				1	1	2	1
Dave Silman	1						1	
Tommy Baldwin					1		1	
Steve Wilkins					0+1		0+1	

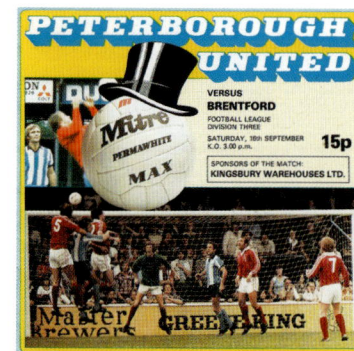

Mike Allen played his 255th and final game for Brentford at London Road in September 1978.

Unused as a substitute

4 occasions	Doug Allder
3 occasions	John Fraser
2 occasions	Jackie Graham
1 occasion	Willie Graham, Dean Smith, Barry Tucker, Paul Walker

Total number of players used during the season 26

Number of goalscorers 12

SEASON 1979-1980

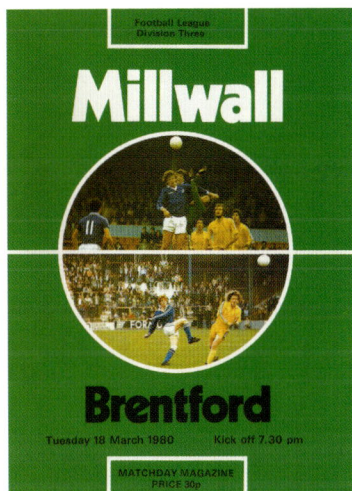

Defender and player of the season, Pat Kruse, scored his third goal of the campaign during the away game at The Den in March 1980.

	League Apps	League Goals	FAC Apps	FAC Goals	FLC Apps	FLC Goals	Total Apps	Total Goals
Steve Phillips	45+1	12	1		2		48+1	12
Pat Kruse	44	3	1		2		47	3
Len Bond	42		1		2		45	
John Fraser	42	4	1		2		45	4
Barry Tucker	41+1		1				42+1	
Danis Salman	39+2	3	1		1		41+2	3
Dave Carlton	38	2	1		2		41	2
Paul Shrubb	34+5	1	0+1		2		36+6	1
Jim McNichol	31	8	1		2		34	8
Jackie Graham	30+1	1	1				31+1	1
Lee Holmes	26+2	6			2	1	28+2	7
Dean Smith	20+2	5	1	1	2		23+2	6
Doug Allder	19+8		1		1+1	1	21+9	1
Bob Booker	9+3	6					9+3	6
Noel Parkinson	9+1						9+1	
Billy Holmes	8+7	2					8+7	2
Tony Funnell	8+1	2					8+1	2
Keith Fear	7+1	2					7+1	2
Trevor Porter	4						4	
Allan Glover	3+1				2		5+1	
Steve Harding	3+1						3+1	
Paul Walker	2+1						2+1	
Willie Graham	1						1	
Iori Jenkins	1						1	

Unused as a substitute

1 occasion

Doug Allder, Bob Booker, John Fraser, Jackie Graham, Willie Graham, Billy Holmes, Paul Shrubb, Dean Smith, Paul Walker

Total number of players used during the season 24

Number of goalscorers 15

PENALTY KICKS TAKEN DURING
FIRST-TEAM FIXTURES

100% Success Rate
(not including players who have only taken one penalty)

Terry Johnson   7 out of 7
Roger Cross   3 out of 3

Other players who took more than one penalty

Penalties		Scored	Missed	Success
14	Steve Phillips	8	6	57%
9	Bobby Ross	7	2	78%
5	Gordon Sweetzer	4	1	80%

One Penalty Attempt only

Scored: Alan Murray, Jim McNichol

Missed: Barry Salvage, Dave Simmons, Steve Aylott, Gordon Riddick, Andy McCulloch.

Bobby Ross

1970-71 v Grimsby (H)	Scored
1970-71 v Southend United (H) (1st penalty)	Scored
1970-71 v Southend United (H) (2nd penalty)	Scored
1971-72 v Peterborough United (H)	X
1971-72 v Newport County (H)	Scored
1971-72 v Darlington (H)	Scored
1971-72 v Southend United (A)	Scored
1971-72 v Exeter City (H)	Scored
1972-73 v Cambridge United (H) (Cup)	X

prior to 1970-71, Bobby Ross scored 4 out of 5 penalties

Alan Murray

1972-73 v Chesterfield (H)	Scored

Roger Cross

1973-74 v Mansfield (H)	Scored
1974-75 v Aldershot (H) (Cup)	Scored
1976-77 v Southend United (A)	Scored

Barry Salvage

1973-74 v Lincoln City (H)	X

Dave Simmons
1974-75 v Torquay United (H)   X

Terry Johnson
1975-76 v Brighton (H) (Cup)   Scored
1975-76 v Workington (H)   Scored
1975-76 v Rochdale (H)   Scored
1975-76 v Wimbledon (A) (Cup)   Scored
1975-76 v Northampton Town (H)   Scored
1976-77 v Southport (A)   Scored
1976-77 v Swansea City (H)   Scored

Steve Aylott
1976-77 v Huddersfield Town (H)   X
(*1st Attempt)

Gordon Riddick
1976-77 v Huddersfield Town (H)   X
(*2nd Attempt)

Gordon Sweetzer
1976-77 v Torquay United (H)   Scored
1976-77 v Hartlepool United (H)   Scored
1977-78 v Reading (H)   Scored
1977-78 v Stockport County (A)   X
1977-78 v Torquay United (H)   Scored

Steve Phillips
1977-78 v Halifax Town (H)   Scored
1977-78 v Swindon Town (A) (Cup)   Scored
1977-78 v Newport County (H)   Scored
1977-78 v Crewe Alexandra (H)   Scored
1977-78 v Rochdale (H)   X
1977-78 v Aldershot (H)   Scored
1977-78 v Barnsley (H)   Scored
1977-78 v Darlington (H)   Scored
1978-79 v Watford (H) (Cup)   X
1978-79 v Watford (H)   Scored
1979-80 v Chesterfield (H)   X
1979-80 v Sheffield Wednesday (A)   X
1979-80 v Southend United (A)   X
1979-80 v Rotherham United (H)   X

Andy McCulloch
1978-79 v Tranmere Rovers (H)   X

Jim McNichol
1979-80 v Rotherham United (A)   Scored

FIRST-TEAM HAT-TRICKS

1970-1971
John Docherty   York City (H)   Won 6-4

1971-1972
John O'Mara   Hartlepool (H)   Won 6-0
John O'Mara   Northampton (H)   Won 6-1
John Docherty   Darlington (H)   Won 6-2

1972-1973
Andy Woon   Port Vale (H)   Won 5-0

1973-1974
Roger Cross   Mansfield Town (H)   Won 4-1
Roger Cross   Chester City (H)   Won 3-0

1976-1977
Gordon Sweetzer   Stockport (H)   Won 4-0
Gordon Sweetzer   Torquay (H)   Won 3-2

1977-1978
Gordon Sweetzer   Crewe (A)   Won 6-4
Steve Phillips   Huddersfield (A)   Won 3-1

1978-1979
Steve Phillips   Chester City (H)   Won 6-0

1979-1980
Bob Booker   Hull City City (H)   Won 7-2

[Above] Bob Booker is mobbed by his team mates after scoring his third goal against Hull City

PLAYERS SENT-OFF DURING FIRST-TEAM FIXTURES

1970-1971
Dick Renwick   Peterborough United (A)

1971-1972
Brian Turner   Hartlepool United (A)

1972-1973   None

1973-1974
Dave Metchick   Plymouth Argyle (A) (FAC)

1974-1975
Jackie Graham   Southport (A)
Paul Bence   Newport County (A)

1975-1976
Terry Johnson   Rochdale (H)
Gordon Sweetzer   Rochdale (H)
Roger Cross   Reading (H)

1976-1977   None

1977-1978
Gordon Sweetzer   Doncaster Rovers (A)
Andy McCulloch   Aldershot (A)

1978-1979
Paul Shrubb   Southend United (A)
Andy McCulloch   Lincoln City (A)

1979-1980
Doug Allder   Sheffield United (H)
Dave Carlton   Colchester United (H)
Pat Kruse   Chesterfield (A)

PLAYERS WHO SCORED ON THEIR DEBUT

Steve Tom
Saturday 14th August 1971   Bury (A)   W 2-0

Roger Cross (second spell)
Saturday 13th January 1973   Rotherham United (H)   D 1-1

Barry Salvage
Saturday 10th February 1973   Port Vale (H)   W 5-0

Dave Metchick
Saturday 29th September 1973 Barnsley (H)   W 5-1

Terry Johnson
Saturday 16th November 1974 Hartlepool (A)   L 2-3

Mickey French (sub)
Saturday 8th February 1975   Barnsley (H)   W 3-0

Gordon Sweetzer (sub) [pictured right]
Saturday 27th September1975 Huddersfield Town (A)   L 2-3

Gary Rolph
Monday 20th December 1976   Colchester (A) FAC   L 2-3

Billy Eames
Monday 25th September 1978 Lincoln City (H)   W 2-1

Lee Holmes
Wednesday 15th August 1979 Southend (A) (FLC)   L 1-2

Billy Holmes (sub)
Saturday 1 September 1979   Chesterfield (H)   W 3-1

GOALKEEPING & GOALS CONCEDED

Chic Brodie

Games Played	Goals Conceded	per game
19	31	1.63

Clean Sheets	Penalties Faced	Penalties Saved
4 (21%)	1	0

Gordon Phillips

Games Played	Goals Conceded	per game
98	114	1.16

Clean Sheets	Penalties Faced	Penalties Saved
38 (39%)	3	1

Keiron Baker

Games Played	Goals Conceded	per game
6	6	1.00

Clean Sheets	Penalties Faced	Penalties Saved
3 (50%)	1	0

Paul Priddy   [pictured left]

Games Played	Goals Conceded	per game
133	173	1.30

Clean Sheets	Penalties Faced	Penalties Saved
33 (25%)	13	3

Garry Towse

Games Played	Goals Conceded	per game
5	8	1.60

Clean Sheets	Penalties Faced	Penalties Saved
2 (40%)	0	0

Steve Sherwood

Games Played	Goals Conceded	per game
66	61	0.92

Clean Sheets	Penalties Faced	Penalties Saved
26 (39%)	2	0

Bill Glazier

Games Played	Goals Conceded	per game
12	19	1.58

Clean Sheets	Penalties Faced	Penalties Saved
1 (8%)	1	0

[Left] Len Bond presents Trevor Porter with a Player of the Month award [Above] Goalie, Paul Priddy

Graham Horn

Games Played	Goals Conceded	per game
3	6	2.00

Clean Sheets	Penalties Faced	Penalties Saved
1 (33%)	0	0

Graham Cox

Games Played	Goals Conceded	per game
4	11	2.75

Clean Sheets	Penalties Faced	Penalties Saved
0	2	0

Tony Burns

Games Played	Goals Conceded	per game
6	13	2.16

Clean Sheets	Penalties Faced	Penalties Saved
1 (17%)	0	0

Len Bond

Games Played	Goals Conceded	per game
130	165	1.27

Clean Sheets	Penalties Faced	Penalties Saved
49 (38%)	13	4

Trevor Porter

Games Played	Goals Conceded	per game
17	36	2.11

Clean Sheets	Penalties Faced	Penalties Saved
2 (12%)	1	0

THE
RESERVES

1974-1975

The reserve team was reinstated for the first time since 1966-67

MID-WEEK FOOTBALL LEAGUE

Tue 27th August   **Southend United (H)**
Lost   2-3   **Simmons (pen), Devonshire**
Priddy, Bence, Tripp, Gary Smith, Gelson, Graham Smith, Stagg, Simmons, Poole, Steve Johnson, Devonshire

Wed 11th September   **Northampton Town (A)**
Won   3-1   **Woon, Fletcher, Poole**

Wed 18th September   **Peterborough United (A)**
Lost   0-5

Tue 1st October   **Watford (H)**
Drew   1-1   **Cross**
Gordine, Harding, Tripp, Gelson, Gary Smith, Filby, Griffin, Cross, Poole, Steve Johnson, Graham Smith Subs: Nelmes, Stephen Dray

Mon 7th October   **Luton Town (A)**
Lost   0-5

Mon 14th October   **Cambridge United (H)**
Won   3-1   **Filby (pen), Woon, Steve Johnson**
Gordine, Harding, Tripp, Nelmes, Gary Smith, Steve Johnson, Stagg, Woon, Poole, Graham Smith, Filby Sub: Griffiths

Tue 22nd October   **Colchester United (A)**
Lost   0-1

Tue 29th October   **Charlton Athletic (H)**
Drew   0-0
Gordine, Griffiths, Tripp, Nelmes, Gary Smith, Cross, Stagg, Woon, Poole, Steve Johnson, Graham Smith Subs: Dray, Cobb

Wed 6th November   **Cambridge United (A)**
Lost   2-3   **Cross, Steve Johnson**

Tue 12th November   **Portsmouth (H)**
Won   3-2   **Poole, Allen, OG**

Wed 4th December   **Gillingham (A)**
Drew   1-1   **Woon**

Wed 11th December   **Millwall (A)**
Won   3-0   **Simmons (2), Cross**

Wed 18th December   **Portsmouth (A)**
Lost   1-2   **Woon**

Tue 7th January   **Peterborough United (H)**
Drew   1-1   **Cross**
Gordine, Tripp, Scales, Steve Johnson, Lawrence, Harding, Poole, Woon, Cross, Graham Smith, Salvage Sub: Stagg

Wed 15th January   **Orient (A)**
Drew   2-2   **Lawrence, Salvage**
Gordine, Steve Johnson, Lawrence, Harding, Scales, Stagg, Poole, Graham Smith, Woon, Cross, Salvage

Wed 5ᵗʰ February　　　　　**Southend United (A)**
Drew　1-1　　　　　　　　**Woon**

Wed 12ᵗʰ February　　　　**Luton Town (H) (Cup)**
Lost　2-3　　　　　　　　**Woon, Nelmes**
Gordine, Nelmes, Tripp, French, Gary Smith, Harding, Potrac, Woon, Poole, Steve Johnson, Stagg Subs: Allen, Lawrence

Tue 25ᵗʰ February　　　　**Luton Town (H)**
Won　3-1　　　　　　　　**Cross (2), Graham**
Gordine, Nelmes, Scales, Harding, Potts, Allen, Graham, Kemp, French, Potrac, Cross Sub: Terry Johnson

Wed 5ᵗʰ March　　　　　　**Watford (A)**
Won　1-0　　　　　　　　**Poole**
Gordine, Nelmes, Riddick, Gary Smith, Tripp, Metchick, Harding, Potrac, Steve Johnson, Bence, Poole Subs: Billy Sweetzer , Stagg

Mon 10ᵗʰ March　　　　　**Colchester United (H)**
Lost　0-3
Gordine, Nelmes, Tripp, Potrac, Gary Smith, Billy Sweetzer, Stagg, Steve Johnson, Simmons, Metchick, Poole

Wed 19ᵗʰ March　　　　　**Gillingham (H)**
Lost　0-1
Gordine, Nelmes, Tripp, Steve Johnson, Gary Smith, Billy Sweetzer, Stagg, Poole, Simmons, Metchick, Harding Subs: Graham, Cross

Tue 25ᵗʰ March　　　　　**Brighton (H)**
Lost　0-2
Gordine, Billy Sweetzer, Tripp, Steve Johnson, Gary Smith, Nigel Smith, Stagg, Poole, Simmons, Metchick, Docherty, Sub: Lawrence

Wed 2ⁿᵈ April　　　　　　**Orient (H)**
Lost　1-3　　　　　　　　**Stagg**
Gordine, Brazier, Tripp, Steve Johnson, Nelmes, Billy Sweetzer, Stagg, Nigel Smith, Poole, Metchick, Newman, Sub: Docherty

Thu 10ᵗʰ April　　　　　　**Charlton Athletic (A)**
Lost　1-2　　　　　　　　**Newman**

Mon 14ᵗʰ April　　　　　　**Brighton (A)**
Lost　0-5

Thu 17ᵗʰ April　　　　　　**Millwall (H)**
Lost　0-1

Wed 30ᵗʰ April　　　　　　**Northampton Town (H)**
Lost　1-3　　　　　　　　**Simmons**
Sherwood, Steve Johnson, Nigel Smith, Billy Sweetzer, Tripp, Stagg, Ballantyne, Metchick, Poole, Simmons, Kerr

1974-75 Final League Table

		P	W	D	L	F	A	Pts
1	Colchester United	26	16	6	4	63	35	38
2	Orient	26	15	7	4	60	25	37
3	Charlton Athletic	26	14	6	6	43	33	34
4	Southend United	26	13	6	7	46	37	32
5	Peterborough	26	12	7	7	53	37	31
6	Luton Town	26	12	7	7	55	40	31
7	Portsmouth	26	12	4	10	51	45	28
8	Brighton	26	11	5	10	48	50	27
9	Watford	26	5	10	11	31	37	20
10	Gillingham	26	6	8	12	34	47	20
11	Cambridge United	26	6	6	14	29	44	18
12	**Brentford**	**26**	**6**	**6**	**14**	**30**	**50**	**18**
13	Northampton Town	26	5	5	16	42	65	15
14	Millwall	26	6	3	17	29	70	15

[Left] Apprentice, Steve Johnson, was a regular for the reserves during the 1974-75 season

Thirty-three year old manager, Mike Everitt, made two substitute appearances for the reserve team – first appearing as a second-half replacement in the game at Northampton Town on 11th September 1974.

Appearances

Steve Johnson (25)
Mickey Tripp (22)
Dave Metchick (13)
Billy Sweetzer (9+1)
Ian Filby (4)
Jackie Graham (3+2)
Peter Gelson (3)
John Fielding (2)
Paul Priddy (2)
John Ballantyne (1)
David Kemp (1)
Gordon Riddick (1)

Barry Gordine (24)
Gary Smith (19+1)
Graham Smith (12)
Dave Simmons (7)
Tony Potrac (4)
Paul Bence (3+1)
Michael Newman (3)
Mickey French (2)
John Docherty (1+2)
Willie Brown (1)
C.Murphy (1)
Steve Sherwood (1)

Richard Poole (24)
Kevin Harding (15+1)
Andy Woon (11)
Nigel Smith (6)
Keith Lawrence (3+3)
Barry Salvage (3+1)
Mike Allen (2+1)
D.Griffin (2)
Paul Griffiths (1+1)
Alan Devonshire (1)
S.Oates (1)
L.Stojanovic (1)

Billy Stagg (23+2)
Alan Nelmes (13+2)
Roger Cross (9+1)
Terry Scales (5)
Stephen Dray (3+2)
Martin Brazier (3)
Peter Cobb (2)
Paul Kerr (2)
Terry Johnson (1+1)
Steve Fletcher (1)
Alan Potts (1)
Mike Everitt (0+2)

Goalscorers

Roger Cross, Andy Woon (6), Dave Simmons (4), Poole (3), Steve Johnson (2), Devonshire, Fletcher, Filby, Allen, Lawrence, Salvage, Nelmes, Graham, Stagg, Newman, OG (1)

1975-1976

MID-WEEK FOOTBALL LEAGUE

Tue 26th August   **Brighton (H)**
Won   2-1   **G.Sweetzer (2)**
Cox, Fielding, Tripp, Ballantyne, Butler, Riddick, French, Kerr, Poole, Gordon Sweetzer, Peett Sub: Docherty

Wed 3rd September   **Southend United (A)**
Lost   1-3   **Ballantyne**

Tue 9th September   **Peterborough (H)**
Lost   0-3
Cox, Salman, Tripp, Ballantyne, Riddick, Billy Sweetzer, Kerr, Butler, Gordon Sweetzer, Poole, Bartlett

Wed 17th September   **Watford (A)**
Drew   0-0

Tue 23rd September   **Charlton Athletic (H)**
Drew   0-0
Priddy, Salman, Tripp, Ballantyne, Riddick, Billy Sweetzer, Kerr, Bartlett, Fielding, Poole. Gordon Sweetzer Sub: Docherty

Mon 29th September   **Luton Town (A)**
Drew   2-2   **Bartlett, Poole**
Priddy, Salman, Lawrence, Billy Sweetzer, Tripp, Ballantyne, Kerr, Horastead, French, Poole, Bartlett

Tue 7th October   **Orient (A)**
Lost   0-3

Mon 13th October   **Cambridge United (A)**
Won   2-1   **Simmons, Kerr**

Wed 22nd October   **Cambridge United (H)**
Lost   2-3   **Gordon Sweetzer (2)**

Wed 29th October   **Gillingham (A)**
Lost   1-4   **Graham**

Tue 18th November   **Millwall (A) (Cup)**
Lost   1-6   **Nigel Smith**

Tue 25th November   **Luton Town (H)**
Lost   1-2   **French**
Cox, Salman, Tripp, Nelmes, Ballantyne, Riddick, French, Kerr, Docherty, Poole, Fielding

Wed 3rd December   **Portsmouth (A)**
Drew   1-1   **Graham**
Cox, Bence, Nelmes, Salman, Tripp, Clark, Riddick, Ballantyne, French, Poole, Graham

Tue 9th December   **Watford (H)**
Lost   0-3

Tue 23rd December   **Northampton Town (H)**
Won   3-1   **Fielding, Riddick, Poole**

Wed 28th January   **Northampton Town (A)**
Lost   2-4   **Poole, Sharp**

Tue 3rd February   **Colchester (A)**
Lost   1-2   McGettigan

Tue 10th February   **Brighton (A)**
Won   3-2   Poole (2), McGettigan

Tue 17th February   **Southend United (H)**
Drew   2-2   Oxley, Poole
Cox, Nelmes, Tripp, Salman, Lawrence, Sharp, Graham, Oxley, Cross, Poole, French Sub: Docherty

Tue 24th February   **Colchester (H)**
Won   5-0   McGettigan (2), Gordon Sweetzer (2), Sharp
Cox, Bence, Lawrence, Sharp, Tripp, Ballantyne, Oxley, Docherty, Gordon Sweetzer, Poole, McGettigan Subs: Graham, Shirley

Tue 2nd March   **Gillingham (H)**
Drew   1-1   McGettigan
Cox, Salman, Tripp, Smith, Lawrence, Sharp, Scales, Oxley, Poole, Terry Johnson, McGettigan Sub: Bence

Tue 9th March   **Orient (H)**
Won   2-1   Oxley, Docherty
Cox, Salman, Tripp, Ballantyne, Lawrence, Sharp, Docherty, Oxley, Barnett, Terry Johnson, McGettigan

Tue 23rd March   **Portsmouth (H)**
Lost   0-1

Wed 31st March   **Charlton Athletic (A)**
Lost   1-4

Tue 6th April   **Millwall (H)**
Lost   1-3
Cox, David Johnson, Lawrence, Docherty, Tripp, Ballantyne, Oxley, Sharp, Poole, McGettigan, Gordon Sweetzer

Tue 27th April   **Millwall (A)**
Drew   2-2   Docherty (pen), Gordon Sweetzer
Cox, Reagan, Sharp, Docherty, Tripp, Nigel Smith, Riddick, Oxley, McGettigan, Poole, Billy Sweetzer

Peterborough (A)   Lost   1-5

1975-76 Final League Table

[Left] Bees reserve keeper Graham Cox

		P	W	D	L	F	A	Pts
1	Watford	26	16	5	5	55	29	37
2	Cambridge United	26	13	8	5	42	32	34
3	Peterborough	26	14	5	7	59	34	33
4	Charlton Athletic	26	15	3	6	65	42	33
5	Southend United	26	13	4	9	37	28	30
6	Gillingham	26	11	7	8	52	33	29
7	Brighton	26	10	7	9	48	44	27
8	Luton Town	26	9	8	9	35	39	26
9	Orient	26	10	4	12	36	37	24
10	Portsmouth	26	9	4	13	33	45	22
11	Millwall	26	7	5	14	47	59	19
12	**Brentford**	**26**	**6**	**7**	**13**	**36**	**54**	**19**
13	Colchester United	26	7	4	15	34	63	18
14	Northampton Town	26	6	1	19	39	65	13

Appearances (as known)

Richard Poole (18)
John Ballantyne (14)
Gordon Riddick (9)
John Docherty (6+3)
Jackie Graham (4)
Tom Sharp (3+1)
Gary Butler (3)
Mike Allen (2)
Alan Peett (1)
David Johnson

Mickey Tripp (18)
Graham Cox (14)
Gordon Sweetzer (8+1)
Paul Priddy (5)
R. Horastead (4)
Dave Simmons (3+1)
Nigel Smith (2+1)
R. Clark (2)
C. Sharp (1)

Danis Salman (16)
Mickey French (10)
Alan Nelmes (8)
Gordon Bartlett (4)
David Oxley (4)
Terry Scales (3+1)
Roger Cross (2+1)
R. Hodges (1)
Reagan

Paul Kerr (15)
Billy Sweetzer (10)
Keith Lawrence (7+1)
John Fielding (4)
Paul Bence (3+1)
Larry McGettigan (3)
J. Norris (2)
Terry Johnson (1)
Shirley

Goalscorers (as known)

Gordon Sweetzer (7), Richard Poole (6), Larry McGettigan (5), John Docherty, David Oxley, Tom Sharp, Jackie Graham (2), John Ballantyne, Gordon Bartlett, Dave Simmons, Paul Kerr, Nigel Smith, Gordon Riddick, Mickey French, John Fielding (1)

1976-1977

MID-WEEK FOOTBALL LEAGUE

Tue 7ᵗʰ September   **Southend United (H)**
Won   3-0   **Walker (2), Evans**
Cox, Fraser, Pritchett, Walker, Sharp, Smith, Scales, Johnson,
French, Cross, Redknapp Subs: Rolph and Evans
Attendance: 79

Tue 21ˢᵗ September   **Cambridge United (H)**
Lost   2-3   **Rolph, Barnett**
Cox, Salman, Sharp, Walker, Hughes, Pritchett, Redknapp, Rich-
ardson, Evans, Rolph, Barnett Sub: Smith
Attendance: 172

Tue 28ᵗʰ September   **Northampton Town (H)**
Lost   3-5   **Rolph, Redknapp, Pritchett**
Cox, Salman, Allen, Sharp, Hughes, Rolph, Redknapp, Walker,
Gordon Sweetzer, Richardson, Pritchett Subs: Smith and French
Attendance: 158

Wed 13ᵗʰ October   **Millwall (H)**
Lost   1-2   **McCulloch**
Cox, Aylott, Fraser, Salman, Sharp, Rolph, Walker, Richardson,
Glover, McCulloch, Gordon Sweetzer Subs: Smith and French
Attendance: 117

Wed 27ᵗʰ October   **Watford (H)**
Won   2-1   **Pritchett, Rolph**
Cox, Salman, Aylott, Smith, Sharp, Lucas, Gary Johnson, Walker,
Bence, French, Pritchett Subs: Evans and Rolph
Attendance: 204

Tue 9ᵗʰ November   **Portsmouth (H)**
Won   1-0   **Sweetzer (pen)**
Cox, Smith, Scales, Salman, Sharp, Walker, Gary Johnson, Lucas,
Rolph, French, Gordon Sweetzer Sub: Bence
Attendance: 39

Wed 24ᵗʰ November   **Northampton Town (A)**
Drew   0-0
Cox, Shrubb, Fraser, Salman, Smith, Sharp, Walker, Scales, Rolph,
French, Gary Johnson
Sub: Cross

Tue 4ᵗʰ January   **Brighton (H)**
Won   3-2   **Scales, Johnson, Sweetzer**
Priddy, Aylott, Sharp, Goldthorpe, Scales, Gary Johnson, Salman,
Gordon Sweetzer, Cross, French, Smith

Wed 9ᵗʰ February   **Gillingham (A)** _(played at Griffin Park)_
Lost   1-2   **Rolph**
Priddy, Aylott, Sharp, Billy Sweetzer, Goldthorpe, Scales, Kelly,
Bence, Evans, Gary Johnson, Rolph

Wed 16ᵗʰ February   **Southend (A) Cup)**
Lost   0-1

Wed 23rd February　　　　　**Charlton (H)**
Lost　1-3　　　　　　　　　**Rolph**
Cox, Aylott, Shrubb, Sharp, Salman, Gary Johnson, Bence, Scales, Terry Johnson, Rolph, Evans

Mon 28th February　　　　　**Charlton (A)**

Wed 9th March　　　　　　　**Millwall (A) (Cup)**
Won　2-0　　　　　　　　　**Salman, Rolph**
Cox, Sharp, Salman, Laws, Billy Sweetzer, Aylott, Gary Johnson, Shrubb, Rolph, Ellis, McCulloch Sub: Smith

Tue 15th March　　　　　　　**Southend (H) (Cup)**

Tue 29th March　　　　　　　**Peterborough (H)**
Lost　0-1
Cox, Brett Walker, Sharp, Billy Sweetzer, Laws, Shrubb, Salman, Ellis, Paul Walker, McCulloch, Rolph Sub: Gary Johnson

Tue 26th April　　　　　　　**Brighton (A)**
Won　2-0　　　　　　　　　**Goldthorpe, Sharp**

Wed 4th May　　　　　　　　**Watford (A)**
Lost　1-2

Thu 5th May　　　　　　　　**Gillingham (H)**
Cox, Sharp, Billy Sweetzer, Salman, Gary Johnson, Aylott, Smith, Terry Johnson, Gordon Sweetzer, Carlton, Phillips

Mon 9th May　　　　　　　　**Millwall (H) (Cup)**

Wed 11th May　　　　　　　**Cambridge United (A)**

Mon 16th May　　　　　　　**Millwall (A)**
Portsmouth (A)　　　　　　　Lost　0-8

Southend (A)　　　　　　　　Won　2-0

Peterborough (A)　　　　　　**No Details**

1976-77 Final League Table

		P	W	D	L	F	A	Pts
1	Portsmouth	20	12	2	6	48	29	26
2	Brighton	20	10	3	7	38	26	23
3	Northampton Town	20	8	7	5	41	37	23
4	Watford	20	9	4	7	35	37	22
5	Charlton Athletic	20	8	5	7	37	24	21
6	Millwall	20	7	6	7	30	32	20
7	Peterborough	20	6	7	7	29	28	19
8	Cambridge United	20	8	2	10	33	39	18
9	Southend United	20	8	1	11	29	32	17
10	**Brentford**	**20**	**6**	**4**	**10**	**25**	**37**	**16**
11	Gillingham	20	5	5	10	22	36	15

During the opening fixture, at home to Southend United on 7th September 1976, manager John Docherty was summoned to the boardroom and his employment was terminated.

The away fixture against Gillingham on 9th February 1977 was switched to Griffin Park due to the pitch at Gillingham's Priestfield stadium being water-logged and unplayable.

Appearances

Mike Allen, Dave Carlton, Morgan Evans, Bobby Goldthorpe, Mike Kelly, Steve Phillips, John Richardson, Tom Sharp, Gordon Sweetzer, Steve Aylott, Graham Cox, John Fraser, Matt Hughes, Laws, Paul Priddy, Gary Rolph, Paul Shrubb, Brett Walker, Mickey Barnett, Roger Cross, Mickey French, Gary Johnson, Stuart Lucas, Keith Pritchett, Danis Salman, Nigel Smith, Paul Walker, Paul Bence, Martin Ellis, Alan Glover, Terry Johnson, Andy McCulloch, Harry Redknapp, Terry Scales, Billy Sweetzer

Goalscorers (as known)

Gary Rolph (6), Keith Pritchett, Paul Walker, Gordon Sweetzer (2), Mickey Barnett, Morgan Evans, Bobby Goldthorpe, Gary Johnson, Andy McCulloch, Harry Redknapp, Danis Salman, Terry Scales, Tom Sharp (1)

1977-1978

MID-WEEK FOOTBALL LEAGUE

Wed 7th September   **Millwall (A)**
Won   4-2   **Walker (2), Willie Graham, Williams**

Tue 20th September   **Cambridge United (H)**
Won   2-1   **Willie Graham, Walker**

Tue 4th October   **Gillingham (H)**
Lost   0-1

Tue 11th October   **Wimbledon (A) (Cup)**
Lost   0-1

Tue 18th October   **Wimbledon (H) (Cup)**
Lost   1-4   **Phillips**
Cox, Aylott, Smith, Merison, Billy Sweetzer, Willie Graham, Walker, Williams, Rolph, Salman, Anderson

Wed 26th October   **Portsmouth (H) (Cup)**
Won   3-0   **Williams (2), Anderson**
Cox, Fraser, Lloyd, Salman, Aylott, Anderson, Walker, Willie Graham, Rolph, Goodchild, Williams

Tue 1st November   **Brighton (A)**
Lost   1-3   **Anderson**

Mon 7th November   **Northampton Town (H)**
Won   3-1   **Gordon Sweetzer, Rolph, Childs**

Tues 22nd November   **Portsmouth (A) (Cup)**
Drew   2-2   **Easterbrook (2)**

Tue 29th November   **Wimbledon (A)**
Won   4-1   **Williams (2), Walker, Rolph (pen)**
Cox, Rolph, Allen, Aylott, Smith, Willie Graham, Walker, Carlton, Goodchild, Childs, Williams

Wed 21st December   **Portsmouth (A)**
Drew   3-3

Tue 3rd January   **Wimbledon (H)**
Won   3-2   **Childs (2), Walker**
Cox, David Nicholson, Andrew Nicholson, Smith, Aylott, Walker, Lovett, Metchick, Childs, Rolph, Williams Sub: Baldwin

Tue 10th January   **Watford (H)**
Won   3-2   **Smith (2), Easterbrook**
Cox, David Nicholson, Lloyd. Smith, Hughes, Walker, Jackie Graham Rolph, Gordon Sweetzer, Childs, Williams Sub: Easterbrook and Alan Nicholson

Tue 17th January   **Portsmouth (H)**
Lost   1-2   **Childs**
Cox, Andrew Nicholson, David Nicholson, Smith, Aylott, Walker, Lloyd, Metchick, Childs, Rolph, Williams Sub: Easterbrook

Wed 25th January   **Northampton Town (A)**
Won   2-1   **Gordon Sweetzer, OG**
Cox, Aylott, Smith, Salman, Walker, Jackie Graham, Phillips, Gordon Sweetzer, Willie Graham, Easterbrook, Rolph, Sub: Kruse

Wed 15th February   **Peterborough (H)**
Won   **3-1**   **Baldwin (2), Childs**
Cox, Aylott, Lloyd, Rolph, Silman, Smith, Walker, Metchick, Baldwin, Carlton, Childs Sub: Salman

Mon 20th February   **Gillingham (A)**
Won   **5-1**   **Sweetzer (2), McCulloch (2) Murray**
Cox, Salman, Smith, Shrubb, Kruse, Walker, Willie Graham, Carlton, Gordon Sweetzer, McCulloch, Murray

Wed 22nd February   **Southend United (A)**   **Drew**   **1-1**
Baldwin
Cox, Rolph, Allen, Smith, Shrubb, Walker, Folley, Phillips, Gordon Sweetzer, Baldwin, Allder Subs: Willie Graham, Salman

Tue 7th March   **Millwall (H)**
Lost   **0-1**
Cox, Rolph, Allen, Smith, Silman, Walker, Lloyd, Metchick, Murray, Jackie Graham, Williams Subs: White, Salman

Mon 13th March   **Brighton (H)**
Lost   **2-3**   **Booker (2)**
Cox, Smith, Allen, Lloyd, Silman, White, Walker, Rolph, Murray, Booker, Willie Graham Subs: Salman, Jackie Graham

Mon 20th March   **Southend United (H)**
Lost   **0-1**
Cox, Smith, Allen, Lloyd, Silman, Walker, Aylott, White, Rolph, Booker, Murray

Thu 30th March   **Peterborough (A)**
Drew   **1-1**   **Baldwin**
Cox, Smith, Lloyd, Silman, Salman, Walker, Aylott, White, Rolph, Baldwin, Murray Sub: Willie Graham

Tue 11th April   **Charlton Athletic (A)**   **Lost**   **1-2**

Wed 19th April   **Cambridge United (A)**

Wed 26th April   **Charlton Athletic (H)**   **Won**   **3-1**
Lloyd, Walker, Murray
Cox, Smith, Allen, Lloyd, Silman, Holyoak, Aylott, Baldwin, Murray, Walker, Rolph

Mon 1st May   **Watford (A)**   **Drew**   **1-1**
Murray
Cox, Aylott, Allen, Kruse, Willie Graham, Silman, Walker, Rolph, Baldwin, Murray, Lloyd

Dave Metchick returned on a non-contract basis during the 1977-78 campaign to assist the reserve team, more than two years after leaving the club.

Former junior, Bobby Childs, played for the reserves on a non-contract basis, 15 years after the striker had appeared for Brentford in the Combination League.

1977-78 Final League Table (last version published)

		P	W	D	L	F	A	Pts
1	Peterborough United	18	9	4	5	40	25	22
2	Brighton	16	10	2	4	35	22	22
3	**Brentford**	**18**	**9**	**3**	**6**	**38**	**29**	**21**
4	Portsmouth	18	7	5	6	34	28	19
5	Charlton Athletic	15	8	2	5	34	29	18
6	Wimbledon	16	7	3	6	31	28	17
7	Millwall	16	6	3	7	25	36	15
8	Gillingham	15	6	3	6	28	40	15
9	Cambridge United*	15	5	5	5	25	22	12*
10	Watford	15	5	2	8	21	26	12
11	Southend United	18	4	4	10	19	33	12
12	Northampton Town	18	4	2	12	18	31	10

Appearances

Graham Cox (26)
Steve Aylott (21)
Danis Salman (11+6)
Dave Silman (9)
Alan Easterbrook (4+2)
Robbie Anderson (3+1)

John Fraser (3)

Johnny Ayris (2)
Billy Sweetzer (2)
Malcolm Folley (1)
Andy McCulloch (1)

Gary Rolph (25)
Willie Graham (15)
Tommy Baldwin (11+1)
Bobby Childs (9)
Cliff White (4+1)
David Nicholson (3)

Gary Goodchild (3)

Bob Booker (2)
Doug Allder (1)
P.Holyoake (1)
A.Faulkener (0+1)

Paul Walker (25)
Derek Williams (13+1)
Mike Allen (11)
Paul Shrubb (5)
Dave Metchick (4)
Dave Carlton (3)

Pat Kruse (2+1)

Terry Glynn (2)
G.Borg (1)
Matt Hughes (1)

Nigel Smith (24)
Barry Lloyd (12)
John Murray (9)
Gordon Sweetzer (5)
Jackie Graham (3+1)
Steve Phillips (3)
Andrew Nicholson (2+1)
Alan Merison (2)
Martin Ellis (1)
Andrew Lovett (1)

Goalscorers (as known)

Derek Williams, Paul Walker (6), Bobby Childs (5), Tommy Baldwin, Gordon Sweetzer (4), Alan Easterbrook, Willie Graham, John Murray (3), Bob Booker, Andy McCulloch, Gary Rolph, Nigel Smith, Robbie Anderson (2), Barry Lloyd, Steve Phillips, OG (1)

1978-1979

MID-WEEK FOOTBALL LEAGUE

Wed 23rd August   **Gillingham (A)**
Lost   1-4

Tue 29th August   **Peterborough United (H)**
Lost   2-4

Wed 13th September   **Northampton (H)**
Lost   0-2

Tue 19th September   **Northampton (A)**
Won   3-0   **Rolph (2), Cox**

Mon 2nd October   **Watford (A)**
Lost   3-5   **Rolph, Williams, Childs**

Tue 10th October   **Southend United (H)**
Lost   1-2
Bond, Johns, Fraser, Brooks, Rolph, Willie Graham, Baldwin, Childs, Booker, Walsh, Allder

Tue 24th October   **Millwall (H) (Cup)**
Drew   2-2   **Childs, Rolph (pen)**
Porter, Shrubb, Fraser, Salman, Silman, Rolph, Williams, Walsh, Childs, Booker, Allder Sub: Baldwin

Tue 31st October   **Charlton (A) (Cup)**
Lost   2-6   **Rolph, Baldwin**
Porter, Rolph, Silman, Salman, Fraser, Willie Graham, Walsh, Collins, Johns, Childs, Allder
Sub: Baldwin

Tue 7th November   **Cambridge United (A)**
Won   2-1   **Allder, Booker**
Porter, Johns, Fraser, Allen, Silman, Rolph, Glover, Willie Graham, Allder, Booker, Murray Sub: Walker

Mon 13th November   **Millwall (A) Cup**
Drew   0-0
Porter, Johns, Fraser, Allen, Silman, Glover, Walker, Willie Graham, Rolph, Booker, Murray Sub: Salman

Wed 22nd November   **Charlton (H) (Cup)**
Drew   1-1   **Rolph**
Porter, Johns, Fraser, Allen, Silman, Walker, Walsh, Rolph, Allder, Booker, Murray

Wed 29th November   **Charlton Athletic (A)**
Won   3-2

Mon 4th December   **Portsmouth (H)**
Won   3-0   **Booker, Willie Graham, Baldwin**
Porter, Johns, Silman, Rolph, Fraser, Willie Graham, Walker, Murray, Walsh, Booker, Baldwin Sub: Williams

Wed 10th January   **Millwall (H)**
Won   4-1   **Rolph (3), Silman**
Porter, Fraser, Silman, Allen, Johns, Shrubb, Walker, Booker, Willie Graham, Allder, Rolph Sub: Salman

Tue 6th February　　　　　　**Southend United (A)**
Lost　1-4　　　　　　　　　**Tucker**

Porter, Rolph, Silman, Allen, Tucker, Carlton, Glover, Willie Graham, Smith, Booker, Phillips

Tue 20th February　　　　　　**Brighton (A)**
Lost　0-1

Porter, Johns, Silman, Allen, Fraser, Walker, Glover, Willie Graham, Rolph, Booker, Allder Sub: Salman

Mon 26th February　　　　　　**Gillingham (H)**
Won　2-0　　　　　　　　　**Booker, Rolph**

Porter, Johns, Fraser, Allen, Silman, Glover, Walsh, Walker, Booker, Rolph, Allder Sub: Willie Graham

Thu 1st March　　　　　　　**Wimbledon (A)**
Won　3-2　　　　　　　　　**Glover, Willie Graham, Allder**

Porter, Johns, Silman, Allen, Fraser, Walker, Glover, Willie Graham Rolph, Booker, Allder
Sub: Salman

Wed 14th March　　　　　　　**Peterborough United (A)**
Lost　0-2

Porter, Johns, Fraser, Allen, Silman, Sartori, Walker, Booker, Rolph, Willie Graham, Allder
Subs: Caddon and Bushell

Mon 19th March　　　　　　　**Wimbledon (H)**
Won　2-0　　　　　　　　　**Walsh, Willie Graham**

Porter, Johns, Silman, Allen, Fraser, Willie Graham, Walker, Walsh, Rolph, Booker, Biggins

Wed 28th March　　　　　　　**Watford (H)**
Lost　0-1

Porter, Johns, Silman, Allen, Fraser, Walker, Willie Graham, Walsh, Rolph, Booker, Biggins Sub: Sartori

Wed 18th April　　　　　　　**Charlton Athletic (H)**
Drew　2-2　　　　　　　　　**Holmes, Smith**

Shrubb, Johns, Allen, Silman, Rolph, Walker, Willie Graham, Booker, Baldwin, Biggins, Holmes Sub: Smith

Wed 25th April　　　　　　　**Cambridge United (H)**
Lost　0-1

Pemberton, Johns, Allen, Silman, Rolph, Walker, Willie Graham, Carlton, Walsh, Booker, Biggins Subs: Smith and Salman

Thu 26th April　　　　　　　**Portsmouth (A)**
Drew　1-1　　　　　　　　　**Booker**

Porter, Johns, Silman, Allen, Fraser, Willie Graham, Walker, Rolph, Holmes, Booker, Allder Sub: Shrubb

Tue 1st May　　　　　　　　**Brighton (H)**
Lost　0-3

Pemberton, Johns, Jackie Graham, Silman, Allen, Walker, Willie Graham Glover, Holmes, Booker, Rolph Sub: Salman

Wed 9th May　　　　　　　　**Millwall (A)**
Lost　1-2

1978-79 Final League Table

		P	W	D	L	F	A	Pts
1	Peterborough	22	13	6	3	37	21	32
2	Southend United	22	13	5	4	45	20	31
3	Brighton	22	13	4	5	42	26	30
4	Charlton Athletic	22	7	9	6	33	30	23
5	Watford	22	8	6	8	30	29	22
6	Northampton Town	22	9	3	10	36	30	21
7	Wimbledon	22	9	2	11	29	42	20
8	Cambridge United	22	6	7	9	27	41	19
9	**Brentford**	**22**	**8**	**2**	**12**	**34**	**40**	**18**
10	Gillingham	22	6	6	10	23	31	18
11	Millwall	22	5	5	12	27	33	15
12	Portsmouth	22	7	1	14	30	51	15

The home game against Watford on 28th March 1979 was held up for 35 minutes while officials attempted to catch a stray dog on the Griffin Park pitch.

Paul Shrubb was named as goalkeeper for the home game against Charlton on 18th April 1979 – he also played in goal for the second half of the game at Portsmouth the following week.

[Left] Bees reserve striker, Bradley Walsh, before finding fame elsewhere

Appearances (as known)

Doug Allder
Len Bond
Caddon
Graham Cox
Willie Graham
Mark Pemberton
Danis Salman
Dean Smith
Derek Williams

Mike Allen
Bob Booker
Dave Carlton
John Fraser
Lee Holmes
Steve Phillips
Gian Franco Sartori
Barry Tucker

Tommy Baldwin
John Brooks
Bobby Childs
Allan Glover
Dean Johns
Trevor Porter
Paul Shrubb
Paul Walker

Gordon Biggins
Bushell
Collins
Jackie Graham
John Murray
Gary Rolph
David Silman
Bradley Walsh

Goalscorers (as known)

Gary Rolph (10), Bob Booker (4), Willie Graham (3), Doug Allder, Tommy Baldwin, Bobby Childs (2), Lee Holmes Graham Cox, Allan Glover, Dave Silman, Dean Smith, Barry Tucker, Bradley Walsh, Derek Williams (1)

1979-1980

MID-WEEK FOOTBALL LEAGUE

Tue 4ᵗʰ September   **Southend United (H)**
Lost 0-2
Porter, Johns, Salman, Glover, Booker, Lee Holmes, Willie Graham, Walker, Smith, Knight, Benning
Sub: O'Callaghan

Wed 12ᵗʰ September   **Portsmouth (A)**
Lost 0-5
Porter, Johns, Booker, Knight, O'Mahoney, Glover, Walker, Willie Graham, Benning, Baldwin, Walsh

Wed 19ᵗʰ September   **Wimbledon (H)**
Lost 0-1
Porter, Johns, Knight, Shrubb, O'Mahoney, Glover, Benning, Walker, Willie Graham, Booker, Smith Sub: Walsh

Tue 25ᵗʰ September   **Cambridge United (H)**
Lost 1-3
Porter, Allder, Salman, Fraser, O'Mahoney, Benning, Walker, Glover, Willie Graham, Booker, Smith

Tue 16ᵗʰ October   **Aldershot (A)**
Drew 2-2   **Salman, Benning**
Porter, Bowen, Salman, Shrubb, O'Mahoney, Willie Graham, Glover, Walker, Benning, Allder, Midmer

Tue 23ʳᵈ October   **Charlton Athletic (H)**
Lost 1-2   **Walker**
Porter, Johns, Glover, Walker, Willie Graham, Benning, Booker, Bowen, O'Mahoney, Billy Holmes, Midmer Sub: O'Callaghan

Thu 15ᵗʰ November   **Brighton (H)**
Lost 1-2   **Booker**
Porter, O'Mahoney, Glover, Shrubb, Jenkins, Walker, Willie Graham, Booker, Billy Holmes, Fear, Benning Sub: Johns

Tue 27ᵗʰ November   **Watford (H)**
Lost 0-1
Porter, Glover, Jenkins, Booker, O'Mahoney, Benning, Walker, Willie Graham, Fear, Lee Holmes, Billy Holmes Sub: Bowen

Tue 4ᵗʰ December   **Millwall (A)**
Won 2-1   **Glover, Salerno**
Porter, O'Mahoney, Allder, Glover, Jenkins, Willie Graham, Salerno, Walker, Billy Holmes, Booker, Benning

Wed 19ᵗʰ December   **Watford (A)**
Drew 1-1   **Lee Holmes**
Porter, Smith, O'Mahoney, Jenkins, Salman, Benning, Walker, W Graham, J Graham, L Holmes, B Holmes, Subs: Walsh, Bowen

Tue 8ᵗʰ January   **Portsmouth (H)**
Lost 0-2
Porter, O'Mahoney, Glover, Jenkins, Salman, Walker, Willie Graham, Benning, Boyd, Bowen, Lee Holmes Subs: Smith and Billy Holmes

Tue 22ⁿᵈ January   **Peterborough (H)**
Drew 1-1   **Smith**
Porter, O'Mahoney, Salman, Jenkins, Kruse, Walker, Benning, Willie Graham, Bowen, Smith, Billy Holmes Subs: Glover and Booker

Tue 29ᵗʰ January   **Northampton (A) (Cup)**
Won 3-0   **Smith, Phillips, Tucker (pen)**

Mon 4ᵗʰ February   **Gillingham (H)**
Lost   2-5   **Booker (2)**
Porter, O'Mahoney, Glover, Jenkins, Salman, Walker, Willie Graham, Benning, Billy Holmes, Booker, Smith Sub: Walsh

Tue 12ᵗʰ February   **Aldershot (H)**
Lost   0-3
Porter, Shrubb, Salman, Jenkins, McNichol, Bowen, Jackie Graham, Willie Graham, Benning, Booker, Billy Holmes, Sub: Glover

Tue 19ᵗʰ February   **Southend United (A)**
Lost   1-2   **Smith**
Porter, Smith, Glover, Fraser, Lee Holmes, Salman, O'Mahoney, Benning, Willie Graham, Booker, Billy Holmes

Thurs 21ˢᵗ February   **Aldershot (A) Cup)**
Lost   1-2   **Booker**
Porter, Glover, Jenkins, Bateman, Walsh, Walker, O'Mahoney, Willie Graham, Lee Holmes, Booker, Hoare Subs: Billy Holmes, Shrubb

Wed 27ᵗʰ February   **Gillingham (A)**
Drew   1-1   **Lee Holmes**
Porter, Jackie Graham, Jenkins, Salman, Bateman, Glover, Smith, Willie Graham, Lee Holmes, Billy Holmes, Booker, Subs: Walsh, Benning

Tue 4ᵗʰ March   **Charlton Athletic (A)**
Drew   2-2   **Billy Holmes, Phillips**
Porter, Glover, Jenkins, Booker, Phillips, Willie Graham, Benning, O'Mahoney, Billy Holmes, Lee Holmes, Smith

Tue 11ᵗʰ March   **Cambridge United (A)**
Drew   2-2   **Booker, OG**
Porter, Lee Holmes, Glover, Jenkins, Davies, O'Mahoney, Walker,

Willie Graham, Benning, Billy Holmes, Booker Sub: Smith

Thu 20ᵗʰ March   **Brighton (A)**
Drew   3-3   **Booker, Smith, Billy Holmes**
Carman, O'Mahoney, Bateman, Jenkins, Walker, Willie Graham, Benning, Allder, Billy Holmes, Smith, Booker

Tue 25ᵗʰ March   **Northampton (A)**
Won   3-0   **Booker, Allder, Smith**
Porter, Salman, Jenkins, Kruse, Carlton, Allder, Walker, Jackie Graham, Willie Graham, Booker, Billy Holmes Subs: Benning, Smith

Mon 21ˢᵗ April   **Peterborough (A)**
Lost   0-4
Porter, Glover, Jenkins, McNichol, Tucker, Parkinson, Walker, Willie Graham, Jackie Graham, Billy Holmes, Phillips

Thu 24ᵗʰ April   **Millwall (H)**
Lost   0-4
Porter, Glover, O'Mahoney, McNichol, Jenkins, Walker, Chandler, Willie Graham, Billy Holmes, Funnell, Benning Subs: Pentland, Maltby

Thu 1ˢᵗ May   **Northampton (H)**
Won   3-0   **Lee Holmes, Walker, Funnell**
Porter, Fraser, Tucker, McNichol, Jenkins, Shrubb, Lee Holmes, Walker, Smith, Carlton, Phillips Sub: Funnell

Mon 5ᵗʰ May   **Wimbledon (A)**
Lost   1-2   **Billy Holmes**
Porter, Glover, Jenkins, McNichol, Tucker, W Graham, J Graham, Benning, Allder, Phillips, Billy Holmes Subs: Shrubb, Carlton

1979-80 Final League Table

[Left] Midfielder, Terry Benning, had signed professional forms with Brentford but never progressed further than the reserves

		P	W	D	L	F	A	Pts
1	Watford	23	16	6	2	63	25	38
2	Charlton Athletic	24	14	5	5	59	41	33
3	Southend United	24	14	5	5	53	38	33
4	Wimbledon	24	10	8	6	44	37	26
5	Portsmouth	24	9	6	9	39	35	24
5	Peterborough	24	9	5	10	42	37	23
6	Gillingham	24	9	5	10	46	45	23
7	Millwall	24	9	4	11	34	39	22
8	Northampton Town	24	9	3	12	30	44	21
10	Brighton	24	8	5	11	40	55	21
11	Cambridge United	24	6	5	13	31	49	17
12	Aldershot	24	6	4	14	41	52	16
13	**Brentford**	**24**	**3**	**7**	**14**	**27**	**51**	**13**

Appearances

Willie Graham (25)
Allan Glover (19+2)
Bob Booker (17+1)
Doug Allder (6)
Jim McNichol (5)
Jeff Bateman (3)
Dave Carlton (2+2)
Tony Funnell (1+1)
S.Chandler (1)

J.Salerno (1)

Trevor Porter (25)
Iori Jenkins (19)
Dean Smith (12+3)
Jackie Graham (6)
Steve Phillips (5)
John Fraser (3)
Bradley Walsh (2+4)
Tommy Baldwin (1)
P.Davies (1)
Marcus O'Callaghan (0+2)

Terry Benning (21+2)
Dave O'Mahoney (19)
Danis Salman (11)
Barry Bowen (5+2)
Dean Johns (4+1)
Tony Knight (3)
Keith Fear (2)
G.Boyd (1)
S.Hore (1)

A.Maltby (0+1)

Paul Walker (21)
Billy Holmes (18+2)
Lee Holmes (10)
Paul Shrubb (5+2)
Barry Tucker (4)
Pat Kruse (3)
S.Midmer (2)
Nigel Carman (1)
Noel Parkinson (1)

S.Pentland (0+1)

Goalscorers

Bob Booker (7), Dean Smith (5), Lee Holmes, Billy Holmes, Paul Walker (3), Steve Phillips (2), Doug Allder, Terry Benning, Tony Funnell, Allan Glover, J.Salerno, Danis Salman, Barry Tucker, OG (1)

JUNIOR AND YOUTH TEAM

SEASON 1970-1971

With the club on the road to recovery in the aftermath of the 1967 takeover crisis, the board felt that the re-introduction of a junior team was a necessity and, under the guidance of Roy Ruffell, the newly-formed line-up made its bow in the opening South-East Counties League fixture, away to Arsenal, on Saturday 15th August 1970. Brentford suffered a 5-1 thumping.

The first home game came seven days later with an 11.00 am kick-off at Griffin Park and 178 people, paying gate receipts of £20, witnessed Paul Devis score in a 2-1 defeat with a line-up of Priddy, Pipe, Futerill, Hillman, Hillier, Wilkinson, Smith, Devis, Emanuel, Dunn and Davidson.

The FA Youth Cup 1st Qualifying tie at home to Viking Sports two weeks later saw the attendance figure doubled, to 344, and a 3-1 success, followed by another qualifying victory at home to Edmonton (4-3 with two goals a-piece from Davidson and Emanuel). Progression to the first round proper saw an exit from the competition at the hands of Crystal Palace by 5-2, with goals by Pipe (pen) and Emanuel, witnessed by just over 200 spectators.

The season ended strongly results-wise, with a run of four wins in five matches, including home victories against Watford by 2-0 and a 3-2 victory over Orient – with Paul Ward (2) and Paul Devis on the scoresheet.

Alongside the creation of an under-14 team, under the guidance of former Bee Ken Horne, who moved across from a similar role with Queens Park Rangers, the other notable highlight of the season saw two of the juniors, 17-year-olds Barry Futerill from Hounslow and Danny Pipe from Bedfont, selected for the London FA in a match against London Universities.

SEASON 1971-1972

The switching of home league fixtures from Griffin Park to Ruislip Manor's ground resulted in a lower profile being given to junior matches, although the FA Youth Cup once again resulted in an appearance in the first round proper, after victories in the qualifying rounds against Wealdstone at home by 3-1 (Fraser with two goals and Devis) and a 2-1 win at Wembley FC (Henderson and Mote).

The first round exit was inflicted in a home tie against Crystal Palace for the second successive season, with a strike from Fraser and an own goal failing to prevent a 4-2 defeat.

Involvement in the Southern Junior Floodlit Cup competition also ended with an exit at the earliest stage – a home tie against Chelsea saw the visitors leave Griffin Park as 3-2 victors after goals from Palfrey and Henderson had proved insufficient to earn a result.

In December 1971 Steve Henderson was chosen to represent an England Youth XI in a private match at Loftus Road against Queens Park Rangers and, with the team now in the hands of new manager Phil Jarrett, the club received an invitation for the junior side to participate in a prestigious end of season youth tournament in Holland.

SEASON 1972-1973

The first signs of fruition from the re-instatement of junior football came with the signings of 15-year-olds Kevin Harding and Richard Poole as apprentices. Both youngsters had spent two years with the club and, with Harding as skipper, the team won the opening South East Counties League match against Ipswich Town – Jess Rossiter scoring the only goal of the game.

An early season set-back, which saw Richard Poole suffer a broken wrist, was off-set by some impressive results – notably a 4-1 League Cup win at Reading (Rossiter (2), Orron and Johnson) and a 2-2 draw with Chelsea (Rossiter and Cotton).

The squad, consisting of N.Oliver and C.Green (goalkeepers), J.Mileham, P.Currie, J.Goodhall, K.Harding, S.Murphy, G.Smith and A.White (defenders), L.Bircham, G.Johnson, T.Byatt, and L.Wicks (midfielders) and strikers R.Cotton, G.Huxley, R.Poole and J.Rossiter, reached the turn of the year with Jess Rossiter leading the scoring charts with seven goals, followed by four-a-piece from Gary Huxley, Roy Cotton and Richard Poole.

Both cup competitions resulted in first round exits, a 2-1 defeat at Bournemouth in the Floodlit Cup and a 4-1 (Rossiter) home defeat to Southampton in the FA Youth Cup.

After both Gary Huxley and Roy Cotton had been selected for the Middlesex Senior FA under-18 Squad, a real coup was achieved in January 1973 as Gary Huxley became the club's first England youth international since Gerry Cakebread 19 years earlier – he made his debut against Scotland.

An Easter invitation to take part in an international youth tournament in Frankfurt saw the successful team return home with the competition trophy.

SEASON 1973-1974

The season got underway in good style – a 2-0 home success (Cotton and Poole) against Watford in the opening South-East Counties fixture was followed a week later by the best result since the re-formation of the juniors, as Queen Park Rangers were thrashed 6-1 with Terry Palfrey hitting four goals (Poole and Cotton scored the others) in the first away game of the campaign. A mixed bag of league results produced an inconsistent season, including:

Home			
Watford	Won	2-0	Cotton, Palfrey
Ipswich Town	Drew	0-0	
Fulham	Won	2-1	Poole (2)
Queens Park Rangers	Lost	0-1	

Richard Poole, number 10, scores Brentford Juniors first goal against Gillingham Juniors at Ruislip Manor on Saturday

West Ham United	Lost	0-3	
Brighton and Hove Albion	Won	2-0	Palfrey, Poole
Gillingham	Won	5-2	Palfrey (2), Poole, Harding, Wicks
Millwall	Won	4-1	Goodall, Wicks, White, Opher
Tottenham Hotspur	Won	3-0	Cotton (2), Smith

Away
Queens Park Rangers	Won	6-1	Palfrey (4), Poole, Cotton
Charlton Athletic	Lost	1-3	Cotton
Crystal Palace	Drew	1-1	Poole
Millwall	Won	2-1	Poole, Wicks
Watford (League Cup)	Won	2-0	Wicks, Cotton
Reading	Lost	1-2	Cotton
Chelsea	Lost	0-2	

Tottenham Hotspur	Lost	0-2	
Gillingham	Won	1-0	Goodall
Arsenal	Lost	1-2	Cotton
Brighton and Hove Albion	Won	2-1	Palfrey
Ipswich Town	Lost	1-3	Poole
West Ham United	Won	1-0	Palfrey
Watford	Won	3-2	Cotton (2), Brown

In the FA Youth Cup first round, a 1-0 home loss was incurred at the hands of Southampton, while Chelsea won a Southern Junior Floodlit first round tie at Griffin Park for the second time in three seasons to inflict a 2-1 defeat, with Currie on the scoresheet.

Roy Cotton provided the highlight of the season by representing England in youth team internationals against Scotland and Wales – scoring in both games. There was no longer a competitive junior team after this season.

DEDICATIONS

ACKNOWLEDGEMENTS, CREDITS AND THANKS

The production of this book has been a collaboration between three life-long Brentford fans: David Lane, Mark Croxford and Greville Waterman.

Countless hours have been spent by Mark Croxford over the past 40 years in keeping and updating his Brentford diary, writing match reports, collecting cuttings and newspaper articles and compiling player profiles and statistics – so when Greville Waterman approached me about Mark's remarkable collection, it soon became clear that with some expansion and adaptation, a wonderful series of books could be published.

The Big Brentford Book of the Seventies is the first volume of a collection that will provide Bees fans with the most thorough retrospective look at each decade possible – books to cherish.

It is fair to say, however, that *The Big Brentford Book of the Seventies* would not have been quite *so* big without the help and enthusiasm of several other key people. I hope you agree that the photos included within this book are simply outstanding, so I really must say a huge thank you to Geoff Buckingham (who was asked to look after Eric White's collection when the former Brentford programme editor died) for agreeing to allow us to use them in this book and the volumes that will follow. Dan Jackson, who produced the wonderful *Positively Brentford* book in 1996, also provided some of the

[Previous pages] Graham Haynes and Geoff Buckingham present Steve Phillips with a Player of the Month award
[Left] Former programme editor, Eric White, with Bill Dodgin

photos, with Martin Holland and Tony Ross providing pictures and cuttings from their personal collections.

The Middlesex Chronicle should be acknowledged and thanked for allowing us to use their newspaper cuttings in the diary sections throughout the book, along with those from other newspapers that the Group now owns. Thanks to Tim Street for helping with that.

Brentford Football Club has been fully supportive too, and we would like to thank Peter Gilham in particular, who was always on hand to help whenever he was asked.

Jackie Graham, a real Brentford legend if ever there was one, provided contact details for some of the other iconic Seventies players that we have tracked down and interviewed for this volume and I'd like to thank John O'Mara and Peter Gelson in particular for being so honest and open about the era.

Former Brentford FC chairman, Dan Tana, provides a wonderful glimpse back to his time at the club and it was a real honour to meet and spend time with him. It has to be said that Dan is a fascinating, visionary man and, as well as remaining heavily involved with European football, he still cares greatly for Brentford.

Other people who deserve thanks include Mark Chapman for providing us with additional photos, Rob Jex for his updated match attendance figures, Phil Lynch for producing a wonderful, nostalgic promotional video for the book and Keith Westcott for obtaining Steve Wilkins's elusive birth date!

David Lane

THE FINAL SAY

"It was the best of times, it was the worst of times" are the opening words from Dickens's *A Tale of Two Cities*. It sums up the Seventies superbly.

The time was spent seesawing between the lower reaches of the Third and Fourth Divisions and was a period when, apart from the delights of watching John O'Mara, Gordon Sweetzer, Steve Phillips and Andy McCulloch, goals were a hard commodity to come across. Highlights were also few and far between with two of the standout moments coming against the same team, albeit eight years apart.

The 2-1 FA Cup Fifth Round defeat at Hull City in February 1971, three weeks after a glorious victory away to Cardiff City in the previous round, was hard to take as the Bees were classically robbed by the referee, who failed to witness the tie-deciding challenge on keeper Gordon Phillips, which ultimately led to our exit. However, the monies accrued from our Cup run finally paid off the £104,000 loan that had been hanging over our heads for four years. Eight years later, on a crisp December afternoon at Griffin Park, a legend was born when Bob Booker scored a hat trick against the Tigers.

[Left and Right] The familiar face of Peter Gilham – a Brentford fan known to all others

Bob was one of a number of players to have played during the decade to have achieved cult status – others were the previously credited O'Mara, Sweetzer, Phillips, McCulloch plus, of course, Peter Gelson, who amassed 516 appearances for the club. Other legendary appearance makers of note during that era include Jackie Graham, Danis Salman, Alan Hawley and Alan Nelmes.

We operated under the guidance of four managers during this period. Frank Blunstone opened the decade and it was Frank who I had the pleasure of working with on my first committee, to raise funds for the Juniors, called The Junior Amenities Fund Committee, together with the legendary Eric White. Frank was followed by Mike Everitt, John Docherty and finally Bill Dodgin (Junior), an absolute and understated gent.

Other personalities who were synonymous with the Seventies were Denis Piggott who performed as Secretary/General Manager/Chief Administrator throughout the period and I believe to have been the unsung hero of the 1967 crisis. He was perceived as a difficult man by many supporters, but I still treasure my customary end of season "thank you" letters from him. Eddie Lyons was another long-serving stalwart at the club as trainer – a nicer, more down to earth guy you couldn't wish to meet.

Travelling to away games gradually got easier as the decade unfolded and the regular overnight coach trips to most points north of Watford (so it seemed) were replaced by same-day trips up the newly extended motorways.

Although the decade may not have been the greatest era Brentford fans have witnessed on the pitch, to say the least, off the field, it was as good as you can get. Socially the players were brilliant and understood the importance of supporting club functions and, in turn, supporting those who supported them on match days. I believe that spirit and unity should be an integral part of any football club, at whatever level, and we were blessed at that time. Indeed, a number of those same players still support the club in a number of ways and there is a real sense of camaraderie after all that time has passed.

As I said it was the best of times and the worst of times. But I have very warm memories of it.

I would like my dedication to be in memory of all those who gave voluntary service to Brentford Football Club and helped make it the wonderful club it is.

Peter Gilham

DEDICATIONS

Mark Croxford
David Lane
Greville Waterman
Dan Tana
Peter Gilham
Jackie Graham
Frank Blunstone
John O'Mara
Peter Gelson
Pat Kruse
Gordon Phillips
Andy McCulloch
Alan Nelmes
Danis Salman
Doug Allder
Alan Hawley
Geoff Buckingham
Tony Ross
Mark Chapman
Phil Lynch
Martin Holland
Sav Kyriacou
Eric White (in memory of)
Graham Haynes (in memory of)
Chris Wickham
Ian Levack (in memory of)
Jim Levack
Paul Slattery
Graham Clark
Christel Maria Knowles (in memory of)
James Walsh
Sharon Hurley

Robert Whale
Gary Piggott
Keith Piggott
John Chandler
John Habes
John Allen
Nigel Allen
Sam Allen
Russell Owen
Lawrence Barnes
Peter Cox
Martin Barrett
Robert Barrett
Mark Saggers
Rob Jex
Ian Anderson
Tony James
David Nott
Phil Murray
Paul Briers
Phil Roker
Trevor Inns
Robert Pullen
Paul Niven
Bernard Jackson
Alan Winter
Graham Huntingford
Barry Huntingford
Bruce Powell
Matthew Connolly
Jeremy Clark
Trevor Cook

Paul Reddick
Peter Keen
Peter Herman
Alan Wheatley
Terry C Smith
Stephen Ellis Turner
Chris Abigail
Stephen Abigail
Sean Londra
David Wheeler
Martin Clive Sexton
John Bosher
Graham Bosher
Ian Ackary
David Smith
Lynne Morgan
Ken Hart
John Stride
Matthew Stride
Clive Dawson
Alan Scott
Jorgen Karlsson
Tony Daly
Lance Yerrell
David Pring
Malcolm Smith
Richard Emmott
Brian Bristow
Simon Allford
Barry Mingard
Nigel Hawkins
John Huggins

Matt Chambers
John Francis Timon (in memory of)
Steve Flanagan
Liam Flanagan
Ralph Tebby
Trevor Lanning
Gary Stenning
John Tulett
Mick Morris
Peter Ilett
Gary Pain
Robert Gothold
Ian Westbrook
Mike Cabble
Colin Martin
Gary (Bert) Wheadon
Simon Johnston
Ron Bibby
James Malcolm
Nicholas Maniatakis
Stephen Armstrong
Diana Wall-McNeill's Family
Kelvin Rush
Jonathan Burchill
Louis McAree
Gary Barrell
Pete Gregorowski
Brian Chidwick
Andrew Vickers
Jeremy Smith
Eric Miller
Stuart Costick
Lee Ashton
Colin Downey
Matthew C Downey
John Hirdle

Peter Wickham
Michael Wickham
Mark Bluck
Darryl Howell
Fred Porter (in memory of)
Graham Rikly
Huw Davies
Fred Larkbey (1917-2000 RIP)
Robert Cleveland
Sheila Carroll
John 'Daddybee' Carroll
John Fenn
Mark Fenn
Sean Mitchell
Mark Barrell
Archie Ryan
Conaill Ryan
Oisin Ryan
Keneth John Secker (in memory of)
John Tickner
Alan Owen
Darrin Romp
Robert Romp
Steve Kirk
Jim O' Reardon
Len Tincknell
Graham Sandys
David Uren
Mark Taverner
Steve Jacobs
Jacqui Laslett
Marc Fisher
Barry Neighbour
Francis G. Wall
Alan Cox
Wayne Dickson

Ian Blackham
Alan Thomas (In loving memory)
Colin Penn
Julian Mann
Michael Gray
Roy Deller (In loving memory)
Denis Spencer (In memory of)
Nicki Finnigan
Steve Tom
Paul Bradley
Stephen Lyall
John Abbett
Christina Maria Thaws
Tony Keen
Micky Clark
Brian Forbes
Oscar Thompson
Dave Fisher
David Newlin
Malcolm Porter
Nick Smith
Mark Walter
Ella Haines
Neil Plunkett
David Lambert
David Hodge
Stephen Boyce
Christopher Boyce
Roger Hailey
Jim Hailey
David Grimmett
Dennis Brown
Rev Rob Day
Mr Michael G Goodchild (dad)
Steven McGhee
Brian Eyles

M A Pension
Philip Mooney
S. Skinner
Stewart Lockie
David Ohl
William Sandy
Graham Tyrrell
Tim Porter
John Gillespie
Tony Thomas
Rupert Wadsworth
Mark Raymond Whelan
Michael Taylor
Nick Logan
Steve Bowry
Dale Harwood
Paul Fenn
Stephen 'Bordeaux Bee' Lewis
Philip Eden
Tommy Gunner Hill (deceased)
Leslie Carlton
Malcolm Pearce
Steven Goater
Victor Boulter
Michael Perkins
Stephen Osbourne
Carl Whitaker
Alan Tilbury
Bill Benn
Gary Marson
Andrew Martin
Adam Hobbs
Francis Barry
The Randall family
Robert Brewer
Daddy Bear
Michael Claydon

Dedicated to Jo, Seb and Darcey, plus my Brentford fan friends who, despite the heartache and perennial disappointments, help make Griffin Park one of the finest places on Earth! **David Lane**

I'd like to dedicate this book to my dad Alf, for teaching me about football and Sylvia, my mum – for packing me off to see my first Brentford game, little realising the addiction she was about to unleash, and Junior Bee Joseph – the next generation. **Mark Croxford**

To my dad, who first took me to Griffin Park in 1965 and is therefore responsible for all the frustration that has followed and to my beloved Miriam, Nick and Becca for all their patience, love and support. **Greville Waterman**